Effective Writing

Second Canadian Edition

University of Windsor

Kemper / Meyer / Van Rys / Sebranek / Holditch

NELSON

NELSON

ISBN-13: 978-0-17-687765-1
ISBN-10: 0-17-687765-7

Consists of Selections from:

Write2, First Canadian edition
Kemper
ISBN 10: 0-17-653389-3, © 2016

Cover Credit:

nopporn/Shutterstock

WRITE 2:
Paragraphs and Essays

CONTENTS

ColorBlind Images/Getty Images

David Henley/Dorling Kindersley/Getty Images

Part 3: Developing Paragraphs 120

Part 4: Developing Essays 178

Dougal Waters/Digital Vision/Getty Images

Part 5: Sentence Workshops 276

S.Borisov/Shutterstock.com

raresirimie/Shutterstock.com

Part 6: Word Workshops 366

Part 7: Punctuation and Mechanics Workshops   440

Renata Sedmakova/Shutterstock.com

Convit/Shutterstock.com

"I write to discover what I think."
—Joan Didion

Lucky Business/Shutterstock.com

1 Writing and Learning

In college and university, the new concepts flooding your way can seem overwhelming. To succeed you must be able to retain new knowledge, connect it to other ideas and subjects, and communicate conclusions with your peers and instructors. Writing can help.

You may not think of writing as a learning tool, but writing can make you a better, more efficient learner. Think about it: Writing allows you to sort through your thoughts, form new and insightful opinions, and communicate what you've learned with others. And these skills translate directly to the workplace. It is no surprise that today's employers place a premium on effective writers.

This chapter is set up in two parts. The first half introduces you to writing as a learning tool, while the second half discusses writing as a means of sharing knowledge. Becoming an effective writer and learner isn't magic, but the result of focus and practice.

What do you think?

What does the quotation on the previous page say about writing? How does it match up with your opinion of writing?

Learning Outcomes

LO1 Write to learn for yourself.

LO2 Write to share learning.

LO3 Consider the range of writing.

LO4 Review writing and learning.

L○1 Writing to Learn

Gertrude Stein made one of the more famous and unusual statements about writing when she said, "To write is to write is to write is to write. . . ." The lofty place that writing held in her life echoes in this line. As far as she was concerned, nothing else needed to be said on the subject.

What would cause a writer to become so committed to the process of writing? Was it fame and recognition? Not really. The real fascination that experienced writers have with writing is the frame of mind it puts them in. The act of filling up a page stimulates their thinking and leads to exciting and meaningful learning.

Changing Your Attitude

If you think of writing in just one way—as an assignment to be completed—you will never discover its true value. Writing works best when you think of it as an important learning tool. Writing doesn't always have to lead to an end product submitted to an instructor.

A series of questions, a list, or a quick note in a notebook can be a meaningful form of writing if it helps you think and understand. If you make writing an important part of your learning routine, two things will happen: (1) You'll change your feelings about the importance of writing, and (2) you'll become a better writer, thinker, and learner.

Speaking & Listening

As a class, discuss this writing experience: Did it help you focus your thinking on the topic? Did you surprise yourself in any way? Could you have written more? If so, about what?

Reflect Write non-stop for five minutes about one of the three topics below. Don't stop or hesitate, and don't worry about making mistakes. You are writing for yourself. Afterward, checkmark something that surprises you or that you learned about yourself.

What are my talents? OR **Where do I want to go?** OR **Have I seized opportunities?**

Keeping a Class Notebook

Keeping a class notebook or journal is essential if you are going to make writing to learn an important part of your learning routine. Certainly, you can take notes in this notebook, but it will also be helpful for reflecting on what is going on in the class. Try these activities:

- Write freely about anything, from class discussions to challenging assignments to important exams.
- Discuss new ideas and concepts.
- Argue for and against any points of view that come up in class.
- Question what you are learning.
- Record your thoughts and feelings during an extended lab or research assignment.
- Evaluate your progress in the class.

Other Classes

Note taking is a common form of writing that is useful in most classes. Always try to record some of your thoughts and feelings alongside the basic notes. This makes note taking more meaningful. (See Chapter 2, LO2, Taking Effective Notes.)

Special Strategies

Writing or listing freely is the most common way to explore your thoughts and feelings about your course work. There are, however, specific writing-to-learn strategies that you may want to try:

Sent or Unsent Messages	Draft messages to someone about something you are studying or reading.
First Thoughts	Record your first impressions about something you are studying or reading.
Role-Play	Write as if you are someone directly involved in a topic you are studying.
Nutshelling	Write down in one sentence the importance of something you are studying or reading.
Pointed Question	Keep asking yourself *why?* in your writing to sort out your thoughts about something.
Debate	Split your mind in two. Have one side defend one point of view, and the other side, a differing point of view.

Practise For one month, make a commitment to writing to learn. In a notebook or on a laptop, take five minutes after or in between classes to write freely about what you just learned. Also, try a few of the strategies on this page as study tools. Afterward, evaluate how writing to learn worked for you. Did you retain more knowledge? Did you come to new conclusions or understandings?

RoJo Images/Shutterstock.com

Review

Writing is called a process because a piece of writing must go through a series of steps before it is ready to share. (See Part 2, The Writing Process and the Traits of Writing.)

LO2 Writing to Share Learning

The other important function of writing is to share what you have learned. When you write to learn, you have an audience of one, yourself; when you write to share learning, you have an audience of many, including your instructors and classmates.

All writing projects (paragraphs, essays, blog entries) actually begin with writing to learn, as you collect your thoughts about a topic. But with a first draft in hand, you turn your attention to making the writing clear, complete, and ready to share with others.

A Learning Connection

As the graphic below shows, improved thinking is the link between the two functions of writing. Writing to learn involves exploring and forming your thoughts; writing to share learning involves clarifying and fine-tuning them.

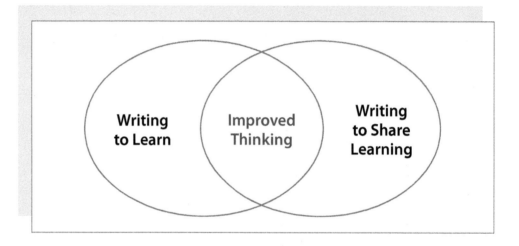

Writing to Learn — Improved Thinking — Writing to Share Learning

Speaking & Listening

As a class, explore the following question: Why is writing often called "thinking on paper"?

Identify Label each scenario below as an example of writing to learn (WL) or writing to share learning (WSL).

_____ 1. Evan freewrites on his laptop about a concept he just learned in his biology course.

_____ 2. Paige writes a blog about last night's basketball game for her school's online newspaper.

_____ 3. Liam lists the pros and cons of a political movement he learned about in a Russian and Eastern studies course.

_____ 4. Brianna e-mails new notes from her book review to her study group.

_____ 5. Mia is revising and editing her personal essay for her creative writing assignment.

Michaelpuche/Shutterstock.com

LO3 Considering the Range of Writing

The forms of writing to share cover a lot of territory as you can see in the chart below. Some of the forms are quick and casual; others are more thoughtful and formal. As a student, your writing may cover this entire spectrum, but the instruction you receive will likely focus on the more formal types.

The Writing Spectrum

Formal and Thoughtful	Multimedia Reports
	Research Papers
	Stories/Plays/Poems
	Responses to Literature
	Persuasive Paragraphs and Essays
	Expository Paragraphs and Essays
	Business Letters
	Personal Narratives
	Blogs
	E-Mails
Casual and Quick	Microblogs
	Text Messages

Insight

Completeness and correctness are perhaps less critical in quick and casual writing, but they are important for all of the other forms on the chart.

React After studying the chart, answer the following questions. Then discuss your responses as a class.

1. What form of writing do you most often engage in?

   _____

   _____

2. How might your writing approach change at different points on the writing spectrum?

   _____

   _____

3. What characteristics do you associate with casual and quick writing? How about formal and thoughtful?

   _____

   _____

LO4 Reviewing Writing and Learning

Consider Answer the following questions about writing as a learning tool. (See LO1, Writing to Learn.)

1. How is writing to learn different from traditional writing assignments?

   _____

   _____

2. What are some ways you can write to learn using your classroom notebook or personal laptop?

   _____

   _____

3. How can pointed questions be used as a writing-to-learn strategy? What about debate?

   _____

   _____

   _____

Answer Answer the following questions about writing to share learning. (See LO2, Writing to Share Learning.)

1. How is writing to share learning different from writing to learn?

   _____

   _____

2. Why is improved thinking considered the link between writing to learn and writing to share?

   _____

   _____

Rank Rank the following forms of writing in order of casual and quick to formal and thoughtful, with 1 being the most casual. (See LO3, Considering the Range of Writing.)

_____ On your personal blog, you write a review of a new restaurant.

_____ You complete a research report on sports in ancient Greece.

_____ You send your friend a text message about your plans for the evening.

_____ You argue for a campus-wide smoking ban in a letter to the editor in your campus newspaper.

> "Reading furnishes the mind only with materials of knowledge;
> it is thinking that makes what we read ours."
> —John Locke

nik40fox/iStockPhoto/Thinkstock

2

Reading and Learning

Reading, as you well know, is a gateway to learning. Textbooks, literature, newspaper articles, and websites have fuelled much of your formal education. It should come as no surprise, then, to discover that reading is an essential learning tool in college and university.

But where much of elementary and secondary school reading material is geared toward gaining a basic understanding of new ideas and concepts, post-secondary reading assignments demand a more active reader. Your instructors will expect you not only to retain new information, but also to compare it to what you already know and reflect on what makes the information important. This chapter is set up to help you become a successful reader.

Learning Outcomes

LO1 Read to learn.
LO2 Use reading strategies.
LO3 Read graphics.
LO4 Review reading and learning.

What do you think?

What message is John Locke trying to get across in his quotation at the top of the page? Do you agree with him?

_____

_____

_____

_____

"Some books are to be tasted, others to be swallowed, and some few are to be chewed and digested."

—Francis Bacon

Traits

Effective writing has strong ideas, clear organization, appropriate voice, precise words, smooth sentences, correct conventions, and a strong design. Use these traits to understand what you read.

Vocabulary

context cues
the words surrounding an unfamiliar term that can help unlock its meaning

LO1 Reading to Learn

Thoughtful, active reading encompasses a number of related tasks: previewing the text, reading it through, taking notes as you go along, and summarizing what you have learned. Active reading gives you control of reading assignments and makes new information part of your own thinking.

Effective Academic Reading

Follow the guidelines listed below for all of your academic reading assignments. A few of these points are discussed in more detail later in the chapter.

1. **Know the assignment:** Identify its purpose, its due date, its level of difficulty, and so on.
2. **Set aside the proper time:** Don't try to read long assignments all at once. Instead, try to read in 30-minute allotments.
3. **Find a quiet place:** The setting should provide space to read and to write.
4. **Gather additional resources:** Keep on hand a notebook, related handouts, Web access, and so on.
5. **Study the "layout" of the reading:** Review the questions in the study guide. Then skim the pages, noting titles, headings, graphics, and boldfaced terms.
6. **Use proven reading strategies:** See LO2, Using Reading Strategies.
7. **Look up challenging words:** Also use context cues to determine the meaning of unfamiliar terms.
8. **Review and paraphrase difficult parts:** Reread difficult sections of the assigned reading, write about them, and discuss them with your classmates.
9. **Summarize what you learned:** Note any concepts or explanations that you will need to study further.

Reflect Which of the tips above do you follow? Which do you not follow? Reflect on one tip that could help you improve your reading.

Using a Class Notebook

To interact thoughtfully with a text, you need to write about it, so reserve part of your class notebook for responses to your readings. Certainly, you can take straight notes on the material (see LO2, Taking Effective Notes) but you should also personally respond to it. Such writing requires you to think about the reading—to agree with it, to question it, to make connections. The following guidelines will help you get started:

- **Write whenever you feel** a need to explore your thoughts and feelings. Discipline yourself to write multiple times, perhaps once before you read, two or three times during the reading, and once afterward.
- **Write freely and honestly** to make genuine connections with the text.
- **Respond to points of view** that you like or agree with and information that confuses you; make connections with other material and record ideas that seem significant.
- **Label and date your responses clearly.** These entries will help you prepare for exams and other assignments.
- **Share your discoveries.** Think of your entries as conversation starters in discussions with classmates.

Special Strategies

Here are some specific ways to respond to a text:

Discuss Carry on a conversation with the author or a character until you come to know him or her and yourself a little better.

Illustrate Use graphics or pictures to help you think about a text.

Imitate Continue the article or story line by trying to write like the author.

Express Share your feelings about a text in a poem.

Insight

If you are a visual person, you may understand a text best by mapping or clustering its important points. (See Chapter 5, LO2, for a sample cluster.)

Practise For one of your next reading assignments, carry out at least two of the reading-response strategies described on this page. When you have finished, reflect on the value of responding to the reading.

Olga Kovalenko/Shutterstock.com

LO2 Using Reading Strategies

To make sure that you gain the most from each reading assignment, employ these additional strategies: paraphrasing, annotation, note taking, and summarizing.

Paraphrasing

Paraphrasing is the act of using your own words to restate an author's original meaning. The value of paraphrasing is difficult to overstate. If you can successfully state an author's ideas in your own words, then you have understood what that author is saying. Paraphrasing is the key skill in note-taking and in summarizing. Paraphrasing works best at the sentence (or very short paragraph) level. As with any skill, paraphrasing ability is developed through practice.

Paraphrasing Tips

- Read and reread the original until you are sure you understand it.
- Write your version of the material without looking at the original.
- Compare your paraphrased version against the original for correctness; pay close attention to numbers and dates, if any, in the original.
- Revise your version, if necessary.

Paraphrase Working with a friend or classmate, read the following sentences and then paraphrase each one. Review each other's paraphrases against the original for correctness.

1. The long process of walking a bill through the Canadian parliament involves three readings in the House of Commons, committee hearings, readings in the Senate, and a final vote in the House of Commons, a process that can take months.

2. Once a soldier in the Canadian infantry, American novelist Raymond Chandler is noted for writing some of the most influential "hard-boiled" detective fiction ever printed, mostly starring private eye Philip Marlowe, who first appeared in Chandler's debut novel, *The Big Sleep*.

3. Cryptozoologists, who search for creatures that most people do not believe exist, say Canada has several such fantastic creatures, one of which is Ogopogo, a water-dwelling creature similar to the Loch Ness monster and which supposedly makes its home in Lake Okanagan in British Columbia, and Champie, a similar creature found in Lake Champlain.

Annotating a Text

Annotating a text allows you to interact with the writer's thoughts and ideas. Here are some suggestions:

- Write questions in the margins.
- Underline or highlight important points.
- Summarize or paraphrase key passages.
- Define new terms.
- Make connections to other parts.

Vocabulary

annotating
the process of underlining, highlighting, or making notes on a text

Annotating in Action

You've Got Hate Mail
by Lydie Raschka

online Check out the full
MindTap version of this essay online.

First I expected it; now I'm scared.

Hate mail confirms a vague, nagging feeling that you've done something wrong. It's a firm tap on the shoulder that says, "The jig is up." So when the first letter came, it was expected. The second, however, was a shock. By the third I was a wreck. How did he know it would take exactly and only three?

So the hate mail is all coming from one person—a man.

I started writing a few years ago, after I had a baby. I haven't completely figured out what led me to writing, but it was probably tied up with my son's birth and the attendant emotions that needed sorting.

Def: related; associated

I like the solitary work life. I write at a table in the bedroom. I send my ideas out into the void. The bedroom seems a safe enough place. I have been told that I am an introvert. What on earth makes me want to communicate with strangers in this perilous way—standing naked in a field?

I can relate to this. Also, it exhibits her fear of people judging her.

"You have to expect these things when you are a writer," my father says about the hate mail. "When you're in the public eye, anyone can read what you write."

The letters are effective and unsettling, to say the least. I have an unusual name, so he thinks I'm foreign. He calls me "Eurotrash." It's a relief because it means he doesn't really know me—although he makes some pretty accurate guesses. He doesn't know that my parents simply like unusual names.

A shortsighted conclusion

Annotate Carefully read the excerpt below from an article by Don Tapscott. Then annotate the text, according to the following directions:

- Circle the main point of the passage.
- Underline or highlight one idea in each paragraph that you either agree with, question, or are confused by. Then make a comment about this idea in the margin.
- Circle all of the words that you are unsure of. Then define or explain these words in the margin.

Digital Generation Will Lead Change
by Don Tapscott

A lot of parents, employers and professors are angry about today's youth. They argue that young people are net-addicted, inattentive and losing their social skills. They are also narcissistic, and a new book even calls them the "Dumbest Generation." My research says none of this is true. I am optimistic about the potential of young people today. I call them the Net Generation, since these older teenagers and young adults are so bathed in bits that they think the Internet is part of the natural landscape. To them, digital technology is no more intimidating than a refrigerator or toaster. For the first time in history, children are more comfortable, knowledgeable and literate than their parents about an innovation central to society. And it is through the use of the digital media that the Net Generation will develop and superimpose its culture on the rest of society.

Evidence is mounting that kids can juggle multiple sensory inputs much more easily than older adults. Rather than our children having dysfunctional brains that can't focus, young people are developing brains that are more appropriate for our fast-paced, complex world. When baby boomers were young they spent many hours a day staring at a television screen, and this passive behaviour influenced the kind of brains they developed. Today, young people spend an equivalent amount of time with digital technologies—being the user, the actor, the collaborator, the initiator, the rememberer, the organizer—which gives them a different kind of brain.

The interactive games that young people play today require both team building and strategic skills. Learning a game and having died (virtually) a hundred times before winning makes them far more determined and more likely to try new ideas and take calculated risks. Young people collaborate constantly through online chats, multi-user video games, and more recently text messages, Facebook and Twitter. For teenagers today, doing their homework is a social and collaborative event involving text messages, instant messages and Facebook walls to discuss problems while the iPod plays in the background.

Already, these kids are learning, playing, communicating, working and creating communities very differently than their parents. They are a force for social transformation. The main interest of the Net Generation is not technology, but what can be done with that technology. I think they are smart, have great values, know how to use collaborative tools, and are well equipped to address many of the big challenges and problems that my generation is leaving them. Overall, their brains are more appropriate for the complex demands of the 21st century.

1

5

10

15

20

25

Tapscott, Don "Digital generation will lead change", *The Toronto Star* (4 July 2012) <www.thestar.com/opinion/editorialopinion/article/1220968–digital-generation-will-lead-change>. Reprinted by permission of the author.

Taking Effective Notes

Taking notes helps you focus on the text and understand it more fully. It changes information you have read about into information that you are working with. Good notes help you paraphrase particularly important points; as discussed earlier, paraphrasing is a key tool used in understanding the text. Personalizing information in this way makes it much easier to remember and use.

Note-Taking Tips

- Use your own words as much as possible (paraphrase).
- Record only key points and details rather than complicated sentences.
- Consider boldfaced or italicized words, graphics, and captions as well as the main text.
- Employ as many abbreviations and symbols as you can (vs., #, &, etc.).
- Decide on a system for organizing or arranging your notes so they are easy to review.

An Active Note-Taking System

To make your note taking more active, use a two-column system: one column (one-third of the page) is for comments, reactions, and questions, and the other (two-thirds of the page) is for your main notes.

Two-Column Notes

You've Got Hate Mail
by Lydie Raschka

March 3

Comments, reactions, questions

At what point would police take action? →

How do other authors and musicians react to hate mail? →

This last bullet is interesting. It reminds me of Stockholm Syndrome—when hostages begin having positive feelings toward their captors. →

Main notes

- The author has received multiple hate letters from the same person; the first included feces.
- She has contacted the post office and the police, who say there is not much they can do.
- The author admits she is vulnerable to people's opinions of her, so much so she takes what the hate mail says seriously.
- Eventually, she admits she feels a connection to the accuser.

Practise Use the two-column note system for one of your next reading assignments. Use the left-hand column to react with questions, comments, and reflections about the information that you record.

Summarizing a Text

Summarizing is the process of identifying and restating—in your own words—the thesis, main points, and conclusion of a document. These points are usually written in the order they appear in the document; however, if the original work is disorganized, the main points can be organized in a more logical order. Main points are written objectively. The purpose of a summary is not to argue with an author's ideas; rather, it is to identify and understand the author's main ideas. (You can always argue the ideas in your own paper.) Although a summary may include a direct quotation from the original document, you should strive to restate the ideas in your own words. If you cannot do that, you likely do not fully understand the information.

Generally, a summary should range from about 5 percent to 30 percent of the length of the original. Summaries of shorter documents that do not include a lot of examples or extended commentary are likely to closer to the 30 percent length while longer documents, with lots of examples, are likely to be closer to 5 percent of the length. However, completeness—identifying and restating all the main ideas— is more important than length.

Formal summaries, those that may be published or read by others, start with one or two sentences that do the following: name the author and the title; identify the source and date of publication; and present the thesis of the article. The main points are presented in your own words and in the author's order or in some logical order. Finally the author's conclusion is presented, in your own words.

Summarizing Tips

- Start with a clear statement of the main point or thesis of the text.
- Include only the essential supporting facts and details (names, dates, times, and places) in the next sentences. Leave out examples, redundancies, definitions, and so on.
- Present the main ideas in the original order, or, if necessary, in a more logical order.
- Remain objective: A summary presents the author's ideas, not what you think about them.
- Tie all of the main points together in a closing sentence.
- Remember to write the thesis, main points, and conclusion in your own words.

Other Classes

In many classes, you'll find summarizing skills useful to help you understand and retain content.

Example Summary

The example below summarizes Lydie Raschka's three-page essay concerning hate mail that she received.

Review

Check out Chapter 10, LO1, for more information on summarizing.

Main points (underlined)	<u>Three occurrences of hate mail from the same sender have left author Lydie Raschka consumed with fear and doubt.</u> Even before the hate mail, Raschka, who admits to being an introvert, struggled with the vulnerability of sharing her writing. She expected hate mail, but, when new letters from the same man kept coming, Raschka contacted the post office and police. Neither helped much. As the unsettling feeling increased, Raschka was unable to continue writing. At some point, she became so consumed by the letters that she began relating to her enemy, even feeling some sympathy for him. For example, he talks in his letters about his aunt and disabled sister; Raschka has a sister and a disabled aunt. <u>In the end, Raschka wishes the sender could realize how much he has in common with her.</u>
Essential supporting facts	
Closing sentence (underlined)	

Summarize Summarize the information in one of the essays in Part 8 of this text or in an essay provided by your instructor. Use the tips and sample above as a guide.

_____
_____
_____
_____
_____
_____
_____
_____
_____
_____
_____
_____

Vocabulary

graphic
a visual representation of information that reveals trends, makes comparisons, shows how something changes over time, and so on

horizontal
parallel to ground level, at right angles to the vertical

vertical
straight up and down, at right angles to the horizontal

LO3 Reading Graphics

In many of your college or university texts, a significant portion of the information will be communicated via charts, graphs, diagrams, and drawings. Knowing how to read these types of graphics will help you become a more effective and informed student. Follow the guidelines listed below when you read a graphic.

- **Scan the graphic.** Consider it as a whole to get an overall idea about its message. Note its type (bar graph, pie graph, diagram, table, and so forth), its topic, its level of complexity, and so on.

- **Study the specific parts.** Start with the main heading or title. Next, note any additional labels or guides (such as the horizontal and vertical axes on a bar graph). Then focus on the actual information displayed in the graphic.

- **Question the graphic.** Does it address an important topic? What is its purpose (to make a comparison, to show a change, and so on)? What is the source of the information? Is the graphic dated or biased in any way?

- **Reflect on its effectiveness.** Explain in your own words the main message communicated by the graphic. Then consider its effectiveness, how it relates to the surrounding text, and how it matches up to your previous knowledge of the topic.

Analysis of a Graphic

Review the vertical bar graph below. Then read the discussion to learn how all of the parts work together.

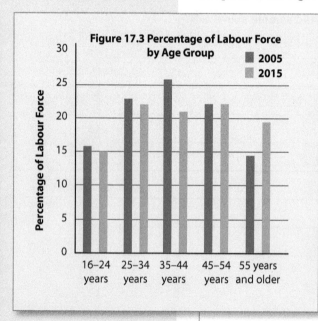

Figure 17.3 Percentage of Labour Force by Age Group

Discussion: This bar graph compares the labour force in 2005 to the labour force in 2015 for five specific age groups. The heading clearly identifies the subject or topic of the graphic. The horizontal line identifies the different age groups, and the vertical line identifies the percentage of the labour force for each group. The key in the upper right-hand corner of the graphic identifies the purpose of the colour coding used in the columns or bars. With all of that information, the graphic reads quite clearly—and many interesting comparisons can be made.

React Read and analyze the following graphics, answering the questions about each one. Use the information in LO3, Reading Graphics, as a guide.

Graphic 1

1. This graphic is called a pictograph rather than a bar graph. What makes it a "pictograph"?

_____

_____

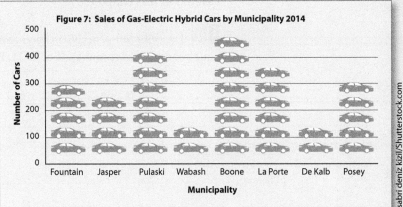

Figure 7: Sales of Gas-Electric Hybrid Cars by Municipality 2014

sabri deniz kizil/Shutterstock.com

2. What is the topic of this graphic?

_____

_____

3. What information is provided on the horizontal line? On the vertical line?

_____

_____

4. What comparisons can a reader make from this graphic?

_____

_____

Graphic 2

1. This graphic is called a line diagram, mapping a structure. What structure does this diagram map?

_____

2. How are the different navigational choices on a complex website shown on this graphic? How might you improve the effectiveness of this graphic?

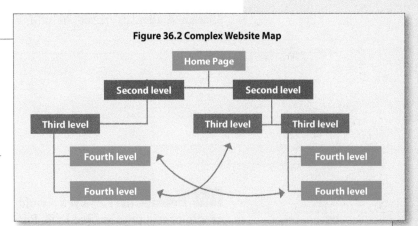

Figure 36.2 Complex Website Map

_____

_____

_____

LO4 Reviewing Reading and Learning

Complete these activities as needed to help you better understand the concepts covered in this chapter.

List Describe some activities you can do in your notebook to better engage with your reading assignments. (See LO1, Reading to Learn.)

_____

_____

_____

_____

_____

Answer What is the purpose of annotating a text? (See LO2, Using Reading Strategies.)

_____

_____

_____

Identify Identify three helpful note-taking tips. (See LO2, Using Reading Strategies.)

1. _____

2. _____

3. _____

List Describe the steps you should take to evaluate the graphics you see in your reading assignments. (See LO3, Reading Graphics.)

_____

_____

_____

_____

_____

> "It's good to rub and polish our brain against that of others."
> —Michel de Montaigne

ColorBlind Images/Getty Images

3

Making the Writing–Reading Connection

Professional writers are well aware of the special connection between writing and reading. Stephen King says, "Reading is the creative centre of a writer's life." Joan Aiken says, "Read as much as you possibly can." William Faulkner said, "Read, read, read. Read everything. . . ." These successful authors know that reading stimulates writing, while their writing stimulates them to read more.

As a student, you need to make your own special connections between writing and reading. This chapter will get you started because it provides three important strategies to enrich your writing and reading.

What do you think?

How can you connect the de Montaigne quotation to the writing process, the reading process, or both?

_____

_____

_____

_____

Learning Outcomes

LO1 Analyze the assignment.

LO2 Use the traits of writing.

LO3 Use graphic organizers.

LO4 Review the writing–reading connection.

L◯1 Analyzing the Assignment

Part of making good choices is understanding in advance what you are dealing with. You would, for example, want to know the basics about a job or an internship before you apply for it. The same holds true for each of your college or university reading and writing assignments. You should identify its main features before you get started on your work.

The STRAP Strategy

You can use the STRAP strategy to analyze your writing and reading assignments. The strategy consists of answering questions about these five features: _subject, type, role, audience,_ and _purpose_. Once you answer the questions, you'll be ready to get to work. This chart shows how the strategy works:

For Writing Assignments		For Reading Assignments
What specific topic should I write about?	**Subject**	What specific topic does the reading address?
What form of writing (_essay, article_) will I use?	**Type**	What form (_essay, text chapter, article_) does the reading take?
What position (_student, citizen, employee_) should I assume?	**Role**	What position (_student, responder, concerned individual_) does the writer assume?
Who is the intended reader?	**Audience**	Who is the intended reader?
What is the goal (_to inform, to persuade_) of the writing?	**Purpose**	What is the goal of the material?

Test Taking

The STRAP questions can help you to quickly understand a writing prompt or a reading selection on a test.

The STRAP Strategy in Action

Suppose you were given the following reading assignment in an environmental studies class.

> Read the essay "To Drill or Not to Drill" in the online readings. Then write a blog entry comparing the reading with what you've learned about oil drilling in class discussions.

Here are the answers to the STRAP questions for this assignment:

Subject: Drilling for oil in the Arctic National Wildlife Refuge

Type: Persuasive essay

Role: Advocate of less drilling, more conservation

Audience: General consumers

Purpose: To persuade readers to accept a new line of thinking

Respond Use the STRAP strategy to complete the assignments below.

Review

Before you begin any reading assignment, you should also consider these issues:

- The importance of the assignment
- The time you have to complete it
- The way the assignment fits into the course as a whole

Assignment 1: Read "Religious Faith Versus Spirituality" by Neil Bissoondath, found in Chapter 42, Comparison–Contrast Essays. Then in your class notebook, respond to the reading, noting its key features and your reactions to them.

Subject: What specific topic does the reading address?

_____

_____

Type: What form *(essay, text chapter)* does the reading take?

_____

_____

Role: What position does the writer assume?

_____

_____

Audience: Who is the intended audience?

_____

_____

Purpose: What is the goal of the material?

_____

_____

Assignment 2: Answer the STRAP questions that follow for a reading assignment in Part 8 of *WRITE 2* or elsewhere. Choose an essay that informs or entertains.

Subject: What specific topic does the reading address?

_____

_____

Speaking & Listening

Work on the second assignment with a partner or a small group if your instructor allows it.

Type: What form *(essay, text chapter)* does the reading take?

_____

_____

Role: What position does the writer assume?

_____

_____

Audience: Who is the intended audience?

_____

_____

Purpose: What is the goal of the material?

_____

_____

L◯2 Using the Traits

Chapter 4, Using the Writing Process and the Traits, goes into great detail about using the **traits** of writing to help you write more effectively. In this chapter, we preview these traits and show how you can use them to help analyze and discuss your reading assignments.

Previewing the Traits

The traits of writing are highlighted below. Each one is an important feature in any reading selection, whether an essay, a chapter, an article, or a piece of fiction. (The questions will help you analyze a reading selection for the traits.)

Traits

Throughout *WRITE 2*, the traits are used to help you read and write.

- **Ideas** The information contained in reading material
  What is the topic of the reading?
  What main point is made?
  What supporting details are provided?

- **Organization** The overall structure of the material
  How does the reading selection begin?
  How is the middle part arranged?
  How does the selection end?

- **Voice** The personality of the writing—how the writer speaks to the reader
  To what degree does the writer seem interested in and knowledgeable about the topic?
  To what degree does the writer engage the reader?
  What is the tone of the reading?

- **Word Choice** The writer's use of words and phrases
  What can be said about the nouns, verbs, and modifiers in the reading?
  Are the words too general, or are they specific and effective?
  Does the writer use figurative language?

- **Sentence Fluency** The flow of the sentences
  What stands out about the sentences?
  Are they varied in length, do they flow smoothly, do they seem stylish, and so on?

- **Conventions** The correctness or accuracy of the language
  To what degree does the writing follow the conventions of the language?

- **Design** The appearance of the writing
  What, if anything, stands out about the design?
  Does it enhance or take away from the reading experience?

Vocabulary

traits
key elements or characteristics

tone
the writer's attitude towards the subject matter

figurative language
metaphors, personification, or other creative comparisons used to describe something or to make a point

Nikada/iStockphoto.com

A Sample Analysis for a Reading Selection

Here is a traits analysis of "A Modest Proposal: Guys Shouldn't Drive Till 25," an argumentative essay posted on the *WRITE 2* MindTap website.

■ **Ideas**

The essay focuses on a bold proposal (rather than a modest one): raising the driving age for males to 25. The writer presents reliable statistics showing the dangers that young male drivers present. She also addresses main objections to her idea as well as many benefits to it.

■ **Organization**

The beginning paragraph uses dramatic statistics to lead up to the proposal.

The middle paragraphs cover main objections, benefits, and exceptions to the idea.

The closing paragraph identifies rules and actions that haven't worked in the past as a dramatic contrast to the writer's bold claim, which the writer restates here.

■ **Voice**

The writer speaks in a friendly, knowing manner. The use of the pronoun "We" in a few paragraphs helps connect the reader with the writer. At times, she speaks in a tongue-in-cheek style. For example, she claims a more fit male population in our "paunchy" society would be a side benefit.

■ **Word Choice**

The word choice reflects an essay intended for a general audience—not too challenging nor too basic. The most challenging terms such as *salient* and *carnage* are defined for the reader.

■ **Sentence Fluency**

The sentences are, for the most part, long, and some of them may require a few readings. The varied sentence beginnings help with the flow of the writer's ideas.

■ **Conventions**

The writer clearly follows the conventions.

■ **Design**

The essay is traditional in design except for one long bulleted list.

Vocabulary

tongue-in-cheek
an expression or idiom meaning "somewhat humourously" or "not to be taken seriously"

Respond Analyze "Spanglish Spoken Here" (Chapter 43) for the traits. To develop your analysis, ask and answer each of the specific questions listed earlier in this chapter, or use the questions as a basic response guide, as is done above. (Use your own paper.)

Speaking & Listening

Work on this activity with a partner or a small group of classmates if your instructor allows it.

Other Classes

See Chapter 5, LO4, Using Graphic Organizers, for eight common graphic organizers that you can use to organize ideas in any class.

LO3 Using Graphic Organizers

Graphic organizers help you map out your thinking for writing and reading assignments. You can, for example, use a Venn diagram or a T-graph to arrange your thinking for a comparison essay that you are about to write or have just read. Other common graphics can help you organize your thinking for problem–solution, cause–effect, and narrative writing and reading.

Graphing a Reading Assignment

Provided below is a time line charting the main actions in a narrative essay found in Chapter 40, Narrative Essays. (A time line identifies the key actions and events, without the related details and explanations.)

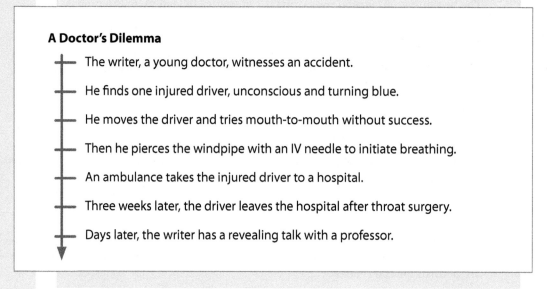

A Doctor's Dilemma

- The writer, a young doctor, witnesses an accident.
- He finds one injured driver, unconscious and turning blue.
- He moves the driver and tries mouth-to-mouth without success.
- Then he pierces the windpipe with an IV needle to initiate breathing.
- An ambulance takes the injured driver to a hospital.
- Three weeks later, the driver leaves the hospital after throat surgery.
- Days later, the writer has a revealing talk with a professor.

Respond In the space provided, use a time line to chart the main actions from the narrative essay "Shark Bait," also found in Chapter 40. (Remember to focus on key actions, without all of the related details.)

Shark Bait

LO4 Reviewing the Writing–Reading Connection

Complete these activities as needed to help you better understand the writing–reading connection.

Analyze Use the STRAP strategy to analyze the following reading assignment. (See LO1, Analyzing the Assignment.)

Read "Overpopulation Is Bad but Overconsumption Is Worse," found in Chapter 44, Argument Essays.

Subject: _____

Type: _____

Role: _____

Audience: _____

Purpose: _____

Analyze Analyze the contents of "Overpopulation Is Bad but Overconsumption Is Worse" for the following traits. (See LO2, Using the Traits.)

Ideas: _____

_____

_____

_____

_____

_____

Organization: _____

_____

_____

_____

_____

Word Choice: _____

_____

_____

_____

"If you start in the right place and follow all the steps,
you will get to the right end."

——Elizabeth Moon

metin Kiyak/iStockPhoto/Thinkstock

4 Using the Writing Process and the Traits

Have you ever climbed to the top of a lighthouse? You can't get there in one step. You can't get there in a straight line, either. But if you've ever completed such a climb and looked out for miles over the ocean, you know it's worth the trip.

Writing is the same way. You can't arrive at a final draft in one step or in a straight line. It's going to take some work and a bit of sweat. You may even feel dizzy sometimes. But if you take the steps in the writing process, you'll reach your destination and see things you've never imagined. This chapter will show you the way.

What do you think?

How can a series of small steps in writing equal a giant leap in thinking?

Learning Outcomes

LO1 Think about writing as a process.

LO2 Learn about the steps in the writing process.

LO3 Learn about the traits of effective writing.

LO4 Connect the process and the traits.

lO1 Understanding the Writing Process

When receiving a writing assignment, most writers ask the same question: How will I *ever* get this done? If you struggle to answer this question, you are not alone. Even professional writers labour for the right answer. But have no fear. A writing project is much less imposing when you approach it as a process rather than as an end product.

This chapter will introduce you to the manageable steps of the **writing process**. Taking those steps one at a time will help you become a better writer and make your next writing assignment a lot less intimidating.

The Process in Action

The writing process is often considered a process of discovery: While you follow it, you will find out what you want to say.

Read/React Read the following quotations from writers who describe the writing process as a means of discovery. Discuss the quotations with a partner or a small group of classmates. Then explain below what one or two of the statements mean to you.

"Writing became such a process of discovery that I couldn't wait to get to work in the morning: I wanted to know what I was going to say."

—Sharon O'Brien

"For most writers, the act of putting words on paper is not the recording of a discovery but the very act of exploration itself."

—Donald Murray

"If you don't allow yourself the possibility of writing something very, very bad, it would be hard to write something very good."

—Steven Galloway

BorisVian/Shutterstock.com
mates/Shutterstock.com
Alexander Kalina/Shutterstock.com

Reactions: _____

_____

_____

_____

_____

_____

_____

_____

Thinking about Your Own Writing

Respond Answer the following questions about your writing experiences. Be sure to explain each of your answers.

1. Rate your experience as a writer by circling the appropriate star:

    negative ★ ★ ★ ★ ★ positive

    Explain. _____

    _____

    _____

    _____

2. What is the easiest part of writing for you? _____

    _____

    _____

    _____

3. What is the hardest part of writing for you? _____

    _____

    _____

    _____

4. What types of writing assignments challenge you the most? _____

    _____

    _____

    _____

5. What is the best thing you have ever written? _____

    _____

    _____

    _____

6. What is the most important thing you have learned about writing?

    _____

    _____

    _____

    _____

    _____

Photo by Kristian Dowling/ Getty Images

Spotlight on Writing

"Sometimes something discouraging can be encouraging. It's all in how you take it."

The writing career of playwright Suzan-Lori Parks nearly fizzled, thanks in part to resistance from her high school English teacher, who recommended she not pursue an English degree because she was a poor speller. "Still am actually," says Parks.

Following that advice, Parks went to college to pursue a chemistry degree, but rediscovered her passion for writing in a fiction workshop. "What you love comes back to you," she says.

Since that time, Parks has become a renowned playwright. In 2002, her play *Topdog/Underdog* was awarded the Pulitzer Prize for Drama, making her the first African American woman to win the award.

LO2 The Steps in the Process

You cannot change a flat tire in one fell swoop—it takes a number of steps to get the job done right. The same goes for writing. If you expect to finish a paper in one broad attempt, you are going to be disappointed by the result. On the other hand, if you follow the steps of the writing process and pace yourself, you'll get the job done right.

Process	Activities
Prewriting	Start the process by (1) selecting a topic to write about, (2) collecting details about it, and (3) finding your focus: the main idea or thesis.
Writing	Then write your first draft, using your prewriting plan and outline as a general guide. Writing a first draft allows you to connect your thoughts about a topic.
Revising	Carefully review your first draft and have a classmate read it as well. Change any parts that need to be clearer, and add missing information.
Editing	Edit your revised writing by checking for style, grammar, punctuation, and spelling errors.
Publishing	During the final step, prepare your writing to share with your instructor, your peers, or another audience.

Explain On the lines below, tell how the writing process explained above compares with your own way of completing writing assignments. Consider what you usually do first, second, third, and so on.

_____

_____

_____

_____

_____

_____

_____

_____

_____

_____

_____

> "The first draft is a skeleton—just bare bones."
>
> —Phyllis Reynolds Naylor

Speaking & Listening

If you are having trouble explaining your process, talk about it with a partner.

The Process in Action

As the chart below indicates, for a major writing assignment you will likely move back and forth among the steps in the writing process. For example, after writing a first draft, you may decide to collect more details about your topic, which is a prewriting activity. Or you may want to apply the revision step more than once, producing multiple drafts that become increasingly clear and complete.

Process Chart

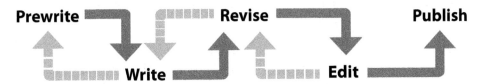

Create In the space provided below, create a chart that shows your own process. Discuss your chart with a partner or small group of classmates.

Reasons to Write

The four main reasons to write are given below. Always use the writing process when **writing to show learning** and when **writing to share**.

Reason	Forms	Purpose
Writing to show learning	Summaries, informational essays	To show your understanding of subjects you are studying
Writing to share	Personal essays, blog postings, short stories, plays	To share your personal thoughts, feelings, and creativity with others
Writing to explore	Personal journals, diaries, unsent letters, dialogues	To learn about yourself and your world
Writing to learn	Learning logs, reading logs, notes	To help you understand what you are learning

Explain Why is using the writing process unnecessary for **writing to explore** and **writing to learn**?

_____

_____

_____

_____

Test Taking

When you respond to a written question on an exam, use an abbreviated form of this process. Spend a few minutes gathering and organizing ideas, then write your response. Afterward, read what you have done and quickly revise and edit it.

LO3 Understanding the Traits of Effective Writing

Think about your favourite song. What makes it great? It's a combination of elements, right? The beat is fresh; the lyrics, inventive; the chorus, catchy.

A combination of elements results in good writing, too. In Chapter 3, you previewed the key elements, or traits, of effective writing:

ideas	word choice	conventions
organization	sentence fluency	design
voice		

In this chapter, you will see how each of these can contribute to the overall quality of a piece of writing. If each trait is skillfully handled, the result will be a successful article, essay, or other text.

The traits of effective writing are described below.

Traits of Effective Writing

■ **Strong Ideas** Good writing contains plenty of relevant information (ideas and details). And all of the information holds the reader's interest.

> In the world of cloud enthusiasts, 1951 was a special year. It marked the last time a new cloud category was recognized by the International Cloud Atlas. But that may soon change. A photograph of wavy, violent-looking clouds over Cedar Rapids, Iowa, is at the heart of a 2009 cloud debate. Many say the picture reveals a new cloud category known as *undulatus asperatus*. Others say it is just another example of an *undulatus* cloud. A review is underway to determine the answer. Will 2009 become the new 1951?
>
> — Johanna Ruiz

1. Rate the passage for ideas by circling the appropriate star:

   weak ★ ★ ★ ★ ★ strong

   Explain. _____

   _____

2. What is the main point? _____

   _____

Other Classes

The traits help you write and read in any subject area. Each discipline has its own ideas and organizational structures that you should learn, and all writing benefits from strong words, smooth sentences, correctness, and effective design.

■ **Logical Organization** Effective writing has a clear overall structure—with a beginning, a middle, and an ending.

> I've experienced all sorts of road trips. Some have been great; others have been lousy. But along the way, I've picked up tips for maximizing the experience. The first is preparation. Before you leave, gather snacks, caffeinated drinks, and a minimum of three of your favorite CDs. Next, carry a notebook to record all the stupid things your friends say. And lastly, drive whatever car is least likely to break down. Now go enjoy the open road!
>
> — T. J. Brown

1. Rate the passage for organization by circling the appropriate star:

   weak ★ ★ ★ ★ ★ strong

   Explain. _____

   _____

2. How is this passage arranged—by time, by order of importance, by logic?

_____

_____

3. What transitional phrases does the writer use? _____

_____

Traits

Transitions (_first, later, for a brief time on the other hand, consequently, alternatively_) establish logical organization by linking ideas.

■ **Appropriate Voice** In the best writing, you can hear the writer's voice—her or his special way of saying things. Using a voice that fits the piece of writing shows that the writer cares about the subject. A lively voice can add interest to a piece of writing; a formal voice can give it an air of gravitas.

> Natural disasters are as ruthless as they are powerful. Too often they leave families, communities, and entire countries broken and helpless. But that's when we must step up and help. You may think one person can't make a world of a difference to people affected by a natural disaster, but you can. Besides donating money, you can give blood, volunteer for relief agencies, and use social media to influence others to help. Will you join the cause?
>
> — Melanie Roberts

Speaking & Listening

Read this model aloud to a partner. Then have the partner read the model. How do your different voices and expression affect the overall impact of the model?

1. Rate the passage for voice by circling the appropriate star:

weak ★ ★ ★ ★ ★ strong

Explain. _____

_____

2. Does the writer seem to care about the topic? Explain. _____

_____

3. How would you identify the voice in this passage—sincere, silly, bored?

_____

_____

■ **Well-Chosen Words** In strong writing, nouns and verbs are specific and clear, and modifiers add important information.

> The swimmer hunched over the starting line, anticipating the start of the race. "Bang!" The sound thrust her into motion. She dived into the pool, darting through the water like a torpedo. As she approached the other end of the pool, she swiftly spun around, kicked her feet off the concrete side, and swam back to the original end of the pool.
>
> — Joel Gutierrez

1. Rate the passage for word choice by circling the appropriate star:

weak ★ ★ ★ ★ ★ strong

Explain. _____

_____

2. Which, if any, specific verbs stand out for you? _____

_____

3. What other words do you find interesting? (Name two.)

_____

_____

The traits help you in two important ways: (1) They name the key elements that you must consider when writing. (2) They provide a vocabulary to discuss writing with your peers.

■ **Smooth Sentences** The sentences in good writing flow smoothly from one to the next. They carry the meaning of the essay or article.

Have you ever sent so many text messages that your thumbs started to ache? If so, you may be suffering from a condition dubbed "Blackberry thumb." It's true. Repetitive stress on your thumbs from texting can cause tendonitis and nerve damage. Doctors say the chance for injury is greater as you age. Naturally, the remedy is to rest your fingers.

— James Jackson

1. Rate the sentences in the passage by circling the appropriate star:
   weak ★ ★ ★ ★ ★ strong

   Explain. _____

   _____

2. In what ways does the writer vary the sentences he uses? _____

   _____

3. Which sentence do you like best? Why? _____

   _____

■ **Conventional Correctness** Strong writing is easy to read because it follows the conventions, or rules, of the language.

Ella Fitzgerald is one of the most famous jazz vocalists in music history. Known as "the First Lady of Song," Fitzgerald made her singing debut at 17 at the renowned Apollo Theater in Harlem, New York. From there, her career went through three progressions—big band, bebop, and mainstream. In all, her recording career lasted 59 years and produced 13 Grammy Awards.

— Chloe Evans

1. Rate the conventions in the passage by circling the appropriate star:
   weak ★ ★ ★ ★ ★ strong

   Explain. _____

   _____

2. What punctuation marks, other than periods, are used correctly in this passage?

   _____

   _____

3. What do the quotation marks show? (See Chapter 38 for help.)

   _____

   _____

■ **Appropriate Design** The design of a document should be determined by its context. In academic writing, the design should follow the guidelines established by the instructor or school. Two common formatting styles are MLA (see Chapter 9, LO3 and LO5) and APA (see Chapter 9, LO4 and LO6).

LaShawna Wilson

Ms. Davis

Forces in Science

February 11, 2015

Physics of Rainbows

"Why are there so many songs about rainbows?" asks the old tune. Perhaps it's because rainbows are beautiful, multicoloured, and huge, arching over cities and mountains. But rainbows have captured human imagination as much because of their mystery as their beauty. In his work with prisms, Sir Isaac Newton demonstrated that something as beautiful and mysterious as a rainbow could be created through the simple property of refraction.

Basics of Refraction

The key to understanding rainbows is refraction. When light passes from one medium to another, it bends. Simply look at a straw in a glass, and the apparent break in the straw when it enters the water demonstrates refraction. Light is bending as it passes through the water, showing the straw in a different place. When light enters a new medium at a sharp angle, the refraction is stronger. That's because one side of the light beam is entering the medium first, thereby slowing down, as the other side of the light beam continues longer at its previous speed. The result is a turnin the angle of the light ("Prism" 13). This effect is demonstrated in Figure 1.

Figure 1: Basic refraction. Light moving from one medium to another slows down. When entering at an angle, the light is more sharply refracted.

Wilson 2

Frequencies and Refraction

Different frequencies of light bend at different angles. The relatively long wavelengths of red light do not bend as much as the relatively short wavelengths of purple light, which is why a prism splits white light into its colours.

A raindrop can do the same thing. Figure 2, derived from the website "How Stuff Works," shows how white light is bent when passing through a raindrop.

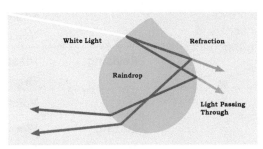

Figure 2: Refraction of light through a raindrop. Note that the purple light exits at a higher angle than the red. Drops lower in the air will reflect violet light to viewers' eyes, while higher drops reflect red light. (Source http://science.howstuffworks.com/rainbow2.htm.)

Bands of Colour

The reason that a rainbow looks like bands of colour is that the observer sees only one colour coming from each droplet. As Figure 2 shows, a droplet that is higher in the sky will refract red into the eyes of the viewer. A droplet that is lower in the sky will refract violet into the viewer's eyes. This same patternholds for all of the colours in between—orange, yellow, green, blue, and indigo. This effect creates the bands of colour that the person sees when looking at the rainbow.

1. Rate the design of these pages (consider headings, margins, and graphics) by circling the appropriate star:

    weak ★ ★ ★ ★ ★ strong

    Explain. _____

    _____

    _____

2. What one design feature stands out for you? _____

    _____

    _____

3. Why is design important for a finished piece of writing?

    _____

    _____

Workplace

Design becomes especially important when you create a workplace document. Using correct format for letters, memos, and reports helps readers understand the content and projects a professional image.

Traits

The first three traits—ideas, organization, and voice—deal with big issues, so they dominate the beginning of the writing process. Word choice, sentence fluency, conventions, and design become important later.

LO4 Connecting the Process and the Traits

The writing process guides you as you form a piece of writing. The writing traits identify the key elements to consider in the writing. This chart connects the two. For example, the chart shows that during prewriting, you should focus on ideas, organization, and voice.

Process	Traits: Activities
Prewriting	**Ideas:** selecting a topic, collecting details about it, forming a thesis
	Organization: arranging the details
	Voice: establishing your stance (objective, personal)
Writing	**Ideas:** connecting your thoughts and information
	Organization: following your prewriting plan
	Voice: sounding serious, sincere, interested, et cetera
Revising	**Ideas:** reviewing for clarity and completeness
	Organization: reviewing for structure/arrangement of ideas
	Voice: reviewing for appropriate tone
Editing	**Word choice:** checking for specific nouns, verbs, and modifiers
	Sentences: checking for smoothness and variety
	Conventions: checking for correctness
Publishing	**Design:** evaluating the format

Think Critically Team up with a classmate to discuss the following questions. Record your answers on the lines below.

1. Which writing trait interests you the most? Why?

_____

_____

_____

2. Which step in the writing process should probably take the most time? Explain. _____

_____

_____

_____

3. How could you use the chart above during a writing project? _____

_____

_____

_____

Monkey Business Images/Shutterstock.com

> "Bring ideas in and entertain them royally, for one of them may be king."
>
> —Mark Van Doren

David Henley/Dorling Kindersley/Getty Images

Prewriting

A process, by definition, is "a series of actions bringing about a result." **Prewriting** is the first action, or step, in the writing process. In many ways, it is the most important one, because it involves all of the decisions you should make before the actual writing. If you do the necessary prewriting and planning, you will be well prepared to work through the rest of the process. If, on the other hand, you jump right into your first draft, you will find it extremely difficult to develop an effective piece of writing.

In this chapter, you will learn about the following prewriting strategies: selecting a specific topic, gathering details about it, forming a focus or thesis, and organizing your support. Completing each one of these activities puts you in control of your writing. And for extended writing assignments, like research papers, thorough prewriting becomes even more important.

Learning Outcomes

LO1 Analyze the assignment.

LO2 Select a topic.

LO3 Gather details about a topic.

LO4 Use graphic organizers.

LO5 Establish a focus.

LO6 Understand patterns of organization.

LO7 Organize your information.

LO8 Review prewriting.

prewriting
the first step in the writing process; preparation for the actual writing

What do you think?

In the quotation above, what does Van Doren mean by "bring ideas in and entertain them royally"? How does this thought relate to prewriting?

_____

_____

_____

_____

LO1 Analyzing the Assignment

Suppose a student writes an essay explaining the main features of a weight-training program, but the instructor really wanted an evaluation of its effectiveness. The student will have missed the purpose of the assignment (*to evaluate*). To make sure that this doesn't happen to you, always analyze your writing assignments.

Using the STRAP Strategy

In Chapter 3, you were introduced to the STRAP strategy for analyzing assignments. This strategy asks you to answer key questions about an assignment.

Subject:	What specific topic should I write about?
Type:	What form of writing (*essay, article, report*) should I use?
Role:	What position (*student, citizen, employee, family member*) should I assume?
Audience:	Who (*classmates, instructor, government official, parent*) is the intended reader?
Purpose:	What is the goal (*to inform, to analyze, to persuade, to share*) of the writing?

Respond Analyze the following assignment using the STRAP strategy.

Assignment: In a class blog posting, reflect on the significance of a social custom from another culture. In your writing, consider the history of the custom, its relationship to similar customs in other cultures, and your reasons for choosing this particular custom.

Subject: What topic should I write about?

_____

_____

Type: What form of writing should I use?

_____

Role: What position should I assume?

_____

Audience: Who is the intended reader?

_____

Purpose: What is the goal of the writing?

_____

Test Taking

For some assignments, you may not find a direct answer to every STRAP question. Use your best judgment when this happens.

Vocabulary

STRAP strategy
a strategy helping a writer identify the key features of an assignment—the subject, type of writing, writer's role, audience, and purpose

Understanding Key Words in Assignments

A key word in a writing assignment identifies the assignment's purpose; more specifically, it tells you what you should do in your writing. For example, in the assignment on the previous page, the key word is *reflect*. Other common key words include *explain, persuade, describe,* and so on. But what exactly does it mean to reflect or explain? The following chart summarizes the meanings and implications of some typical key terms.

Common Key Words

Here are key words that you will find in many of your assignments.

Analyze	Break down a topic into its parts.
Argue or persuade	Defend a position with logical arguments and support.
Compare	Show the similarities and differences.
Describe	Show in detail what something or someone is like.
Evaluate	Consider the truth, usefulness, or value of something.
Explain or inform	Give reasons, list steps, or discuss something.
Reflect	Share your well-considered thoughts and feelings about a topic.
Summarize	Restate someone else's ideas briefly in your own words.

Tip

Once you find out the due date for the assignment, set up a schedule to complete your work. Be sure to give yourself enough time for each step in the writing process—prewriting, writing, revising, and editing.

Identify Circle the key word in each of the following assignments. Then explain how this key word will direct your writing. (The first one is done for you.)

1. In a movie review suitable for a school publication, (evaluate) one of Quentin Tarantino's later films.

   To evaluate a movie means to identify its main features, its strengths and weaknesses, and its value (whether or not it is worth seeing).

2. In a personal essay, describe a time when the "better angels of your nature" took control.

3. Write an editorial to your local newspaper, arguing for or against a piece of immigration legislation.

4. Explain in an informational essay the causes of a serious health condition affecting a large number of people.

Select a topic.

> "There are few experiences quite so satisfactory as getting a good idea...."
>
> —Lancelot Law Whyte

A topic for an extended assignment such as a research paper must be broad enough to offer plenty of information. For a more limited assignment (a one- or two-page essay), the topic should be more specific.

LO2 Selecting a Topic

Personal essayist Andy Rooney of *60 Minutes* fame stated, "I don't pick subjects so much as they pick me." He was lucky in that he could write about anything that interested him, and he came across so many interesting subjects that they seemed to "pick" him. You are not so lucky in most of your writing assignments because your choices are usually limited. Even so, always try to select a topic that you have strong feelings about. Otherwise, you will find it very difficult to do your best work.

Narrowing Your Choices

Some assignments will tell you specifically what you should write about, but in most cases, they will identify a general subject area that serves as a starting point for a topic search. This graphic shows how the selecting process should work, moving from the general subject area to a specific topic.

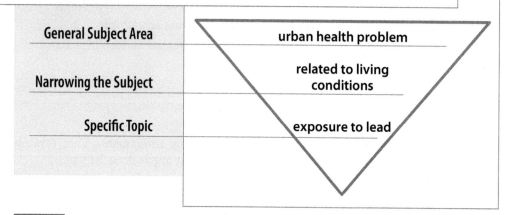

Assignment: Analyze the causes and effects of an urban health problem.

General Subject Area	urban health problem
Narrowing the Subject	related to living conditions
Specific Topic	exposure to lead

Choose Identify a specific topic for the following assignment. (Use the example above as a guide.)

Assignment: In a persuasive essay, argue for or against a new or proposed mode of transportation.

1. What is the general subject area?

2. How can you narrow this subject?

3. What is one specific topic that you could write about?

Selecting Strategies

If you can't think of a suitable topic for an assignment, be sure to review your class notes, your text, and relevant websites for ideas. You may also want to use a selecting strategy to help you identify possible topics.

Clustering Begin a cluster with the general subject area or a narrowed subject. Circle it and then cluster related words around it.

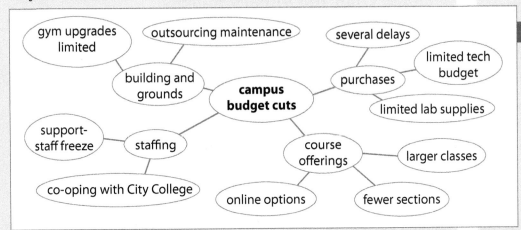

Extend

If one of the clustering ideas interests you, write freely about it for 5 minutes to see what you can discover.

Freewriting Write non-stop for 5–10 minutes about your assignment to discover possible topics. Begin by writing down a particular thought about the assignment. Then record whatever comes to mind without stopping to judge, edit, or correct your writing.

Developing a Dialogue Create a dialogue between yourself and another person to identify possible topics for a writing assignment.

Practise Use the format below to create a dialogue for the following writing assignment. Afterward, circle any possible writing ideas. (Use your own paper to continue the conversation.)

Vocabulary

dialogue
a composition in the form of a written conversation

Assignment: Write a brief personal essay in which you reflect on something that really bugs you about school life or the workplace.

You: _So, what is one thing that really bugs you about school?_____

Other person: _____

_____

You: _____

_____

Other person: _____

_____

L○3 Gathering Details

After selecting a writing topic, you'll need to learn as much as you can about it. Writing your first draft will go smoothly if you have collected plenty of information about your topic, so use strategies like those below and on the next page to gather facts and details.

Deciding What You Already Know

To review what you already know about a topic, try one of these strategies:

Five W's of Writing Answer the five W's (who? what? when? where? and why?) to identify basic information about your subject. Add *how?* to the list for more thorough coverage.

Listing List your first thoughts about your topic as well as questions about it. Work rapidly, recording ideas non-stop for as long as you can.

Clustering Create a cluster with your specific topic as the starting point.

Focused Freewriting Write freely about your topic for at least 5 minutes to see what thoughts and feelings you can uncover. Keep writing for as long as you can.

Dialoguing Discuss your topic in a creative dialogue between you and another person of your choice.

Explore Using one of the strategies above, collect your first thoughts about one of the topics listed here. (Use your own paper if you need more room.)

- an aspect of school or work that I really don't like
- the benefits (or drawbacks) of taking online post-secondary courses
- a promising career choice
- a particular trend in fashion or music
- a favourite vacation spot
- the best pet

Bomshtein/Shutterstock.com

Collecting Additional Information

For most writing assignments, gathering your own thoughts will just be a starting point, unless, of course, you're writing about a personal experience. Conducting primary and secondary research is the main way to learn more about a topic. Here is the main difference between the two types of research:

> **Primary research** consists of information you gather by observing the topic in action, participating in it, and so on.

> **Secondary research** consists of learning what others have already written about the topic.

Questioning

Your questions will naturally guide your search for additional information about a topic. Whether your topic is a **problem** (school budget cuts), a **policy** (graduation requirements), or a **concept** (a weight-training program), the questions in the following chart will lead you to pertinent facts and details.

	Description	Function	History	Value
Problems	What is the problem?	Who or what is affected by it?	What or who caused it?	What is its significance?
Policies	What are the most important features?	What is the policy designed to do?	What brought this policy about?	What are its advantages and disadvantages?
Concepts	What type of concept is it?	Why is it important?	When did it originate?	What value does it hold?

Collect Fill in the first blank below with a specific topic. (See the previous activities in this chapter for ideas.) Then indicate the topic's category—either a problem, policy, or concept. Finally, choose two appropriate questions from the chart above and answer them. (You may have to do some quick research to answer your questions.)

Topic: _____   Category: _____

Question 1: _____   Question 2: _____

_____   _____

Answer: _____   Answer: _____

_____   _____

Citation

You need to document properly any secondary sources you use in your writing. See Chapter 9 for more information.

Vocabulary

primary research information gained through firsthand experience such as participating, observing, or interviewing

secondary research information gained through reading what others have learned about a topic

LO4 Using Graphic Organizers

Researching a topic is one thing; keeping track of all of the new information is quite another. To remember key points, take notes, write summaries (see Chapter 2, LO2, Using Reading Strategies), or use a graphic organizer.

Sample Graphic Organizers

Timeline Use for personal narratives to list actions or events in the order they occurred.

Subject: _____

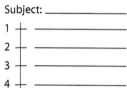

1
2
3
4

Process Diagram Use to collect details for science-related writing, such as the steps in a process.

Topic: _____

Step 1
↓
Step 2
↓
Step 3

Line Diagram Use to collect and organize details for informational essays.

Specific Topic
Main Point   Main Point
Details | Details | Details | Details

Venn Diagram Use to collect details to compare and contrast two topics.

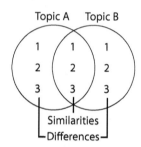

Topic A   Topic B

Similarities
Differences

Cause–Effect Organizer Use to collect and organize details for cause–effect essays.

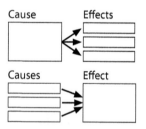

Cause   Effects

Causes   Effect

Problem–Solution Web Use to map out problem–solution essays.

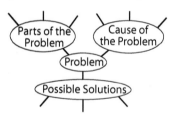

Parts of the Problem   Cause of the Problem
Problem
Possible Solutions

Evaluation Chart Use to collect supporting details for essays of evaluation.

Subject:

Points to Evaluate	Supporting Details
1	
2	
3	
4	

Cluster Use to collect details for informational essays.

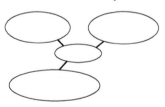

Tip

A graphic organizer helps you to put the information you are collecting in good order.

Choose Identify the best graphic organizer for collecting information about each of the following topics.

1. A personal experience that changed your thinking

   Graphic organizer: _____

2. The features of a new recycling system

   Graphic organizer: _____

3. Vandalism in the dormitories

   Graphic organizer: _____

4. Effects of a specific oil spill

   Graphic organizer: _____

5. Examining two similar movies

   Graphic organizer: _____

Complete Use the appropriate graphic organizer to record information about one of the topics above. (You may have to do more research to help you fill in the graphic organizer.)

Chapter 5 Prewriting

LO5 Establishing a Focus

There are really two parts to prewriting. Part one involves selecting an appropriate topic and collecting information about it. Part two deals with planning how to use this information in the actual writing. To initiate this plan, you must establish a writing focus.

Choosing the Special Part of a Topic

A skilled photographer decides how to focus or centre the subject before taking a photograph. You should do the same before you begin writing. A thoughtful focus dictates what information to include in your writing, as well as what information to leave out.

Suppose you were writing an essay on the effects of the 2010 Winter Olympics on the city of Vancouver. To focus your writing and enhance its interest, you could cover how the winter games have affected a particular business or industry.

Topic: Effects of 2010 Winter Olympics on the City of Vancouver

Focus: The effect of the games on a particular business or industry.

Review Develop a focus for each of the following topics. When finished, have a partner rate the effectiveness of each focus. Make sure the focus is clear, reasonable, and worth developing.

1. **Topic:** My personal ambitions
   Focus:

   weak ★ ★ ★ ★ ★ strong

   _____

2. **Topic:** Barbie dolls
   Focus:

   weak ★ ★ ★ ★ ★ strong

   _____

3. **Topic:** Canadian art museums
   Focus:

   weak ★ ★ ★ ★ ★ strong

   _____

4. **Topic:** Media violence
   Focus:

   weak ★ ★ ★ ★ ★ strong

   _____

Forming a Working Thesis

You will state your focus in a thesis statement for an essay and in a topic sentence for a paragraph. It is very difficult to create a perfect thesis statement or topic sentence on your first try. You may have to write two, three, or even four versions of a thesis statement until it says exactly what you want it to say. In the prewriting stage, create a "working" thesis or topic sentence that will guide you as you write. As you work through the writing process, be open to changing your working thesis or topic sentence. The following formula can be used to write a working thesis or topic sentence.

A specific topic	**+**	A particular attitude, feature, or part	**=**	An effective working thesis statement or topic sentence
Biking to school		Better than driving		Biking to school is better than driving.

Create Identify a focus and then write a working topic sentence or thesis statement for each of the following assignments.

1. **Writing assignment:** Paragraph describing a specific type of exercise

   Specific topic: Pilates

   Focus: _____

   Topic sentence: _____

   _____

2. **Writing assignment:** Paragraph explaining a type of ethnic food

   Specific topic: Japanese cuisine

   Focus: _____

   Topic sentence: _____

   _____

3. **Writing assignment:** Essay reflecting on a modern social problem

   Specific topic: Affordable living spaces

   Focus: _____

   Thesis statement: _____

   _____

4. **Writing assignment:** Essay analyzing a favourite or important movie

   Specific topic: (Your choice)

   Focus: _____

   Thesis statement: _____

   _____

Vocabulary

thesis statement
the main idea in an essay, highlighting a special part or feature of a topic or expressing a particular attitude towards it

topic sentence
the sentence that expresses the main idea in a paragraph

Chapter 5 Prewriting

LO6 Understanding Patterns of Organization

After identifying your thesis, you'll need to decide how to organize the information that supports it. You have many patterns of organization to choose from. Here's how to proceed:

1. **Study your working thesis.** It will usually indicate how to organize your ideas. For example, consider the following working thesis:

   > Viewers love *The Simpsons* because the show **parodies** daily life in North America.

   As a point to be proved, this thesis suggests arranging the information by order of importance. As an idea to be shared and explained, it suggests a deductive organization of supporting information.

2. Then **review the information you have gathered.** Decide which ideas support your thesis and arrange them according to the appropriate method of organization. For example, if you are trying to prove a point about *The Simpsons*, you would arrange your reasons either from most important to least important or vice versa, depending on your purpose and your audience.

Patterns of Organization

Listed below are some of the common patterns that you will use in your writing.

- Use **chronological order** (time) when you are sharing a personal experience, telling how something happened, or explaining how to do something.

- Use **spatial order** (location) for descriptions, arranging information from left to right, from top to bottom, from the edge to the centre, and so on.

- Use **order of importance** when you are taking a stand or arguing for or against something. Arrange your reasons either from most important to least important or the other way around.

- Use **deductive organization** when writing to an audience that is neutral or receptive to the main idea in your essay. In this type of organization, you begin with your thesis statement and follow it with reasons, examples, and facts that support your main idea.

- Use **inductive organization** when writing to a skeptical or hostile audience. In this type of organization, you present your support first and conclude with your thesis statement.

- Use **compare–contrast organization** when you want to show how one topic is different from and similar to another one.

3dfoto/Shutterstock.com

Choose Study each of the following thesis statements. Then choose the method of organization that the thesis suggests. Explain each of your choices.

Speaking & Listening

Work on this activity with a partner if your instructor allows it.

1. **Thesis statement:** The Seawall makes Vancouver different from any other Canadian city.

   Appropriate method of organization: _____

   Explain: _____

   _____

2. **Thesis statement:** I am Korean, but I am Canadian, too.

   Appropriate method of organization: _____

   Explain: _____

   _____

   _____

3. **Thesis statement:** Multicultural education is vital to a society made up of many different peoples.

   Appropriate method of organization: _____

   Explain: _____

   _____

   _____

4. **Thesis statement:** I did something totally out of character for me; I jumped off a bridge with nothing more than a giant rubber band attached to my ankles.

   Appropriate method of organization:

   Explain: _____

   _____

   _____

5. **Thesis statement:** (Choose one that you wrote in the exercise at the end of LO5.)

   Appropriate method of organization: _____

   Explain: _____

   _____

   _____

"The essay is a literary device for saying almost everything about almost anything."
—Aldous Huxley

LO7 Organizing Your Information

Here are three basic strategies for arranging your supporting information after identifying an appropriate pattern of organization.

> **Make a quick list** of main points.
>
> **Create an outline**—an organized arrangement of main points and subpoints.
>
> **Fill in a graphic organizer**, arranging main points and details in a chart or diagram. (See LO4.)

> "Complicated outlines tempt you to think too much about the fine points of organization, at a time when you should be blocking out the overall structure."
>
> —Donald Murray

Using a Quick List

A quick list works well when you are writing a short piece, such as a paragraph, or when your planning time is limited. Here is a quick list for an informational essay about comets. (The main pattern of organization is chronological.)

Sample Quick List

Topic sentence: The appearance of comets in the night skies has puzzled people for thousands of years.

- very early on, thought to be planets
- Aristotle, the result of air escaping from atmosphere
- by 15th & 16th centuries, thought to be heavenly bodies
- all along, considered a sign of impending disaster
- really a gaseous body around a core of ice and dust
- head hundreds of miles in diameter; tail millions of miles in length

Create Write a thesis statement and a quick list for an essay explaining why a certain book is one of your favourites.

Thesis statement: _____

_____

_____

Quick list:

_____

_____

_____

_____

_____

3dfoto/Shutterstock.com

Using an Outline

An effective outline shows how ideas fit together and serves as a blueprint for your writing. Topic and sentence outlines follow specific guidelines: If you have a "I," you must have at least a "II." If you have an "A," you must have at least a "B," and so on. You can also customize an outline to meet your own needs.

Sample Customized Outline

What follows is the first part of a customized outline that includes main points stated in compete sentences and supporting details stated as phrases.

Thesis statement: American activist Charlotte Perkins Gilman rejected commonly held notions of male superiority.

1. Gilman's beliefs did little to prepare her for domestic life.
   - in 1884, married Charles W. Stetson
   - gave birth to a daughter
   - visited California shortly after to mentally and emotionally recuperate
   - while there, wrote a book about a pregnant woman locked in a room

2. During the next stage in her life, Gilman became a leading feminist.
   - delivered speeches on women's rights
   - following a divorce in 1894, edited *Impress* for Women's Press Associate
   - from 1895-1900, continued lecturing on women's rights
   - in 1896, a delegate to the National Socialist and Labour Congress in London

---

Create Develop the first part of a customized outline for an essay about television viewing. A thesis statement and two main points are provided. Put the main points in a logical order and make up two or three details to support each one.

Thesis statement: Unregulated television viewing has harmful effects on young viewers.

Main points: Television is reactive, requiring no skill or thinking. Television viewing takes away from study and reading time.

1. _____

   - _____

   - _____

   - _____

2. _____

   - _____

   - _____

   - _____

Vocabulary

customize
to change or alter

unregulated
not controlled

LO8 Reviewing Prewriting

Complete these activities as needed to help you better understand the key prewriting strategies.

Choose Select a specific topic for the following general subject area. (See LO2, Selecting a Topic.)

1. General subject area: a helpful website _____

   _____

2. Narrowing the subject: _____

   _____

3. Specific topic: _____

   _____

Write In the blank boxes provided, write out the formula for writing a working thesis. Then write a working thesis for the topic you identified in the question above. (See LO5, Establishing a Focus.)

	+		=		

Organize Identify the best pattern of organization for developing each of the following working thesis statements. (See LO6 and LO7.)

1. **Thesis statement:** Believe it or not, the environment can take care of itself.

   Pattern of organization: _____

   _____

2. **Thesis statement:** The animated movie *Fantasia* may be more than 60 years old, but it is a timeless work of art.

   Pattern of organization: _____

   _____

> "You have to write a lot; let the words flow. . . ."
>
> —Benjamin Percy

Evgeny Trofimov/Thinkstock

6

Drafting

When developing a piece of writing, you don't have to get it right the first time, the second time, or even the third time. Knowing this should help you feel less anxious about writing first drafts. You have a singular task at this point in the process—connecting your thoughts and feelings about your topic. These thoughts and feelings don't have to be perfectly worded or in the best order; they just have to be put on paper so you have something to work with.

Of course, drafting goes most smoothly when you have done the necessary prewriting, including information gathering, focusing, and organizing. Prewriting provides a road map for the writing that follows.

If you remember to approach a first draft as your *first look* at an emerging writing idea, you'll do fine. This chapter provides many additional tips and guidelines about the drafting process.

What do you think?

How can Benjamin Percy's advice about writing a lot and letting the words flow be applied to writing a first draft?

_____

_____

_____

_____

_____

Learning Outcomes

LO1 Follow a drafting plan.

LO2 Form a meaningful whole.

LO3 Create an effective opening.

LO4 Write a strong thesis statement.

LO5 Develop the middle part.

LO6 Write a strong closing.

LO7 Review drafting.

Vocabulary

singular
one of a kind, unique

emerging
coming into being, still forming

Traits

In order to do your best work, you must have strong feelings about your topic. As you work, let your voice develop.

LO1 Following a Drafting Plan

When writing a first draft, you're writing to see how well you match up with the topic and if your initial planning still makes sense.

Writing a first draft helps you decide how to proceed with your writing idea. If you're lucky, everything will turn out just as you had planned, and you'll continue to develop your writing. On the other hand, you may discover that you need to learn more about the topic, adjust your focus, or start over.

A Writing Plan

Use the following points as your drafting guide.

- Focus on developing your thoughts and feelings, not on trying to produce a final copy.
- Follow your prewriting and planning notes, and also feel free to include new ideas that come to mind as you write.
- Continue writing until you cover all of your main points or until you come to a logical stopping point.
- Express yourself honestly and sincerely, using other sources of information to support what you have to say.

Write Answer the following questions related to the drafting process.

1. Why is a first draft commonly called a rough draft?

   _____

   _____

2. In what way does writing a first draft set in motion the rest of the writing process?

   _____

   _____

3. Some instructors suggest turning down the resolution on your computer if you have trouble writing a first draft. How do you think this action would help?

   _____

   _____

Avoiding Writer's Block

Writer's block is the condition of not knowing what to say in a piece of writing. You've got pen in hand or fingers on the keyboard, but the words just won't come. It's quite natural to experience writer's block every once in a while. But your chances of facing this condition are greatly reduced if you know a lot about your topic and have strong feelings about it. That is why prewriting is so important.

Strategies to Try

When writer's block strikes, try one of these strategies to get the words flowing.

1. **Write as if you are in a conversation with the reader.** Don't worry about sounding academic or correct. Instead, talk to the reader.

2. **Write non-stop in short, fluid bursts of 3–5 minutes.** Don't worry about making mistakes, or you'll stop the flow of ideas.

3. **Start in the middle.** The traditional Latin term for such a beginning is *in media res* (literally, "in the middle of things"). Don't waste time with building an elaborate opening. Just identify your topic or focus, if necessary, and go from there.

Write Develop the first part of a draft in which you discuss something in everyday life that bugs you (*noisy eaters, sniffers and coughers, braggarts, barking dogs*). Use one of the strategies above to get started.

_____

_____

_____

_____

_____

_____

_____

_____

_____

LO2 Forming a Meaningful Whole

Writer Lillian Hellman said, "There are a thousand ways to write, and each is as good as the other if it fits you." That is certainly true when writing a first draft, once you understand that it doesn't have to be perfect. You must also understand that when developing a first draft, your goal is to form a meaningful whole or a complete initial writing.

Forming a meaningful whole for a paragraph means including a topic sentence, body sentences, and a closing sentence. For an essay, it means including an opening paragraph (with a thesis statement), multiple supporting paragraphs, and a closing paragraph.

"Just get it on paper, and then we'll see what to do with it."
—Maxwell Perkins

Graphically Speaking

The graphics below show the structure of both basic forms of writing.

Paragraph Structure

Topic Sentence

A **topic sentence** names the topic.

Detail Sentences

Detail sentences support the topic.

Closing Sentence

A **closing sentence** wraps up the paragraph.

Essay Structure

Opening Paragraph

The **opening paragraph** draws the reader into the essay and provides information that leads to a **thesis statement**. The thesis statement tells what the essay is about.

Middle Paragraphs

The **middle paragraphs** support the thesis statement. Each middle paragraph needs a topic sentence, a variety of detail sentences, and a closing sentence.

Closing Paragraph

The **closing paragraph** finishes the essay by revisiting the thesis statement, emphasizing an important detail, providing the reader with an interesting final thought, and/or looking toward the future.

LO3 Creating an Effective Opening

In many situations, first impressions are important—say, for instance, when you're interviewing for a job or introducing yourself to a roommate or a co-worker. First impressions are important in writing, too, because the first few ideas help set the tone for the rest of the piece. The information that follows will help you make a positive impression in the opening part of your essays.

The Basic Parts

The opening paragraph (or part) of an essay usually does these three things: (1) identifies the topic, (2) engages the reader, and (3) states the thesis. Before stating your thesis, you may also need to include a sentence or two of background information.

Starting Strategies

Listed below are a few strategies to help you introduce the topic and engage the reader.

- Begin with a surprising or little-known fact about the topic.

  > Thousands of babies are born each year with alcohol-related defects, making fetal alcohol syndrome one of the leading causes of intellectual disability.

- Ask an interesting or challenging question about the topic.

  > What exactly do the signs held up by homeless people tell us?

- Start with a telling quotation.

  > "We live here and they live there," Bigger Thomas says in *Native Son.* "We black and they white. They got things and we ain't. They do things and we can't."

- Share a brief, dramatic story.

  > It was May 1945. World War II had just ended and Yugoslavia had been overtaken. The town of Vrhnika, Yugoslavia, was no longer safe. Russian and communist troops would break into houses, take what they wanted, and even kill.

- Open with a bold statement.

  > Barbie's breasts and spacious mansion helped cause the decay of today's youth, or so say some experts.

Jon Le-Bon/Shutterstock.com

"The best advice on writing I've ever received is 'Knock 'em dead with the lead sentence.'"
—Whitney Balliett

Vocabulary

tone
the writer's attitude toward his or her topic

engage
attract, instill interest

Once the beginning part is set, you'll find it much easier to develop the rest of your writing.

degenerative
gradual loss of use or function

conscientious
caring, hard-working

debilitating
weakening, draining the strength or health

Sample Opening Paragraph

Analyze Carefully read the following opening paragraph from an essay about a **degenerative** bone disease called Legg-Calvé-Perthes (pronounced leg-cal-VAY-PER-theez). Then answer the questions below.

Allie Mason acted like a typical high school student. She was bubbly, energetic, and extremely friendly. She was also a **conscientious** student, belonged to the Art Club, and enjoyed golfing. What set Allie apart was a **debilitating** physical condition that caused one of her legs to be noticeably shorter than the other one and forced her to limp. As a result, she had to endure endless medical procedures and missed out on typical school activities such as gym and dances. She also had to endure more than her share of insensitive remarks. She remembered, "My classmates would tease me and call me names." Their comments obviously hurt, especially those made by her friends. The reason for Allie's suffering was Legg-Calvé-Perthes, a painful bone disease that truly challenges the sufferer.

1. What strategy does the writer use to introduce the topic and engage the reader?

   _____

2. What, if any, background information is provided about the topic?

   _____

3. What special part of or feeling about the topic is identified in the thesis statement?

   _____

Create Write a sample opening paragraph for an essay about one of the topics that you worked with in Chapter 5, Prewriting. Use your own paper if you need more room.

_____

_____

_____

_____

_____

_____

_____

LO4 Developing an Effective Thesis Statement

Your thesis is the most important sentence in your essay or paragraph: It states the overall purpose or central idea of your writing. In an essay, your thesis is the last sentence of your introduction; in a paragraph, your thesis is your topic sentence.

The Basic Parts

A thesis typically has three different parts:

1. **The specific topic** is the main subject of your essay. Always make sure that your topic is narrow enough (see Chapter 5, LO2, Selecting a Topic).

2. **The "point"** is the main idea that your essay is expressing about the topic. Your "point" will change depending on the purpose of your writing (see Chapter 5, LO1, Analyzing the Assignment).

3. **The overview of support** lists the evidence that the essay uses to prove the point. This overview serves as a map for your readers and should correspond with the organization of the essay (see Chapter 5, LO6, Understanding Patterns of Organization).

If expressed as a formula, a thesis should look like this...

Learning Outcome

Develop an effective thesis statement.

Review

Essays that follow inductive organization (see Chapter 5, LO6) do not have a thesis stated in the introduction.

Review

Make sure your overview of support uses parallel structure (see Chapter 29, LO3).

Specific Topic		Your Point		Overview of Support		Thesis Statement
fighting in professional hockey	+	should not be banned	+	not as dangerous as it is depicted in the media _____ helps protect players from unsafe play	=	Fighting should not be banned from the NHL because it is no more dangerous than other parts of the game and actually helps protect players from unsafe play.

Not all thesis statements provide an overview of support. This is typically the case for shorter essays and paragraphs. Consider the following example.

Specific Topic		Your Point		Overview of Support		Thesis Statement
nuclear deterrence	+	the only way to prevent other countries from using their own nuclear weapons	+	X	=	Nuclear deterrence is the only way of preventing other countries from using nuclear weapons.

As you work through this textbook, you will encounter different rhetorical modes (e.g., narration, argumentation, cause–effect). These different forms of writing may require you to change this thesis formula in subtle ways. For more information, see the various chapters in Parts 3 and 4.

Fill in the Blank Using the thesis formula provided, fill in the missing blanks in the following table. Remember, not all thesis statements include an overview of support.

A Specific Topic	+ Point	+ Overview of Subgroups	= Thesis Statement
	The greatest superheroes earn their powers through personal determination.		There are three common ways that superheroes gain their superpowers: birth, accident, or—the greatest of way of all—personal determination.
Print and e-books			Although some people think reading print books or e-books is an either/or decision, both are convenient at different times and place.
History of oil contamination in the Niger delta		As a result of sabotage, theft, and corporate mismanagement	
Social media			Some people claim social-networking sites are bad for society, but the benefits of social media greatly outweigh any shortcomings.
			The idea of a perfect bicycle is relative because different styles of bicycles serve different purposes.

A Specific Topic	+	Point	+	Overview of Subgroups	=	Thesis Statement
Visiting the ship museum *CSS Acadia*						Stepping aboard the *CSS Acadia* is like stepping back in time.
The process of water purification		Water purification makes water safe to drink		Pre-treatment, coagulation, filtration, disinfection		
						Applying stage makeup is a multiple-step process that helps actors portray their characters.
						Beyond the aesthetic loss, the loss of farmland is putting our economy and food supply at risk for future generations. The Canadian public must take greater measures to pressure the country's farmland.
						Young people today are still getting married—but they're taking their time walking down the aisle.

Create Write a thesis statement to go along with the opening paragraph that you wrote in LO3. Use your own paper if you need more room.

A Specific Topic	Your Point	Overview of Support	Thesis Statement

Chapter 6 Drafting

L◯5 Developing the Middle Part

In the middle paragraphs, you should develop all of the main points that support your thesis statement. Use your planning (quick list, outline, graphic organizer) as a general guide when you develop this part of an essay. Here are a few tips for getting started:

> "When your writing is filled with details, it has a lot more impact."
>
> —Ivan Levison

- **Keep your thesis statement in mind as you write.** All of your main points should support or advance this statement.
- **Develop each main point in a separate paragraph (or two).** State the main point in the form of a topic sentence and follow with detail sentences that support it.
- **Use plenty of details** to fully explain your points.
- **Use your own words,** except on those few occasions when you employ a quotation to add authority to your writing.
- **Be open to new ideas that occur to you,** especially if they will improve your essay.
- **Try any of the basic methods of development listed below** that are appropriate to your topic.

Basic Methods of Development

The paragraphs in the middle part of an essay should, among other things, *explain, describe, define, classify,* and so on. What follows is a list and definitions of these basic methods of development.

Other Classes

Most writing assignments use one of these basic writing words to identify the key focus of your work—to *describe,* to *explain,* and so on.

Narrating — sharing an experience or a story

Describing — telling how someone or something appears, acts, or operates

Explaining — providing important facts, details, and examples

Analyzing — carefully examining a subject or breaking it down

Comparing — showing how two subjects are similar and different

Defining — identifying or clarifying the meaning of a term

Reflecting — connecting with or wondering about

Evaluating — rating the value of something

Arguing — using logic and evidence to prove something is true

Analyze Read two different essays from Part 8. On your own paper, list the different patterns of development that the writer uses in the middle paragraphs of her or his writing. For example, the writer may *explain* in one or more paragraphs, *reflect* in another, and so on.

Christopher Halloran/Shutterstock.com

Sample Middle Paragraph

Analyze Carefully read the following middle paragraph from an essay on Legg-Calvé-Perthes. Then answer the questions below.

Tip

Keep your reader in mind as you write. Try to anticipate and answer any questions your audience may have about your topic.

Legg-Calve-Perthes is both rare and mysterious. The disease affects only 5 of every 100 000 children, usually when they are between the ages of five and twelve. While boys suffer from the disease far more frequently than girls do by a ratio of 4 to 1, when girls do develop Legg-Calvé-Perthes, they tend to suffer more severely from it. At this point, researchers are not really sure of the cause of the disease. They are, however, fairly certain that it is not genetic. They also know that a reduction of blood flow at the hip joint contributes to the disease and causes the bone tissue to collapse or react in other strange ways. Usually, the rounded part of the femur bone that fits into the hip joint becomes deformed. In Allie's case, the top of her femur bone grew to double its normal size, a condition that produced extreme pain when she tried to walk. It's hard to imagine how Allie or anyone else is able to deal with this condition during the active childhood years.

1. What specific part or special feature of the topic is identified in the topic sentence?

   _____

   _____

2. What basic pattern (or patterns) of development does the writer use in this paragraph?

   _____

   _____

Create Write a middle paragraph to go along with the opening paragraph that you wrote earlier. You may either carry out some quick research or simply make up details to complete your paragraph. Use your own paper if you need more room.

_____

_____

_____

_____

_____

_____

_____

Traits

You may need to write two or three versions of your closing, adjusting your word choice and the flow of your sentences, before it says exactly what you want it to say.

LO6 Writing a Strong Closing

While the opening part of your writing offers important *first* impressions, the closing part should offer important *final* impressions. More specifically, it should help the reader better understand and appreciate the importance of your topic or thesis.

The Working Parts

Consider the strategies below when writing your closing. In most cases, you will want to use more than one of them; whatever you choose to do, your closing must flow smoothly from your last middle paragraph.

- Remind the reader of the thesis.

  > Legg-Calvé-Parthes is like a cancer in the ways it affects an individual and her or his family.

- Summarize the main points or highlight one or two of them.

  > Ultimately, both Alan and Bigger (two literary characters) fail to gain real control over the outside forces in their lives. Alan **forfeits** his interest in life, and Bigger forfeits life itself.

- Reflect on the explanation or argument you've presented in the main part.

  > It would be a shame to lose these amazing creatures (humpback whales). We don't want their mysterious song to be a thing of the past. And we can't turn to zoos when the numbers shrink to a precious few.

- Offer a final idea to keep the reader thinking about the topic.

  > If the Canadian government fails to address climate change, global warming may reach the point of no return and the environment may never recover.

FloridaStock/Shutterstock.com

Sample Closing Paragraph

Analyze Carefully read the following closing paragraph for an essay on Legg-Calvé-Perthes. Then answer the questions below.

> Legg-Calvé-Perthes is like a cancer in the ways it affects an individual and her family. In Allie's case, the debilitating effects started with Allie's painful efforts to walk and they have continued with attempts to address the condition with operations, therapy, and braces. Through all of this, she and her family have missed out on so much. Her mother had to quit her job, and her sister felt ignored. As Allie recalled, "My sister has always felt jealous of all of the attention I get from my parents." But knowing that the condition should, in time, resolve itself certainly must help sufferers like Allie meet each new challenge. It must also help them to know that young people suffering from Legg-Calvé-Perthes usually do quite well in the long term.

1. In what way does the first sentence remind the reader of the thesis statement?

   _____

   _____

2. What other strategy or strategies does the writer use?

   _____

   _____

Create Write a closing paragraph to go along with the opening and middle paragraphs that you have written in this chapter. Use the sample above and the information in LO6 as a guide.

_____

_____

_____

_____

_____

_____

_____

_____

_____

"Make your writing useful."
—William Zinsser

L○7 Reviewing Drafting

Complete these activities as needed to help you better understand key strategies in this chapter.

Answer What are two things that you can do if you get stuck when drafting? (See LO1, Following a Drafting Plan.)

1. _____
2. _____

List What are the three main things that you should accomplish in the opening part of an essay? (See LO3, Creating an Effective Opening.)

1. _____
2. _____
3. _____

List What are the three main parts of a thesis statement? (See LO4, Writing a Strong Thesis Statement.)

1. _____
2. _____
3. _____

Answer Answer these questions about the basic patterns of development a writer may use. (See LO5, Developing the Middle Part.)

1. What does it mean to narrate in a paragraph? _____

2. When explaining, what types of information will a writer include? _____

3. When a writer evaluates, what is she or he actually doing? _____

List What are two strategies that you can use to develop a closing? (See LO6, Writing a Strong Closing.)

1. _____
2. _____

BlueSkyImage/Shutterstock.com

> "If [you] write a lot, that's good.
> If [you] revise a lot, that's even better."
> —Toni Morrison

7 Revising

You would never expect a musician to perform or record a song after putting lyrics and music together for the first time. In fact, the real work would have just begun. There would be questions to answer: Does the song have potential? If so, what needs to be done to get it performance-ready? Then would come the work of arranging and practising the song, again and again, until everything—lyrics, rhythm, timing, beat—was just right.

In the same way, you should never expect to share a first draft of your writing as if it were a finished piece. You still have a lot of work ahead of you—reviewing your writing, and then revising any confusing, incomplete, or out-of-order parts. Each revision you make brings you closer to an effective piece of writing.

This chapter provides guidelines and strategies for revising a first draft, with the traits of strong writing, and a fine finished draft, in clear view.

Learning Outcomes

LO1 Understand the revision process.

LO2 Recognize the traits of strong writing.

LO3 Check for completeness.

LO4 Check for coherence.

LO5 Learn the basics of peer reviewing.

LO6 Review revision.

What do you think?

In the quotation, why does Morrison state that revising a lot is even better than writing a lot?

_____

_____

_____

> "If you haven't revised, you're not finished."
>
> —Patricia T. O'Conner

Traits

Don't pay undue attention to surface issues—usage, spelling, punctuation—at this point in the process. Instead, focus on the bigger picture: the organization, voice, and content of your writing.

LO1 Understanding Revision

Revising is the process of improving the message in your writing. To make the best revising decisions, follow these guidelines:

- **Take some time away from your writing.** This will help you see your first draft more clearly, with a fresh outlook.

- **Read your first draft a number of times,** silently and out loud, to get an overall impression of your work.

- **Have a trusted peer or two react to your writing.** Their questions and comments will help you decide what changes to make.

- **Check your overall focus or thesis.** Decide if it still works and if you have provided enough support for it.

- **Then review your work, part by part.** Pay special attention to the opening, since it sets the tone of your writing, and the closing, since it serves as your final word on the topic.

- **Plan a revising strategy** by deciding what you need to do first, second, and third.

Select Put a check mark by the statements below that clearly refer to revising.

- [ ] **1.** Reviewing the opening part to make sure it effectively introduces your thesis

- [ ] **2.** Looking up a specific comma rule

- [ ] **3.** Adding supporting details in one of your paragraphs

- [ ] **4.** Changing the order of two parts to strengthen your message

- [ ] **5.** Replacing one word with a synonym

- [ ] **6.** Deleting a part that is not really related to your thesis

- [ ] **7.** Moving a prepositional phrase from the beginning to the end of a sentence

- [ ] **8.** Rewriting the closing so it more effectively ties everything together

Additional Considerations

What follows are two additional aspects of the revising process to consider.

Revisit Your Purpose and Audience

Before you revise a first draft, be sure to have the purpose of your writing clearly in mind: Are you writing to explain, to persuade, to describe, or to share? With a clear understanding of the purpose, you will find it much easier to know what changes to make. Also consider your readers: Have you anticipated and answered the questions they may have about the topic?

Understand the Basic Revising Moves

You have four basic ways to make changes in your writing—adding, cutting, rewriting, or reordering information. Each change or improvement that you make will bring you closer to a strong finished piece.

Add information to . . .
- make a supporting point more convincing.
- complete a specific explanation.
- improve the flow of your writing.

Cut information if it . . .
- doesn't support the thesis.
- seems repetitious.

Rewrite information if it . . .
- seems confusing or unclear.
- appears too complicated.
- lacks the proper **voice**.

Reorder information if it . . .
- seems out of order.
- would have greater impact in another spot.

Vocabulary

voice
a writer's manner of expression, the "sound" of his or her words (A strong voice signals an interested, knowledgeable writer.)

React Carefully read this first draft. As you will see, it has a number of problems. Then follow the directions below the writing.

> Winning the lottery must be everyone's number one dream! If I won the lottery, my life would be wonderful. First, I'd travel to other countries. I've always wanted to go to Italy and eat spaghetti in a gondola. Yeah I'm definitely going to keep buying those lottery tickets. Then I'd buy a retooled Mustang with a stardust paint job. My dad says that old Fords have mechanical problems. But he's just an old dude who doesn't know cars. Everyone knows Mustangs are totally hot-looking cars. I'd buy my mom a car, too. She'd probably want a dull, dependable car like a Volvo or something dull like that, but a Jeep is something I'd talk her out of undoubtedly for sure. Some 4x4 action would spice up her life.
>
> 1. **Underline** one sentence or idea that could be improved if information were added.
>
> 2. **Put** a line through one idea that should be cut because it is unnecessary.
>
> 3. **Draw** a wavy line under one idea that should be rewritten because it is unclear.
>
> 4. **Circle** one idea that should be moved; draw an arrow to show where you would move it.

Rewrite Rewrite this paragraph, making the changes that you marked on the original. Feel free to make other changes as well. Afterward, share your revised writing with your classmates.

LO2 Recognizing Strong Writing

The traits of effective writing were introduced in Chapters 3 and 4. The traits-based checklist below can serve as an effective guide when you revise. If your writing doesn't "pass" certain descriptors, then you should make the necessary changes.

> "There is no such thing as good writing, only good rewriting."
>
> —Louis Brandeis

Revising Checklist

Ideas

☐ **1.** Does an interesting and relevant topic serve as a starting point for the writing?

☐ **2.** Is the writing focused, addressing a specific feeling about or a specific part of the topic? (The focus is usually expressed in the thesis statement.)

☐ **3.** Are there enough specific ideas, details, and examples to support the thesis?

☐ **4.** Overall, is the writing informative?

Organization

☐ **5.** Does the writing form a meaningful whole—with opening, middle, and closing parts?

☐ **6.** Does the writing follow a logical pattern of organization?

☐ **7.** Do transitions connect ideas clearly?

Voice

☐ **8.** Does the writer sound informed about and interested in the topic?

☐ **9.** In addition, does the writer sound sincere and genuine?

Word Choice

☐ **10.** Does the word choice clearly fit the purpose and the audience?

☐ **11.** Does the writing include specific words as much as possible?

Sentence Fluency

☐ **12.** Are the sentences clear and do they flow smoothly?

☐ **13.** Are the sentences varied in terms of their beginnings and length?

Traits

Word choice and sentence fluency are not as important as the other traits at this point. But they become very important during the editing step.

React Carefully read the following paragraphs from a persuasive essay. Then answer the questions below that address the first three traits: *ideas, organization, and voice*. (Use your own paper for your answers.)

Learn to Earn

Lack of student motivation is a main topic of discussion when it comes to today's underachieving schools. The experts ask, how can we motivate our students to learn? And how can we keep them in school long enough to prepare for the twenty-first century workplace? These questions are especially important in urban areas, where the drop-out rate is alarming, especially among non-native English students. One answer appears quite logical: Give them money. In other words, if we want our students to succeed in school, we should pay them.

Students, in one way, are already bribed to attend school. The whole point of academic scholarships is based on receiving a monetary reward for being a good student. Calling a cash award a "scholarship" doesn't alter the fact that what's being offered is money. Presently, only the best students or the best athletes pick up all the cash. That does not seem fair. What about the student that doesn't want to go to college? Why not pay everyone for going to school the same way they would get paid for doing any other job?

Many students drop out of school because they are forced to work to help support their families. When it comes to choosing between going to school or going to work, the latter usually wins out for practical reasons. If these same students were paid a minimum wage for attending school, they wouldn't have to worry about choosing between education and keeping their jobs. In the long run, it would probably be less expensive to keep these students in school by paying them than to have them drop out of school with no skills.

Ideas

1. Is the topic relevant and interesting? Explain.

2. Is the focus or thesis of the essay clear? Explain.

3. Does the essay contain a variety of specific details? Explain.

Organization

1. Does the first paragraph include the key elements of an effective opening? (See Chapter 6, LO3, Creating an Effective Opening.) Explain.

2. Do these paragraphs follow a logical pattern of organization? If so, which one? (See Chapter 5, LO6 and LO7.)

Voice

1. Does the writer sound informed and interested in the topic? Explain.

2. Does the writer sound sincere and honest? Explain.

LO3 Checking for Completeness

Your instructors expect you to support the main points in your essays with plenty of details. Details help you develop complete explanations and arguments.

"The first great gift we can bestow on others is a good example."
—Thomas Morell

Types of Details

The following list identifies the common types of details.

Facts and statistics give specific information that can be checked.

> Legg-Calvé-Perthes affects only 5 of every 100 000, usually when they are between the ages of five and twelve.

Examples demonstrate or show something.

> Donald, who is two years younger than I am, has always been more daring. (main point)
>
> When we were younger, he was the first to jump off the cliffs at the quarry. (example)

Definitions explain new terms.

> The *Canadian Oxford Dictionary* defines sexual harassment as "harassment in a workplace involving the making of unwanted sexual advances, obscene remarks, demands for sexual favours in return for advancement, etc."

Reasons answer "why" after a main point.

> Watching television is a **reactive** activity. (main point)
>
> It takes absolutely no skill or thinking. (reason)

Quotations provide the thoughts of people knowledgeable about the topic.

> Tuyen stated, "In the Chinese tradition, the superior person assumes loving responsibility for the inferior, and the inferior person shows respect and obedience to the superior."

Reflections offer the writer's thoughts.

> For most young people, growing up means being told to act like an adult while being treated like a child. It means receiving an abundance of advice but having little patience. It means wanting to be independent but realizing just how dependent you are.

Identify In the essay "Learn to Earn," record one example of each type of detail listed below. (Use your own paper if you need more room.)

Fact: _____

Example: _____

Reason: _____

Quotation: _____

Levels of Detail

Effective essays are thorough, meaning that they contain the appropriate level of information to fully explain or develop each main point. Here are three basic levels of detail in writing.

> **Level 1:** A **controlling sentence** names a topic (usually a topic sentence) or makes a main point.
>
> **Level 2:** A **clarifying sentence** explains a level 1 sentence.
>
> **Level 3:** A **completing sentence** adds details to complete the point.
>
> **Note:** To "complete" some main points, a writer may add another level of detail (level 4).

Details in Action

The passage that follows uses three different levels of detail. Notice that the level 1 sentence (a topic sentence) is supported by three level 2 sentences. Two level 3 sentences complete the last level 2 sentence.

> **(Level 1)** Legg-Calvé-Perthes is both rare and mysterious. **(Level 2)** The disease affects only 5 of every 100 000 children, usually when they are between the ages of five and twelve. **(Level 2)** Boys suffer from the disease far more frequently than girls do, by a ratio of 4 to 1, which makes Allie's experience all the more unusual. **(Level 2)** At this point, researchers are not really sure of the cause of the disease. **(Level 3)** They are, however, fairly certain that it is not genetic. **(Level 3)** They also know that a reduction of blood flow . . .

Identify Carefully read the following passage; then label its levels of detail. (Work on this activity with a partner if your instructor allows it.)

> (_____) Plato, an ancient Greek philosopher and educator, was the first to write about the lost continent of Atlantis in his book *Critias*. (_____) Most scholars agree that Plato's book includes only legendary events, not real history. (_____) When Plato described Atlantis, he painted a picture of a people of fabulous wealth who ruled over a great and wonderful empire. (_____) He also claimed that the continent of Atlantis sank beneath the sea in one day's time.

Write Write a paragraph of at least five or six sentences about one of the following topics: *types of sports fans, your favourite type of music, the best piece of technology ever invented, the one time you really "roughed it."* Afterward, label your sentences with the numbers 1, 2, or 3, depending on the level of detail they represent.

Chapter 7 Revising

> "I tell [students] to use transitions, to start each paragraph with an interlocking nut, a thread, so that the story is seamless."
>
> —Steve Lovelady

LO4 Checking for Coherence

When a paragraph or essay is coherent, all of its ideas work together and flow smoothly from one point to the next. Transitions, or linking words and phrases like *such as, on the other hand,* and *in addition,* help create coherence because they connect ideas. Transitions can show location or time, compare and contrast things, and so on.

Words used to show location:

above	behind	down	on top of
across	below	in back of	onto
against	beneath	in front of	outside
along	beside	inside	over
among	between	into	throughout
around	beyond	near	to the right
away from	by	off	under

Words used to show time:

about	during	next	today
after	finally	next week	tomorrow
afterward	first	second	until
as soon as	immediately	soon	when
at	later	then	yesterday
before	meanwhile	third	

Words used to compare things (show similarities):

also	in the same way	likewise
as	like	similarly

Words used to contrast things (show differences):

although	even though	on the other hand	still
but	however	otherwise	yet

Words used to emphasize a point:

again	for this reason	particularly	to repeat
even	in fact	to emphasize	truly

Words used to conclude or summarize:

all in all	finally	in summary	therefore
as a result	in conclusion	last	to sum up

Words used to add information:

additionally	and	equally important	in addition
again	another	finally	likewise
along with	as well	for example	next
also	besides	for instance	second

Words used to clarify:

for instance	in other words	put another way	that is

Linking Words and Phrases in Action

Note the use of transitions in the following passages. Each one adds to the coherence and readability of the ideas.

Traits

Use transitions as needed in your writing to help your reader follow your train of thought. But be careful not to overuse them. Too many transitions can actually get in the way and draw undue attention to themselves.

- Jazz ballet provides me with all of the exercise that I need. *To begin with,* it combines gymnastics with dance. All of the gymnastic-like splits, leaps, kicks, and high jumps provide the ultimate cardiovascular workout. *(The transition is used to add information.)*

- Alan experiences the pressure of working as a clerk at Bryson's Appliance Store. The customers are demanding, and the many products and brand names are confusing. *Later,* under hypnosis, he admits that his "foes" are the myriad brand names he is challenged to locate. *(The transition is used to show time.)*

- In response to Motz's idea that Barbies make girls dependent on males, I say, "Phooey." I played with the dolls for years, and I have often been free from any type of romantic attachment. *In fact,* I am now a happy single girl. *(The transition emphasizes a point.)*

Identify Circle the transition or transitions used in each of the following passages. In the space below each passage, identify the purpose of the transition—*to show location, to show time,* and so on.

- Humpbacks, like other whales, must migrate. Some humpbacks begin their journey in October. Mature females accompanied by their yearling calves set off first. Next, the immature males and females begin the journey. . . .

- American art museums represent a confusing mix of public and private interests. Without question, however, the primary function of the museum is to serve the public.

- What set Allie apart was a debilitating physical condition that caused one of her legs to be noticeably shorter than the other one. As a result, she had to endure endless medical procedures, . . .

- This crude tent-like structure was to be my home. Around the base, four strong poles stick straight up. On the top, a crisscrossing of long branches and thatch serves as a roof. . . .

Review Review the paragraph you may have written in response to the assignment at the end of LO3, looking for transitions. Did you use any? If not, could the paragraph benefit from a transition or two? Which ones?

Andresr/Shutterstock.com

Having your peers react to your writing helps you decide what changes need to be made. They can tell you if your writing keeps their interest, answers their main questions about the topic, and makes sense from start to finish.

The Role of the Writer

1. **Have a complete piece of writing to share.** Make a copy for each group member.

2. **Set the scene.** Make a few introductory comments about your work. But don't say too much.

3. **Read your work out loud.** Don't stop to explain anything; just read the text as clearly as you can.

4. **Afterward, listen carefully to the reactions.** Answer any questions. Don't try to defend yourself or your writing. Just listen and take notes on important points.

5. **Ask for help.** If you have concerns about certain parts of the piece, invite the group to offer thoughts or ideas.

The Role of the Listeners/Responders

1. **Pay careful attention during the reading.** Take brief notes if you think it would help. Then read the text silently.

2. **React positively and constructively.** Instead of saying "Nice start," for example, say something more exact, such as "Sharing that dramatic story in the beginning really made me take notice."

3. **Comment on specific things you noticed.** Saying "It would be good to add more style to your writing" isn't very helpful. But saying "Many of the sentences start in the same way" gives the writer a specific idea for improving the writing.

4. **Question the writer if you are unsure of something.** "What is the purpose of . . . ?" or "Why did you start the . . . ?"

5. **Show that you are really interested in helping.** Have at least one positive comment and one suggestion to offer. Also listen to others' comments and add to them.

Write Develop a first draft in which you reflect and/or comment upon a current event in any area of life—political affairs, the environment, sports, entertainment, and so on. (Use your own paper if you need more room.)

_____

_____

_____

_____

_____

_____

_____

_____

_____

_____

_____

_____

_____

_____

_____

_____

_____

_____

_____

_____

_____

Ljupco Smokovski/Shutterstock.com

Share Review your first draft in a peer-responding session, following the guidelines on the previous page. (Work with one partner or a small group of your peers.) Then list two helpful suggestions that were made.

1. _____

_____

2. _____

_____

Chapter 7 Revising

LO6 Reviewing Revision

Complete these activities as needed to help you better understand the revision process.

List List below the four basic revising moves. (See LO1, Understanding Revision.)

1. _____

2. _____

3. _____

4. _____

Identify What questions should you ask about your writing to check it for effective organization? Identify two of them. (See LO2, Recognizing Strong Writing.)

1. _____

2. _____

Identify Identify the type of detail used in each of the following examples. (See LO3, Checking for Completeness.)

1. _____ According to *Modern Style* magazine, a face-lift costs $5000–$15 000; nose jobs are $4000–$8000; and hair transplants are $6000–$10 000.

2. _____ Charlotte Perkins Gilman contributed to the women's movement. *(main point)* She developed the idea of collective child care and attacked misconceived notions of womanhood and motherhood.

Tell Circle the transitions used in each passage and tell the purpose of each one: to show time, to emphasize a point, and so on. (See LO4, Checking for Coherence.)

1. The assortment of food whisking by me is astonishing. Below me, a father and his two sons are just completing their third trip to the food court. _____

2. I made French toast this morning for my family. It was a treat, and they praised my cooking. Afterward, we all watched an old movie. _____

3. A tactful person expresses herself not only sensitively, but truthfully as well. Doctors, for example, must be truthful when dealing with their patients and the patients' families.

_____

> "I love the taste of words. They have a taste and a weight and a colour as well as a sound and a shape." —Philip Pullman

A Carmichael/Stone/Getty Images

8

Editing

There's a time during the writing process when **editing** for style and correctness makes the most sense; that time comes after you have done everything possible to make your main message logical and complete. Always think content before anything else.

Editing writing is like buffing out the smudges and scratches on a car after it's been painted. The buffing is certainly important, but only after the main work—the actual painting—is complete.

The first part of this chapter provides tips for checking the word choice and sentence fluency in your writing. The second part provides, among other things, strategies for editing for correctness and a discussion of academic versus informal writing.

What do you think?

How can Pullman's quotation serve as a guide for selecting words for your writing?

Learning Outcomes

LO1 Understand the basics of word choice.

LO2 Learn about sentence fluency.

LO3 Learn how to check for correctness.

LO4 Edit academic writing.

LO5 Use a common errors list.

LO6 Review editing.

Vocabulary

editing
the step in the writing process when you check the style (word choice and sentence fluency) and correctness of your revised writing

LO1 Understanding Word Choice

When it comes to word choice, the first **rule of thumb** is to use words that fit the audience and the purpose of your writing. For example, the words used in a personal essay would not necessarily be appropriate for a report or research paper. Word choice is also called **diction**.

Pay special attention to your choice of nouns and verbs, as well as to any jargon words that you use, since together they create much of the meaning and style of your writing. The information that follows serves as a guide to selecting nouns and verbs and to using jargon.

Using Specific Nouns

Insight

To build a strong working vocabulary for your writing, do these three things: (1) become a regular reader; (2) keep a vocabulary notebook, recording new and interesting words as you come across them; and (3) learn how to use a thesaurus and a dictionary.

Nouns name people, places, objects, and ideas, and they range from the very general (*man* or *drink*) to the very specific (*Wayne Gretzky* or *mango juice*). Notice how the nouns become more specific from left to right in the chart below. In writing, specific nouns almost always work better than general ones.

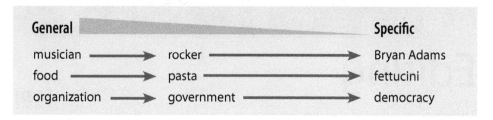

General		Specific
musician →	rocker ────────→	Bryan Adams
food →	pasta ────────→	fettucini
organization →	government ──────→	democracy

Complete Fill in the blanks below with nouns that become more specific.

General ◢◣ Specific

People:

_____ _____ _____

_____ _____ _____

Objects:

_____ _____ _____

_____ _____ _____

Ideas:

_____ _____ _____

_____ _____ _____

Extend

On your own paper, write five or six sentences about one of your favourite classes or one of your best jobs. Afterward, underline the nouns that you have used; then replace at least two of these nouns with more specific ones.

Using Specific Verbs

Action verbs tell what is happening in a sentence. A specific action verb like *examine* usually works better than a general one like *look* because it is more exact. Listed below are a few additional synonyms for *look*; each one is more exact and interesting.

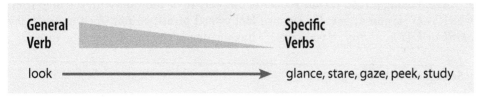

General Verb   **Specific Verbs**

look ———————————➤ glance, stare, gaze, peek, study

Complete List three or four specific verbs for two of the following general verbs: *give, laugh, think,* or *make*. Use the example above as a guide.

General
verb: _____   Specific
verbs: _____

General
verb: _____   Specific
verbs: _____

_____   _____

_____   _____

Watch for "Be" Verbs

Overusing "be" verbs (*is, are, was,* and *were*) can weaken your writing, so always look for ways to use action verbs.

Sentence with a "be" verb:

Maria Posada **is** the supervisor of the nursing trainees.

Sentence with an action verb:

Maria Posada **supervises** the nursing trainees.

Revise Rewrite each of the following sentences so that it contains a specific action verb rather than a "be" verb. (You can often form an action verb from another word in the sentence.)

Sentence with a "be" verb: Pierre Trudeau was an advocate of personal freedoms.

Sentence with an action verb: _____

_____

Sentence with a "be" verb: Scooters are a dominant feature of modern European traffic.

Sentence with an action verb: _____

_____

Diction is not restricted to word choice, but refers also to phrases or figures of speech that a writer chooses to use. Determining an appropriate diction for your writing requires you to think carefully about who your intended audience is and the kind of language your audience understands and uses.

Extend

Circle the main verbs that you used in the sentences you wrote for the Extend feature on the previous page. Replace at least two or three of these verbs (including "be" verbs) with more specific action verbs.

Vocabulary

synonyms
words having similar meaning

affect
in psychology, the
experience of emotion a
person feels, or the display
of that emotion by a person

corespondent
a legal term for a person
involved in adultery

Using Jargon

Jargon is a set of words or phrases that have very specific meanings for very specific groups. For most people, *affect* is a verb that means to influence or have an effect upon someone or something. In psychology, however, affect means something completely different.

Avoid using jargon if your reader is unlikely to be familiar with the field from which that jargon arises. Do not use Hollywood pirate jargon, such as *walk the plank* or *keel haul him*, if your reader has no idea of the meaning of the terms.

Sentence with legal jargon:

Bill was Mary's corespondent in her divorce case.

Sentence without legal jargon:

Bill was the man identified in the court case as having an affair with Mary.

Revise Rewrite the following sentences to use standard, jargon-free language.

Sentence with hockey jargon: When the fight was over, the players delayed the game further by looking for their chicklets on the ice.

Sentence without hockey jargon: _____

_____

Sentence with electrical jargon: As a new homeowner, one of your first jobs should be to find out where your consumer unit is.

Sentence without electrical jargon: _____

_____

LO2 Writing Fluent Sentences

Your writing will have a strong style if the sentences are fluent—if they flow smoothly from one idea to the next. To achieve sentence fluency, vary the length of your sentences as well as the way they begin. Note how the sentences in the following passage flow smoothly:

> Fred's Sandwich Shop opens in the back onto an alley. Last night, while cutting veggies in the kitchen, I happened to see a man in a tailored suit and a townie in a T-shirt and jeans meet in the alley behind our dumpster. They were not more than 20 feet away from me. Without any real caution, the townie handed the man a roll of bills, and in return, received a package wrapped in brown paper. A quick examination of the goods and a simple nod signalled the end of the transaction, and they both went their separate ways. This whole drug deal took less than 45 seconds.
>
> **Discussion:** The passage reads well because, among other things, no two sentences start in the same way, and the sentences vary in length from 9 to 33 words.

Create In the space provided below, narrate an exciting or surprising event that you witnessed. Try to write at least five or six sentences.

_____

_____

_____

_____

_____

_____

_____

_____

_____

_____

_____

Review Circle the first two or three words in each of your sentences. Also count the number of words in each sentence. Then decide if you need to vary some of the beginnings or lengths of your sentences to make them more fluent. If so, rewrite the passage on your own paper.

Learning Outcome

Learn about sentence fluency.

Traits

Sentences that all sound the same become too predictable and are actually hard to read.

Phecsone/Shutterstock.com

A Closer Look at Fluency

One way to achieve sentence fluency is to combine series of shorter sentences into longer ones that read more smoothly. Combining sentences is one of the keys to becoming a better writer, helping you to present your ideas in a more sophisticated way.

Read Study the three short sentences that follow. Then notice how the ideas flow more smoothly when they are combined.

Shorter Sentences

Last weekend, Moira prepared lunches at Brighton Hall.
Brighton Hall is a local community centre.
The lunches consisted of soup and sandwiches.

Combined Sentence

Last weekend, Moira prepared lunches of soup and sandwiches at Brighton Hall, a local community centre.

Create Follow the directions below to combine the following sentences in various ways. (Add, delete, or change words as necessary.)

1. There was a power failure.
2. The power failure hit the school.
3. The power failure hit without warning.
4. The failure left the lower-level classes completely in the dark.
5. The failure left the tech-ed classes without operable equipment.
6. The failure left the cafeteria with half-cooked food.

1. Combine the first three sentences.

   _____

   _____

2. Combine the last three sentences.

   _____

   _____

3. Combine sentences three and four using the word *which* to introduce one of the ideas.

   _____

   _____

4. Complete this sentence:

   When the power failure hit, _____

   _____

Vocabulary

sophisticated
improved and polished

Fluency Trouble

Pay special attention to the following two problems.

Slow-Moving Sentences

If too many of your sentences contain passive verbs, your writing will plod along. To fix this problem, edit the sentences so that they contain active, forward-moving verbs. (See Chapter 32, LO3, Voice of the Verb, for more information.)

Sentence with Passive Verb:

> The 16-ounce porterhouse was dragged along the kitchen counter by the Chihuahua. *(The subject "porterhouse" is being acted upon.)*

Sentence with Active Verb:

> The Chihuahua dragged a 16-ounce porterhouse along the kitchen counter. *(The subject "Chihuahua" is performing the action.)*

Sentences with Qualifiers

If you use too many qualifiers in your sentences (*maybe, it seems to me, I think*), you will sound unsure of yourself. To sound confident, simply omit these words.

Sentence with Qualifiers:

> Although McDonald's is a leading fast-food chain, *it seems to me* that it has *maybe* introduced some healthy alternatives to fried food.
> *(The qualifiers create uncertainty.)*

Sentence without Qualifiers:

> Although McDonald's is a leading fast-food chain, it has introduced some healthy alternatives to fried food.
> *(Removing the qualifiers creates assurance.)*

Edit Rewrite these sentences to fix the fluency challenges discussed above.

1. Ryan Braun was being held at first base by Albert Pujols. The pitcher was signalled by the catcher Yadier Molina to throw a pitch out.

   _____

   _____

2. I think that Queen Elizabeth II is the monarch of the United Kingdom, but, if I'm not mistaken, the prime minister actually governs the country.

   _____

   _____

"While I grumble about the imperfections of spell-checkers, mine does find those embarrassing word repetitions (*the the*) I can't see myself."

—Patricia T. O'Conner

Most writers have a fairly short list of errors they routinely make—such as confusing *effect* with *affect* or making pronoun agreement errors. Look at your own previously graded assignments to create your own short list of routine errors, and use that list to direct much of your editing.

LO3 Checking for Correctness

Mechanical correctness should be the last element that you address in a piece of writing. When editing for correctness, you check your writing for punctuation, capitalization, spelling, and grammar errors.

Strategies for Editing

When checking for errors, examine your writing word for word and sentence by sentence. The following strategies will help you edit thoroughly and effectively.

- If possible, first set your writing aside for a day or two.
- Work with a clean copy of your writing, one that incorporates your revisions and stylistic changes.
- Check one element at a time—spelling, punctuation, and so on.
- For spelling, start at the bottom of the page to force yourself to look at each word. (Remember that your spell-checker will not catch all errors. In particular, most spell-checkers are set for U.S. spelling. Also, your spell-checker will not highlight errors with homonyms.)
- For punctuation, circle all the marks to force yourself to look at each one.
- Read your work aloud at least once, noting any errors as you go along.
- Refer to a list of common errors (see LO5) or a short personal list of errors you often make.
- Have an editing guide (see Parts 5, 6, and 7 in this text) and a dictionary handy.
- Ask a trusted classmate to check your work as well.

Preview When you have questions about punctuation, grammar, or any other convention, turn to Parts 5, 6, and 7 in *WRITE 2*. This part of the book is divided into three major workshops. Answer the following questions about this section.

1. What are the names of the three workshops in this section?

   _____

   _____

   _____

2. How will these workshops prove helpful when you are editing your writing?

   _____

   _____

   _____

3. Which one or two of these workshops will you probably turn to more than the others? Why?

   _____

   _____

   _____

Using Editing Symbols

You can use editing symbols to mark errors in your writing. Listed in the margin are some of the most common symbols.

Edit Use the editing symbols in the margin to mark the errors in the following piece and show how they should be corrected. The first error has been marked for you.

When we lived on Maple street, we had a neighbour who seemed to have

two personalities his name was Mr. Bunde. I worked for him one Summer

while I was in grade school, cutting his lawn and doing other yard work.

After a few months of working for him I'd had more than enough. In

general, he was a nice enough guy and he likes to joke around some of

the time. Unfortunately, it was hard to tell if he was really kidding or

if his mood was suddenly changing. When he was in one of his moods

I couldn't do anything rite. Sometimes he would complain about other

neighbors and he would expect me to agree with him, even though he

new they were my friends. I not only have to concentrate on my work but

I also had to be on my guard, trying to predict Mr. Bundes mood. Why

did I have to work for him

Edit Use the editing symbols to mark errors in this writing sample and show how they should be corrected. The first error has been marked for you.

During the last few decades‸this Nation has become obsessed with dieting and

caloric intake. While many of us are counting calories, not everyone understands

what it is were are counting. by definition, a calorie is a measure of the heat

similar to that required to raise the temperature of one gram of water by one

degree Celsius. Our bodies can be thought of as biocemical machines that burn

the food we eat for fuel The amount of burning that takes place is measured

in calories. how much energy is produced by burning calories is determined

by how active we are. By just sitting and resting we expend about a calorie

minute. That means that just to stay alive our body it must burn 1440 calories

per day. The more active we are, the more calories we will up burn. How many

calories do we burn up when we engage hard exercise.

Vocabulary

caloric intake
the total number of calories taken in

expend
use up, burn

LO4 Editing Academic Writing

Everyday writing may have an informal style, but academic writing should have a semiformal writing style. The following information identifies the basics of these two styles.

Informal

An informal style is a somewhat relaxed style of writing often used when communicating via e-mail, letters, blogs, narratives, personal essays, and so on. This style is often signalled by the following:

- **contractions** (*I'll, she's, can't*)
- **popular expressions** (*Can you believe that!*)
- **cliches** (*blew his top*)
- **first-person references** (*It took me a long time . . .*)
- **occasional fragments** (*Not if I can help it.*)

Semiformal

A semiformal style is a careful, all-purpose writing style used in most academic essays, articles, reports, and papers. This style is signalled by the following:

- **few contractions** (*A strict vegetarian will not . . .*)
- **carefully chosen words** (*The recycled lumber can withstand . . .*)
- **few, if any, cliches**
- **few, if any, first-person references** (*The election proved . . .*)
- **carefully constructed sentences**

Respond Decide if each of the following passages demonstrates an informal or a semiformal style of writing. Explain each of your choices.

1. Science fiction is not always, as some people believe, a second-rate, comic-book literary genre.

   _____ Informal   _____ Semiformal

   _____

   _____

2. We were really scared when the cops pulled us over on the Confederation Bridge. Who wouldn't be?

   _____ Informal   _____ Semiformal

   _____

   _____

3. Elderly people in Edmonton often struggle to pay their utility bills during the coldest months of the year. One utility advocacy group reports that . . .

   _____ Informal   _____ Semiformal

   _____

   _____

Learning Outcome

Edit academic writing.

Insight

The level of language used by your friends may be much different from the level of language expected in academic writing. Develop the ability to shift into semiformal language as needed.

Extend

On your own paper, write the same brief message twice, using a different writing style for each version. You can choose two of these three styles: very personal, informal, and semiformal.

Vocabulary

cliches
overused expressions or ideas, such as *sharp as a tack*

genre
category, type, or class

Use a common errors list.

LO5 Using a Common Errors List

You can find top-ten lists covering just about any topic: top business schools, top crime novels, even top angry comedians. Here is a list of ten common writing errors to watch for. (The corrections are shown in blue.) Turn to this list whenever you edit your writing.

Throughout the semester, list in a notebook other errors that you commonly make. Then be sure to refer to this list whenever you are editing your writing.

1. **Missing Comma after Long Introductory Phrase(s)**

   Because of the fitness craze in this country, many people are suffering from sore muscles and pulled tendons.

2. **Confusing Pronoun Reference**

   While Serena met with Ms. Randall, her cellphone rang two different times.   Ms. Randall's

3. **Missing Comma in a Compound Sentence**

   For job-searching advice, consulting a school's placement service is a good first step, but there are many other options to consider as well.

4. **Missing Comma(s) with a Non-Restrictive Phrase or Clause**

   Travelling, which is usually tiring, is absolutely brutal when you experience flight delays or cancellations.

5. **Comma Splices**

   People are affected differently by the sun. Each person's system produces different amounts of skin pigment or melanin.

6. **Subject–Verb Agreement Errors**

   Every one of the senators wants the president to call a special meeting.

7. **Missing Comma in a Series**

   Stephen Hawking became a renowned physics professor, author, and theorist despite suffering from **ALS**.

8. **Pronoun–Antecedent Agreement Errors**

   Neither Carlos nor Manny has completed his first-aid requirements for the job.

9. **Missing Apostrophe to Show Ownership**

   The left front tire on Martha's car needs to be replaced.

10. **Misusing *Its* and *It's***

    It's a fact that a hummingbird beats its wings more than 75 times a second.

non-restrictive
extra, not necessary (A non-restrictive phrase or clause is set off by commas because it offers extra information, or information that is not necessary to understand the basic sentence. See Chapter 35, LO4.)

ALS
amyotrophic lateral sclerosis, a disease of the nervous system that controls muscle movement

antecedent
the noun that a pronoun refers to

LO6 Reviewing Editing

Complete these activities as needed to help you better understand the editing process.

Write In the space provided below, write two or three sentences about your favourite restaurant. Afterward, underline the nouns and circle the verbs in your writing. Replace any general words with more specific ones. (See LO1, Understanding Word Choice.)

```
_____

_____

_____
```

Explain In the space provided below, explain what is meant by these two sentence problems (see LO2, Writing Fluid Sentences).

Slow-moving sentences: _____

_____

Sentences with qualifiers: _____

_____

Edit Edit the following sentences using the symbols in LO3 to mark the errors.

London is a fascinating city, its filled with historical buildings such as the british museum and st

pauls cathedral

Explain The two basic writing styles are informal and semiformal. Explain the differences between the two styles. (See LO4, Editing Academic Writing.)

Answer Answer the following questions about the common errors list in LO5, Using a Common Errors List.

1. What punctuation mark is often missing in compound sentences? _____

_____

2. What is an antecedent, and what word in the sentence must it agree with? _____

_____

Learning like never before.

4LTR
P·R·E·S·S

www.nelson.com/student

"In my excitement and naiveté as an amateur filmmaker, I got lost in the creative
process and neglected to follow proper accreditation"
— From Shia LaBeouf's Twitter Account

cinemafestival/Shutterstock.com

cinemafestival/Shutterstock.com

9

Plagiarism and Documentation

In 2014, actor–director Shia LaBeouf was accused of plagiarism. LaBeouf released a short film that took large portions of dialogue from a comic book published four years earlier. LaBeouf had failed to acknowledge the cartoonist in the film's credits.

While LaBeouf quickly apologized, his critics began to find instances of plagiarism in his other work. Since those accusations, LaBeouf has declared that he was "retiring" from acting and has appeared publicly wearing a paper bag on his head (see photo). While the exact motive for LaBeouf's bizarre behaviour is unclear, these accusations have called into question his professional integrity both as an actor and a filmmaker.

Plagiarism has serious consequences in the academic world as well. This chapter is designed to help you avoid plagiarism in your own work through proper documentation.

What do you think?

Read the quotation on the top of the page from LaBeouf's Twitter account. Does the fact that he didn't *intend* to steal make him any less guilty of plagiarism? Explain.

_____

_____

_____

Learning Outcomes

LO1 Understand the definition and consequences of plagiarism.

LO2 Review documentation styles.

LO3 Practise documenting sources using MLA guidelines.

LO4 Practise documenting sources using APA guidelines.

LO5 Review MLA formatting guidelines.

LO6 Review APA formatting guidelines.

Vocabulary

plagiarism
using the words or ideas of another person without giving them credit

documentation
acknowledging the use of outside sources in a piece of academic writing

Review

See Chapter 10 to review the differences between paraphrasing, summarizing, and quoting.

LO1 Understanding Plagiarism and Its Consequences

Plagiarism occurs when a student submits the work of another person and presents it as his or her own. While penalties differ from institution to institution, plagiarism is always a serious offence.

Identifying Plagiarism

Learning to identify plagiarism is the first step to avoiding it in your own writing. The chart below provides common examples of both intentional and unintentional plagiarism. Keep in mind that plagiarism can occur regardless of intention. This means you can be punished for plagiarizing even when you have done so by accident.

Intentional Plagiarism	Unintentional Plagiarism
■ purchasing an essay (in part or whole) from a website or another student	■ forgetting to give citations for sources that you have used
■ piecing together an essay by copying and pasting sentences or paragraphs stolen from the Internet (or other sources)	■ forgetting to use quotation marks for direct quotations (even if you provide a citation)
■ on group assignments, letting your partner do all the work and still claiming that you did your fair share	■ insufficient paraphrasing by not changing the words or sentence structure enough (even if you provide a citation)
■ submitting an assignment—either the same or very similar—more than once (even if it is for a different class)	■ using someone else's ideas or concepts (from a text, from a fellow student, etc.) without giving them credit (even if you properly paraphrase the ideas)
■ selling or permitting others to copy your work	■ allowing a tutor to write part of an assignment

Identify Put an X by each scenario that describes a situation in which a student has committed plagiarism.

1. Oswald buys a "plagiarism-free" essay from a website called customessay.ca. _____

2. Selina takes a sentence directly from a magazine article. She properly cites the source but doesn't put quotation marks around the sentence. _____

3. Joe takes an idea from a magazine article. He doesn't cite the source because he is stating the idea in his own words. _____

4. Hugo convinces his tutor to write a couple paragraphs of his paper. He hands the paper in the next day without changing them. _____

5. Pamela lets her friend do the work on a group assignment. Her friend says she is okay with Pamela claiming that they both did an equal amount of the work. _____

6. Edward carefully paraphrases and provides an in-text citation for the sources he used in his research paper but doesn't hand in a bibliography. _____

7. Victor takes a few sentences from a webpage and uses them in his paper. He changes the wording of the sentences slightly and properly cites the Web page. _____

8. Lexx borrows an essay from a friend. Before submitting the paper, he changes some of the wording and inserts a few of his own ideas. _____

Vocabulary

citation
acknowledging you have used an outside source in your own writing

direct quotations
an exact reproduction of the words of a sources used in your own writing

paraphrase
reproduction of the ideas of a source in your own words

Reviewing the Consequences of Plagiarism

Become familiar with the plagiarism policy of your college or university. Your course syllabus is a good place to start: Instructors often include a copy of the plagiarism policy. You could also do an Internet search that includes the name of your institution and "plagiarism policy."

Review Review the plagiarism policy of your college or university. In the space provided, write out the consequences of plagiarism at your school.

Avoiding Plagiarism

Now that you know what plagiarism is and its consequences, the rest of the chapter is devoted to helping you avoid plagiarism in your own work. Consider the following strategies.

1. Start early! Many students plagiarize because they "ran out of time."

2. Be familiar with proper citation format (see the remainder of this chapter).

3. Give credit and citations for everything—it's better to give too much credit than not enough.

4. Make sure you have access to the sources you are using so you can easily check page numbers. Save a PDF to your computer, or make a photocopy of articles you use as source material.

5. Make sure you double-check all of your paraphrasing (see Chapter 10, LO2, for tips on how to paraphrase properly).

6. Choose a topic that interests you. Many students plagiarize because they view the assignment as boring and a "waste of time."

7. Do not give other students copies of your work.

8. Understand what the definitions of plagiarism are; ignorance is not an excuse.

Sign To complete this section, sign the declaration below.

I fully understand the definitions of plagiarism, and accept the consequences if I choose to plagiarize on any of my assignments.

Signed: _____

LO2 Introduction to Documentation

Reviewing Documentation Styles

To avoid plagiarism, you must provide proper documentation for any print or electronic sources you use in your writing.

Print Sources	Electronic Sources
■ Books	■ Web pages
■ Magazines	■ Blogs
■ Journals	■ E-mails
■ Newspapers	■ Tweets
■ Anthologies	■ YouTube videos
■ Encyclopaedias	■ Digital images
■ Dictionaries	■ Articles in online journals
■ Government Publications	■ Articles in online magazines
■ Pamphlets	

Tip

See LO3 for detailed look at MLA style and LO4 for APA style.

In all of your classes, you will be required to follow a specific documentation style. Documentation styles provide instructions on how to acknowledge outside sources correctly. Two common documentation styles are MLA (Modern Language Association) and APA (American Psychological Association). The MLA style is typically used in the humanities while APA is used in the social sciences.

List Make a list of all of the classes you are currently taking. Determine which documentation style you are using for each (MLA, APA, or other). If you are unsure, be sure to check with your instructor or a librarian. Write your answers in the space provided below.

Class	Documentation Style

Respond The example essay "Pot Prohibition in Canada: End the War on Weed" (see Chapter 22, LO3) was written for a psychology class. Which documentation style does it follow? How do you know?

Respond The example essay "On-Ice Fighting: Protecting NHL Players since 1917" (see Chapter 22, LO1) was written for a philosophy class. Which documentation style does it follow? How do you know?

Vocabulary

documentation
acknowledging the use of outside sources in a piece of academic writing

Comparing MLA and APA Styles

Despite a number of small differences, both MLA and APA follow the convention of using (1) an in-text citation and (2) a bibliography entry to acknowledge an outside source.

In-Text Citations	Bibliography Entries
■ Appear in the body of your writing ■ Indicate to your reader that you have used the words or ideas of another person ■ Follow a paraphrase, direct quotation, or summary ■ State the author's last name along with page number (MLA) or year of publication (APA).	■ Appear on a separate page at the end of your essay ■ Contain all relevant publication information so that your reader can easily find the source

To better understand the relationship between an in-text citation and a bibliography entry, consider the following sentence taken from the essay about on-ice fighting in professional hockey (see Chapter 22, LO1).

> The author of this study concluded that **"the fights aren't causing the concussions"** and that the risk of injury from fighting itself is actually quite low **(Stinson)**.

The quotation marks and the last name indicate to the reader that these words do not *belong* to the author of this essay. Instead, the author has taken the words and ideas of another person (as indicated by the last name) from an outside source and used it in his or her writing.

Now flip to the page of works cited at the end of the essay (Chapter 22, LO1). The in-text citation corresponds with the following MLA entry as indicated by the last name.

> **Stinson**, Scott. "Brawls 'Aren't Causing' Head Trauma: Doctor." *National Post*, 21 Oct. 2011, www.news.nationalpost.com/sports/nhl/expert-fighting-isnt-causing-the-concussions. Accessed 14 Feb. 2014.

If the readers wanted to find this article, they could do so by locating the October 21, 2011 issue of the *National Post* online. Including the date of access is optional, but if changes have been made to the source since its original publication, the date confirms the version you consulted.

Practise Pick an in-text citation from the example essay "Pot Prohibition in Canada: End the War on Weed" (Chapter 22, LO3). Then find the corresponding entry in the references page. Finally, use a web browser to locate the source using the information provided.

L○3 MLA Style

Works Cited Page

The works cited page appears at the end of your essay. It lists in alphabetical order by author's surname all the outside sources used in your essay. Each entry should provide enough information for your reader to locate each source. See the examples below for three common entry models.

Entry for Basic Source (e.g., a book)

Author's Last Name, First Name. *Title of the Book in Italics*. Publisher, year of publication. (Use "P" or "UP" instead of "Press" or "University Press" in the publisher's name.)

Aarseth, Espen. *Cybertext: Perspectives on Ergodic Literature*. Johns Hopkins UP, 1997.

Entry for Journal Article in an Online Database

Author's Last Name, First Name. "Title of Article in Quotation Marks." *Journal Title in Italics*, volume, issue, publication date, location within the issue. *Name of the Online Database in Italics*, URL. (Optional: Access Date.)

Budra, Paul. "American Justice and the First-Person Shooter." *Canadian Review of American Studies*, vol. 34, no. 1, 2004, pp. 1-12. *Project Muse*, www.muse-jhu-edu.ezproxy.library.yorku.ca/article/168567/pdf. Accessed 16 Apr. 2015.

Entry for a Web Source

Editor or Author's Last Name, First Name (if available). "Page, Document, or Posting Title in Quotation Marks." *Website Title in Italics*. Publisher (can be omitted if the publisher and the website title are the same, as in the case of newspapers), Publication Date, URL. (Optional: Access Date.)

McGee, Maxwell. "Beyond Earth: The Alpha Centauri Connection." *Gamespot*, CNET Networks, 14 Apr. 2014, www.gamespot.com/articles/beyond-earth-the-alpha-centauri-connection/1100-6418924. Accessed 27 Dec. 2015.

Create Create works cited entries for the following sources. Follow the model entries above, paying close attention to the placement of punctuation marks and spacing.

1. An article written by Blackbeard Thatch titled Grapeshot and You. The article was published in 1997 in a journal titled *The New Journal of Piracy* volume 3, issue 9 on pages 13–19. You downloaded the article from the database JSTOR on December 21, 2015, and the URL was www.jstor.org/stable/njp019970309.

2. A book titled *Empire of Blue Water: Captain Morgan's Great Pirate Army, the Epic Battle for the Americans, and the Catastrophe that Ended the Outlaws' Bloody Reign* written by Stephan Talty. The book was published by Three Rivers Press on April 22, 2008.

3. An article posted on the website *Booty Bay* on October 21, 2012, titled Flag Making: The Definitive Guide. Julia Geeson wrote this article. You couldn't find the publisher, but the URL is www.bootybay.ca/flag-making-definitive. You downloaded the article on January 11, 2016.

MLA In-Text Citations

In-text citations appear in the body of your essay to indicate material that has been borrowed from an outside source. For MLA style, in-text citations usually list (1) the last name of the author who wrote the material, and (2) the page number where the material is from. Using the author's last name, readers can find the full source information on the works cited page.

Author's last name and page number in parenthesis

Typically, the author's last name and the page number are placed in parentheses followed by a period.

Open meditation focuses on cultivating "mindfulness" which involves "*maintaining complete awareness of all conscious thoughts, perceptions and actions*" (Rychlak 223).

In this example, the quotation marks indicate that the author has borrowed the words of another person. See Chapter 10 for more information on properly quoting an outside source.

Author name cited in sentence, page number in parenthesis

Another common way to present the material is to name the author in the preceding sentence.

White notes that meditation is one of the oldest spiritual practices (67).

In this example, the author has paraphrased the outside material as opposed to quoting it directly. See Chapter 10 for more information on how to paraphrase.

No author name and/or page number

In some cases (e.g., electronic sources) you may have a source without an author. Use a shortened version of the source title instead.

Meditation became popular in the West with the introduction of transcendental meditation ("Alterations of Consciousness" 189).

Other times, usually with electronic sources, you may be without a page number. In these instances, just use the author's last name.

Meditation became popular in the West with the introduction of transcendental meditation (White).

Note that some online sources provide paragraph or section numbers that could guide your readers to a specific section. The abbreviations *sec.* or *par.* can be used instead of a page number. You do not need to count paragraphs for a reference if the source does not contain numbered paragraphs.

Create For each of the following excerpts, write a sentence that uses part of the excerpt and an in-text citation. If you are unsure how to properly paraphrase or quote, see Chapter 10, LO2 and LO3.

1. *Unlike traditional cannonballs, grapeshot is a mass of smaller balls jammed together into a canvas bag. When fired from a canon, the individual balls spread out in a way similar to a blast from a shotgun shell. Grapeshot is most useful at short range against masses of infantry.* Quotation taken from page 19 of "Grapeshot and You" (see earlier exercise for full source information for article by Blackbeard Thatch).

2. *The pirates voted on how many shares of treasure each pirate would get. The captain got five or six shares to the common pirate's one; the master's mate got two; the cabin boy one-half. Skilled tradesmen were well compensated: The carpenter who'd be responsible for fixing any breaches of the hull from cannonballs or storm damage was often paid 150 pieces of eight; the surgeon and his "chest of medicaments" got 250.* From page 188 of *Empire of Blue Water* (see earlier for full source information for book by Stephan Talty).

3. *The Jolly Roger is a flag design used to identify a ship and its crew as pirates. The most popular design is a skull and crossbones on a pure black background. Common variations on this design include replacing the bones with two crossed cutlasses.* From the third paragraph of "Flag Making: The Definitive Guide" (see earlier exercise for full source information for article by Julia Geeson).

Tip

Entry models for other types of sources can be found online. Purdue University provides an excellent website on APA style (owl.english .purdue.edu), as does the American Psychological Association (www .apastyle.org).

L◯4 APA Style

References Page

The references page appears at the end of your essay. It lists all the outside sources used in your essay. Each entry should provide enough information for your reader to locate each source. See the examples below for three common entry models.

Entry for Basic Print Source (e.g., a book)

Author's Last Name, Initials. (Publication Year). *Title of the book in italics*. Publication City, Province, Territory, or Country: Publisher.

Aarseth, E. (1997). *Cybertext: Perspectives on ergodic literature*. Baltimore, MD: Johns Hopkins University Press.

Entry for Journal Article in an Online Database

Author's Last Name, Initials. (Publication Year). Title of article. *Journal Title in Italics, Volume*(issue), page numbers. Retrieved from http://www .websitename.com/entire/url

Budra, P. (2004). American justice and the first-person shooter. *Canadian Review of American Studies, 34*(1), 1–12. Retrieved from http://www. projectmust.edu/articles/vol34/first-person

If an article appears with a DOI (digital object identifier), use the following model.

Author's Last Name, Initials. (Publication Year). Title of article. *Journal Title in Italics, Volume*(issue), page numbers. doi: code

Budra, P. (2004). American justice and the first-person shooter. *Canadian Review of American Studies, 34*(1), 1–12. doi: 1827397 / 012384719235

Entry for an Online Document

Author's Last Name, Initials. (Publication Date). *Page, Document or Posting Title*. Retrieval statement with URL.

McGee, M. (2014). *Beyond earth: The alpha centauri connection*. Retrieved from http://www.gamespot.com/articles/beyond-earth-the-alpha-centauri-connection/

Create APA reference entries for the following sources. Follow the model entries above, paying close attention to the placement of punctuation marks and spacing.

1. An article written by Blackbeard Thatch titled Grapeshot and You. The article was published in 1997 in a journal titled *The New Journal of Piracy* volume 3, issue 9 on pages 13–19. You downloaded the article from the database JSTOR on December 21, 2015.

2. A book titled *Empire of Blue Water: Captain Morgan's Great Pirate Army, the Epic Battle for the Americans, and the Catastrophe That Ended the Outlaws' Bloody Reign* written by Stephan Talty. The book was published by Three Rivers Press on April 22, 2008, in New York.

3. An article posted on the website *Booty Bay* on October 21, 2012, titled Flag Making: The Definitive Guide. Julia Geeson wrote this article. You couldn't find the publisher. You downloaded the article on January 11, 2014. The URL is www.bootybay.com/flagmaker

APA In-Text Citations

In-text citations appear in the body of your essay to indicate material that has been borrowed from an outside source. APA in-text citations usually list (1) the last name of the author who wrote the material and (2) the publication date of the material. Using the author's last name, readers can find the full source information on your references page.

Author's last name and page number in parenthesis

Typically, the author's last name and the publication date are placed in parentheses, separated by a comma and followed by a period.

Those who practise concentrative meditation focus their attention on one, unchanging object (**Rychlak, 1997**).

In this example, the author has paraphrased the outside material as opposed to quoting it directly.

Author name cited in sentence, publication year in parenthesis

Another common way to present the material is to the name the author in the preceding sentence followed by the publication year in parenthesis.

White (1974) notes that meditation is one of the oldest spiritual practices.

No author name and/or publication date

In some cases (e.g., electronic sources), you may have a source without an author. Use a shortened version of the source title instead. Use the abbreviation *n.d.* for sources that do not list a publication date.

Meditation became popular in the West with the introduction of transcendental meditation (**"Alterations of consciousness," n.d.**).

Page or paragraph numbers

When referring a specific part of a source, add the abbreviation *p.* (for page number) or *para.* (for paragraph).

Open meditation focuses on cultivating "mindfulness" which involves "maintaining complete awareness of all conscious thoughts, perceptions and actions" (Rychlak, 1997, **p. 223**).

In this example, the quotation marks indicate that the author has taken the words or ideas of another person. See Chapter 10, LO3, for more information on quoting an outside source.

Create For each of the following, write a sentence that uses part of the excerpt and an in-text citation. If you are unsure how to properly paraphrase or quote, see Chapter 10.

1. *Unlike traditional cannonballs, grapeshot is a mass of smaller balls jammed together into a canvas bag. When fired from a canon, the individual balls spread out in a way similar to a blast from a shotgun shell. Grapeshot is most useful at short range against masses of infantry.* Quotation taken from page 19 of "Grapeshot and You" (see earlier exercise for full source information).

2. *The pirates voted on how many shares of treasure each pirate would get. The captain got five or six shares to the common pirate's one; the master's mate got two; the cabin boy one-half. Skilled tradesmen were well compensated: The carpenter who'd be responsible for fixing any breaches of the hull from cannonballs or storm damage was often paid 150 pieces of eight; the surgeon and his "chest of medicaments" got 250.* From page 188 of *Empire of Blue Water* (see earlier exercise for full source information).

3. *The Jolly Roger is a flag design used to identify a ship and its crew as pirates. The most popular design is a skull and crossbones on a pure black background. Common variations on this design include replacing the bones with two crossed cutlasses.* From the third paragraph of "Flag Making: The Definitive Guide" (see earlier exercise for full source information).

Chapter 9 Plagiarism and Documentation

Documentation: More Practice

Create Create reference or works cited entries for the following sources. Use MLA or APA style, whichever is more relevant to your particular area of study. For any model entries not covered in this chapter, check out examples of current guidelines at the Purdue Online Writing Lab (owl.english.purdue.edu).

1. A book by Ben Hornigold and Calico Jack titled *How to Speak Pirate*. Published by Galleon Press in Port Royal in 2006.

2. An article published in *The Globe and Mail* titled Beyond Booty: Pension Planning for Pirates by Olivia Arrson. It was published on May 14, 2014, on page A9.

3. On a website, you are using a page called "Disinfecting Wounds with Rum." You can't find the name of the author or the publisher, or the publishing date. The website is called The Golden Age and the URL is www.goldenage.org/ disinfecting-wounds-with-rum. You downloaded the article on July 7, 2016.

4. An e-mail by William Kid sent to Charles Vane on December 7, 2015. The subject line is "Tips on Training Your Parrot."

5. An essay titled "Hiding Treasure in Style" by John Silver published in a larger anthology called *"X" Marks the Spot*. The anthology was edited by Mary Read and published in London, England, by Banana Press in 2015. The essay appears on pages 1723–1891.

Create Type up both a works cited page (MLA) or references page (APA) using the entries you created above. Remember to organize the entries alphabetically and follow the formatting conventions for MLA (LO3) and APA (LO4).

Write The following excerpts are taken from the five sources in the exercise you have just completed. For each, write short paragraph that uses part of the excerpt and an in-text citation. If you are unsure how to properly paraphrase or quote, see Chapter 10.

Vocabulary

aficionado
a devotee, fan, or enthusiast

1. *September 19th is International Talk like a Pirate Day: Every year, pirate aficionados gather at local bars and taverns to drink grog and speak like pirates. From page 65 of How To Speak Pirate.*

2. *Burying your treasure, or booty, in multiple locations is the most important rule for pirates planning to retire. By splitting your treasure into multiple piles and hiding them in different locations, the loss of one chest isn't overly problematic. From page A9 of "Beyond Booty: Pension Planning for Pirates."*

3. *Before applying rum to the wound, take a long sip directly from the bottle. Next, pour the rum directly from the bottle onto the wound. Make sure the wound is fully covered. Apply liberally. Take another long sip from the bottle. From the third paragraph of the web article "Disinfecting Wounds with Rum."*

4. *Behavioural reinforcement is the most important aspect of parrot training. Need to find a strong reinforcer for your pet. I recommend choosing food. From the fourth paragraph of the email "Tips on Training Your Parrot."*

5. *A treasure map is very important for remembering where you buried treasure. Do not make copies of the map. Only have one copy and keep it on your person at all times. From page 1758 "Hiding Treasure in Style."*

LO5 MLA Formatting

In addition to documentation rules, MLA style also provides guidelines for formatting your final paper (see style.mla.org/formatting-papers/). A complete paper following MLA style is provided in Chapter 22, LO1. Included below for quick reference are the first and last pages of an example essay, annotated to demonstrate the basic MLA formatting rules.

MLA Paper (First Page Excerpt)

Add 1.25 cm margin between top of page and running head.

Do not provide a title page.

Snowp 1

List your full name, instructor's name, course title, and date of submission. Only provide this information on the first page.

Provide your last name and corresponding page number in the top right corner of every page.

Jonathan Snowp

Dr. Jeo Merment

English 270

30 October 2016

Do not underline or put the title in bold or italics.

Double space and centre your title.

Vancouver's Post-Modern Identity:

Contradictory Representations in *Everything's Gone Green* and *City of Glass*

Vancouver author Douglas Coupland remarked in an interview with *Maclean's* magazine that "there is no core [to Vancouver], it's all margin" (Wood 70). This quotation is significant because it establishes the identity that Coupland attributes to Vancouver in many of his works, including *Everything's Gone Green*, a film dealing with many issues exclusive to the city, and *City of Glass*, a photo journal/essay about Vancouver. Therefore, according to Coupland, Vancouver could be seen as a post-modern city in that its identity is fragmented and contradictory thereby dissolving any (modernist) notion of a cultural city "core" (Delany 3-4). Coupland sees Vancouver's post-modern nature not as problematic, but as positive, a sentiment which is evident in both *Everything's Gone Green* and *City of Glass*. However, there are also apparent contradictions between these two texts in their conflicting representations of poverty and substance abuse in Vancouver. Ultimately, these discrepancies can be accounted for by the differing contextual circumstances of these texts.

Everything's Gone Green and *City of Glass* share a positive attitude towards Vancouver's post-modern identity: "The city's [post-modern nature is its] greatest blessing" (Wood 70). For example, both texts seem to argue that conceptualizing Vancouver in this way is productive because it provides a way of coming to terms with the fragmented nature of the city. More specifically, through a post-modern identity, many traditional (modernist) assumptions about

Use a double space between the title and the first line of your essay.

Choose a legible font like Times New Roman or Arial. Pick font size "12."

Be sure to double-space the entire document.

Justify the left side of the page.

Use double space between paragraphs.

Hit the "tab" key to indent your paragraphs.

Put any titles of outside sources in italics.

Leave only one space after periods.

Leave the right side of the page ragged, not justified.

Use square brackets when you make changes to a direct quotation.

MLA Works Cited List

Provide your last name and corresponding page number in the top left corner.

Put your works cited on a separate page.

Works Cited

Centre the title. Do not italicize, underline or bold.

Busta, Caroline. "Douglas Coupland: Everywhere Is Anywhere Is Anything Is Everything." *Artforum International*, vol. 52, no. 9, 2014, www.artforum.com/inprint/id=46397. Accessed 21 Nov. 2014.

Coupland, Douglas. *City of Glass: Douglas Coupland's Vancouver*. Douglas and McIntyre, 2000.

Organize entries alphabetically by author's last name. If no author name is given, use the title of the source instead.

Delany, Paul. "Vancouver as a Postmodern City." *Vancouver: Representing the Postmodern City*, edited by Paul Delany, Arsenal Pulp P, 1994, pp. 1-25.

Italicize titles of works that are published as a whole (e.g., books, films, plays, periodicals).

"Douglas Coupland: everywhere is anywhere is anything is everything." *Vancouver Art Gallery*, www.vanartgallery.bc.ca/the_exhibitions/exhibit_coupland.html. Accessed 21 Nov. 2014.

Double space the entire page. Do not add extra space between entries.

Fiske, John. "Culture, Ideology, Interpellation." *Literary Theory: An Anthology.* 2nd ed., edited by Julie Rivkin and Michael Ryan, Blackwell Publishing, 2004, pp. 1268-73.

Add a paragraph indent (1.25 cm) for any lines after the first.

Follow MLA guidelines for listing publishing information.

Fox, Paul, director. *Everything's Gone Green*. Astral Media, 2007.

Lacken, Felladark. "Vancouver: Mapping the Rainy City." *Rain City*, 2 Nov. 2013, www.raincity.ca/mappingrainycity. Accessed 11 May 2015.

Miller, Stephen. "The Grid: Living in Hollywood North." *Vancouver: Representing the Postmodern City,* edited by Paul Delany, Arsenal Pulp P, 1994, pp. 1-25.

Put article or essay titles that are a part of a larger work in quotation marks.

Put titles of the larger work in italics.

Rivkin, Julie, and Michael Ryan. "The Politics of Culture." *Literary Theory: An Anthology.* 2nd ed., edited by Julie Rivkin and Michael Ryan, Blackwell Publishing, 2004, pp. 1233-34.

Set margins to 2.5 cm on all sides.

Wood, Chris. "Douglas Coupland Praises Vancouver's Dynamism." *Maclean's*, Nov. 2000, pp. 70-71.

LO6 APA Formatting

In addition to documentation rules, APA style also provides guidelines for formatting your final paper. A complete paper following APA style is provided in Chapter 22, LO3. Included below for quick reference are an example title page, abstract, body, and references, annotated to demonstrate the basic APA formatting rules.

APA Title Page

Write "Running Head:" followed by a shortened version of your title in capital letters.

Provide a page number in the top right corner of every page.

Use a readable font like times new roman (size 12) for the entire paper.

Do not underline or put the title in bold or italics.

APA Abstract Page

Make sure shortened version of title appears in the top left corner of all pages after the title page.

Write "Abstract" in the centre of the page.

Underneath, provide a short overview (around 200 words) of your paper.

Summarize the problem addressed in the paper.

identify participants and methods.

State overall purpose of the study.

Note results of study and conclusion.

Add 1.25 cm margin between top of page and running head.

List the essay's title, your full name, and your school's name in the centre of the title page. This information, as well as the rest of the essay, should be double spaced.

Running Head: FACE IDENTIFICATION AND DISGUISES   1

Face Identification and Surveillance Camera Technology:
The Influence of Sunglasses and Hats

Feedber R.M. Hambersonth

University of Toronto

FACE IDENTIFICATION AND DISGUISES   2

Abstract

Closed circuit television (CCTV) surveillance cameras are a common technology used today; however, people caught on camera may be difficult to identify, especially when their faces are unfamiliar and/or if they are wearing a disguise. This study examines the effect of disguises on participants' ability to identify suspects from a photo array of faces based on a still image taken from a surveillance video. Forty-five participants, undergraduate psychology students, were shown surveillance videos (and still images taken from the videos) containing suspects wearing no disguise, a hat, or a hat and sunglasses. Participants then had their accuracy levels measured by their ability to correctly pick the suspect's face out of a photo array. A number of significant effects were found, and it was concluded that as the degree of disguise increases, participant accuracy decreases. Future research needs to be done in this area in order to provide further explanations.

APA Body Pages

Define any acronyms using parenthesis.

FACE IDENTIFICATION AND DISGUISES   3

Face Identification and Surveillance Camera Technology:

The Influence of Sunglasses and Hats

Surveillance cameras, or closed circuit television (CCTV) security cameras, are a common technology used today (Bruce, Henderson, & Greenwood, 2012). CCTV systems are installed in most stores, malls, and shopping centres with the objective of helping to identify, and potentially deter, individuals who commit crimes (Bruce et al., 2012). It is assumed that once a person is caught on tape, they can easily be identified, or their identify can be verified, from the recorded images; furthermore, this technology removes the problems typically associated with eyewitness memory (Henderson, 2011). However, a review of the literature demonstrates that individuals captured on video images are difficult to identity, especially when the faces are unfamiliar and if the suspect is wearing a disguise. The problems are further compounded by other technological issues such as the quality of the CCTV images and the size of the area monitored.

FACE IDENTIFICATION AND DISGUISES   6

Discussion

Summary

The first hypothesis stated that increasing the degree of disguise (no disguise, hat, hat and sunglasses) would lead to lower identification accuracy, and this hypothesis is supported by the results. The second hypothesis stated that there would be a difference in accuracy when using still images versus moving video.

As indicated by the results, statistical significance was found between the different type of disguises for both the still image condition and the moving video condition and therefore the first hypothesis was supported. As noted by figure 6, the results were most clear for the still image condition: they support the prediction that as the disguise increases from no disguise, to hat, to hat and sunglasses, participant accuracy decreases. This is likely due to the fact that as disguise increases, obvious facial

---

Sidebar notes:

Define any acronyms using parenthesis.

Hit the "tab" key to indent your paragraphs.

Justify the left side of the page.

Restate your title in the top centre of the page following your abstract.

Use a double space between the title and the first line of your essay.

When providing an in-text citation for three or more authors, list all names the first time you cite the source. Afterwards, you may simply list the first author's name followed by "et al." See the following citation for an example.

In-text citation for one author.

Leave only one space after periods.

Leave the right side of the page ragged, not justified.

Centre and bold level one headings.

Left align and bold level two headings.

8

group for the still image condition. These results support the conclusions of Patterson and Baddeley (1977) and Henderson et al. (2001).

However, as indicated by Figure 6, for the video condition, the hat group is less accurate than the hat and sunglasses group There is not much difference, however, and that difference is not statistically significant. Furthermore, statistical significance was found (post hoc) for the no disguise group and the hat group a finding which supports the general prediction that there will be a difference when a disguise is added.

Clearly reference figures in the text.

Figure 6

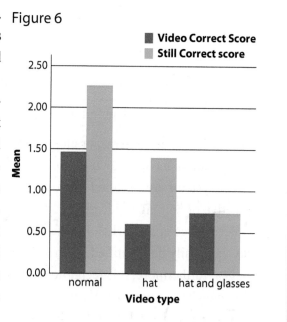

APA References List

10

References

Centre the title. Do not italicize, underline, or bold.

Put your references on a separate page.

Set margins to 2.5 cm on all sides.

Organize entries alphabetically by author's last name. If no author name is given, use the title of the source instead.

Follow APA guidelines for listing publishing information.

Add a paragraph indent (1.25 cm) for any lines after the first.

Bruce, V., Henderson, Z., & Greenwood, K. (2012). Verification of face identities from images captured on video. *Journal of Experimental Psychology: Applied, 5*(4), 339-360.

Henderson, Z. (2011). Matching the faces of robbers captured on video. *Applied Cognitive Psychology, 15,* 445-464.

Houston, K. A., Hope, L., Memon, A., & Read, J. D. (2013). Expert Testimony on Eyewitness Evidence: In Search of Common Sense. *Behavioral Sciences & The Law, 31*(5), 637-651. doi:10.1002/bsl.2080.

McLeod, S. (2009, February 3). Eyewitness Testimony. Retrieved November 21, 2014, from http://www.simplypsychology.org/eyewitness-testimony.html.

Patterson, K. & Baddeley, A. (1977). When face recognition fails. *Journal of ExperimentalPsychology: Human Learning and Memory, 3,* 406-417.

Shepherd, J., Ellis, H., & Davies, G. (1982). *Identification evidence: A psychological evaluation.* Aberdeen, Scotland: University of Aberdeen Press.

Wise, R. A., Sartori, G., Magnussen, S., Safer, M. A., Byk, D., & Hogan, E. (2014). An examination of the causes and solutions to eyewitness error. *Frontiers In Psychiatry,* 51-8. doi:10.3389/fpsyt.2014.00102.

Yarmey, A. D. (2014). Eyewitness recall and photo identification: A field experiment. *Psychology, Crime and Law, 10*(1), 53-68.

"I try to leave out the parts that people skip."
—Elmore Leonard

gwycech/Shutterstock.com

10

Summarizing Source Material

Knowing how to summarize accurately and effectively is a powerful instrument in a writer's toolbox. So much of writing involves responding to other writing or incorporating it as support for your own text. In either case, effective summary helps a reader to grasp how those sources relate to your ideas.

In this chapter, you'll learn to write a paragraph summarizing a source. You'll also learn how paraphrasing is similar to and different from summarizing, and how to correctly and effectively use quotations.

Learning Outcomes

LO1 Learn to summarize.

LO2 Learn to paraphrase.

LO3 Learn to use quotations.

What do you think?

Consider the photo and quotation. What does each make you think alone? What do they make you think together?

Citation

Whether summarizing, paraphrasing, or quoting, always take care to give credit to the original source. For more information on crediting sources, review Chapter 9 on MLA and APA citation styles.

Incorporating Source Material

Obviously you cannot expect your reader to be familiar with every source you reference in your work. To do justice to the ideas you borrow, you must both cite them accurately and communicate them faithfully—summarizing, paraphrasing, or quoting, as appropriate for your purposes.

In this chapter, we will use the following original material from the preface to the book *Crime: Its Cause and Treatment,* by Clarence Darrow, originally published in 1922 by Thomas Y. Crowell Co. The full text of the book is available for free online at http://www.gutenberg.org/ebooks/12027.

Example Source Material

The physical origin of such abnormalities of the mind as are called "criminal" is a comparatively new idea. The whole subject has long been dealt with from the standpoint of metaphysics. Man has slowly banished chance from the material world and left behavior alone outside the realm of cause and effect. It has not been long since insanity was treated as a moral defect. It is now universally accepted as a functional defect of the human structure in its relation to environment.

My main effort is to show that the laws that control human behavior are as fixed and certain as those that control the physical world. In fact, that the manifestations of the mind and the actions of men are a part of the physical world.

I am fully aware that this book will be regarded as a plea or an apology for the criminal. To hold him morally blameless could be nothing else. Still if man's actions are governed by natural law, the sooner it is recognized and understood, the sooner will sane treatment be adopted in dealing with crime. The sooner too will sensible and humane remedies be found for the treatment and cure of this most perplexing and painful manifestation of human behavior. I have tried conscientiously to understand the manifold actions of men and if I have to some degree succeeded, then to that extent I have explained and excused. I am convinced that if we were all-wise and all-understanding, we could not condemn.

LO1 Summarizing

The purpose of a summary is to provide the main ideas of a source, condensed, in your own words. Summarize whenever you need to include an extended set of ideas or information about your topic, all from a single source. To prepare a summary, follow these steps.

1. Reread and jot down key words from the source.

2. Restate the main point in your own words.

3. Add key supporting points, leaving out examples, details, and long explanations.

4. Restate objectively, excluding your own commentary.

5. Check your completed summary against the original source, adding quotation marks around any exact phrases you have borrowed.

Sample Summary

It is a relatively new idea that criminal activity results from a mental rather than a moral defect. Only recently has even insanity gained recognition as a mental problem. Yet the human mind is part of the physical world. The natural laws that determine physical reality equally affect human behaviour. Recognizing this will sooner lead to "sensible and humane" solutions to criminal activity. To understand prevents condemnation.

Respond

1. Circle the main point in the sample summary and in the original text. Then underline and number the supporting points in the sample summary and the original.

2. Are there any other details from the original that you believe should have been included in the summary? Explain.

Practise

3. Choose another set of paragraphs from the original text online, or from a text assigned by your instructor, and write a summary paragraph. When finished, compare your summary with another student's.

LO2 Paraphrasing

While a summary's goal is to condense the ideas of a source, the purpose of a paraphrase is to recast the entire passage in your own words. As a result, a paraphrase is generally longer than a summary. A paraphrase follows the structure of the original source, simplifying and clarifying the wording. To write a paraphrase, follow these steps.

1. Review the original source for an overall sense of it.

2. Proceed sentence by sentence through the original,

    a. stating the ideas in your own words, defining any terms as necessary,

    b. editing for clarity, taking care not to change the meaning, and

    c. putting any direct quotations in quotation marks.

3. Check your final paraphrase against the original for accuracy.

Sample Paraphrase

That criminal behaviour results from a physical source is a new idea. It has previously been considered a subject of metaphysics (beyond the material world). Although humans have come to recognize cause and effect in all other aspects of the world, behaviour has been left outside. Until recently, even insanity was considered a "moral defect." Now, however, we recognize it as a functional problem with physical origins.

The causes of human behaviour are as absolute as the physical laws controlling the world because the mind and the actions from it are part of that physical world.

Obviously, this argument will be viewed as "a plea or an apology" for criminals, making the case that they are not to blame. But if human actions are determined by physical laws, the sooner we accept this, the sooner we can develop a sane approach to dealing with crime. From this understanding, we can find "sensible and humane" treatments to this vexing, troublesome problem of human behaviour. If we had all wisdom and all understanding, surely we could no longer condemn.

Practise Return to the selection you summarized on the previous page. Write a paraphrase of that same selection. Then compare your summary to your paraphrase.

L◯3 Using Quotations

Unlike a summary, which condenses a source in your own words, or a paraphrase, which restates that source in your own words, a quotation exactly reproduces the words of a source. Quotations should be used infrequently, to avoid making your text seem a patchwork of other people's ideas. However, they can be used in your writing to accomplish the following:

- Lend authority by including the exact words of a respected expert.
- Add colour by using particularly well-worded phrases from the source.
- Include sentences or phrases that could not be expressed as well in other words.
- Provide specific examples from a source.

To make a quotation, follow these steps.

1. Be fair to the author, using her or his words as intended, not taking them out of context to seemingly support your point.

2. Copy the quoted passage word for word, enclosing it in quotation marks and making the source evident either in your text or as a parenthetical note.

3. Use ellipses to indicate any words you left out of the original; use square brackets to indicate changes you made to spelling, capitalization, or grammar.

Example Quotations

The following text incorporates specific wording to lend authority and colour.

Not so very long ago, humans viewed nearly every physical phenomenon as having a spiritual origin. Every rock, tree, and stream seemed to possess its own willful spirit. As human understanding has expanded, however, it has "slowly banished chance from the material world and left behavior alone outside the realm of cause and effect" (Darrow, ii).

The following example demonstrates use of ellipses and brackets to create a condensed quotation from a longer original.

"[I]f man's actions are governed by natural law, the sooner it is recognized and understood, the sooner will sane treatment be adopted…, [t]he sooner too will sensible and humane remedies be found…" (Darrow, iii).

Practical Application

Read Read the following selection, noting its main idea and supporting points.

On Different Degrees of Smallness.

Topic Sentence | We shall find that in our processes of calculation we have to deal with small quantities of various degrees of smallness.

Body Sentences | We shall have also to learn under what circumstances we may consider small quantities to be so minute that we may omit them from consideration. Everything depends upon relative minuteness.

Before we fix any rules let us think of some familiar cases. There are 60 minutes in the hour, 24 hours in the day, 7 days in the week. There are therefore 1440 minutes in the day and 10080 minutes in the week.

Obviously 1 minute is a very small quantity of time compared with a whole week. Indeed, our forefathers considered it small as compared with an hour, and called it "one minùte," meaning a minute fraction—namely one sixtieth—of an hour. When they came to require still smaller subdivisions of time, they divided each minute into 60 still smaller parts, which, in Queen Elizabeth's days, they called "second minùtes" (i.e. small quantities of the second order of minuteness). Nowadays we call these small quantities of the second order of smallness "seconds." But few people know why they are so called.

Closing Sentence | Now if one minute is so small as compared with a whole day, how much smaller by comparison is one second!

Source: Thompson, Silvanus Phillips. *Calculus Made Easy.* London: MacMillan, 1914. Print.

Respond Write a journal entry in response to the selection above. Include specific quotations where possible, taking care to cite that information.

Summarize or Paraphrase Write a summary or paraphrase of the selection (your choice). Compare yours with another student's and discuss any major differences.

_____

_____

_____

_____

_____

_____

The study habit that sets you apart.

www.nelson.com/student

Part 3 Developing Paragraphs

"To write about people you have to know people, to write about bloodhounds you have to know bloodhounds, to write about the Loch Ness monster you have to find out about it."
—James Thurber

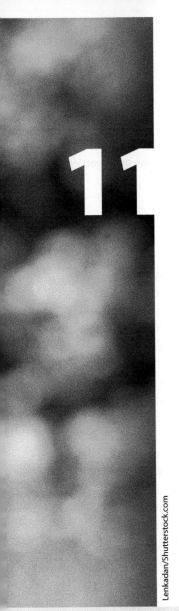

11 Description and Narration

What sets human beings apart from other animals is, among other things, our curiosity. We have a deep-seated need to know what is happening around us, what things look like, and what our world means. It is not an exaggeration to say that the world as we know it would not exist if people weren't obsessed with a need to know.

Whenever you describe a particular topic or explore some aspect of your life, you are satisfying, in one small way, your innate curiosity. In the first part of this chapter, you will analyze a descriptive paragraph and then write a paragraph of your own. In the second part, you will analyze a narrative paragraph before recalling and writing about one of your own memorable experiences.

As you develop each of your paragraphs in this section, you will learn valuable strategies that you can apply to all of your writing, including establishing a focus, using specific details, and following a clear pattern of organization.

What do you think?

What does Thurber's quotation say about the importance of research in the writing process, especially as it applies to descriptive writing?

Learning Outcomes

L◯1 Analyze a descriptive paragraph.

L◯2 Write a descriptive paragraph.

L◯3 Analyze a narrative paragraph.

L◯4 Write a narrative paragraph.

L◯5 Review description and narration.

Vocabulary

innate
inborn or automatic

Analyze a descriptive paragraph.

LO1 Analyzing a Descriptive Paragraph

When writing a description, you are using words to represent a topic. An effective description creates a clear, interesting image in the reader's mind.

Read/React Read the following descriptive paragraph; then answer the questions at the bottom of the page.

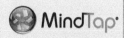 MindTap®

Check online for another example of a descriptive paragraph.

Matchmaker, Matchmaker

The **topic sentence** identifies the topic and focus of the paragraph.

One particular Capewell photo is proudly displayed in our house. It is a portrait-style black-and-white photograph of two people neatly attired in their best military uniforms, and it was taken during World War II in a small studio in Leicester, England. One of the individuals is wearing the uniform of the British Royal Air Force; the other, the uniform of the Royal Canadian Air Force.

Body sentences share descriptive details plus interesting background information about the topic.

Both people are clearly very happy. The person positioned to the left has huge dimples, an infectious smile, and bright, dark eyes. The one to the right has a more understated smile and lighter, happy eyes. The first has thick, wavy black hair worn in a fashionable turned-under military style; the second has neatly trimmed fairer hair. What makes this photograph so special to our family is the occasion that prompted it. It is my great-grandparents' wedding picture. My great-grandmother was born in England and my great-grandfather was born in Canada, and they were both on leave to get married. Their honeymoon had to wait until after the war.

The **closing sentence** re-establishes the importance of the topic.

This photograph is one of the few keepsakes that we have left from their military experience and wedding day, and we take very special care of it.

1. What does the paragraph describe?

_____

_____

_____

portrait
a photograph or painting showing the face and perhaps the upper part of the body

keepsakes
small items reminding people of specific events or times

2. What physical features of the two people are highlighted?

Specific Features	Woman	Man

LO2 Writing a Descriptive Paragraph

The next three pages provide guidelines for writing a descriptive paragraph, starting with the prewriting step below.

Prewriting

List/Select Under each category below, list potential topics. Then circle the one topic that you will describe in your paragraph. On the lines provided at the bottom of the chart, explain the reason for your choice.

Favourite Keepsakes	Special Photographs	Indispensable Tools or Gadgets
_____	_____	_____
_____	_____	_____
_____	_____	_____
_____		
_____		

Collect Study your topic; list specific details that describe it. Try to list them in a logical order: from top to bottom, bottom to top, side to side, and so on.

_____

_____

_____

_____

_____

_____

_____

_____

_____

Create Write a topic sentence for your paragraph following this formula:

A specific topic	**+** a particular feeling, feature, or part	**=** an effective topic sentence
a Capewell photograph	proudly displayed in our house	One particular Capewell photo is proudly displayed in our house.

_____

_____

Review

You can strengthen your paragraph by including sensory details. See Chapter 17, LO2, and Chapter 20, LO4, for more information.

Traits

The basic paragraph organizational structure can be expanded into an essay structure with an opening, a middle, and a closing.

Writing

Write Create a first draft of your descriptive paragraph, using the following paragraph outline as a guide.

Paragraph Outline

Topic Sentence: Begin with your topic sentence from the previous page.

Body Sentences: Follow with sentences that describe and explain your topic. Organize your details according to the order that you determined during prewriting.

Closing Sentence: Write a sentence that sums up the topic's essential meaning.

Revising

Revise Read your paragraph and, if possible, have someone else read it as well. Then use the following checklist to guide your revision. Keep revising until you can check off each item in the list.

Ideas

- [ ] **1.** Does my paragraph describe a special keepsake, photo, or tool?
- [ ] **2.** Do I include plenty of specific details?
- [ ] **3.** Do I include background information to tie the details together?

Organization

- [ ] **4.** Does my topic sentence name the topic and focus of the paragraph?
- [ ] **5.** Do the body sentences present details in a logical order (top to bottom, left to right, most important to least important)?
- [ ] **6.** Does my closing sentence tell what the object means to me?

Voice

- [ ] **7.** Does my writing voice reflect my feelings about the topic?
- [ ] **8.** Does my voice sound knowledgeable?

Editing

Edit Create a clean copy of your revised paragraph and use the following checklist to check it for word choice, sentence fluency, and conventions.

Word Choice

- [ ] **1.** Have I used specific nouns and verbs? (See Chapter 8, LO1.)
- [ ] **2.** Have I used specific modifiers? (See Chapter 17, LO4.)

Sentence Fluency

- [ ] **3.** Have I varied the beginnings and lengths of sentences? (See Chapter 25, LO2.)
- [ ] **4.** Have I combined short, choppy sentences? (See Chapter 25, LO1.)

Conventions

- [ ] **5.** Have I avoided fragments and run-ons? (See Chapter 27, LO1 and LO2; Chapter 28, LO2.)
- [ ] **6.** Do I use correct verb forms (*he saw,* not *he seen*)? (See Chapter 32, LO4.)
- [ ] **7.** Do my subjects and verbs agree (*she speaks,* not *she speak*)? (See Chapter 26, LOs 1–4.)
- [ ] **8.** Have I used the right words (*their, there, they're*)?
- [ ] **9.** Have I capitalized first words and proper nouns and adjectives? (See Chapter 39, LO1.)
- [ ] **10.** Have I used commas after long introductory word groups? (See Chapter 35, LO2.)
- [ ] **11.** Have I carefully checked my spelling?

L○3 Analyzing a Narrative Paragraph

The starting point for all writers is their own story. Everything they create stems, in some way, from their own experiences. Keeping this point in mind gives you a new perspective whenever you read someone else's writing.

Read/React Read the following narrative paragraph; then answer the questions at the bottom of the page.

MindTap

Check online for another example of a narrative paragraph.

Attention!

The **topic sentence** identifies the topic and focus of the paragraph.	Mr. Brown, my junior high gym teacher, did not allow any goofing around in his class. Unfortunately two of my friends learned this the hard way. At the end of the first day of flag football, Mr. Brown blew his whistle to signal that time was up. Most of us knew enough to stop and fall in line. He had made it very clear on the first day of class that when he blew his whistle, we had to stop whatever we were doing. Immediately! Randy Steger and Joe Johnson, being brave or stupid, decided to test Mr. Brown, so
Body sentences share details about the memory.	they continued throwing a football to each other. With fire in his eyes, "the drill sergeant" quickly sent us in and went after the two transgressors. We all watched from the locker-room doorway while Mr. Brown gave them an earful and then made them duckwalk across the field. After 10 yards or so, we could tell that duckwalking was not easy because they were already struggling. He sent them
The **closing sentence** brings the experience to a satisfying ending.	in after another 10 yards when their duckwalk had turned into more of a crawl. We couldn't help giving a few duck calls when Randy and Joe got into the locker room, but we didn't "quack" too loudly. We didn't want Mr. Brown to make us walk like a duck, or any other animal.

1. This paragraph (1) shares a specific experience and (2) introduces you to a memorable individual. What details stand out about either of these characteristics? Name two.

   _____

   _____

2. What questions, if any, do you have about the experience?

   _____

   _____

3. What is the tone of this paragraph (serious, sarcastic, interesting/entertaining)? Explain.

   _____

   _____

Vocabulary

transgressors
people who act in violation of (against) the rules or laws

duckwalk
to walk in a crouching or squatting position

tone
the writer's attitude toward the topic

LO4 Writing a Narrative Paragraph

The next three pages provide guidelines for writing a narrative paragraph, starting with prewriting below.

Prewriting

Select List below four or more experiences that you have had with memorable individuals. Consider school-related, work-related, sports-related, and family-related experiences. Circle the one experience that you would like to share in a narrative paragraph. On the lines that follow, explain the reason for your choice.

_____   _____   _____
_____   _____   _____

_____

_____

_____

_____

_____

_____

Gather Gather details for your paragraph by answering the 5 W's and H about the experience.

Who? _____

_____

What? _____

_____

When? _____

_____

Where? _____

_____

Why? _____

_____

How? _____

Prewrite A timeline is another method of gathering details about the event you have chosen. Most stories are told in a linear fashion, from start to finish. To prepare for your story, begin listing details on a timeline. (Leave space between events to add new details as they occur to you.)

Timeline

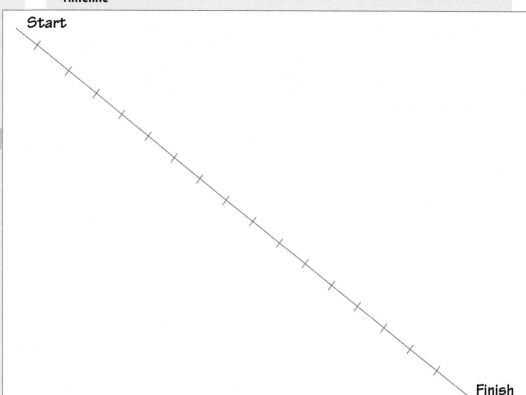

Review

In most cases, narrative paragraphs are arranged chronologically or according to time (see Chapter 5, LO6). Remember to use transitions to help your paragraph flow smoothly from one point to the next (see Chapter 7, LO4, and Chapter 17, LO2).

Prewrite A sensory chart is another productive way to gather details to use in a personal narrative. As you recall the event, write details of sight, sound, smell, touch, and taste in the appropriate column. (See Chapter 17, LO2, and Chapter 20, LO4, for review.)

Sensory Chart

Sight	Sound	Smell	Touch	Taste

Writing

Write Create the first draft of your narrative paragraph, using the following paragraph outline as a guide.

Paragraph Outline

Topic Sentence: Begin with a topic sentence that identifies the topic and focus of your paragraph. (See LO2 for a formula to follow.)

Body Sentences: Write sentences that cover the 5 W's and H of the experience. Be sure to include plenty of specific details.

Closing Sentence: Write a sentence that brings the experience to a satisfying or natural stopping point. (See Chapter 6, LO5, and Chapter 17, LO3, for suggestions.)

Review

If you choose to use dialogue in your narrative paragraph, review Chapter 17, LO5.

Valentin Agapov/Shutterstock.com

Revising

Revise Read your paragraph and, if possible, have someone else read it as well. Then use the following checklist to guide your revision. Continue making improvements until you can check off each item in the list.

Ideas

☐ 1. Does my paragraph share a specific experience related to a memorable person?

☐ 2. Have I answered the 5 W's and H about the experience?

☐ 3. Do I include plenty of specific details, including sensory details? (See Chapter 17, LO2.)

Organization

☐ 4. Does my topic sentence name the topic and focus of the paragraph?

☐ 5. Do the body sentences present details in chronological (time) order? (See Chapter 5, LO6.)

☐ 6. Have I used transitions to connect my sentences? (See Chapter 7, LO4.)

☐ 7. Does my closing sentence bring the experience to a satisfying end? (See Chapter 6, LO5, and Chapter 17, LO3.)

Voice

☐ 8. Does my voice reflect my feelings about the topic?

☐ 9. Does my voice create interest in the reader?

Editing

Edit Create a clean copy of your revised paragraph and use the following checklist to check it for style and conventions.

Words

☐ 1. Have I used specific nouns and verbs? (See Chapter 8, LO1.)

☐ 2. Have I used specific modifiers? (See Chapter 17, LO4.)

Sentences

☐ 3. Have I varied the beginnings and lengths of sentences? (See Chapter 25, LO2.)

☐ 4. Have I combined short, choppy sentences? (See Chapter 25, LO1.)

Conventions

☐ 5. Have I avoided fragments and run-ons? (See Chapter 27, LO1 and LO2; Chapter 28, LO2.)

☐ 6. Have I used dialogue and quotations properly? (See Chapter 17, LO5.)

☐ 7. Do I use correct verb forms (*he saw*, not *he seen*)? (See Chapter 32, LO4.)

☐ 8. Do my subjects and verbs agree (*she speaks*, not *she speak*)? (See Chapter 26, LOs 1, 2, 3, and 4.)

☐ 9. Have I used the right words (*their, there, they're*)?

☐ 10. Have I capitalized first words and proper nouns and adjectives? (See Chapter 39, LO1.)

☐ 11. Have I used commas after long introductory word groups? (See Chapter 35, LO2.)

☐ 12. Have I carefully checked my spelling?

LO5 Reviewing Description and Narration

Describe Select an interesting photograph from one of your textbooks or from a periodical (newspaper or magazine). In the space below, list in a logical order specific details that describe it. Then, on your own paper, develop a descriptive paragraph about the photo. (See LO2, Writing a Descriptive Paragraph.)

_____

_____

_____

_____

_____

_____

_____

_____

Narrate Identify below your strongest early memory. Next, identify the basic details about the experience by completing the 5 W's and H chart. Then, on your own paper, write a narrative paragraph about the experience. (See LO4, Writing a Narrative Paragraph.)

Who?	
What?	
When?	
Where?	
Why?	
How?	

Built for the way you learn.

WRITE2

www.nelson.com/student

> "Knowledge is of two kinds: We know the subject ourselves
> or we know where we can find information upon it."
>
> —Samuel Johnson

Todd Davidson/Illustration Source

Illustration and Process

The best informational writing succeeds because it (1) focuses on an interesting topic and (2) provides plenty of supporting facts and examples. This fact holds true for newspaper stories, magazine articles, text chapters, blogs, and academic essays. Readers of informational texts want to be engaged and informed.

In this chapter, you will read examples of two basic forms of informational writing: illustrating a main point and explaining a process. Each one is intended to be interesting and informative. After each sample, you will write an illustration or process paragraph of your own.

Learning Outcomes

LO1 Analyze an illustration paragraph.

LO2 Write an illustration paragraph.

LO3 Analyze a process paragraph.

LO4 Write a process paragraph.

LO5 Review illustration and process.

What do you think?

According to the Johnson quotation, what are the two kinds of knowledge? How does the quotation relate to informational writing?

Vocabulary

engaged
fully and actively occupied

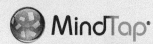

Learning Outcome

Analyze an illustration paragraph.

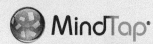

Check online for another example of an illustration paragraph.

LO1 Analyzing an Illustration Paragraph

Illustrating in writing is the process of clarifying or explaining with examples. Think of the examples in this type of writing as the legs that support the table-top, or main point.

Read/React Read the following illustration paragraph; then answer the questions below.

Late to the Show

The **topic sentence** states the topic and focus.

Body sentences give examples that illustrate or support the topic sentence.

The **closing sentence** reflects on the main point and keeps the reader thinking.

Young people today are still getting married—but they're taking their time to walk down the aisle. The average age for first marriages in the 1970s was 21 for women and 23 for men, compared to 26 for women and 28 for men in 2009. In fact, the traditional route to adulthood—finishing school, starting a career, and marrying—is being pushed back altogether. That's not to say young people aren't dating, or even living together. Studies show that two-thirds of couples live together before getting married, a fact that causes older generations quite a bit of anxiety. But this is merely an example of a new calculated approach to marriage. The whirlwind romances of yesteryear are being replaced with lengthy courtships, as couples take years to sort out personal and financial issues before tying the knot. Still, the fact that today's twentysomethings approach marriage differently than older generations did does not mean that they don't value marriage. Nor does it ensure that their marriages will be any more or less successful.

"Late to the Show," model student paragraph

Ysbrand Cosijn/Shutterstock.com

1. What is the main point of this paragraph?

   _____

2. List at least three examples that support the main point.

   _____

3. Are the *ideas* clear in this paragraph?   unclear ★ ★ ★ ★ ★ clear

   Explain._____

   _____

4. How well is the paragraph organized?   poorly ★ ★ ★ ★ ★ well

   Explain._____

   _____

5. How effective is the *voice* of this paragraph?   ineffective ★ ★ ★ ★ ★ effective

   Explain._____

   _____

LO2 Writing an Illustration Paragraph

Prewriting

Select To select a topic for your paragraph, answer the following question:

What is your favourite type of television show, movie, music, literature, magazine, or Internet feature?

_____

_____

Focus Then decide on a feature of this topic that you could illustrate in your paragraph. Explain your choice below.

_____

_____

_____

Identify List at least four examples that illustrate this feature.

_____

_____

_____

_____

_____

Create On the lines below, write a topic sentence for your paragraph. Be sure that your sentence identifies the topic and the feature you are going to illustrate. (See Chapter 11, LO2, for a formula to follow.)

_____

_____

Writing

Write Develop a first draft of your illustration paragraph, using the outline below as a guide. Be sure to refer to the sample for additional help.

Paragraph Outline

Topic Sentence: Begin with the topic sentence that you wrote on the previous page.

Body Sentences: Present the supporting examples that you have listed. Include explanations or background information as needed to connect the examples.

Closing Sentence: Write a sentence that reflects on the main point or keeps the reader thinking about your topic.

Revising

Revise Read your paragraph and, if possible, have someone else read it as well. Then use the following checklist to guide your revision. Continue making improvements until you can check off each item in the list.

Ideas

☐ **1.** Does my paragraph address an interesting topic?

☐ **2.** Have I included at least four examples that illustrate the topic?

☐ **3.** Do I include additional background details as needed?

Organization

☐ **4.** Does my topic sentence name the topic and focus of the paragraph?

☐ **5.** Are the body sentences presented in a logical order?

☐ **6.** Does my closing sentence sum up the topic and keep the reader thinking about the topic?

Voice

☐ **7.** Does my voice reflect my feelings about the topic?

☐ **8.** Does my voice create interest in the topic?

Editing

Edit Create a clean copy of your revised paragraph and use the following checklist to check it for style and conventions.

Word Choice

☐ **1.** Have I used specific nouns and verbs? (See Chapter 8, LO1.)

☐ **2.** Have I used specific modifiers? (See Chapter 17, LO4.)

Sentence Fluency

☐ **3.** Have I varied the beginnings and lengths of sentences? (See Chapter 25, LO2.)

☐ **4.** Have I combined short, choppy sentences? (See Chapter 25, LO1.)

Conventions

☐ **5.** Have I avoided fragments and run-ons? (See Chapter 27, LOs 1 and 2; Chapter 28, LO2.)

☐ **6.** Do I use correct verb forms (*he saw*, not *he seen*)? (See Chapter 32, LO4.)

☐ **7.** Do my subjects and verbs agree (*she speaks*, not *she speak*)? (See Chapter 26, LOs 1–4.)

☐ **8.** Have I used the right words (*their, there, they're*)?

☐ **9.** Have I capitalized first words and proper nouns and adjectives? (See Chapter 39, LO1.)

☐ **10.** Have I used commas after long introductory word groups? (See Chapter 35, LO2.)

☐ **11.** Have I carefully checked my spelling?

Chapter 12 Illustration and Process

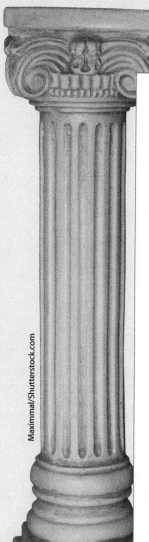

Maximmal/Shutterstock.com

MindTap®

Check online for
another example
of a descriptive
paragraph.

Vocabulary

cobbled
uneven, rough

cityscape
the part of a city viewed,
the sights in part of a city

LO3 Analyzing a Process Paragraph

Process paragraphs explain how to do something (*apply for a passport*) or how
something works (*photosynthesis*). The paragraph that follows explains how to do
something.

Read/React Read the following process paragraph, then answer the questions
below.

Two Steps Forward, One Step Back

**The topic
sentence**
introduces the
process.

**Body
sentences**
explain the
materials
needed and the
steps to follow.

**The closing
sentence**
provides the
reader with a
final thought
about the topic.

Walking the streets of Rome for the first time requires   *1*
patience and a sense of adventure. Before you set out, be sure to
put on a comfortable pair of shoes. Roman streets, at least the most
interesting ones, are cobbled. Also dress in light layers, even if you
see most of the natives dressed in heavy coats. They must have   *5*
thinner blood than the rest of us. Then plan a route on a street map
by circling the sites you want to visit and the streets you need to
follow. As you start, enjoy all that the cityscape has to offer. Then
within the first 10 or 15 minutes, expect to get lost. Roman streets,
other than the main thoroughfares, are never straight, seldom   *10*
marked, and rarely labelled on the street map you have in hand.
When you get lost, you can try to retrace your steps or continue
on. If you are at all adventurous, just keep going and enjoy what
that part of the city has to offer. You won't be disappointed, and
sooner or later, you'll come across a plaza or church square that will   *15*
be marked on your map. Once you get your bearings, proceed, but
again, expect to get lost in no time at all. You can continue in this
way from plaza to plaza, enjoying the sites that you come across as
well as stopping for some refreshments or a meal. When you've had
enough, find a taxi or tram for the return trip—you'll never find
your way by foot.

1. What specific feeling about the topic is expressed in the topic sentence?

_____

_____

2. What steps are offered for the walking tourist in Rome?

_____

_____

_____

_____

LO4 Writing a Process Paragraph

Prewriting

Select Complete the following sentence starters in at least two ways. (Avoid food-related topics.)

1. I learned the hard way how to . . .

   _____   _____

2. I may be one of the few people who knows how to . . .

   _____   _____

3. In case of an emergency, I would like to be able to . . .

   _____   _____

4. From the six sentences you have just written, choose a topic and explain your choice.

   _____

Collect Identify the materials needed and the steps in your process.

Materials	Steps

Create Write a topic sentence for your paragraph. This sentence should identify the topic and focus of your writing. (See Chapter 11, LO2, for a formula to follow.)

_____

_____

Writing

Write Create a first draft of your process paragraph, using the following paragraph outline as a guide.

Paragraph Outline

Topic Sentence: Begin with the topic sentence that you wrote on the previous page.

Body Sentences: First, write about any materials that may be needed. Then clearly explain the steps to complete the process. Add other information as needed to connect all of your ideas.

Closing Sentence: Write a sentence that sums up the process.

Revising

Revise Read your process paragraph and, if possible, have someone else read it as well. Then use the following checklist to guide your revision. Continue to make improvements until you can check off each item in the list.

Ideas

☐ **1.** Have I selected an interesting process to explain?

☐ **2.** Do I identify the necessary materials and provide all of the steps?

Organization

☐ **3.** Does my topic sentence identify the topic and focus of my paragraph?

☐ **4.** Have I put the body sentences that explain the steps in order?

☐ **5.** Does my closing sentence effectively sum up the process?

Voice

☐ **6.** Does my writing voice sound knowledgeable?

☐ **7.** Does my voice create interest in this process?

Editing

Edit Create a clean copy of your revised paragraph and use the following checklist to check it for style and conventions.

Words

☐ **1.** Have I used specific nouns and verbs? (See Chapter 8, LO1.)

☐ **2.** Have I used more action verbs than "be" verbs? (See Chapter 32, LO1.)

Sentences

☐ **3.** Have I varied the beginnings and lengths of sentences? (See Chapter 25, LO2.)

☐ **4.** Have I combined short, choppy sentences? (See Chapter 25, LO1.)

Conventions

☐ **5.** Have I avoided fragments and run-ons? (See Chapter 27, LO1 and LO2; Chapter 28, LO2.)

☐ **6.** Do I use correct verb forms (*he saw,* not *he seen*)? (See Chapter 32, LO4.)

☐ **7.** Do my subjects and verbs agree (*she speaks,* not *she speak*)? (See Chapter 26, LOs 1–4.)

☐ **8.** Have I used the right words (*their, there, they're*)?

☐ **9.** Have I capitalized first words and proper nouns and adjectives? (See Chapter 39, LO1.)

☐ **10.** Have I used commas after long introductory word groups? (See Chapter 35, LO2.)

☐ **11.** Have I carefully checked my spelling?

LO5 Reviewing Illustration and Process

Illustrate Fill in the top blank with a career that truly interests you. Then write four statements that illustrate or explain your choice. On your own paper, write an illustration paragraph about this career. (See LO2, Writing an Illustration Paragraph.)

Career: _____

    Example: _____

    Example: _____

    Example: _____

    Example: _____

List On the top blanks, list possible topics for a paragraph explaining how something works. Consider pieces of technology, features on the Internet, a natural phenomenon *(evaporation)*, or a governmental process *(how to become a Canadian citizen)*. Circle the one that you would like to write about.

Next, list any materials needed and the steps taken to complete the process. Then, on your own paper, write a paragraph explaining the process. (See LO4, Writing a Process Paragraph.)

Topics (how something works)

_____ _____ _____

Materials

_____

_____

Steps

_____

_____

_____

_____

_____

_____

_____

> "My father told me that words and letters hold the secrets of the universe. That in their shape and sounds I could find everything, could see beyond myself to something special . . . perfect."
>
> —Eliza, in the movie *Bee Season*

Dougal Waters/Digital Vision/Getty Images

Definition and Classification

Each new course presents you with a set of words and concepts to learn. (Just think of all of the vocabulary lists you've received over the years.) One of the best ways to understand these new terms and topics is to write about them. Writing extended definition and classification paragraphs allows you to do just that.

Both of these types of writing require you to research a word or concept and then understand and synthesize the information you have gathered. As you develop these paragraphs, you may consult several sources—from traditional dictionaries and other print sources to a variety of online sites. As you hunt down information, your topic will take shape before you.

Learning Outcomes

LO1 Analyze a definition paragraph.

LO2 Write a definition paragraph.

LO3 Analyze a classification paragraph.

LO4 Write a classification paragraph.

LO5 Review definition and classification.

Vocabulary

extended
fully explained, added to

classification
systematic or organized grouping

synthesize
combine multiple ideas to form new understandings

What do you think?

How can words "hold the secrets of the universe"?

_____

_____

_____

_____

LO1 Analyzing a Definition Paragraph

A definition paragraph explains a new or, perhaps, a misunderstood term. This type of paragraph may include a dictionary definition, the history of the term, examples of the term in use, related words, and so on. Providing extended definitions like this is an important part of academic writing.

Read/React Read this definition paragraph, then follow the directions at the bottom of the page.

Frontpage/Shutterstock.com

Vocabulary

globetrotting
traveling often
and widely

A Word of Warning

The **topic sentence** identifies the term and focus of the paragraph.

Body sentences explore the term in a number of ways.

The **closing sentences** keep the reader thinking about the term.

One word in medical reports strikes fear into people everywhere, and that word is *pandemic*. One report might say, "The threat of a pandemic flu hitting North America exists"; another one might say, "The World Health Organization has raised the level of the influenza pandemic alert." Who wouldn't be scared by threats such as these? So what exactly is a pandemic and where did this word come from? A pandemic is an "infectious disease covering a wide geographic area and affecting a large proportion of the population." Being "infectious" is a key feature because a disease cannot become a pandemic unless it can be spread by humans over a very wide area. So influenza can be pandemic, but cancer cannot. Some people use *pandemic* interchangeably with *epidemic*. But an epidemic doesn't become pandemic until it covers an extremely widespread area, such as a series of countries. *Pandemic* comes from the Greek *pandēmos:* The Greek root *pan* means "every" or "all" and *demos* means "common people." Thus, *pandēmos* means "all the people," so the connection with pandemic is clear. Two pandemics that are often cited are the Black Death during the Dark Ages and the flu pandemic in 1918 that killed from 40 to 50 million people. Recent pandemics include Ebola and HIV. Here's a scary final thought: Globetrotting provides an easy way for pandemics to occur.

This paragraph defines *pandemic* by providing the following types of details. Identify each detail from the paragraph.

Dictionary definition: _____

_____

History of the word: _____

_____

Examples: _____

_____

Related word: _____

_____

Explanations: _____

_____

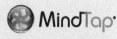

Check online
for another
example of a
definition
paragraph.

LO2 Writing a Definition Paragraph

The next three pages provide guidelines for writing a definition paragraph, starting with prewriting below.

Prewriting

Identify Read a few articles (online or in print) about medical, scientific, or technological topics. On the lines below, list four to six terms you encountered that sparked your interest. Then circle one term that you would be interested in writing about. On the lines that follow, explain the reason for your choice.

_____   _____   _____

_____   _____   _____

_____

_____

_____

Collect On the lines below, gather information for your paragraph. Look for the following types of details:

Dictionary definitions	History of the word	Related words
Examples	Quotations	Explanations
Interesting facts	Personal definition	What the word means to others

_____

_____

_____

_____

_____

_____

_____

_____

_____

Writing

As the model in the APA
In-Text Citations section
in chapter 9 shows,
definition writing is key to
science.

Write Create a first draft of your paragraph, using the outline that follows as a guide.

Paragraph Outline

Topic Sentence: Write a topic sentence that names the term and identifies a personal feeling or special feature about it. (See the formula on Chapter 11, LO2.)

Body Sentences: Write sentences that explore the term in a variety of different ways. Organize the details in a logical way, perhaps starting with the dictionary definition.

Closing Sentence: Write a sentence that leaves the reader with a final thought about the term.

Revising

Revise Read your paragraph and, if possible, have someone else read it as well. Then use the following checklist to guide your revision. Keep revising until you can check off each item in the list.

Ideas

- [ ] **1.** Does my paragraph focus on an interesting term?
- [ ] **2.** Do I explore the term in a number of different ways?

Organization

- [ ] **3.** Does my topic sentence name the term and the focus of the paragraph?
- [ ] **4.** Are the body sentences arranged in a logical way?
- [ ] **5.** Does my closing sentence leave the reader with an interesting final thought?

Voice

- [ ] **6.** Does my writing voice demonstrate a clear understanding of the term?
- [ ] **7.** Does my voice engage the reader?

Editing

Edit Create a clean copy of your revised paragraph and use the following checklist to check it for style and conventions.

Word Choice

- [ ] **1.** Have I used specific nouns and verbs? (See Chapter 8, LO1.)
- [ ] **2.** Have I used more action verbs than "be" verbs? (See Chapter 32, LO1.)

Sentence Fluency

- [ ] **3.** Have I varied the beginnings and lengths of sentences? (See Chapter 25, LO2.)
- [ ] **4.** Have I combined short, choppy sentences? (See Chapter 25, LO1.)

Conventions

- [ ] **5.** Have I avoided fragments and run-ons? (See Chapter 27, LOs 1 and 2; Chapter 28, LO2.)
- [ ] **6.** Do I use correct verb forms (*he saw*, not *he seen*)? (See Chapter 32, LO4.)
- [ ] **7.** Do my subjects and verbs agree (*she speaks*, not *she speak*)? (See Chapter 26, LOs 1–4.)
- [ ] **8.** Have I used the right words (*their, there, they're*)?
- [ ] **9.** Have I capitalized first words and proper nouns and adjectives? (See Chapter 39, LO1.)
- [ ] **10.** Have I used commas after long introductory word groups? (See Chapter 35, LO2.)
- [ ] **11.** Have I carefully checked my spelling?

LO3 Analyzing a Classification Paragraph

A classification paragraph identifies the types or varieties of something. Classifying is a common form of thinking and writing used in the sciences.

Read/React Read the following classification paragraph, then answer the questions at the bottom of the page.

Nighttime Blues

The **topic sentence** identifies the topic and focus.

Body sentences provide examples that classify the topic.

The **closing sentence** provides a final thought.

Most people are familiar with eating disorders and learning disorders, but they may not be quite as familiar with sleeping disorders. Experts in the field identify four basic types of sleep disorders. The first one, insomnia, is linked to the other disorders because it covers the inability to fall asleep or stay asleep at night. Sleep apnea is another sleep disorder, and it is characterized by snoring, snorting, and even gasping. These irritating sound effects are produced when the sufferer tries to force air through a blockage of the airway during sleep. Narcolepsy, a third disorder, is characterized by excessive sleepiness during the day. It is caused by a chemical imbalance in the part of the brain that controls sleeping and staying awake. One narcoleptic stated that the sleepiness can come on suddenly in much the same way as an epileptic attack comes on. The fourth type of sleep disorder is restless leg syndrome. People suffering from this disorder feel a twitching, pulling, or aching in their legs, which forces them to move or kick them. The syndrome most often strikes during the night, but it can also occur during the day. Exploring the basics of sleeplessness makes it clear why we have sleep disorder clinics: There are a lot of people who aren't getting a good night's sleep.

1. What are the topic and focus of the paragraph?

_____

_____

2. How many types of the topic are identified? What are they?

_____

_____

_____

3. How does the closing connect with the beginning?

_____

_____

_____

MindTap

Check online for another example of a classification paragraph.

LO4 Writing a Classification Paragraph

Learning Outcome

Write a classification paragraph.

Prewriting

Select On the blanks that follow, list possible topics as they come to mind. Try to fill in the entire chart with ideas. Afterward, review your list and circle one topic that you would like to write about in a classification paragraph. (Two ideas are provided for you.)

Types of . . .

weight trainers		
instructors		

Collect Complete the following chart to gather details for your paragraph. In the first column, list the types of your topic. In the second column, explain or define each one. (You may have to do some quick research to gather information.)

Types/Varieties	Explanation/Definition

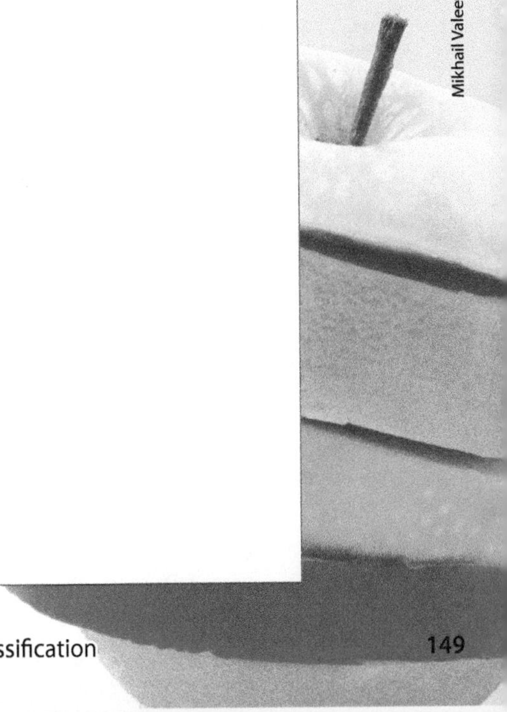

Mikhail Valeev/Shutterstock.com

Writing

Write Create a first draft of your classification paragraph, using the following outline as a guide.

Paragraph Outline

Topic Sentence: Write a sentence that identifies the topic and focus of your paragraph. (See Chapter 11, LO2, for a formula.)

Body Sentences: Write sentences that name and explain each type. Add information as needed to tie everything together.

Closing Sentence: Write a sentence that connects with the beginning or that keeps the reader thinking about the topic.

Revising

Revise Read your paragraph and, if possible, have someone else read it as well. Then use the following checklist to guide your revision. Keep making improvements until you can check off each item in the list.

Ideas

☐ **1.** Does my paragraph focus on an interesting or important topic?

☐ **2.** Do I fully explain or classify the important types or varieties of the topic?

☐ **3.** Do I include plenty of specific details to explain each type?

Organization

☐ **4.** Does the topic sentence name the topic and focus of my writing?

☐ **5.** Are the body sentences arranged in a logical way?

☐ **6.** Does my closing sentence bring the paragraph to a satisfying end?

Voice

☐ **7.** Does my writing voice show my interest in the topic?

☐ **8.** Do I sound knowledgeable about the topic?

Editing

Edit Create a clean copy of your revised paragraph and use the following checklist to check it for style and conventions.

Words

☐ **1.** Have I used specific nouns and verbs? (See Chapter 8, LO1.)

☐ **2.** Have I used specific modifiers? (See Chapter 17, LO4.)

Sentences

☐ **3.** Have I varied the beginnings and lengths of sentences? (See Chapter 25, LO2.)

☐ **4.** Have I combined short, choppy sentences? (See Chapter 25, LO1.)

Conventions

☐ **5.** Have I avoided fragments and run-ons? (See Chapter 27, LOs 1 and 2; Chapter 28, LO2.)

☐ **6.** Do I use correct verb forms (*he saw,* not *he seen*)? (See Chapter 32, LO4.)

☐ **7.** Do my subjects and verbs agree (*she speaks,* not *she speak*)? (See Chapter 26, LOs 1–4.)

☐ **8.** Have I used the right words (*their, there, they're*)?

☐ **9.** Have I capitalized first words and proper nouns and adjectives? (See Chapter 39, LO1.)

☐ **10.** Have I used commas after long introductory word groups? (See Chapter 35, LO2.)

☐ **11.** Have I carefully checked my spelling?

Learning Outcome

Review definition and classification.

LO5 Reviewing Definition and Classification

Define On the first blank line below, identify a term that interests you from one of your classes. Next, fill in the remaining blanks as you collect details that will help you define and explain the term. (Complete at least four of the categories.) Then, on your own paper, develop a definition paragraph about the term. (See LO2, Writing a Definition Paragraph.)

Term: ____________________

Dictionary definition: ____________________

____

Personal definition: ____________________

____

History of the word: ____________________

____

Related words: ____________________

____

Quotations: ____________________

____

Classify At the top of the chart below, list two or three topics related to style (e.g., fashion trends). Consider topics that can be broken down into types or varieties. Circle the one that you would like to write about. Next, complete the chart by identifying the types of your topic and an explanation of each one. Then, on your own paper, write a classification paragraph about the topic. (See LO4, Writing a Classification Paragraph.)

__________ __________ __________

Types/Varieties	Explanation/Definition

flashfilm/Digital Vision/Thinkstock

"Understanding is a two-way street."
—Eleanor Roosevelt

Cause–Effect

We lead cause–effect lives. One person shops for a scooter *(effect)* because he can't afford a car *(cause)*. Another person is still driving the car she bought over a decade ago *(effect)* because she's driven it only occasionally and kept it well maintained *(cause)*. Someone else has had it with a neighbour's barking dog *(cause)*, so she's looking for a new apartment *(effect)*.

A lot of academic writing deals with causes and effects as well. Stated in another way, writing often deals with the logical relationship between events and outcomes. Cause–effect writing requires analytical thinking and planning to complete.

Learning Outcomes

LO1 Analyze a cause–effect paragraph.

LO2 Write a cause–effect paragraph.

LO3 Review cause–effect paragraphs.

What do you think?

How would you explain Eleanor Roosevelt's contention that "understanding is a two-way street"? How can this statement relate to causes and effects?

LO1 Analyzing Cause-Effect Paragraphs

Two starter sentences identify the type of thinking involved in cause–effect writing: *Because of . . . , we now . . .* or *Since . . . happened, we have had to . . . .* Keep this thought pattern in mind as you read and analyze cause–effect writing.

Read/React Read the following cause–effect paragraph, then answer the questions at the bottom of the page.

Africa Studio/Shutterstock.com

Problems in Print

The **topic sentence** identifies the topic and focus of the paragraph.

Body sentences explore the causes and effects.

The **closing sentence** expands on the main point.

Students interested in pursuing a career in traditional journalism may want to think carefully about this decision. The reason is simple: Fewer and fewer people are buying newspapers. Most of them, instead, are getting all or most of their news on the Internet. Fewer buyers of newspapers and magazines mean less income from subscriptions and newsstand sales. Fewer readers also mean fewer ad dollars, a main source of income for publishers. As a result, newspapers are going out of business or cutting back; and magazines are folding. This state of affairs has left publishers unsure about how to re-form for survival. News sources do offer electronic alternatives to their print products, but readers get this news for free or pay a limited fee that in no way offsets the huge losses publishers are experiencing. Because of this situation, there simply are not enough jobs for experienced journalists, let alone recent graduates. So prospective journalism students must realize that their chances of working in a traditional newsroom are slim to none. However, all is not lost. The Internet may offer exciting new career options for journalists, especially those who are strong researchers and communicators and well versed in the new opportunities that the information age has to offer.

1. What are the topic and focus of this paragraph?

   _____

   _____

2. What are the main causes and effects explained in the paragraph?

   Causes: _____

   _____

   _____

   Effects: _____

   _____

   _____

Read/React Read the following cause–effect paragraph; then answer the questions at the bottom of the page.

Instant Impact

Topic Sentence

On the final play of a crucial NFL game in the 1998–1999 season, New York Jets quarterback Vinny Testaverde lunged forward for the winning touchdown over the Seattle Seahawks. A replay of the play showed the ball was more than a foot short of the goal line. The blown call cost the Seahawks a playoff berth and pushed the NFL to reinstate an instant-replay system for disputed calls, a decision that has had far-reaching effects on the game today. Some observers point to the Testaverde touchdown as the sole reason the NFL, out of guilt, adopted a replay system. Technological improvements in the system, however, definitely influenced the decision. Back in 1986, when the NFL first adopted a replay system, officials were stuck looking at limited camera angles on a grainy replay screen. Sometimes officials' television monitors malfunctioned, causing embarrassingly long delays in action. In 1992, the NFL ditched replay altogether. But by 1999, television technology improved dramatically. Now officials could see the replay from a half dozen angles, making calls a lot easier to judge. And with the explosion of high-definition images, replays became clearer than ever. In 1999, 195 plays were reviewed, and 57 were reversed. Those numbers have steadily increased, meaning more and more bad calls are being corrected and fewer games are being decided by incorrect judgments. Opponents of instant replay point out how challenges break the flow of an already choppy game. While this is true, the Seahawks of 1998 surely would have welcomed the break in action.

Causes

Effects

Closing Sentence

Debby Wong/Shutterstock.com

1. What are the topic and focus of this paragraph?

_____

_____

2. Are the *ideas* clear in this paragraph?   unclear ★ ★ ★ ★ ★ clear

Explain. _____

_____

3. How well is the paragraph organized?   poorly ★ ★ ★ ★ ★ well

Explain. _____

_____

4. How effective is the *voice* of this paragraph?   ineffective ★ ★ ★ ★ ★ effective

Explain. _____

_____

LO2 Writing a Cause-Effect Paragraph

To write a cause–effect paragraph, use the guidelines on the next three pages, starting with prewriting below.

Prewriting

Select In the first column, list careers or jobs that you are interested in or have had some experience with. In the second column, explain the status of each one. Afterward, put a check next to the job that you would like to write about in a cause–effect paragraph. On the lines at the bottom of the chart, explain the reason for your choice. (One example is provided.)

Careers or Jobs	Status
journalist	Career opportunities are shrinking and changing.

Consider To plan your paragraph, consider the causes and effects of the current status of your topic. You may have one main cause and multiple effects, multiple causes and one main effect, or multiple causes and effects.

Causes	Effects

Writing

Write Create a first draft of your cause–effect paragraph, using the following outline as a guide.

Paragraph Outline

Topic Sentence: Begin with a topic sentence identifying your topic and focus. (See Chapter 11, LO2 for a helpful formula.)

Body Sentences: Explain the causes and effects of the topic. Arrange these ideas in a logical way, dealing with causes first and then effects, or vice versa.

Closing Sentence: Write a sentence that revisits or expands upon the main point.

Test Taking

By practising cause–effect writing now, you will be better prepared for cause–effect writing prompts on tests.

Revising

Revise Read your paragraph and, if possible, have someone else read it as well. Then use the following checklist to guide your revision. Keep making improvements until you can check off each item in the list.

Ideas

☐ **1.** Does my paragraph address an interesting and timely topic?

☐ **2.** Do I provide appropriate and clear "cause and effect" information?

Organization

☐ **3.** Does my topic sentence identify the topic and focus of my paragraph?

☐ **4.** Do the body sentences follow a logical order—causes first, then effects, or effects first, then causes?

☐ **5.** Does my closing sentence revisit or expand upon the main point?

Voice

☐ **6.** Do I sound knowledgeable about the topic?

☐ **7.** Does my voice create interest in the topic?

Editing

Edit Create a clean copy of your revised paragraph and use the following checklist to check it for style and conventions.

Word Choice

☐ **1.** Have I used specific nouns and verbs? (See Chapter 8, LO1.)

☐ **2.** Have I used specific modifiers? (See Chapter 17, LO4.)

Sentence Fluency

☐ **3.** Have I varied the beginnings and lengths of sentences? (See Chapter 25, LO2.)

☐ **4.** Have I combined short, choppy sentences? (See Chapter 25, LO1.)

Conventions

☐ **5.** Have I avoided fragments and run-ons? (See Chapter 27, LO1 and LO2; Chapter 28, LO2.)

☐ **6.** Do I use correct verb forms (*he saw,* not *he seen*)? (See Chapter 32, LO4.)

☐ **7.** Do my subjects and verbs agree (*she speaks,* not *she speak*)? (See Chapter 26, LOs 1–4.)

☐ **8.** Have I used the right words (*their, there, they're*)?

☐ **9.** Have I capitalized first words and proper nouns and adjectives? (See Chapter 39, LO1.)

☐ **10.** Have I used commas after long introductory word groups? (See Chapter 35, LO2.)

☐ **11.** Have I carefully checked my spelling?

Vocabulary

timely
well-timed,
important now

LO3 Reviewing Cause-Effect Paragraphs

Learning Outcome

Review cause–effect paragraphs.

Brainstorm Fill in the following chart with causes and effects related to this photograph of a shantytown.

Causes	Effects

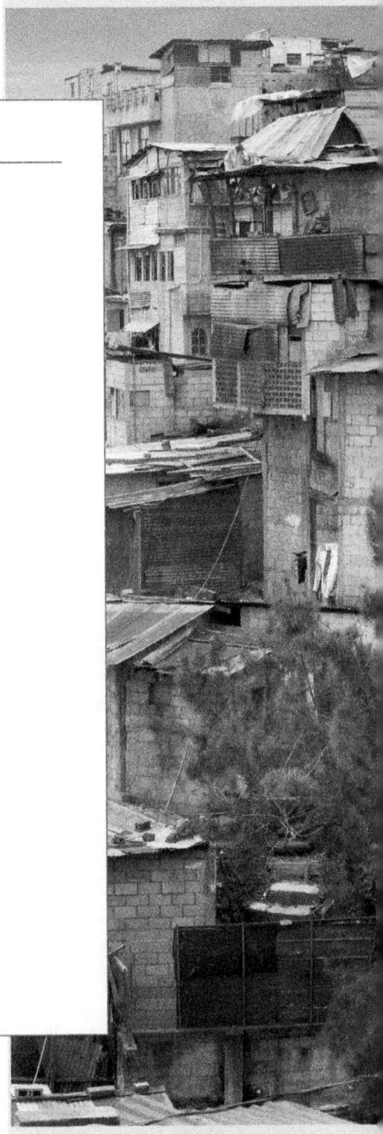

Charles Harker/Shutterstock.com

On the lines below, write a topic sentence for a cause–effect paragraph about the shantytown. Then write the paragraph on your own paper. (See LO2, Writing a Cause–Effect Paragraph.)

Topic Sentence: ______________________________

____

____

Your online study partner.

MindTap®

www.nelson.com/student

> "In theory, there is no difference between theory and practice. In practice there is."
>
> —Yogi Berra

15
Comparison–Contrast

In Lewis Carroll's *Alice in Wonderland*, the Mad Hatter wonders aloud, "Why is a raven like a writing desk?" A few pages later, we learn that this riddle has no answer. But the riddle does tickle the mind, so much so that Sam Loyd later quipped that a raven was like a writing desk "because Poe wrote on both."

When you note the similarities between two things—a raven and a writing desk, for example—you are comparing them. When you note the differences, you are contrasting them. A paragraph that compares and contrasts two things creates a strong understanding of both subjects.

Learning Outcomes

LO1 Analyze a comparison–contrast paragraph.

LO2 Write a comparison–contrast paragraph.

LO3 Review comparison–contrast paragraphs.

What do you think?

In what other ways is a raven like a writing desk? Write as many as you can think of.

_____

_____

_____

_____

LO1 Analyzing a Comparison–Contrast Paragraph

Comparison–contrast writing may emphasize both the similarities and differences between two topics, or it may focus more attention on how the topics are either alike or different.

Read/React Read the following comparison–contrast paragraph, then answer the questions at the bottom of the page.

matka_Wariatka/Shutterstock.com

Vocabulary

advocacy
active support, arguing in favour of something

Order in the Court

The **topic sentence** identifies the topics and focus of the paragraph.

Body sentences share details about the two topics.

The **closing sentence** provides a final thought about the topics.

Both solicitors and barristers serve the public in the British legal system, but they do so in different ways. Someone in Great Britain seeking legal help contacts a solicitor, who will usually be part of a law firm. A solicitor then serves as a client's legal representative, providing legal guidance and advice, and even representing a client in some court cases. When a client needs specialized legal help and advocacy before the high court, a solicitor will contact a barrister. Unlike a solicitor, a barrister has no attachment to any firm but instead is a member of chambers, a group of barristers who share legal aides and such. A barrister's main responsibility is to argue a client's case before a judge and jury, so his or her independence from any firm provides an unbiased voice in the law proceedings. When in "uniform" in front of the judge and jury, barristers have traditionally worn elaborate horsehair wigs, stiff white collars, and long gowns. Although solicitors are now gaining more responsibility before the courts, this legal division of power has served the British public well for ages.

1. What are the topics of this paragraph?

   _____

2. Does the paragraph focus on similarities, differences, or both? Explain.

   _____

   _____

3. What are two important things that you learned about the topics?

   _____

   _____

   _____

Read the following comparison–contrast paragraph; then answer the questions at the bottom of the page.

College and High School

The **Topic sentence** identifies the topics and focus of the paragraph.

Body sentences compare two topics.

The **closing sentence** provides a final thought about the topics.

After a very short period of time in college, I realized that college grades and college professors were not the same as high school grades and high school teachers. I was used to having all of my assigned work graded, and I was shocked when my professor assigned work and did not collect it or mark it. Sometimes the professor did collect the work and mark it, so I soon realized that I had better have my work done all the time. In high school when I was getting lower grades on tests, I always had the opportunity to increase my marks by getting high grades for my homework. In college my professors have specific grades allocated for tests and exams that make up a large portion of final grades. It seemed in high school that I could pass by merely skimming through with D's, but in my program at college, I learned a D grade is not enough to pass. Looking back on my high school days, I have to admit now that some of my teachers gave me marks for a good effort. Today I know that a good effort and a good attitude are helpful especially if I ask professors for extra help. But as far as grades are concerned, more important than effort is the content and quality of the work I hand in. College has been an adjustment. Now that I know the rules of the game, my grades have improved, and when I can't make it to class, I never ask, "Did I miss anything important?"

From CONNELLY/FISHER, Get Writing, 1E. © 2009 Nelson Education Ltd. Reproduced by permission.

1. Use the traits of writing to evaluate the effectiveness of this paragraph (see Chapter 4, LO3, for review).

2. Consider the following chart, which shows the three organizational patterns for a comparison–contrast paragraph: point-by-point, subject-to-subject, and similarities–differences.

Point-by-Point
Beginning
Point 1 — Subject 1 / Subject 2
Point 2 — Subject 1 / Subject 2
Point 3 — Subject 1 / Subject 2
Ending

Subject-to-Subject
Beginning
Subject 1
Subject 2
Ending

Similarities-Differences
Beginning
Similarities
Differences
Ending

What pattern of organization does this paragraph use?

_____

What pattern of organization does the earlier sample paragraph, "Order in the Court," use?

_____

Vocabulary

point-by-point pattern of organization a pattern in which the author discusses one point of comparison for both subjects before moving on to the next point

subject-by-subject pattern of organization a pattern in which the writer first discusses the characteristics of one subject, then the characteristics of the second subject

similarities–differences pattern of organization a pattern in which the writer discusses all the ways in which the subjects are similar, then the ways in which they are different

LO2 Writing a Comparison–Contrast Paragraph

To write a comparison–contrast paragraph, follow the guidelines on the next three pages, starting with prewriting below.

Prewriting

Select Think of jobs or positions that are closely related. For example, within the dental profession, there are dental assistants and dental hygienists. In the automotive field, there are automotive technicians and car mechanics. After listing a number of related jobs, circle the pair you would like to write about in a comparison–contrast paragraph.

Related Jobs or Positions

Collect In the space provided below, gather information about your two topics. Consider training, job description, opportunities, and so on. (Use your own paper if you need more room.)

Job or Position One: _____   Job or Position Two: _____

Plan Decide how you will organize your paragraph: Are you going to share all the information about one topic and then about the other (subject-by-subject)? Are you going to cover the two topics point by point, first showing how they compare or contrast in terms of training, then in terms of job description, and so on (point-by-point)?

Writing

Write Create a first draft of your comparison–contrast paragraph, using the following outline as a guide.

Paragraph Outline

Topic Sentence: Begin with a topic sentence that identifies the related topics and focus of your paragraph. (See Chapter 11, LO2, for a formula.)

Body Sentences: Develop the body sentences, following your planning at the bottom of the previous page.

Closing Sentence: Write a sentence (or two) that provides a final thought about the topics.

Revising

Revise Read your paragraph and, if possible, have someone else read it as well. Then use the following checklist to guide your revisions. Keep making improvements until you can check off each item in the list.

Ideas

☐ **1.** Does my paragraph address two related jobs in a field that interests me?

☐ **2.** Do I provide an adequate number of important similarities and/or differences?

Organization

☐ **3.** Does my topic sentence identify the topics and focus of the paragraph?

☐ **4.** Do the comparisons and/or contrasts follow a logical order?

☐ **5.** Does my closing sentence provide an important final thought about the topics?

Voice

☐ **6.** Do I sound knowledgeable about the topics?

☐ **7.** Does my voice engage the reader?

Editing

Edit Create a clean copy of your revised paragraph and use the following checklist to check it for style and conventions.

Words

☐ **1.** Have I used specific nouns and verbs? (See Chapter 8, LO1.)

☐ **2.** Have I used specific modifiers? (See Chapter 17, LO4.)

Sentences

☐ **3.** Have I varied the beginnings and lengths of sentences? (See Chapter 25, LO2.)

☐ **4.** Have I combined short, choppy sentences? (See Chapter 25, LO1.)

Conventions

☐ **5.** Have I avoided fragments and run-ons? (See Chapter 27, LO1 and LO2; Chapter 28, LO2.)

☐ **6.** Do I use correct verb forms (*he saw*, not *he seen*)? (See Chapter 32, LO4.)

☐ **7.** Do my subjects and verbs agree (*she speaks*, not *she speak*)? (See Chapter 26, LOs 1–4.)

☐ **8.** Have I used the right words (*their, there, they're*)?

☐ **9.** Have I capitalized first words and proper nouns and adjectives? (See Chapter 39, LO1.)

☐ **10.** Have I used commas after long introductory word groups? (See Chapter 35, LO2.)

☐ **11.** Have I carefully checked my spelling?

LO3 Reviewing Comparison–Contrast Paragraphs

Prewrite Complete the Venn diagram below on two comparable subjects. Write two subjects on the lines provided. In the centre section, list similarities between the two subjects. In each outer section, list details that are unique to that subject.

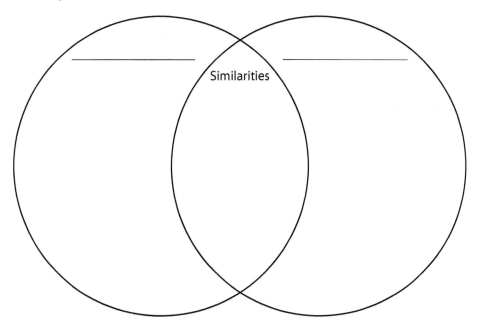

Similarities

Choose three or more points to compare and contrast. Then choose a pattern of organization. Use a point-by-point pattern, a subject-to-subject pattern, or a similarities-and-differences pattern.

Point-by-Point		Subject-to-Subject	Similarities-Differences
Beginning		Beginning	Beginning
Point 1	Subject 1	Subject 1	Similarities
	Subject 2		
Point 2	Subject 1		
	Subject 2	Subject 2	Differences
Point 3	Subject 1		
	Subject 2		
Ending		Ending	Ending

Draft Write a paragraph using the prewriting above. Follow the steps outlined in the chapter (see LO2, Writing a Comparison–Contrast Paragraph).

The information you need, the textbook you want.

WRITE2

www.nelson.com/student

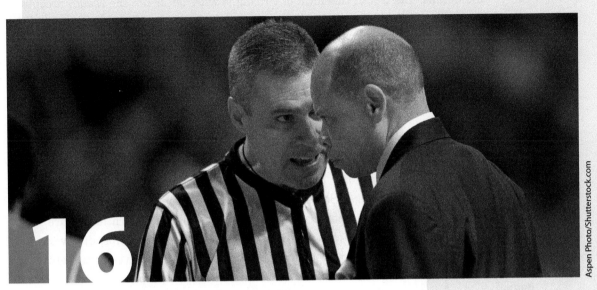

"You're entitled to your own opinion. But you're not entitled to your own facts."

—Daniel Patrick Moynihan

Aspen Photo/Shutterstock.com

16

Argument and Problem–Solution

Writing is really thinking on paper. When you explain or describe, you are demonstrating your ability to understand information. When you compare or classify, you are involved in analyzing, a higher level of thinking. When you persuade, you move even higher up the thinking food chain.

Writing persuasively involves presenting an argument for or against a particular point of view. In order to form a thoughtful opinion, you first must thoroughly understand and analyze the subject. Developing a problem–solution paragraph is a closely related form of writing because it involves analyzing and recommending.

You'll be expected to write persuasively, drafting arguments and presenting solutions to problems, in almost all of your college course work, so the strategies that you learn in this chapter will prove very helpful.

What do you think?

What does Moynihan have to say about the relationship between opinions and facts?

_____

_____

_____

Learning Outcomes

LO1 Analyze an argument paragraph.

LO2 Write an argument paragraph.

LO3 Analyze a problem–solution paragraph.

LO4 Write a problem–solution paragraph.

Vocabulary

food chain
the connection from the lowest life forms to the highest; here, a metaphor for different levels of thinking

LO1 Analyzing an Argument Paragraph

An argument paragraph expresses an opinion and supports it with reliable facts and details. The test of this form of writing is whether or not the reader accepts the validity of the argument.

Read/React Read the following argument paragraph; then answer the questions at the bottom of the page.

A Case for Social Media

The **topic sentence** states the writer's opinion.

Some people claim social-networking sites are bad for society, but the benefits of social media greatly outweigh any shortcomings. Social networks connect and reconnect friends, families, and colleagues on a global scale. In return, users are able to create and strengthen individual relationships, discover new ideas and opportunities, and express themselves creatively.

Body sentences provide support for the writer's position.

A Pew Internet report found that 60 million people received help from people in their social networks to solve major life issues, including illnesses, job turnover, and housing searches. Social networks also power information gathering and social change. In 2009, election protestors in Iran used Twitter to defy government control of phones and the news media. Twitter provided an outlet for spreading real-time information and awareness around the globe. Opponents say social networks offer a space for cyber bullying, identify theft, and sex offenders, but network sites have responded by adding age limitations and privacy controls.

The **closing sentence** reinforces the writer's position.

"Networking is not about hunting. It is about farming. It's about cultivating relationships," says business entrepreneur Dr. Ivan Misner. Likewise, social-networking sites cultivate a closerknit community, and society is better off for it.

1. What is the writer arguing for or against?

_____

2. What part of the paragraph addresses a counterargument?

_____

3. How would you rate the effectiveness of this argument? Explain your choice.

weak									strong
1	2	3	4	5	6	7	8	9	10

_____

_____

Bloomua/Shutterstock.com

MindTap

Check online for another example of an argument paragraph.

LO2 Writing an Argument Paragraph

To write an argument paragraph, follow the guidelines on the next three pages, starting with prewriting below.

Prewriting

Select In the space that follows, list activities (hobbies, sports, other pastimes) that you participate in or have strong feelings about. Then circle one that you could write about persuasively in an argument paragraph.

Activities:

_____

_____

Form After thinking about the topic, write a working opinion statement. (You can always adjust or change it later on.) Use the formula below as a guide.

Topic	+	position	=	opinion statement
Barbed hooks		should be banned from lure fishing to protect the fish stock		Barbed hooks should be banned from lure fishing to protect the fish stock.

_____

_____

Collect Fill in the chart below with two or three supporting details (facts, statistics, quotations, and so on), and, if possible, one main counterargument.

Supporting Details

1. _____

2. _____

3. _____

Counterargument

_____

_____

_____

Writing

Write Create a first draft of your argument paragraph, using the following paragraph outline as a guide.

Other Classes

Argument writing is key to both social sciences and natural sciences.

Vocabulary

reaffirm
to restate in order to emphasize or stress

Paragraph Outline

Topic Sentence: Begin with your opinion statement from the previous page.

Body Sentences: Write sentences that develop the supporting details you listed on the previous page. Work in a counterargument if you feel it is necessary. (Note how the sentences in the sample paragraph flow from one to another.)

Closing Sentence: Write a sentence that reaffirms your opinion.

Revising

Revise Read your paragraph and, if possible, have someone else read it as well. Then use the following checklist to guide your revision. Keep making improvements until you can check off each item in the list.

Ideas
- [ ] **1.** Does my paragraph address a timely and/or important topic?
- [ ] **2.** Do I provide a convincing argument (opinion and supporting points)?
- [ ] **3.** Do I address an important counterargument (optional)?

Organization
- [ ] **4.** Does my opinion statement make a reasonable claim?
- [ ] **5.** Are the body sentences presented in a logical order?
- [ ] **6.** Does the closing sentence reaffirm my opinion or position?

Voice
- [ ] **7.** Does my writing voice reflect my feelings about the topic?
- [ ] **8.** Do I sound logical and knowledgeable?

Editing

Edit Create a clean copy of your revised paragraph. Then edit your writing for style and conventions using the following checklist as a guide.

Vocabulary

reasonable
practical and intelligent

Word Choice
- [ ] **1.** Have I used specific nouns and verbs? (See Chapter 8, LO1.)
- [ ] **2.** Have I used specific modifiers? (See Chapter 17, LO4.)

Sentence Fluency
- [ ] **3.** Have I varied the beginnings and lengths of sentences? (See Chapter 25, LO2.)
- [ ] **4.** Have I combined short, choppy sentences? (See Chapter 25, LO1.)

Conventions
- [ ] **5.** Have I avoided fragments and run-ons? (See Chapter 27, LO1 and LO2; Chapter 28, LO2.)
- [ ] **6.** Do I use correct verb forms (*he saw,* not *he seen*)? (See Chapter 32, LO4.)
- [ ] **7.** Do my subjects and verbs agree (*she speaks,* not *she speak*)? (See Chapter 26, LOs 1–4.)
- [ ] **8.** Have I used the right words (*their, there, they're*)?
- [ ] **9.** Have I capitalized first words and proper nouns and adjectives? (See Chapter 39, LO1.)
- [ ] **10.** Have I used commas after long introductory word groups? (See Chapter 35, LO2.)
- [ ] **11.** Have I carefully checked my spelling?

Chapter 16 Argument and Problem–Solution

LO3 Analyzing a Problem–Solution Paragraph

Problem–solution paragraphs and essays can be expository or persuasive. If the problem and solution happened in the past, the writing is expository. If the essay focuses on a current problem, the writing is persuasive.

Read/React Read the following problem–solution paragraph; then answer the questions at the bottom of the page.

© Glenn Bo/iStockphoto.com

Lead Alert

The **topic sentence** states the topic and focus of the paragraph.

Body sentences explain the problem and offer one or more solutions.

The **closing sentence** reminds readers of the importance of the problem.

Young children unprotected from almost any amount of lead may suffer serious health problems. Lead poisoning can lead to everything from headaches and periods of confusion to learning disabilities and behavioural problems. As the Alliance for Healthy Homes reports, the problem of lead poisoning is most acute in large urban areas where families live in substandard housing. Inner city dwellings built before 1960 likely contain lead-based paints, the major source of the problem. If the lead paint in these dwellings is peeling, very young children will eat the paint chips, but even the dust from the paint is potentially harmful. It can settle on anything, and eventually get in the mouths of the very young. Unfortunately, once someone suffers from lead poisoning, there are no complete cures. The best solution for families is to take preventative measures such as daily house cleaning and regular washing of hands. Long-term measures include painting over old lead paint, but without sanding beforehand. The Mayo Clinic website on lead poisoning reminds renters that they have rights protecting their health and safety. Landlords by law are required to find and address sources of lead. Growing up poor is hard enough. Problems only become magnified if the living conditions expose dwellers to the dangers of lead.

1. What are the topic and focus of the paragraph?

   Topic: _____ **Focus:** _____

2. What are the two things that you learned about the problem?

   _____

   _____

3. What two or three solutions did you learn about?

   _____

   _____

   _____

Vocabulary

acute
intense, serious, or sharp

preventative
intended to prevent

LO4 Writing a Problem–Solution Paragraph

To write a problem–solution paragraph, use the next three pages as a guide, starting the prewriting below.

Prewriting

Select List two or three problems in your community—lack of public transportation or noise pollution. Also list two or three problems related to school life such as *crowded classrooms* or *limited access to courses*. Then circle one that you could write about in a problem–solution paragraph.

Community-related problems:	School-related problems:

Collect Gather information for your paragraph by following the directions below.

Problem

State the problem: _____

Identify who is affected by it: _____

_____

Identify the causes of the problem: _____

_____

_____

Explain its significance: _____

_____

Solutions

State two or three possible solutions, and circle the best one:

_____

_____

_____

_____

Writing

Other Classes

Problem–solution writing is key to both social sciences and natural sciences.

Write Create a first draft of your problem–solution paragraph, using the following paragraph outline as a guide.

Paragraph Outline

Topic Sentence: Start your paragraph with a clear statement of the problem. (See the formula in LO2 for help.)

Body Sentences: Write sentences that explain the problem and offer the best solutions. You may want to lead up to the best solution. Include additional explanations as necessary to connect your ideas.

Closing Sentence: End with a sentence that reminds the reader about the importance of the problem.

Revising

Revise Read your paragraph and, if possible, have someone else read it as well. Then use the following checklist to guide your revision. Keep making improvements until you can check off each item in the list.

Ideas

☐ **1.** Does my paragraph address an important current problem?

☐ **2.** Do I effectively explore the problem and solutions?

☐ **3.** Do I offer additional explanations as needed?

Organization

☐ **4.** Does my topic sentence clearly identify the problem?

☐ **5.** Are the body sentences arranged in a logical way?

☐ **6.** Does my closing sentence stress the importance of the problem?

Voice

☐ **7.** Do I sound interested in and knowledgeable about the problem?

☐ **8.** Do I speak sincerely to the reader?

Editing

Edit Create a clean copy of your paragraph; then use the following checklist to edit your writing for style and conventions.

Word Choice

☐ **1.** Have I used specific nouns and verbs? (See Chapter 8, LO1.)

☐ **2.** Have I used specific modifiers? (See Chapter 17, LO4.)

Sentence Fluency

☐ **3.** Have I varied the beginnings and lengths of sentences? (See Chapter 25, LO2.)

☐ **4.** Have I combined short, choppy sentences? (See Chapter 25, LO1.)

Conventions

☐ **5.** Have I avoided fragments and run-ons? (See Chapter 27, LOs 1 and 2; Chapter 28, LO2.)

☐ **6.** Do I use correct verb forms *(he saw,* not *he seen)*? (See Chapter 32, LO4.)

☐ **7.** Do my subjects and verbs agree *(she speaks,* not *she speak)*? (See Chapter 26, LOs 1–4.)

☐ **8.** Have I used the right words *(their, there, they're)*?

☐ **9.** Have I capitalized first words and proper nouns and adjectives? (See Chapter 39, LO1.)

☐ **10.** Have I used commas after long introductory word groups? (See Chapter 35, LO2.)

☐ **11.** Have I carefully checked my spelling?

"I never travel without my diary. One should always have something sensational to read on the train."
—Oscar Wilde

17 Narrative Essay

Memories seemingly alter reality, taking your mind to another time and place. They can flood your brain for hours, make a lengthy car ride go by in a flash, or get you through a particularly mind-numbing classroom lecture. When your mind drifts to that special place and remembers a past experience, you are reflecting on your own unique story.

An essay that shares a memory or story from your own life is called a personal narrative. The goal of such writing is to bring the memory to life with details that will help the reader see, hear, touch, and taste the experience.

This chapter will guide you through the process of writing a narrative essay about an important past experience.

What do you think?

What sensational stories might be included in the diary of your own life?

_____

_____

_____

_____

_____

_____

_____

_____

_____

_____

_____

_____

_____

_____

_____

_____

_____

Learning Outcomes

LO1 Understand narrative essays.

LO2 Plan a narrative essay.

LO3 Write the first draft.

LO4 Revise the first draft.

LO5 Edit the essay.

LO6 Reflect on the experience.

Demetrio Carrasco/Dorling Kindersley/Getty Images

LO1 Reviewing a Narrative Essay

A narrative essay tells a story. In the following essay, a writer shares a personal story about a memorable experience.

Read/React Read the following essay. Then complete the analysis on the next page.

Tripped Up Road Trip

The **opening paragraph** starts in the middle of the action.

Jammed in our aging royal blue Chevy Astro van with no 1
air conditioning, no radio, and limited legroom, sat my parents,
my two sisters, and our beloved golden retriever, Max. It was mid-
June and we were travelling along historic Route 66 near the New
Mexico–Arizona border, on our way to Grand Canyon National 5
Park.

The first **middle paragraph** uses dialogue to push the story along.

This was not exactly my idea of a fun family vacation. Sweat
beads trickled down my brow, and a feeling of dread washed over
me as I noticed the low-battery sign blinking on my mp3 player.
Couldn't we go to a resort with a swimming pool? "Just six hours 10
left," Mom commented from the front seat. Six hours? You could
watch *Avatar* twice in that same amount of time.

The next **paragraph** describes the key moment in the narrative.

What happened next seemed like a scene from a bad comedy
movie. Out of nowhere, grayish smoke billowed from under the
hood of the van and up the windshield, completely blocking my 15
dad's view of the road. As Dad pulled off to the side, Max started
barking, startling my slumbering sisters, who started screaming
as smoke spilled into the car through the open windows. When the
car was parked, I flung open the door and ran out into the desert
sun. This was the worst vacation ever. 20

The **closing paragraph** describes the action that followed the key moment and provides closure.

Dad discovered the engine had overheated, and we were
stuck. "Is this thing going to blow up?" asked my younger sister
Michelle. "I have, like, a bunch of clothes in there." Luckily Mom
had brought a cooler stocked with bottled water and snacks, so
we survived the hot sun while we waited for a tow truck. It must 25
have been a funny sight for the truck driver when he pulled up.
All six of us sat in a circle, sweating and looking miserable. We
did eventually make it to the Grand Canyon, but not before Mom
admitted, "A pool would feel really nice right now."

MindTap

Log in to MindTap for another example of a narrative essay.

A Closer Look

This essay relied on three basic building blocks of narrative writing: action, dialogue, and description. **Action** suggests the use of active verbs to describe what is happening. *Out of nowhere, grayish smoke billowed from under the hood of the van.* **Dialogue** reveals the unique personalities of the people involved in the story. *"I have, like a bunch of clothes in there," said Michelle.* And **description** uses vivid details to describe people, places, and things. *Sweat beads trickled down my brow.*

Analyze Reread the essay on the previous page. As you do, record any examples of action, dialogue, and description in the following chart.

Action	Dialogue	Description

Explain What type of sensory detail are you most interested in hearing about from a writer? Why?

_____
_____
_____
_____
_____

Chapter 17 Narrative Essay

LO2 Prewriting: Planning

In your own essay, you will write about an experience from your past. Think of a time, a place, or an event that sticks out as a particularly memorable moment in your life.

Selecting a Topic

Select In the space below, list four experiences from your own life to consider for a narrative essay. Next, consider each experience and ask yourself why each is important to you. Put a star by the event that had the greatest impact on who you are today.

1. _____   2. _____

3. _____   4. _____

Using Chronological Order

Once you have selected a topic, think carefully about the order of events in your memory. Almost all narrative essays are arranged chronologically, or according to time.

Identify Use the timeline below to list the main details of your topic in chronological (time) order.

1. _____

2. _____

3. _____

4. _____

5. _____

6. _____

7. _____

8. _____

Gathering Details

The most vivid narrative essays use plenty of sensory details. Such details allow the reader to picture, hear, and touch what you describe. The following chart describes the sensory details in a narrative essay about a special memory.

Traits

The best dialogue captures a person's unique voice, so write the way a speaker actually speaks.

Sights	Sounds	Smells	Tastes	Textures
ceiling fan	buzz of the phone	eggs frying	burn of the bourbon drink	lump in the throat
egg in the frying pan	conversation with Mom			watery eyes
sparkle of brown eyes	Grandpa's deep laugh			
arthritic hands				

Gather Complete the sensory chart below. Collect any sights, sounds, smells, tastes, or textures about your subject in the appropriate column.

Sights	Sounds	Smells	Tastes	Textures

Other Classes

Though some academic forms of writing restrict use of personal pronouns, *I, you,* and *we,* are acceptable in narrative essays.

LO3 Writing: Creating a First Draft

In a first draft you follow your plan and organize your details to create a narrative essay. Provided below is a sample narrative essay about a memorable moment in a writer's life.

Read/React Read the essay, noting how the writer created an effective opening and closing for his personal narrative.

Remembering Grandpa

Opening paragraph

It was sometime after eight o'clock on a Saturday morning when I received the call about my grandfather's death. I was already awake, cracking eggs into a frying pan, when my cellphone buzzed on the countertop. A little early for a phone call, I thought. It was my mom. "Are you awake?" she asked, her voice cracking. Sensing her distress, I asked what was wrong. She told me my grandfather had suffered a stroke during the night and didn't make it.

Middle paragraph 1

After talking through the funeral plans, I wobbled over to my cushy, leather couch and stared blankly at the circulating blades on the ceiling fan. Memories of my grandfather spun around in my head, like the time he taught me how to throw a curveball, and the fishing trip we took together in northern Ontario, and the day he poured me a Coke, but instead mistakenly handed me his glass of bourbon and ice.

Middle paragraph 2

Of course, those were old memories. By the time I reached college, Grandpa wasn't as active anymore. Tired and overworked from his years of hard labour at the steel yard, his back eventually gave out and his joints swelled up with arthritis. He lived alone in the modest two-bedroom home he built for my grandmother after they married. But even after she was gone, he never lost the sparkle in his brown eyes. Nor did he lose his sense of humour, punctuated by a deep baritone laugh.

Closing paragraph

And so I sat there, staring at the ceiling and reminiscing about Grandpa. Sure, I had a lump in my throat and tears filled my eyes; but I felt thankful for the memories of times we had together, and hopeful that one day I could be as good a grandfather as he had been to me.

Creating an Opening Paragraph

The opening paragraph should capture attention and lead the reader into the story. Here are some strategies for beginning your narrative:

- **Set the stage.**
  Show where things happen. Describe the place by using precise details that appeal to the five senses.

  > It was sometime after eight o'clock on a Saturday morning when I received the call about my grandfather's death.

- **Jump into the action.**
  Quickly establish the setting, introduce the characters and topic, and have them do or say something.

  > Jammed in our aging royal blue Chevy Astro van with no air conditioning, no radio, and limited legroom, sat my parents, my two sisters, and our beloved golden retriever, Max.

- **Focus on an interesting detail.**
  Offer a powerful sensory detail to introduce a surprising part of the story.

  > I should have listened to my brother. I never should have walked in that room.

Review

If you are having difficulty creating an opening paragraph or developing a thesis statement, review Chapter 5, LO5 and LO6, and Chapter 6, LO3.

Once you have your reader's attention, lead up to your thesis statement. Here is a formula to use as you create your thesis statement.

Memorable Event		Effect on Your Life		Thesis Statement
Caught up in a surge of raw emotion from the crowd	+	I felt just how strong the pull of "mob mentality" can be.	=	Caught up in a surge of raw emotion from the crowd, I felt just how strong the pull of "mob mentality" can be.

Review

If you need to review thesis statements, see Chapter 5, LO5 and Chapter 6, LO4.

Most narrative essays do *not* state a thesis in the introduction. However, they do have a main idea, theme, or "take-away" message that is implied rather than stated directly. See the two sample narrative essays in this chapter for examples.

Write Create your opening paragraph. Start with a sentence that uses one of the strategies above. Then write sentences that continue to introduce the story.

_____
_____
_____
_____
_____

Use transition words
to move the story
along in time order.
Here are some
transition words that
show time: after /
at / before / during
/ finally / first / later
/ next /next week /
now / second / soon /
suddenly / third / then
/ today / until / when /
while / yesterday

Creating Middle Paragraphs

Write In your middle paragraphs, provide support for your thesis statement by
- telling the story using action, description, and dialogue (review your time line for the most important facts)
- drawing the reader in with details (mine your sensory chart)
- explaining the significance of what happened

Review

See Chapter 6, LO5, for
more suggestions on
how to develop your
middle paragraphs.

Creating a Closing Paragraph

The closing paragraph should explain the outcome of the narrative. Consider the following strategies:

Review

See Chapter 6, LO6, to review other effective closing strategies.

- **Use a final piece of dialogue.**
  Close with an appropriate quotation from someone involved in the narrative.
- **Explain the event's impact.**
  In a sentence, describe how you or the world around you changed after the experience.
- **Reveal a new understanding.**
  Explain what you learned from the experience.

Write Create the closing paragraph for your narrative essay.

Adding a Title

Make sure to add an attention-getting title. Here are three simple strategies for writing narrative-essay titles.

- **Use a phrase from the paragraph:** Remembering Grandpa
- **Use alliteration, the repetition of a consonant sound:** Whale Watchers
- **Use a play on words:** Tripped Up

Speaking & Listening

Have your partner read your essay aloud. Then complete the response sheet.

LO4 Revising: Improving the Writing

Revising your first draft involves adding, deleting, rearranging, and reworking parts of your writing. Revision begins with a peer review.

Peer Review

Sharing your writing at various stages is important, especially when you review and revise a first draft. The feedback that you receive will help you change and improve your essay.

Respond Complete this response sheet after reading the first draft of a classmate's essay. Then share the sheet with the writer. (Keep your comments helpful and positive.)

Essay title: _____

Writer: _____ Reviewer: _____

1. Which part of the essay seems to work best—opening, middle, or closing? Why?

_____

_____

_____

2. Which part of the essay needs work—opening, middle, or closing? Why? _____

_____

_____

_____

3. Which details in the story caught your attention? Name three.

a. _____

b. _____

c. _____

4. Does the writer include appropriate dialogue? Explain.

_____

_____

_____

5. Identify a phrase or two that show the writer's level of interest.

_____

_____

_____

MindTap

For more information, check out the Online Bonus Chapter on peer reviewing.

Adding Specific Verbs and Modifiers

You can strengthen your essay by adding specific verbs and modifiers. Such improvements in word choice make your writing more interesting.

Verbs	
General	Specific
grew	swelled
came	advanced
run	sprint
lives	roams
wear	adorn

Modifiers	
General	Specific
baseball hat	flat-billed New York Yankees hat
curly hair	wavy auburn hair
sweet sauce	tangy barbecue sauce

Revising in Action

Read aloud the unrevised and then the revised version of the following excerpt. Note how specific verbs and adjectives make the writing come alive.

> ~~I walked~~ _{wobbled} over to my _{cushy, leather} couch and stared blankly at the _{circulating} blades on the _{ceiling} fan.

Revise Improve your writing, using the following checklist and your partner's comments on the response sheet. Continue working until you can check off each item in the list.

Ideas

☐ 1. Do I focus on one specific experience or memory?

☐ 2. Do I include sensory details and dialogue?

☐ 3. Do I use specific verbs and modifiers?

☐ 4. Do I include a main theme, idea, or "take away" message?

Organization

☐ 5. Does the essay have an opening, a middle, and a closing?

☐ 6. Is the story organized chronologically?

☐ 7. Have I used transitions to connect my sentences?

Voice

☐ 8. Is my interest in the story obvious to the reader?

☐ 9. Does my writing voice fit my personality?

Chapter 17 Narrative Essay

LO5 Editing: Correcting Your Writing

The main work of editing is correcting your revised first draft.

Quotation Marks and Dialogue

Dialogue enlivens a story and reveals the personalities of its characters. When you recall or create conversations between people using the speaker's exact words, you must use quotation marks before and after the **direct quotation.** However, when you use an **indirect quotation**—one that does not use the speaker's exact words—quotation marks are not needed. See the examples that follow.

Direct Quotation

Before we left class, our instructor said, **"Next week's final will be comprehensive."**

Indirect Quotation

I recall the instructor saying **that the final would be comprehensive.**

Note: The word *that* often indicates dialogue that is being reported rather than quoted.

Practise   Read the sentences below. Place quotation marks ("") before and after the speaker's exact words in direct quotations. If the sentence contains no direct quotations, write "C" for correct on the blank following the sentence.

---

1. Who is your favourite actress? asked Veronica. _____

2. The salesman suggested that I should take the truck for a test drive. _____

3. Frank said that if we want to make it in time, we should leave by noon. _____

4. On my way out today, Jessie said, I forgot my cellphone. _____

5. Pull over to the side of the road, said the police officer. _____

6. After glancing at her test score, Jillian said, Spring break can't come soon enough. _____

7. And with this new cellphone model, said the saleswoman, you can play music, get driving directions, and check your e-mail. _____

8. Jana said that she loves her new summer dress. _____

Apply   Read your narrative essay. If you included any direct quotations, make sure they are properly marked with quotation marks. If you did not use any direct quotations, you should consider adding one or two to reveal the uniqueness of the people in your story.

Punctuation of Dialogue

As you edit your narrative essay, check for the correct punctuation of dialogue. In general, there are three rules you should follow.

> ■ **When a period or comma follows the quotation, place the period or comma *before* the quotation mark.**
>> "You should check your voice messages," advised Mr. Lee.
>> "As you will soon discover," advised Reggie, "the wrap station in the cafeteria is the best choice for lunch."
>
> ■ **When a question mark or an exclamation point follows the quotation, place it *before* the quotation mark if it belongs with the quotation. Otherwise, place it after.**
>> I asked Sheryl, "Where can I get some good poutine?"
>> Did you hear Veronica say, "I quit"?
>
> ■ **When a semicolon or colon follows the quotation, place it after the quotation mark.**
>> Trey only said, "I have other plans"; he didn't mention his fear of heights.

Correct In each sentence that follows, correct the punctuation and capitalization of the quotations.

1. "Let's focus on solutions, not problems", offered Haley.

2. Jack promised he would, "Try his best to make it;" however, I know he's not coming.

3. "It's not the size of the dog in the fight", suggested Mark Twain ", it's the size of the fight in the dog."

4. "It's about time you showed up"! exclaimed Karen.

5. "Should I apply for the job"? asked my roommate.

6. What did you mean when you said, "There is more to the story than you think?"

7. "We are doing everything in our power to regain your trust", said the company spokesperson.

Apply Read your narrative essay. Closely check the punctuation of your dialogue.

Editing an Essay

Before you finish editing your revised essay, you can practise by editing the following model.

Edit Read the following narrative essay, looking at the areas listed in the checklist on the next page. Also refer to the list of common errors Chapter 8, LO5. Correct the model using the marks listed to the left. One correction has been done for you.

Correction Marks

ℐ	delete
d̲	capitalize
Ɗ	lowercase
∧	insert
∧̂	add comma
? ∧	add question mark
word ∧	add word
⊙	add period
◯	spelling
⌓	switch

jo Crebbin/Shutterstock.com

Whale Watchers

On a sunny afternoon off the coast of Vancouver Island, my friend Natalie   *1*
and I set off on our great whale watching adventure. In the winter months,
some 20 000 gray whales migrate through the Pacific waters along the coast
of british columbia, and we wanted to see the majestic creatures in there
natural habitat.   *5*

As we stepped aboard the 30-metre tour boat nicknamed "Night and
Day", Natalie reminded me to take some medication to prevent seasickness.
Good thing she did, because the captain announced we would hit 6-foot swells
on our journey. Their were about 40 other passengers onboard with us.

About 15 minutes off the shoreline, a passenger shouted, "There she   *10*
blows"! Indeed, about 20 metres ahead of us, I seen a spray of white water
rocket vertically from the ocean surface we had spotted our first whale! As
the boat crept closer, we could see the bumpy gray backs of two more whales
rising above the undulating waves. I was so excited that high-fived Natalie so
hard it made my hand sting.   *15*

We ended up seeing five diffrant gray whales two packs of dolphins,
and too many gulls to count. seeing this beautiful sea life in the wild was an
experience I'll never forget. Learning that the whales are endangered goes to
show that we must boost our efforts to protect them from extinction.

Correcting Your Essay

Now it's time to correct your own essay.

Edit Prepare a clean copy of your essay and use the following checklist to look for errors. Continue working until you can check off each item in the list.

Editing Checklist

Word Choice

☐ **1.** Have I used specific nouns and verbs? (See Chapter 8, LO1.)

☐ **2.** Have I used more action verbs than "be" verbs? (See Chapter 32, LO1.)

Sentence Fluency

☐ **3.** Have I used sentences with varying beginnings and lengths? (See Chapter 25, LO2.)

☐ **4.** Have I avoided improper shifts in sentences? (See Chapter 29, LO2.)

Conventions

☐ **5.** Have I avoided fragments and run-ons? (See Chapter 27, LO1 and LO2; Chapter 28, LO2.)

☐ **6.** Do I use correct verb forms (*he saw,* not *he seen*)? (See Chapter 32, LO4.)

☐ **7.** Do my subjects and verbs agree (*she speaks,* not *she speak*)? (See Chapter 26, LO5 1–4.)

☐ **8.** Have I used the right words (*their, there, they're*)?

☐ **9.** Have I capitalized first words and proper nouns and adjectives? (See Chapter 39, LO1.)

☐ **10.** Have I used commas after long introductory word groups and to separate items in a series? (See Chapter 35, LO2.)

☐ **11.** Have I correctly punctuated any dialogue? (See Chapter 17, LO5.)

☐ **12.** Have I carefully checked my spelling?

Documentation Checklist

Format

☐ **1.** Have I followed the proper formatting conventions? (See Chapter 9, LO5 and LO6.)

In-Text Citation

☐ **2.** Have I properly documented any sources in the body of my writing? (See Chapter 9, LO1–LO4.)

Bibliography

☐ **3.** Do I have a references or works cited page? (See Chapter 9, LO1–LO4.)

Kenneth Sponsler/Shutterstock.com

LO6 Reviewing Narrative Writing

Complete these activities as needed to help you better understand how to write narrative essays.

Fill In Description, especially relating to the five senses, makes up a key component of narrative writing. Imagine you are at the carnival in the picture on this page. What sensory details—sights, smells, sounds, and so on—might you experience? Fill in as many as you can in this sensory chart. (See LO2, Prewriting: Planning.)

Sights	Sounds	Smells	Tastes	Textures

Explain What are the three key elements of narrative writing? What purpose does each element serve?

_____

_____

_____

_____

_____

_____

Sort Circle the transitions that *show time*.

after	below	before	near	next	then

> "The essence of the beautiful is unity in variety."
> —William Somerset Maugham

S.Borisov/Shutterstock.com

18

Classification Essay

Say you're starting a flower garden, but you don't know what type of flowers you want to plant. You've got hundreds of options, and you feel overwhelmed. What should you do? Your best plan might be to break down the wide variety of available flowers into categories, or subgroups, that fit your preferences. Think about the colour, shape, style, and growing patterns that will work best in your garden. And, eventually, narrow down your choices to a more manageable list.

A classification essay works in the same way: It breaks down a multi-faceted topic into manageable subgroups, so that you can look at the individual components and consider the relationships between them.

Learning Outcomes

LO1 Understand classification essays.

LO2 Plan a classification essay.

LO3 Write the first draft.

LO4 Revise the essay.

LO5 Edit the essay.

LO6 Reflect on the experience.

What do you think?

Reread the quotation at the top of the page. How might there be unity in variety? Explain.

L◯1 Reviewing a Classification Essay

A classification essay analyzes a topic by breaking it down into different categories or types.

Read/React Read the following essay. Then complete the analysis on the next page.

Malchev/Shutterstock.com

With Great Power: Three Superhero Origin Stories

The **opening** gets the reader's attention and establishes criteria for dividing the topic into subgroups.

William Shakespeare once wrote: "Some are born great, some achieve greatness, and some have greatness thrust upon them" (2.5.135-7). Shakespeare obviously wasn't talking about superhero origin stories, but he might as well have been. <u>This quotation is useful in classifying the three common ways that superheroes gain their superpowers: by birth, by accident, or, the greatest of way of all, by personal determination.</u> 1

Many superheroes are born with innate powers. These heroes are typically non-human and may be aliens, mutants, supernatural creatures (like werewolves or vampires), or divinely chosen. Since they are "born great," these characters often have to hide their powers from the rest of the world or risk being alienated. The most famous hero in this group is Superman. While he pretends to be human, assuming the guise of "Clark Kent," he was actually born on the planet Krypton. His alien heritage grants him extraordinary abilities like flight, super-strength, super-speed, and Xray vision. 10

15

The **middle paragraphs** describe the subgroups, explain their distinct traits, and show the relationships between them.

Unlike heroes who are born great, another group of superheroes start life as painfully ordinary until greatness is "thrust upon them." Usually, these heroes are granted amazing powers completely at random after a freak accident, such as a science experiment gone wrong. For example, with a *ZAP!* of radiation, socially inept nerds, like Bruce Banner or Peter Parker, are transformed into their mighty alter egos, the Incredible Hulk and the Amazing Spiderman, both of whom have a wide range of extraordinary powers. 20

25

The **closing** reunites the subgroups for a final look at the topic.

Some would argue that the final group are not "real" superheroes because they are born ordinary and never granted powers later in life. However, the fact that they are never given powers actually makes these superheroes the greatest of all: They have to "achieve greatness" through their own determination. Rather than being handed their extraordinary skills and abilities, their transformation into a hero depends entirely on personal effort and willpower. The superhero who most fits this archetype is Batman. In response to his parents' tragic murder, he honed his body and mind to a state beyond human perfection. Additionally, he is the only founding member of the Justice League, the most famous superhero team in DC comics, without any "real" superpowers. 30

35

Indeed, his incredible intellect and resolve allow him to hold his own in a universe populated by superheroes with godlike abilities.

People assume that the greatest superheroes are the ones *40* who are born with or given the strongest powers. This is incorrect. The greatest superheroes are those without any powers who transcend their human limitations and transform themselves into superheroes. These heroes remind us that with enough effort and willpower, anyone can be a superhero. *45*

Works Cited

Shakespeare, William. "Twelfth Night." *The Norton Anthology of English Literature*. 8th ed. Ed. Stephen Greenblatt. New York: Norton, 2006. 510–72. Print.

A Closer Look

List Complete the chart below by writing the name of each type of superhero, a definition, and details about it.

Different Types of Superheroes	Definition	Details / Examples
Subgroup 1		
Subgroup 2		
Subgroup 3		

Explain The writer chose to distinguish each subgroup by definition, example, and description. What other features or points could the writer have used to distinguish the different types of superheroes? Explain.

_____

_____

_____

_____

_____

_____

Olga Lyubkina/Shutterstock.com

LO2 Prewriting: Planning

In your own classification essay, you will explore the categories, or subgroups, of a topic of your choice. These two pages will help you select a topic and gather details about it.

Explore Read through the "Essentials of Life" list below. Select four general subject areas you would like to explore. Then, for each subject, write a possible topic. An example has been done for you.

Essentials of Life

food	intelligence	resources
clothing	personality	energy
shelter	senses	money
education	emotions	government
work	goals	laws
entertainment	health	rights
recreation	environment	science
religion	plants	measurement
family	animals	machines
friends	land	tools
community	literature	agriculture
communication	arts	business

1. Subject Area:

Clothing _____

Topic:

Types of Athletic shorts _____

2. Subject Area:

_____

Topic:

Types of _____

3. Subject Area:

_____

Topic:

Types of _____

4. Subject Area:

_____

Topic:

Types of _____

5. Subject Area:

_____

Topic:

Types of _____

Select Review the topics you've listed above and select one that has three to six types (a number you could comfortably cover in a classification essay).

Researching Your Topic

Once you have selected a topic, you may need to find out more about it. Search Internet sites, encyclopedias, school texts, and other sources as necessary. As you break down your topic into types or categories, consider the following points:

Types or categories should be

- **exclusive**, which means that one example doesn't fit into more than one category, and
- **consistent**, which means that examples of each category have the same traits.

Organize In this chart, write your topic within the parentheses. Then list the subgroups, or types, in the first column, define each in the second column, and provide details about each in the third.

Types of ( )	Definition	Details
Subgroup 1		
Subgroup 2		
Subgroup 3		
Subgroup 4		

Citation

When looking for evidence to use in your writing, always carefully record the title, author's name, and publication information for each source. Even if you don't use a source in your final paper, staying organized will help you later when creating your works cited page.

See Chapter 9, Plagiarism and Documentation, for more information about citation.

Other Classes

In all classes, research and classification are critical.

Vocabulary

exclusive category a type that does not overlap with other types

consistent category a type that contains examples that share the same traits

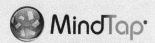

Log in to MindTap for another example of a classification essay.

LO3 Writing: Creating a First Draft

After you have completed planning and gathering information, you are ready to start the drafting stage. Provided below is another sample classification essay.

Read/React Read the essay, noting how the writer classified the topic into distinct subgroups.

Classification Essay

Vegetarian Diets: What and Why?

Opening paragraph

Thesis statement

We often make the mistake of putting all vegetarians into the same category. Oh, they're just those people who don't eat meat, we say. <u>While this is true—the majority of vegetarians do eliminate meat from their diets—we fail to recognize important distinctions in vegetarian diets. We also fail to recognize the different motives that influence vegetarians to eat certain foods over others.</u> 1

  5

Types of Vegetarians

There are four main types of vegetarian diets: total, vegan, lacto-vegetarian, and lacto-ovo-vegetarian. The total-vegetarian diet includes only plant-based foods—no meat, fish, eggs, dairy products, or honey. A vegan diet, like the total-vegetarian diet, includes only food from plant sources; but those who adhere to this diet go a step farther by never using animal products such as leather, wool, and silk. Meanwhile, lacto-vegetarian diets include dairy products but no eggs or meat, while lacto-ovo-vegetarian diets include both eggs and dairy products but no meat. To a non-vegetarian, these differences between vegetarian diets may seem small, but they are consequential to the people who subscribe to them. 10

  15

Reasons and Differences

The reasons for choosing any of these vegetarian diets is often based on an individual's values and beliefs. Three factors especially influence this choice: health, animal rights, and religion. Vegetarian diets are associated with lower cholesterol levels, lower risks of heart disease and cancer, and a higher life expectancy. Many people are attracted by these promised health benefits. Other people become vegetarians because of their concern for animals. They believe that killing animals for food is cruel and unnecessary and that eating plants is the only humane diet choice. Finally, some people become vegetarians because of their religious beliefs. Jainism and other Hindu sects, for example, do not allow the killing or consumption of animals. 20

  25

  30

Closing Paragraph

It is unfair, then, to regard all vegetarians as like-minded. As a group, vegetarians espouse diverse values and beliefs, which in turn influence their diet choices. Likewise, non-vegetarians hold various food preferences for many different reasons. The food we eat is indeed a personal choice, influenced by a host of factors worthy of examination. 35

Reading Using the Traits

Analyze the essay on the facing page using the traits, the key elements found in effective writing

Review

If you need to review the traits and a sample reading analysis, see Chapter 3, LO2.

Ideas:

_____

_____

_____

_____

Organization:

_____

_____

_____

_____

Voice:

_____

_____

_____

_____

Word Choice:

_____

_____

_____

Sentence Fluency:

_____

_____

_____

Conventions:

_____

_____

Design:

_____

_____

Review

See Chapter 6, LO3, if you are having difficulty creating an opening paragraph.

Creating an Opening Paragraph

The objective of the opening paragraph is to gain the reader's attention, introduce the topic, and present your thesis statement. Here are some strategies for beginning your essay:

■ **Challenge a common perception.**

> We often make the mistake of putting all vegetarians into the same category.

■ **Begin with a question.**

> What makes a baseball so hard to hit?

■ **Use a quotation.**

> Comedian Phyllis Diller once joked, "My idea of exercise is a good brisk sit."

Write Create your opening paragraph. Start with a sentence that uses one of the strategies above. Then write sentences that build to your thesis statement.

Writing a Thesis Statement

Once you have your reader's attention, lead up to your thesis statement. Here are a few things to keep in mind when writing a thesis statement for a classification essay:

(1) Mention the **specific topic** that your essay will be discussing. In the body of your essay, you will be breaking this topic up into categories and discussing each in more detail. (See Chapter 5, LO5, for tips on how to narrow your topic, if you need to.)

(2) If appropriate, provide an **overview of the subgroups**. Doing so will help your reader understand the overall organization of your essay.

(3) State your **point** about the classification. Remember, your point is the main idea or attitude you want to convey about your topic.

If expressed as a formula, this thesis statement would look like this:

Review

If you need to review thesis statements, see Chapter 5, LO5, and Chapter 6, LO4.

A Specific Topic	+	Overview of Subgroups	+	Point	=	Thesis Statement
different levels of physical activity		different people pursue different levels of physical activity		those who follow exercise programs are significantly healthier than those who do not		While different people pursue different levels of physical activity, those who follow an exercise program are the healthiest.
different ways that superheroes get their powers		superheroes get their powers through birth, accident, or personal determination		the greatest superheroes earn their powers through personal determination		There are three common ways that superheroes gain their superpowers: by birth, by accident, or, the greatest of way of all, by personal determination.

Write Use the preceding formula to create your thesis statement.

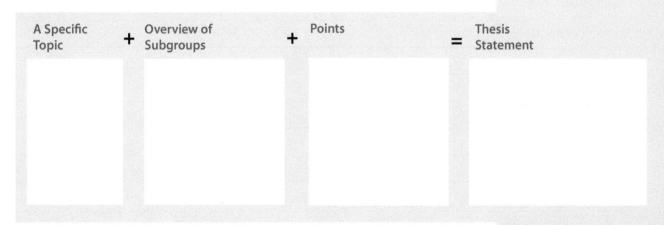

A Specific Topic	+	Overview of Subgroups	+	Points	=	Thesis Statement

Review

See Chapter 6, LO5, for suggestions on how to develop your middle paragraphs.

Traits

Transition words that classify:

one type / a second / a third / the last / the simplest / a more complex / an advanced / the most complex / the most common / a less common / a rare / a very rare / the earliest / a later / a recent / the newest

Creating Middle Paragraphs

Write Refer to the chart in LO2, Prewriting: Planning, to help organize the middle paragraphs of your essay. Use the paragraphs to describe the subgroups of your topic and their respective traits. Include a topic sentence in each paragraph and use transitional words or phrases (like those listed in the margin) to help your writing flow.

Creating a Closing Paragraph

The closing paragraph should bring the subgroups together again for a final look at the topic. Consider showing how the subgroups are related to one another, or leave the reader with some other thought.

Review

See Chapter 6, LO6, to review effective closing strategies.

Write Answer the following questions to help you sum up your essay.

1. What characteristics do the subgroups have in common?

   _____

   _____

2. What is a key difference between the subgroups?

   _____

   _____

Write Create the closing paragraph for your classification essay.

_____

_____

_____

_____

_____

_____

_____

_____

_____

_____

_____

_____

_____

Adding a Title

Make sure to add an attention-getting title. Here are three simple strategies for creating one.

- **Describe the classification:** Three Types of Greatness: Superhero Origin Stories
- **Think creatively:** Vegetarian Diets: What and Why?
- **Use a play on words:** Fast Ballers

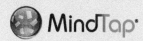

LO4 Revising: Improving the Writing

Revising your first draft involves adding, deleting, rearranging, and reworking parts of your writing. Revision begins with a peer review.

Peer Review

Sharing your writing at various stages is important, especially when you review and revise a first draft. The feedback that you receive will help you change and improve your essay.

Respond Complete this response sheet after reading the first draft of a classmate's essay. Then share the sheet with the writer. (Keep your comments helpful and positive.)

Essay title: _____

Writer: _____ Reviewer: _____

1. Which part of the essay seems to work best—opening, middle, or closing? Why?

   _____

   _____

2. Which part of the essay needs work—opening, middle, or closing? Why? _____

   _____

   _____

   _____

3. Do the middle paragraphs explain the distinct traits of the subgroups? Explain.

   _____

   _____

4. Name two of your favourite details.

   _____

   _____

5. Identify a phrase or two that shows the writer's level of interest.

   _____

   _____

Clarifying Special Terms

Depending on the topic, your essay may contain special terms or words that are unfamiliar to your reader. Keep this potential problem in mind and always clarify such terms in the text of your essay. Consider the following strategies:

- **Provide an actual definition.**

  > A person with a sedentary lifestyle exercises fewer than three times per week.

- **Use an appositive before or after the term.**

  > The pitcher threw a slider, a pitch that breaks sideways and downward at a slower speed than a straight fastball. (The appositive is set off with a comma and defines the term *slider* in this example.)

- **Give word clues.**

  > The African vuvuzelas blared throughout the stadium, a collective buzz from thousands of plastic horns. (Words like *African, blared, buzz, plastic,* and *horns* help the reader understand what *vuvuzelas* are.)

Revising in Action:

Read aloud the unrevised and then the revised version of the following excerpt. Note how the specific words energize the writing.

> Some baseball pitchers will throw a knuckleball, an extremely slow pitch with little to no spin
>
> Tim Wakefield, a pitcher for the Boston Red Sox, now retired, was known for throwing mostly knuckleballs. Many batters are fooled by this specialty pitch because of its wacky movement.

Respond Improve your writing, using the following checklist and your partner's comments on the response sheet. Continue until you can check off each item.

Ideas

- ☐ **1.** Do I focus on one specific topic?
- ☐ **2.** Do I name and define the types or categories of the topic?
- ☐ **3.** Do I provide details about the traits of each type?
- ☐ **4.** Have I clarified any special terms?

Thesis

- ☐ **5.** Do I mention a specific topic?
- ☐ **6.** Do I provide an overview of the subgroups?
- ☐ **7.** Do I make a point about the classiciation?

Organization

- ☐ **8.** Does my essay have effective opening, middle, and closing paragraphs?
- ☐ **9.** Do I use transition words and phrases to show the relationship between types?

Voice

- ☐ **10.** Does my voice sound knowledgeable and interested?

appositive
a word or phrase that identifies or renames a preceding noun or pronoun

LO5 Editing: Correcting Your Writing

The main work of editing is correcting your revised draft.

Before you begin editing your revised essay, you can begin by editing the following model.

Editing an Essay

Edit Read the following classification essay, looking for problems listed in the checklist on the next page. Also refer to the list of common errors in Chapter 8, LO5. Correct the model using the marks listed to the left. The first correction has been done for you.

Correction Marks

ɘ   delete

d̲   capitalize

Ð   lowercase

∧   insert

∧̓   add comma

?   add question
∧   mark

word   add word
∧

⊙   add period

⬭   spelling

⌇   switch

Fast Ballers

What makes a baseball so hard to hit? Well, besides being the size of an orange   1
and travelling at faster velocities than vehicles on the 401 baseballs do funny
things in the air depending on the way their thrown. There are four main types of
pitches thrown by baseball players. Each with different speeds and trajectories.

The most frequently thrown pitch is a fastball. As its name suggests, fastball   5
travel at the highest velocity of any pitch. Generally a fastball's trajectry is
straight through the air and into the catcher's glove.

A second type of pitch, a changeup, is used to trick hitters into thinking its
a fastball. However, the changeup is thrown at a much slower speed and tails
slightly downward as it reaches the plate.   10

A third pitch is called a curveball. It is hard to hit because it travels with
topspin that causes it to curve sharply both laterally and downward. A hitter
might think a curveball is coming right at them before it curves over the plate
and into the strike zone. Because of a curveball's trajectory, its slower than a
fastball but faster than a changeup.   15

A fourth comman pitch is called a slider. The slider is similar to a curveball in
that it break laterally and downward as it reaches the batter. However, a slider's
break is shorter than a curveball's. It is also thrown at a faster speed than a curveball.

When a pitcher is able to throw all four of these pitches hitting becomes a
guessing game for the batter. if the batter is expecting a fastball but receives a   20
changeup, he or she might swing to early. No wonder baseballs is so hard to hit.

Correcting Your Essay

Now it's time to correct your own essay.

Edit Prepare a clean copy of your essay and use the following checklist to look for errors. Continue working until you can check off each item in the list.

Editing Checklist

Words

- ☐ **1.** Have I used specific nouns and verbs? (See Chapter, 8, LO1.)
- ☐ **2.** Have I used more action verbs than "be" verbs? (See Chapter 32, LO1.)

Sentences

- ☐ **3.** Have I used sentences with varying beginnings and lengths? (See Chapter 25, LO2.)
- ☐ **4.** Have I combined short choppy sentences? (See Chapter 25, LO1.)
- ☐ **5.** Have I avoided improper shifts in sentences? (See Chapter 29, LO2.)
- ☐ **6.** Have I avoided fragments and run-ons? (See Chapter 27, LO1 and LO2; Chapter 28, LO2.)

Conventions

- ☐ **7.** Do I use correct verb forms (*he saw,* not *he seen*)? (See Chapter 32, LO4.)
- ☐ **8.** Do my subjects and verbs agree (*she speaks,* not *she speak*)? (See Chapter 26, LOs 1–4.)
- ☐ **9.** Have I used the right words (*their, there, they're*)?
- ☐ **10.** Have I capitalized first words and proper nouns and adjectives? (See Chapter 39, LO1.)
- ☐ **11.** Have I used commas after long introductory word groups and to set off extra information? (See Chapter 35, LO2.)
- ☐ **12.** Have I carefully checked my spelling?

Documentation Checklist

Format

- ☐ **1.** Have I followed the proper formatting conventions? (See Chapter 9, LO5 and LO6.)

In-Text Citation

- ☐ **2.** Have I properly documented any sources in the body of my writing? (See Chapter 9, LO1–LO4.)

Bibliography

- ☐ **3.** Do I have a references or works cited page? (See Chapter 9, LO1–LO4)

Create Prepare a clean final copy of your essay and proofread it.

LO6 Reviewing Classification Writing

Complete these activities as needed to help you better understand how to write classification essays.

Classify Study the photo on this page. In the first column of the chart below, break down the peppers into subgroups, or types. Then define each type in the second column and write at least one detail about each in the third.

Roman Rvachov/Shutterstock.com

Types of Peppers	Definition	Details
Subgroup 1		
Subgroup 2		
Subgroup 3		

Match Draw a line from each sentence starter below to the correct description on the right.

1. The opening of a classification essay should . . .

2. The middle of a classification essay should . . .

3. The closing of a classification essay should . . .

- reconnect the subject and its subgroups and present the reader with a final thought.

- introduce the topic and lead up to the thesis statement.

- describe the subgroups and traits relating to those subgroups.

> "The vision must be followed by the venture. It is not enough to stare up the steps—we must step up the stairs."
>
> —Vance Havner

John Lumb/Shutterstock.com

19

Process Essay

From the beginning of this book, you have approached writing as a process. You know that tackling a writing challenge in one giant step won't get the job done. Instead, it takes a series of steps to create a thoughtful and polished piece of writing. Like good writing, many of the great accomplishments we see around us are born out of a process.

By definition, a process is a series of actions or operations that produce a particular result. In this chapter, you will describe or explain a process; you will lay out its steps and write about it clearly enough for your least knowledgeable reader to understand it.

Learning Outcomes

LO1 Understand process essays.

LO2 Plan a process essay.

LO3 Write the first draft.

LO4 Revise the essay.

LO5 Edit the essay.

LO6 Reflect on the experience.

What do you think?

Reread the definition of a process at the beginning of the second paragraph. Describe the steps you take to get ready for school or work in the morning.

Tip

This essay outlines a sequential process: All of the steps must be followed in a specific order to have a successful outcome.

See the essay in LO3 for an example of a non-sequential process.

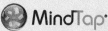

Log in to MindTap for another example of a process essay.

LO1 Reviewing a Process Essay

A process essay explains how something works by laying out the specific steps that will take you to a particular result.

Read/React Read the following essay. Then complete the analysis on the next page.

Making Dirty Water Drinkable

Opening paragraph

One of the most overlooked luxuries of living in Canada is access to clean drinking water. Statistics show roughly one-eighth of the world's population lacks access to safe water supplies, while as many as 2.5 billion people live without sanitized water. Untreated water is full of unhealthy chemicals and contaminants that, if consumed, lead to uncomfortable and sometimes fatal disease, including dysentery and diarrhea. <u>Water purification plants remove these harmful impurities through a process of pre-treatment, coagulation, filtration, and disinfection, making our water safe to drink.</u>

Thesis Statement

1

5

10

First step in the process

The first step in water purification is pre-treatment. During pre-treatment, water is pumped in from its source and screened to remove any large twigs, leaves, or other debris before reaching the holding tanks. Next, coagulation begins. Coagulation removes dirt and other particles from the water by adding a chemical that forms sticky particles called "floc." The floc combines with dirt particles as the water moves to a sedimentary basin. Once inside the basin, the combined weight of the dirt and floc mixture causes it to sink to the floor as sedimentation. The sedimentation is then removed from the water, giving water its clear, colourless quality.

15

20

Final step in the process

While coagulation removes the sedimentation from the water, the filtration phase pushes the remaining particles and unsettled sedimentation through filters of sand or charcoal. Filtration reduces particles in the water by 90 to 95 percent. Lastly the water is pumped to a disinfection tank. During disinfection, chlorine is added to kill any lingering viruses or bacteria. Some treatment plants also introduce fluorine into the water to prevent tooth decay. After the process is completed, the water is tested for safety and then released from the plant for safe consumption.

25

Closing paragraph

Make no mistake: The process of water purification in treatment plants is vitally important to the health of consumers. By removing dirt and sludge through pre-treatment and coagulation, then filtering the lingering particles, and finally disinfecting with chlorine and other chemicals, water purification plants make certain that the water our bodies desperately need to survive will do its job.

30

35

Jonutis/Shutterstock.com

A Closer Look

This essay discusses the process of purifying dirty water. The writer explains each step in chronological order, using transitions to move logically from one step to the next.

Respond Use the STRAP strategy to complete the assignments below.

Reread "Making Dirty Water Drinkable" and answer the following questions.

Subject: What specific topic does the reading address?

_____

_____

Type: What form (*essay, text chapter*) does the reading take?

_____

_____

Role: What position does the writer assume?

_____

_____

Audience: Who is the intended audience?

_____

_____

Purpose: What is the goal of the material?

_____

_____

Identity Reread the essay, paying attention to the steps in the process. Then, in the graphic below, briefly describe each step and the transition word (or words) used to introduce it.

Topic: Purifying dirty water

Transitions	Steps
1.	
2.	
3.	
4.	
5.	
6.	

Traits

Transition words used to show time:
after / before / finally / first / second / third / then / later / next / when / once / while

Workplace

Process writing is practical writing. In the workplace, the ability to give clear instructions means getting a project done correctly.

L○2 Prewriting: Planning

In your own process essay, you will explain how something works or is made. The topic information below will help you select a process to write about.

Selecting a Topic

Use the following ideas to generate possible process-essay topics.

> Consider a process that
> - relates to your major or academic concentration;
> - keeps you healthy or unhealthy;
> - relates to your favourite entertainment—sports, music, theatre, and so on;
> - is in the news; or
> - impacts the world around you.

Select   On the lines below, list four potential topics for your process essay. They may be topics you know a lot about or ones you need to research more thoroughly. Circle the one you would like to write about.

1. _____   2. _____

3. _____   4. _____

Researching a Process

Once you have selected a topic, review what you know about it. If necessary, supplement your information with additional research.

Identify   Complete the research questions below.

1. What is the process?_____

2. Why is it important? _____

   _____

3. What steps are needed to complete it?_____

   _____

4. What is the outcome? _____

   _____

Gathering Details

You can use a timeline to gather details about the steps in your process. The following example lists the steps needed to kill a zombie.

Topic: Killing a zombie		
		Steps
1		Build your physical strength and endurance
2		Find a blunt tool or weapon
3		Repeatedly swing your weapon at the zombie's head
4		Ensure that the brain is destroyed
5		Outcome: Dead zombie

Gather Complete the timeline below. Start by writing down the topic of your process essay. Then fill in the steps that will complete the process and bring you to the desired outcome. (Use your own paper if you are writing about a process with more than six steps.)

Topic: _____

Steps

1 _____ _____

2 _____ _____

3 _____ _____

4 _____ _____

5 _____ _____

6 _____ _____

7 _____ **Outcome:** _____

LO3 Writing: Creating a First Draft

Creating a first draft puts all your planning and gathering into concrete form. Provided below is a sample process essay about water treatment.

Read/React Read the essay, noting how the writer uses the opening paragraph to describe the significance of the process, and then uses the middle paragraphs to explain its steps in chronological order.

MindTap

You will find another example of a process essay online.

Flunking with Style

Opening paragraph

Thesis Statement

People often remark that succeeding in school takes plenty of hard work. The remark implies that failure is a product of general idleness and zero motivation. This is an opinion I'd like to challenge. My long and checkered past in numerous educational institutions has taught me that to fail grandly, to fail extravagantly, to go down in truly blazing splendour, requires effort and imagination. <u>To fail your year in the grand style, you must antagonize your teachers, disdain your studies, and cheat on your work. Keep the following guidelines in mind.</u>

First step in the process

The first step, antagonizing your teachers, isn't difficult if you keep in mind what it is that teachers like: intelligent, interested, even enthusiastic faces in front row centre. Show that you're bored before the class begins by slouching in a desk at the back of the room. Wear your [headphones], and don't forget to turn up the volume when the teacher starts to talk. Carry on running conversations with your seatmates [and on your smart phone]. Aim an occasional snort or snicker in the teacher's direction when she's putting a complex point on the board. Above all, never volunteer an answer and respond sullenly with an "I dunno" if the teacher has the nerve to ask you a question. Before long, you'll have that teacher bouncing chalk stubs off your head. Once you've earned the loathing of your instructors, you'll be well on your way to a truly memorable failure.

Second step in the process

The second step, disdaining your studies, is easy to master. They're probably B-O-R-I-N-G anyway. First, don't buy your books until close to midterm and keep them in their original condition; don't open, read, or note anything in them. Better yet, don't buy your texts at all. Second, never attempt to take notes in class. Third, stop going to class completely, but have lots of creative excuses for missed assignments: "My friend's aunt died"; "My gerbil's in a coma"; "My boyfriend was in another car wreck"; "My dog ate the lab report"; "I've got mono." You can bet your teachers will be really amused by these old standbys. By now you are well on your way to disaster.

Final step in the process

The third step, cheating, will deliver the *coup de grâce* to your academic career. Should an instructor be so sadistic as to assign a research paper, just copy something out of a book that the librarian will be happy to find for you. Your instructor will be astonished at the difference between the book's polished professional prose and your usual halting scrawls; you're guaranteed a zero. During

1

5

10

15

20

25

30

35

your exams, sit at the back and crane your neck to read your classmate's paper. Roll up your shirtsleeves to reveal the answers you've tattooed all over your forearms. Ask to be excused three or four times during the test so you can consult the notes you've stashed in the hall or the washroom. Be bold! Dig out your old wood-burning kit and emblazon cheat notes on the desk. If you want to ensure not just failure but actual expulsion, send in a ringer—a look-alike—to write the exam for you! *40*

45

Closing paragraph

    If you follow these guidelines, you will be guaranteed to flunk your year. Actively courting failure with verve, with flair, and with a sense of drama will not only ensure your status as an academic washout but will also immortalize you in the memories of teachers and classmates alike. The challenge is yours. Become a legend—pick up the torch and fall with it! *50*

Source: "Flunking with Style" by Nell Waldman, from Sarah Norton and Nell Waldman, eds., *Canadian Content* (Toronto: Holt, Rinehart and Winston, 1988). Reprinted with permission from the author.

Reading Using the Traits

Analyze the essay "Flunking with Style" using the traits, the key elements found in effective writing. Use your own paper if you need more room.

Ideas:

_____

Organization:

_____

Voice:

_____

Word Choice:

_____

Sentence Fluency:

_____

Conventions:

_____

Design:

_____

Review

If you need to review the traits and a sample reading analysis, see Chapter 17, LO2.

Traits

The tone of an essay is the attitude that writer expresses towards the topic. What is the tone of "Flunking with Style"? Find words, phrases, or sentences that demonstrate the tone.

Creating an Opening Paragraph

Capture your reader's attention in the first line of your essay. Introduce the topic, state its importance, and then provide a thesis statement. Here are some strategies for beginning your essay:

Review

See Chapter 6, LO3, if you are having difficulty creating an opening paragraph.

Building Interest:

- **Find an eye-popping statistic.**

    Roughly one-eighth of the world's population lacks access to safe water supplies, while as many as 2.5 billion people live without sanitized water.

- **Connect to the reader.**

    Saving for the future may seem impossible while you're in school.

- **Make a bold statement.**

    Simply put, cheese packs some powerful eating enjoyment.

- **Ask a question.**

    Have you ever wondered how a dolphin, an air-breathing creature, is born at sea?

- **Begin with action.**

    Your chest tightens, throat clenching and unclenching; your tongue undulates, mouth opening and closing; and vibrating puffs of air burst forth—you speak.

Write Create your opening paragraph. Start with a sentence that uses one of the strategies above. Then write sentences that build to your thesis statement.

Writing a Thesis Statement

Once you have your reader's attention, lead up to your thesis statement. Here are a few things to keep in mind when writing a thesis statement for a process essay:

(1) Mention the **specific process** that your essay will be discussing. See Chapter 5, LO5, for suggestions on how to focus your thesis statement.

(2) Provide an **overview of the main steps** involved in the process, if possible. Doing so will help your reader understand the overall organization of your essay. However, providing an overview may not always be practical if there are too many steps.

Review

See Chapter 5, LO5, if you need to review how to create a working thesis statement.

(3) State what the **outcome** of the process so your reader knows what will happen if the steps are followed correctly.

If expressed as a formula, the thesis statements for "Making Dirty Water Drinkable" and "Flunking with Style" would look like this:

A Specific Process	Overview of Main Steps	Outcome	Thesis Statement
water purification	(1) pre-treatment (2) coagulation (3) filtration (4) disinfection	Safe drinking water	Water purification plants remove harmful impurities through a process of pre-treatment, coagulation, filtration, and disinfection, making our water safe to drink.
failing a class with style	(1) anger teachers (2) hate your studies (3) cheat on your work	Failing grade	To fail your year in the grand style, you must antagonize your teachers, disdain your studies, and cheat on your work.

Write Use the following formula to create your thesis statement.

A Specific Process	Overview of Main Steps	Outcome	Thesis Statement

Review

See Chapter 6, LO4, for more information about making a "point" in your thesis statement.

Another way of creating a thesis statement for a process essay is to make a **point** about the process. This is often done in situations where there are multiple ways of accomplishing a given task and you want to make the point that your way is the best.

Process and Outcome	Point about Process	Thesis Statement
Synchronizing your blog, newsfeed, and social media	Not as difficult to do as people think	Setting your blog, newsfeed, and social media to automatically synchronize is actually very easy.

Process and Outcome	Point about Process	Thesis Statement
Killing a zombie by destroying its brain	Most efficiently done with repeated blows to the head with a blunt weapon	While there are many ways to kill a zombie, using a blunt weapon is the most effective.

Write Use the following formula to create a thesis statement that makes a point about your process.

Process and Outcome	Point about Process	Thesis Statement

Creating Middle Paragraphs

Write Clearly describe each step in the process. Present the steps in a way that your least knowledgeable reader will be able to follow and understand; be sure to define any special terms. If any special equipment is needed, or if there are any safety issues involved with the procedure, include this information. Also remember to create topic sentences for your paragraphs and use transitional words or phrases to make the writing flow.

Review

See Chapter 6, LO5, for suggestions on how to develop your middle paragraphs.

Review

See Chapter 6, LO6, to review effective closing strategies.

Creating a Closing Paragraph

The final paragraph should help to "set" the process in the reader's mind. You might review the most important details and end by restating your main point, or you might conclude with a reminder of the significance of the process.

Write Create the closing paragraph for your process essay.

Adding a Title

Make sure to add an attention-getting title. Here are two simple strategies for creating one.

- **Use alliteration:** Fighting the Flu
- **Describe the process:** Making Cheese; Making Dirty Water Drinkable

LO4 Revising: Improving the Writing

Revising your first draft involves adding, deleting, rearranging, and reworking parts of your writing. Revision begins with a peer review.

Peer Review

Sharing your writing at various stages is important, especially when you review and revise a first draft. The feedback that you receive will help you change and improve your essay.

Respond Complete this response sheet after reading the first draft of a classmate's essay. Then share the sheet with the writer. (Keep your comments helpful and positive.)

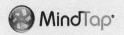
Essay title: _____

Writer: _____ Reviewer: _____

1. Which part of the essay seems to work best—opening, middle, or closing? Why?

   _____

   _____

   _____

2. Which part of the essay needs work—opening, middle, or closing? Why? _____

   _____

   _____

   _____

   _____

3. Do the middle paragraphs clearly present each step of the process? Explain.

   _____

   _____

   _____

4. Do you understand the process after reading the essay?

   _____

   _____

5. Identify a phrase or two that shows the writer's level of interest.

   _____

   _____

Using Transitions That Show Time Order

Transitions or linking words connect ideas by showing the relationships between them. In process writing, time-order transition words provide the link between the steps of the process and add coherence to the writing overall. Refer to the following list of time-order transition words as you revise your essay: *before, during, after, next, finally, first, second, third, then, later, when, once, while, at, meanwhile*

Traits

Transition words signal organization and improve sentence fluency.

Revising in Action

Read aloud the unrevised and then revised version of the following excerpt. Note how time-order transition words tie the steps of the process together while improving the flow of the writing.

> During pre-treatment,
> The first step in water purification is pre-treatment. Water is pumped in from
>
> Next, c
> its source. Coagulation begins. Coagulation removes dirt and other particles
>
> from the water by adding a chemical that forms sticky particles called "floc."
>
> Once inside the basin,
> . . . The combined weight of the dirt and floc mixture causes it to sink to the
>
> floor as sedimentation.

Revise Take a break from your writing. Then come back to it with fresh eyes. If possible, have a friend or family member read the essay and then follow your written instructions to perform the process while you watch to see what may not be clear. Then review your writing with the following checklist. Keep polishing until you can answer every question with a "yes."

Revising Checklist

Ideas:

☐ **1.** Do I explain an interesting process?

☐ **2.** Do I include all the steps in the process?

Thesis:

☐ **3.** Do I identify a specific process?

☐ **4.** Do I provide an overview of the main steps?

☐ **5.** Do I note the outcome?

☐ **6.** If appropriate, do I make a point about the process?

Organization:

☐ **7.** Does the essay have effective opening, middle, and closing paragraphs?

☐ **8.** Are the steps in a logical order?

☐ **9.** Have I used time-order transitions to connect my ideas?

Voice:

☐ **10.** Do I use an informed, respectful voice?

☐ **11.** Does my interest in the topic come through?

LO5 Editing: Correcting Your Writing

The main work of editing is correcting your revised draft.

Editing an Essay

Before you finish editing your revised essay, you can practise by editing the following model.

Edit Read the following process essay, looking for problems listed in the Editing Checklist. Also refer to the list of common errors in Chapter 8, LO5. Correct the model using the marks to the left. The first correction has been done for you.

Correction Marks

⌐ delete

d capitalize
=

D lowercase

∧ insert

∧ add comma

? add question
∧ mark

word add word
∧

⊙ add period

⬭ spelling

⎍ switch

Fighting the Flu

Flu season is a bummer. For some people, ~~its~~ it's downright dangerous.   *1*
Every year in Canada, influenza is responsible for 12 000 hospitalizations
and around 3500 deaths. Many people opt to receive a yearly flu vaccine,
which reduce there chances of getting the flu. The type of influenza vaccine
given out each year are created through a multi-faceted process.   *5*

The first step is surveyllance. Throughout the year, scientists survey the
globe to predict which strains of the influenza virus will dominate the next flu
season. A vaccine can protect against three different strains, so this step helps
decide which strains to put in the vaccine. Next, the World Health Organization
confirms the dominant strains and submits their recommendation to health   *10*
regulators like Health Canada and the Food and drug Administration (FDA).
Health These Organizations then distributes seeds of the three strains to
manufacturers for production.

After surveillance and strain selection, the manufacturing of vaccines begins.
In this step, each virous strain is produced separately. Later combined to make   *15*
one vaccine. Manufacturing begins by injecting millions of chicken eggs with the
virus strains, which develop. The virus fluid is then given a chemical treatment,
so that the virus is disrupted and will stop spreading. What's left of the strain is
combined. With the other two strains. Lastly, the regulatory organizations tests
the vaccine concentrate to make sure it is acceptable for immunization.   *20*

The result is an influenza vaccine that is distributed in viles and syringes
to clinics throughout the world during flu season. After the vaccine is injected
it takes about two weeks for a body to develop immunity to the three strains.
When flu season ends, the process of creating next year's vaccine begins again.

Correcting Your Essay

Now it's time to correct your own essay.

Edit Create a clean copy of your essay and use the following checklist to look for errors. Continue working until you can check off each item in the list.

Editing Checklist

Word Choice

- ☐ **1.** Have I used specific nouns and verbs? (See Chapter 8, LO1.)

- ☐ **2.** Have I used more action verbs than "be" verbs? (See Chapter 32, LO1.)

Sentence Fluency

- ☐ **3.** Have I varied the beginnings and lengths of sentences? (See Chapter 25, LO2.)

- ☐ **4.** Have I combined short choppy sentences? (See Chapter 25, LO1.)

- ☐ **5.** Have I avoided improper shifts in sentences? (See Chapter 29, LO2.)

Conventions

- ☐ **6.** Have I avoided fragments and run-ons? (See Chapter 27, LO1 and LO2; Chapter 28, LO2.)

- ☐ **7.** Do I use correct verb forms (*he saw*, not *he seen*)? (See Chapter 32, LO4.)

- ☐ **8.** Do my subjects and verbs agree (*she speaks,* not *she speak*)? (See Chapter 26, LOs 1–4.)

- ☐ **9.** Have I used consistent verb tense in all steps? (See Chapter 29, LO2.)

- ☐ **10.** Have I used the right words (*their, there, they're*)?

- ☐ **11.** Have I capitalized first words and proper nouns and adjectives? (See Chapter 39, LO1.)

- ☐ **12.** Have I used commas after long introductory word groups? (See Chapter 35, LO2.)

- ☐ **13.** Have I carefully checked my spelling?

Documentation Checklist (see Chapter 9)

Format

- ☐ **1.** Have I followed the proper formatting conventions? (See Chapter 9, LO5 and LO6.)

In-Text Citation

- ☐ **2.** Have I properly documented any sources in the body of my writing? (See Chapter 9, LO1–LO4.)

Bibliography

- ☐ **3.** Do I have a references or works cited page? (See Chapter 9, LO1–LO4.)

Create Prepare a clean copy of your essay and carefully proofread it.

LO6 Reviewing Process Writing

Complete these activities as needed to help you better understand how to write process essays.

Reflect on the experience.

Learning Outcome

Organize Think about your professional goals. What do you want to do? Where do you want to work? How can you get there? In the graphic below, identify your goal and lay out five steps to achieving it. For each step, write a transition word or phrase that links the first steps to the second and so on. (See LO4 for a list of time-order transition words.)

Goal: _____

Transitions	Steps
1	
2	
3	
4	
5	

Learning like never before.

www.nelson.com/student

"The murals in restaurants are on par with the food in museums."
—Peter De Vries

DreamPictures/Taxi/Getty Images

20

Comparison–Contrast Essay

The photo above is full of contrasts: bare glass versus painted brick, straight lines versus curves and jags, tan walls versus an explosion of colour, architecture versus painting. The photo also contains some surprising comparisons. The building and the mural both serve the neighbourhood. There are buildings painted in the mural.

An essay that examines similarities and differences is called a comparison–contrast essay. By looking at the similarities and differences between two things, you can come to understand both things better.

This chapter will guide you through the process of writing an essay that compares and contrasts two places that you know well.

What do you think?

What similarities and differences are there between artwork and food?

Learning Outcomes

LO1 Understand comparison–contrast essays.

LO2 Plan a comparison–contrast essay.

LO3 Write the first draft.

LO4 Revise the essay.

LO5 Edit the essay.

LO6 Reflect on the experience.

L○1 Reviewing a Comparison–Contrast Essay

A comparison–contrast essay shows the similarities and differences between two subjects. In the following essay, a writer compares his bedroom to his sister's.

Read/React Read the following essay. Then complete the analysis on the next page.

Life in a War Zone

The **opening** catches the reader's interest and leads to the **thesis statement**.

"How do you ever find anything in here?" my sister asks. We're looking for her cellphone, which I borrowed last night, and which I left in my room. "It's like a bomb went off." She's right. Compared to Amaya's room, mine is a disaster. Maybe that's because I'm a guy. Maybe that's because I only sleep there. The differences between my room and Amaya's tell a lot about who we are. *5*

The first **middle paragraph** describes one subject.

I couldn't survive in my sister's room. For one thing, it's pink. She's three years younger than me, and she's still into pink, though the princess posters are down and posters of pop stars cover everything. It's like a hundred people staring at you. *10* Amaya has three chests of drawers, neatly closed, and a closet full of clothes, some of which belong to her friends. She's also got Grandma's old vanity, with three big mirrors and little drawers for makeup. Weirdest of all, she manages to get dirty clothes in the hamper, which means you can see the floor. *15*

The second **middle paragraph** describes the other subject.

Now, Amaya couldn't survive in my room, either. The walls are black. I painted them that way in protest when Amaya painted hers pink. I've got no posters on the walls, only some old high-school art projects I did and never took down. There's just one chest of drawers, and the drawers are never closed, and the clothes are *20* hanging out or stacked on top. I don't have a hamper, so my floor is the hamper. The only important thing in my room is my bed, because that's where I crash. Of course, the bed is never made.

The **closing** sums up the comparison and contrast, providing an additional perspective.

Our two different rooms show our different personalities. Amaya thinks a lot about how she looks and what people think of *25* her. She also spends a lot of time in her room. I don't care about my looks. Engines are my thing, building them and fixing them, which means grease, which means fashion can't be a priority. Amaya might think my room is a health hazard, but I'd die in her room. (By the way, we did find her cellphone, not because I knew where *30* I put it, but because I decided to call it.)

A Closer Look

This essay used a subject-by-subject pattern of organization, describing one subject before moving to the other. This organizational pattern works best when focusing on the contrasts between two subjects.

Analyze Reread the essay on the previous page. As you do, use the following T-chart to analyze the essay. In the first column, write details that describe the author's room. In the second column, write details that describe his sister's room.

Vocabulary

subject-by-subject pattern of organization
a pattern in which one subject is fully described before moving on to the other

Author's Room	Sister's Room

Explain The writer of the essay creates a parallel description of his sister's room and his own room. What do you think a "parallel description" is?

LO2 Prewriting: Planning

In your own essay, you, too, will compare and contrast two places that you know well. Because you will be using subject-by-subject organization, choose two places with interesting contrasts. The activity below will help you select two places to write about.

Selecting a Topic

Select After each general heading, write the names of two specific places you know enough about to compare and contrast. Then select the two places you would most like to write about in your essay.

Buildings	1. _____	2. _____
Businesses	1. _____	2. _____
Natural wonders	1. _____	2. _____
Neighbourhoods	1. _____	2. _____
Restaurants	1. _____	2. _____

Describing the Places

Describe Answer each question below, jotting down details about the two places.

1. What three adjectives best describe this place?

    Place 1: _____

    Place 2: _____

2. What is the main feature of this place?

    Place 1: _____

    Place 2: _____

3. What is the feeling you get in this place?

    Place 1: _____

    Place 2: _____

4. Why do you want to write about this place?

    Place 1: _____

    Place 2: _____

Gathering Details

A Venn diagram will help you gather more details as you plan your comparison–contrast essay. The following diagram compares and contrasts two restaurants, listing unique details about each as well as similarities.

Venn Diagram

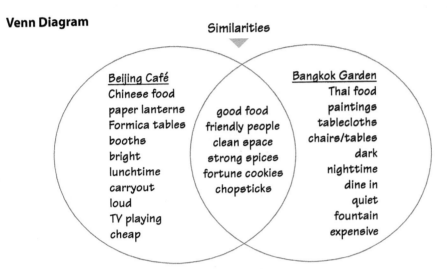

Similarities

Beijing Café
Chinese food
paper lanterns
Formica tables
booths
bright
lunchtime
carryout
loud
TV playing
cheap

good food
friendly people
clean space
strong spices
fortune cookies
chopsticks

Bangkok Garden
Thai food
paintings
tablecloths
chairs/tables
dark
nighttime
dine in
quiet
fountain
expensive

Gather Complete the Venn diagram below. Write the name of one place in one circle and the name of the other place in the other. Next, list the details specific to each place. In the overlapping part, write the things that the two places have in common.

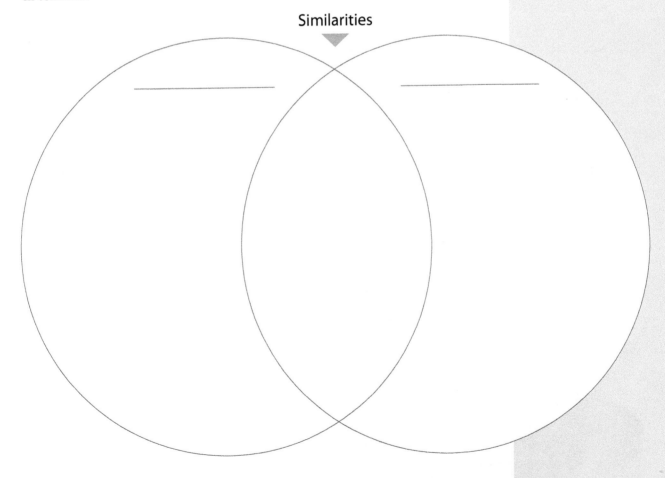

Similarities

LO3 Writing: Creating a First Draft

Creating a first draft puts all of your planning and gathering into concrete form. Provided below is a sample essay that is organized subject by subject.

Read/React Read the essay, noting how the writer created an effective opening and closing for the subject-by-subject comparison.

Two Tastes of Asia

Opening paragraph

What's the difference between Chinese and Thai food? That's what I wondered when a Thai restaurant opened just down the street from my favourite Chinese restaurant. Soon, I had two favourites. <u>The difference between Chinese and Thai cuisine is only the start of the differences between the Beijing Café and the Bangkok Garden.</u>

Thesis statement

Subject 1

The Beijing Café has been my favourite because of its inexpensive food and bright, busy atmosphere. The food is excellent, from the sizzling Chairman Mao's chicken to the extra spicy Szechuan vegetables, and lunch portions are priced below $5. Such prices mean the restaurant has basic decorations like paper lanterns and a utilitarian interior, with Formica tables and plastic booths. The fluorescent lights overhead make the place bright, and the constant traffic of people on lunch break makes the place a loud, busy hangout.

Subject 2

The Bangkok Garden offers a completely different experience. The food is similar to Chinese food, but with coconut milk and different spices. The prices, though, are higher, partly because Bangkok Garden is more of a dinner place. The walls are covered in elegant paintings and tapestries, and candles give a warm glow to cloth-covered tables. As a result, the Bangkok Garden is a quieter spot, more for dates than for high-schoolers on a lunch break.

Closing paragraph

Both restaurants have great food and friendly staff, and both offer chopsticks and fortune cookies. As I've said, they both are favourites of mine. When I'm hungry at lunchtime and need a quick, inexpensive, and delicious meal, I go with friends over to the Beijing Café. And when I'm hungry at dinnertime and want a romantic dinner, I head to the Bangkok Garden. At first, it seemed a waste to have a Chinese restaurant and a Thai restaurant so close together, but they are more different than they are alike.

Jacek Chabraszewski/Shutterstock.com

Creating an Opening Paragraph

The opening paragraph needs to capture the reader's attention and introduce your thesis statement. Here are some strategies for beginning your essay.

Review

See Chapter 6, LO3, if you are having difficulty creating an opening paragraph.

Opening Strategies:

- **Start with a surprising statement.**
  My two favourite restaurants feature food from the other side of the world.
- **Begin with a question.**
  What's the difference between Chinese and Thai food?
- **Use a quotation.**
  "You will soon have two favourites," read the fortune cookie.
- **Share an anecdote.**
  The first time I walked into Bangkok Garden, I was nervous. . . .

Writing a Thesis Statement

To create a thesis statement for your essay, follow this formula.

Review

If you need to review thesis statements, see Chapter 5, LO5, and Chapter 6, LO4.

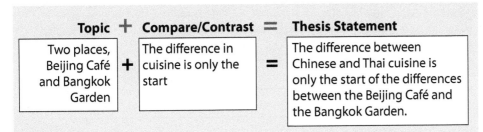

Topic	+	Compare/Contrast	=	Thesis Statement
Two places, Beijing Café and Bangkok Garden	+	The difference in cuisine is only the start	=	The difference between Chinese and Thai cuisine is only the start of the differences between the Beijing Café and the Bangkok Garden.

Write Create your opening paragraph. Start with a sentence that uses one of the strategies above. Then write sentences that build to your thesis statement.

Creating Middle Paragraphs

Write Refer to the Venn diagram you completed earlier as part of LO2 as you develop the middle two paragraphs of your essay. Use one paragraph to describe the first place and another to describe the second place, creating topic sentences for each. Use the transitional words at the left to make your writing flow.

Studio DMM Photography, Designs & Art/Shutterstock.com

Creating a Closing Paragraph

The closing paragraph of your essay should sum up the comparison and contrast and provide a final thought for the reader.

Write Answer the following questions to help you sum up your essay.

1. What key similarity do the two places exhibit?

   _____

   _____

2. What is the key difference between the two places?

   _____

   _____

3. What have I learned from writing this essay?

   _____

   _____

Review

See Chapter 6, LO6, to review effective closing strategies.

Write Create the closing paragraph for your comparison–contrast essay.

_____

_____

_____

_____

_____

_____

_____

_____

_____

_____

_____

_____

Adding a Title

Make sure to add an attention-getting title. Here are three simple strategies for creating one.

- **Use a phrase from the essay:** Cars Have Souls
- **Point to a similarity or difference:** Great Food, Worlds Apart
- **Use the word "versus":** Pink Versus Black

Speaking & Listening

Have your partner read your essay aloud. Then complete the response sheet together.

 MindTap·

For more information, check out the Bonus Online Chapter on peer reviewing.

LO4 Revising: Improving the Writing

Revising your first draft involves adding, deleting, rearranging, and reworking parts of your writing. Revision begins with a peer review.

Peer Review

Sharing your writing at various stages is important, especially when you review and revise a first draft. The feedback that you receive will help you change and improve your essay.

Respond Complete this response sheet after reading the first draft of a classmate's essay. Then share the sheet with the writer. (Keep your comments helpful and positive.)

Essay title: _____

Writer: _____ Reviewer: _____

1. Which part of the essay seems to work best—opening, middle, or closing? Why?

   _____

   _____

   _____

   _____

2. Which part of the essay needs work—opening, middle, or closing? Why? _____

   _____

   _____

3. Which contrasting points about the two subjects caught your attention? Name three.

   a. _____

   b. _____

   c. _____

4. Name two favourite details.

   a. _____

   b. _____

5. Identify a phrase or two that shows the writer's level of interest.

   _____

   _____

   _____

Adding Sensory Details

Your essay will be stronger if you show similarities and differences, rather than just telling about them. Consider the sensory details listed below and used to describe one of the restaurants in the essay "Two Tastes of Asia." Build your own chart of sensory details to enhance your writing.

Senses	Sensory Detail
Sight	paper lanterns, bright, fluorescents
Hearing	sizzle, loud, traffic
Smell	chicken, Szechuan vegetables
Taste	extra spicy
Touch	plastic booths

Revising in Action

Read aloud the unrevised and revised version of the following excerpt. Note how adding sensory details makes the description much richer.

> *sizzling*   *extra spicy*
> The food is excellent, from the Chairman Mao's chicken to the Szechuan
>
> vegetables, and lunch portions are priced below $5. Such prices mean the
>
> *like paper lanterns*   *Formica*
> restaurant has basic decorations and a utilitarian interior, with tables
>
> *plastic*
> and booths. . . .

Revise Improve your writing, using the following checklist and your partner's comments on the response sheet. Continue revising until you can check off each item in the list.

Ideas

☐ **1.** Do I compare two places?

☐ **2.** Do I include sensory details that make the places come to life?

Organization

☐ **3.** Does my opening capture the reader's interest and present a thesis statement?

☐ **4.** Have I used a subject-by-subject pattern in the middle part?

☐ **5.** Have I used transitions to connect my sentences?

☐ **6.** Does my closing sum up the comparison and contrast effectively?

Voice

☐ **7.** Do I sound knowledgeable about my subjects?

☐ **8.** Is my interest obvious to the reader?

Vocabulary

sensory details
what can be seen, heard, smelled, tasted, or touched.

LO5 Editing: Correcting Your Writing

The main work of editing is correcting your revised draft.

Editing an Essay

Before you start editing your revised essay, practise editing the following model.

Edit Read this comparison–contrast essay, looking for problems listed in the checklist on the facing page. Also refer to the list of common errors Chapter 8, LO5. Correct the model using the marks listed to the left. One correction has been done for you.

Correction Marks

ℐ	delete
d	capitalize
D̸	lowercase
∧	insert
⌃	add comma
? ∧	add question mark
word ∧	add word
⊙	add period
◯	spelling
∿	switch

A Commuter's Best Friend

spend

I ~~spends~~ much of my day in my car, an ice-blue Toyota Prius. Its a hybrid   1

which means it's much better for my commute to school than my old Taurus.

Still, I loved that old beater. It carried me safely and faithfully. Through many

winters. Aside from being the same colour, my new Prius and my old Taurus

couldn't be more different.   5

The Taurus was a fifteen-year-old workhorse it had four doors, room for

six, and a trunk to hold all their stuff. The interior is no-frills, with manual

windows, a stereo and tape deck, and two speakers. Nothing is digital. In its

last years, the Taurus been leaking every fluid I put in it, but still it soldiered

on—getting probably twenty miles to the gallon.   10

The Prius is brand new and a little delicate. It weighs about half as much

as the Taurus, and though it has four doors, it really has room only for four

people. It has power everything and a GPS navagation system. As I back up

the Prius the digital console even shows me a picture of what's behind me.

this hybrid is super quiet in the city and gets about twice the mileage of the   15

Taurus.

I think cars have souls, and my taurus was a good friend to me. It read

me a lot of books on tape, and it never left me stranded when I needed it. I'm

still getting used to this Prius, and I hope we'll be friends, too. Heaven knows,

we spend plenty of time together.   20

TIM MCCAIG/iStockphoto.com

Correcting Your Essay

Now it's time to correct your own essay.

Edit Prepare a clean copy of your essay and use the following checklist to look for errors. Continue working until you can check off each item in the list.

Other Classes

You can use this checklist for editing your writing in any class.

Editing Checklist

Word Choice

☐ **1.** Have I used specific nouns and verbs? (See Chapter 8, LO1.)

☐ **2.** Have I used more action verbs than "be" verbs? (See Chapter 32, LO1.)

Sentence Fluency

☐ **3.** Have I used sentences with varying beginnings and lengths? (See Chapter 25, LO2.)

☐ **4.** Have I combined short choppy sentences? (See Chapter 25, LO1.)

☐ **5.** Have I avoided improper shifts in sentences? (See Chapter 29, LO2.)

Conventions

☐ **6.** Have I avoided fragments and run-ons? (See Chapter 27, LO1 and LO2, Chapter 28, LO2.)

☐ **7.** Do I use correct verb forms (*he saw,* not *he seen*)? (See Chapter 32, LO4.)

☐ **8.** Do my subjects and verbs agree (*she speaks,* not *she speak*)? (See Chapter 26, LOs 1–4.)

☐ **9.** Have I used the right words (*their, there, they're*)?

☐ **10.** Have I capitalized first words and proper nouns and adjectives? (See Chapter 39, LO1.)

☐ **11.** Have I used commas after long introductory word groups and to set off extra information? (See Chapter 35, LO2.)

☐ **12.** Have I carefully checked my spelling?

Documentation Checklist

Format

☐ **1.** Have I followed the proper formatting conventions? (See Chapter 9, LO5 and LO6.)

In-Text Citation

☐ **2.** Have I properly documented any sources in the body of my writing? (See Chapter 9, LO1–LO4.)

Bibliography

☐ **3.** Do I have a references or works cited page? (See Chapter 9, LO1–LO4.)

Create Prepare a clean final copy of your essay and proofread it.

LO6 Reviewing Comparison Writing

Complete these activities as needed to help you better understand how to write comparison–contrast essays.

Paul Matthew Photography/Shutterstock.com

Compare/Contrast Consider the woman and child in this photograph. How are they alike? How are they different? Fill in the following Venn diagram, describing the two people.

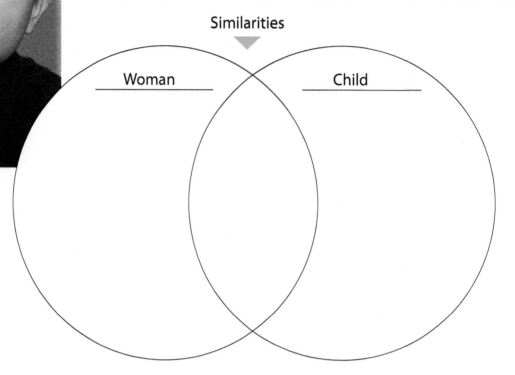

Similarities

Woman   Child

Match For each organizational pattern below, draw a line to connect it to its description.

1. Similarities–differences

2. Point-by-point

3. Subject-by-subject

- an organizational pattern focusing first on one subject and then on the other

- a pattern in which one point of comparison is discussed for both subjects before moving on to the next point

- an organizational pattern dealing with how subjects are alike and how they are different

Sort Circle transitions that *contrast*:

| although | as well | like | much as | otherwise | while | similarly |

"The cause is hidden. The effect is visible to all."

—Ovid

© Julia Christe/fstop/Corbis

21 Cause–Effect Essay

Why? It's such a simple word, but it digs deep. When you ask *why*, you are searching for the cause of something. And there are many different causes. A mother who asks why her son has cancer likely needs a different answer than a researcher who asks the same question.

This chapter is all about asking *why* in the form of an essay. You'll read essays that explore the causes and effects of phenomena in the world, and you'll write a similar essay yourself. All the while, keep asking *why?*

Learning Outcomes

LO1 Understand cause–effect essays.

LO2 Plan a cause–effect essay.

LO3 Write the first draft.

LO4 Revise the essay.

LO5 Edit the essay.

LO6 Reflect on the experience.

What do you think?

What are the possible causes of the fire in the photo above? What are the likely effects?

_____

_____

_____

_____

_____

_____

_____

LO1 Reviewing a Cause–Effect Essay

A cause–effect essay discusses why something happens (the causes) and what results (the effects). In the following essay, a writer looks at the causes and effects of a spicy diet.

Read/React Read the following essay. Then complete the analysis on the next page.

Why Eat That Stuff?

The **opening** catches the reader's attention and leads to the **thesis statement**.

I love spicy food. In fact, I have a theory that food gets better the closer you get to the equator. At the poles, people eat seal blubber and lutefisk, but at the equator, people eat tacos and teriyaki, curry and jalapenos. People who don't like spicy foods wonder what all the fuss is about. There are many reasons people use spices in their foods, and many benefits from doing so.   *1*

5

The first **middle paragraph** discusses causes.

The main reasons for using spice are to make food taste better and to help preserve it. Without salt, pepper, and other basic spices, foods taste bland. In the Middle Ages, explorers like Marco Polo set up trade routes to get desperately needed spices for European foods. Some spices were worth their weight in gold. These spices didn't grow in northern climates, and they weren't needed as much for food preservation as in the equatorial regions, but people still wanted them for taste.   *10*

The second **middle paragraph** discusses effects.

New studies show that spicy foods also have surprising health benefits. A recent study published in the *British Journal of Medicine* showed that women who added hot peppers to their food ate fewer calories in later meals than women who didn't. At the University of California, Los Angeles, scientists found that the substance curcumin, which makes tumeric yellow, clears plaque out of brains, helping stop Alzheimer's disease. And at the State University of New York, researchers found that capsaicin—what makes hot peppers hot—causes endorphins to be released, making the eater feel happy. Other studies show that capsaicin might even help kill off cancer cells in the digestive tract.   *15*

20

25

The **closing** sums up the causes and ties them back to the opening.

So, when I order a Szechuan chicken lunch special, extra hot, why do I do it? Well, partly it's because of the taste—I've grown to really love hot food. Partly it's for the health benefits that I'm getting eating it. But, to be honest, partly it's because I like to see the look of horror on my friends' faces when I start sweating but keep shovelling it in.   *30*

Vocabulary

lutefisk
pickled fish; traditional Norwegian dish

plaque
unhealthy buildup of material

Szechuan
spicy type of food from the Szechuan region of China

A Closer Look

This essay first looks at causes of eating spicy foods, and then looks at effects. This pattern works best for an essay that focuses equally on both cause and effect.

Analyze Reread the essay "Why Eat That Stuff?" As you do, fill in the cause–effect chart below. On the left, write causes of eating spicy food and draw lines to connect them. On the right, write effects of eating spicy foods. Start with the causes and effects in the essay, but feel free to add causes and effects of your own.

Causes	Effects

Explain Do you like to eat spicy foods or not? Explain why you do or do not like to eat spicy foods. Describe the effects you experience if you eat something spicy.

LO2 Prewriting: Planning

You will be writing a cause–effect essay about some lifestyle choice. You need a topic that interests you and that you know a good deal about—or are willing to find out about. You also need a topic that has specific causes and effects.

Selecting a Topic

Brainstorm In each column below, brainstorm possible topics for your cause–effect essay. Sample topics have been provided in each category. Try to think of three or four more topics in each. Then select one topic that you would like to explore, tracing causes and effects.

Lifestyle Choices

Eating	Activities	Style	Pastimes	Habits
vegetarianism	rock climbing	dreadlocks	suduko	smoking

Freewrite After you select a topic that you would like to write a cause–effect essay about, freewrite about the topic. Write about causes of it and effects from it. Then review your freewriting to make sure this is a topic you want to explore. If it is not, choose a new topic and freewrite about it.

Gathering Details

As you gather details about your topic, think of what you already know and what you need to find out. Do whatever research it takes for you to find out about your topic. Then complete a cause–effect chart, like the one below, listing the causes and effects of your topic.

Cause–Effect Chart

Topic: Vegetarianism

Causes	Effects
Concern for animals	Vegans vs. ovo-lacto
Opposition to "factory farming"	Greater awareness
Healthful lifestyle	Greater health
Home-grown food	More sustainable lifestyle
Personal preference	Need for proteins
Peer pressure/social reasons	Struggles in society

Gather Complete the following cause–effect chart by writing your topic at the top and listing causes and effects in their columns.

Cause–Effect Chart

Topic: _____

Causes	Effects

LO3 Writing: Creating a First Draft

Creating a first draft puts all of your planning and gathering into concrete form. Provided below is a sample essay that is organized subject by subject.

Read/React Read the essay, noting how the writer created an effective opening and closing for the cause–effect essay.

Herbivore, Carnivore, or Omnivore?

Opening paragraph

Thesis statement

"We've spent thousands of years getting to the top of the food chain, so why go back to eating leaves?" That's what people sometimes ask vegans and vegetarians, wondering why anyone would choose a meat-free diet. Vegetarians have many reasons for choosing a meat-free diet, but the diet results in the same basic benefits. — 1

— 5

Causes

Every vegetarian is unique, with unique reasons for eating what they eat. Many see animals as more than meat—creatures with intelligence and feelings. These vegetarians don't like the idea of killing animals for food, especially not in the overcrowded and inhumane factory farms of today. Other vegetarians reject modern North American eating habits, with too much meat and too few vegetables. The U.S. Department of Agriculture recommends that people "go lean on protein" and eat even less fat. However, average Americans eat 16 percent of their daily calories in proteins and 44 percent in fat; Canadian diets are not much different. Vegetarians seek a healthier diet and a more sustainable lifestyle. And for some, it's just a matter of personal preference. They just would rather have a salad. — 10

— 15

Effects

For most vegetarians, their choice has very positive effects. Vegetarians have to think about what they eat and where it comes from, and therefore they tend to eat better quality food and less of it. As a result, vegetarians are often slimmer than omnivores and less prone to arteriosclerosis and colon cancer—caused by fatty red meats. Vegetarians feel they live a more sustainable lifestyle, with less impact on the natural world. Still, vegans and vegetarians have their struggles. Many restaurants have meat in just about every dish, including soups and salads, making it a challenge to eat out. Ads and consumer culture also push vegetarians to eat meat. And vegetarians have to be careful to find proteins that can replace those that others get from eating meat. — 20

— 25

— 30

Closing paragraph

The vegetarian lifestyle offers numerous benefits physically and spiritually to a person who chooses it. But the lifestyle isn't for everyone. People with poor impulse control will have a hard time resisting the flow of society at large. And growing children and adolescents must be careful to get enough of the proteins and fats they need to keep growing. The lifestyle doesn't work for everyone, but some people wouldn't have it any other way. — 35

Creating an Opening Paragraph

The opening paragraph needs to capture the reader's attention and introduce the thesis statement. Here are some strategies.

Opening Strategies:

- **Start with an interesting quotation:**
  "We've spent thousands of years getting to the top of the food chain, so why go back to eating leaves?"

- **Begin with a startling fact:**
  For more than four millennia, the "meat of the Orient" hasn't been meat at all, but soybeans.

- **Share an anecdote:**
  When I decided to become a vegetarian, my friends looked at me as if I had joined a cult.

- **Begin with a question:**
  How many animals does the average American eat in a year?

Writing a Thesis Statement:

To create a thesis statement for your essay, follow this formula.

Topic	+	Causes or Effects	=	Thesis Statement
vegetarianism		different reasons for choosing it, but the same benefits		Vegetarians have many reasons for choosing a meat-free diet, but the diet results in the same basic benefits.

Write Create your opening paragraph. Start with a sentence that uses one of the strategies above. Then write sentences that build to your thesis statement.

Traits

Using a variety of details strengthens your ideas and broadens your thinking.

Review

See Chapter 6, LO3, if you are having difficulty creating an opening paragraph.

Review

If you need to review thesis statements, see Chapter 5, LO5, and Chapter 6, LO4.

Creating Middle Paragraphs

Write Refer to the cause–effect chart you created earlier as you develop the middle two paragraphs of your essay. Use one paragraph to describe the causes of the lifestyle choice and another to describe the effects of it. Create a topic sentence for each paragraph. Use transition words from the list at the left to make your writing flow.

Traits

Transitions that show causes and effects:
as a result / because / consequently / due to the fact that / every time that / inevitably / resulting in / since / therefore

Review

See Chapter 6, LO5, for suggestions on how to develop your middle paragraphs.

Studio DMM Photography, Designs & Art/Shutterstock.com

Creating a Closing Paragraph

The closing paragraph of your essay should revisit the causes and effects of the topic and connect to the ideas in the introduction.

Review

See Chapter 6, LO6, to review effective closing strategies.

Write Answer the following questions to help you sum up the causes and effects.

1. What is the most important cause of the lifestyle choice?

   _____

   _____

2. What is the most important effect?

   _____

   _____

3. What final point could you leave your reader with?

   _____

   _____

Write Create the closing paragraph for your cause–effect essay.

_____

_____

_____

_____

_____

_____

_____

_____

_____

Adding a Title

Make sure to add an attention-getting title. Here are three simple strategies for writing titles.

- **Ask a question:** Why Eat That stuff?
- **Use the word "or":** Herbivore or Carnivore
- **Repeat the sounds of letters:** Staying in Step

Speaking & Listening

Have your partner read your essay aloud. Then complete the response sheet together.

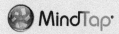

For more information, check out the Bonus Online Chapter on peer reviewing.

LO4 Revising: Improving the Writing

Revising your first draft involves adding, deleting, rearranging, and reworking parts of your writing. Revision begins with a peer review.

Peer Review

Sharing your writing at various stages is important, especially when you review and revise a first draft. The feedback that you receive will help you change and improve your essay.

Respond Complete this response sheet after reading the first draft of a classmate's essay. Then share the sheet with the writer. (Keep your comments helpful and positive.)

Essay title: _____

Writer: _____ Reviewer: _____

1. Which part of the essay seems to work best—opening, middle, or closing? Why?

   _____

   _____

   _____

2. Which part of the essay needs work—opening, middle, or closing? Why? _____

   _____

   _____

   _____

3. Which cause–effect details caught your attention? Name three.

   a. _____

   b. _____

   c. _____

4. Write two other details that might be included.

   a. _____

   b. _____

5. Identify a phrase or two that shows the writer's level of interest.

   _____

   _____

   _____

Using a Variety of Details

Your essay will be stronger if you use a variety of details to support your point. Different types of details provide different types of support.

Facts ground your essay in reality.

> The U.S. Department of Agriculture recommends that people "go lean on protein" and eat even less fat.

Statistics quantify facts.

> However, average Americans 16 percent of their daily calories in proteins and 44 percent in fat.

Quotations from an expert lend support to your point.

> Chris Woolston of the Consumer Health interactive says, "Fatty, unbalanced, and oversized: That, in a nutshell, is the American diet."

Anecdotes share an experience from real life.

> After a week without meat, some vegetarians report that the smell of cooking hamburger makes them sick.

Revising in Action

Read aloud the unrevised and revised version of the following excerpt. Note how adding in facts and statistics makes the essay much stronger.

> Other vegetarians reject modern American eating habits, with too much meat and too few vegetables. Vegetarians seek a better diet and a more sustainable lifestyle.
>
> The U.S. Department of Agriculture recommends that people "go lean on protein" and eat even less fat. However, the average American eats 16 percent of calories in proteins and 44 percent in fat.

Revise Improve your writing, using your partner's comments on the response sheet and including sensory details. Continue revising until you can answer *yes* to each question in the following checklist.

Revising Checklist

Ideas:

1. Do I focus on an interesting lifestyle choice?
2. Do I trace the causes and effects of the lifestyle choice?

Organization:

3. Do I have an effective opening, middle, and closing?
4. Have I used one paragraph for causes and the other for effects?
5. Have I used transitions to connect my sentences?

Voice:

6. Do I sound knowledgeable about and interested in my topic?

Traits

Using a variety of details strengthens your ideas and broadens your thinking. Just remember to properly cite any outside sources that you use in your paper. See Chapter 9 for more information.

LO5 Editing: Correcting Your Writing

The main work of editing is correcting your revided draft.

Editing an Essay

Before you edit your revised essay, you can practise by editing the following model.

Correct Read the following cause–effect essay, looking for problems. Correct the model using the marks listed to the left. One correction has been done for you.

Correction Marks

♉	delete
d	capitalize
Ð	lowercase
∧	insert
ᐱ	add comma
⸮	add question mark
word ∧	add word
⊙	add period
⬭	spelling
∿	switch

Staying in Step

People have many different ways to stay in shape, from jogging to   1
swimming to bike riding. Different people gravitate toward different types of
exercise. Recently, when I was trying to chose a type of exercise, I decided on *choose*
walking. Many factors made me chose walking over other forms of exercise
walking has changed my life in a number of ways.   5

Walking appealed because of its simplicity, safety, cost, and sociability.
While other types of exercise require special equipment or special training
walking is an activity I do every day anyway. I've been walking since I was
1 year old. It requires only normal cloths, comfortable shoes, and a sidewalk.
Walking also ain't dangerous like swimming, and walking isn't hard on the   10
knees like joging. To walk, I don't have to belong to a special club or rent any
special equipment. And when I walk, I walk with friends, and we talk.

Walking regularly has helped me a lot. First of all, I've dropped ten
pounds, I also toned up my legs and the most important muscle of all, my
heart. Beyond these benefits, walking has gave me a chance to talk with best   15
friends about all kinds of things. It has brung us closer. Walking also connects
me to my community. Many people stop me and say they see me walking and
feel they know me. I also like the way that walking connects me to Nature and
Weather. Rain or shine, I feel it when I'm walking.

So you can keep your fancy weight machines and thigh busters. I choose   20
walking because it is simple, safe, cheap, and fun. Walking has rewarded
me with health and happiness walking is a habit that many people should
learn.

Correcting Your Essay

Now it's time to correct your own essay. Use the checklist below.

Apply Create a clean copy of your essay and use the following checklist to search for errors. When you can answer *yes* to a question, check it off. Continue working until all items are checked.

Editing Checklist

Word Choice

☐ **1.** Have I used specific nouns and verbs? (See Chapter 8, LO1.)

☐ **2.** Have I used more action verbs than "be" verbs? (See Chapter 32, LO1.)

Sentence Fluency

☐ **3.** Have I varied the beginnings and lengths of sentences? (See Chapter 25, LO2.)

☐ **4.** Have I combined short choppy sentences? (See Chapter 25, LO1.)

☐ **5.** Have I avoided improper shifts in sentences? (See Chapter 29, LO2.)

Conventions

☐ **6.** Have I avoided fragments and run-ons? (See Chapter 27, LO1 and LO2; Chapter 28, LO2.)

☐ **7.** Do I use correct verb forms *(he saw,* not *he seen)*? (See Chapter 32, LO4.)

☐ **8.** Do my subjects and verbs agree *(she speaks,* not *she speak)*? (See Chapter 26, LOs 1–4.)

☐ **9.** Have I used the right words *(their, there, they're)*?

☐ **10.** Have I capitalized first words and proper nouns and adjectives? (See Chapter 29, LO1.)

☐ **11.** Have I used commas after long introductory word groups? (See Chapter 35, LO2.)

☐ **12.** Have I punctuated dialogue correctly? (See Chapter 17, LO5.)

☐ **13.** Have I carefully checked my spelling?

Documentation Checklist

Format

☐ **1.** Have I followed the proper formatting conventions? (See Chapter 9, LO5 and LO6.)

In-Text Citation

☐ **2.** Have I properly documented any sources in the body of my writing? (See Chapter 9, LO1–LO4.)

Bibliography

☐ **3.** Do I have a references or works cited page? (See Chapter 9, LO1–LO4.)

Create Prepare a clean final copy of your essay and proofread it.

Henglein and Steets/Cultura/Getty Images

LO6 Reviewing Cause–Effect Writing

Complete these activities as needed to help you better understand how to write cause–effect essays.

Analyze Look at the photograph to the left. Think about the causes and effects shown in it. Fill in the following cause–effect chart with your observations.

Cause–Effect Chart

Topic: _____

Causes	Effects

Freewrite Using your answers in the cause–effect chart above, freewrite about the reason the man is riding the child's car and what is likely to result.

_____
_____
_____
_____
_____
_____
_____
_____

Charlene Key/Shutterstock.com

> "Nothing is as frustrating as arguing with someone who knows what he's talking about."
>
> —Sam Ewing

Argument Essay

Have you ever dismissed a political ad for its over-the-top bias? Or left a lecture shaking your head because you just weren't convinced? Building a persuasive argument is difficult. Convincing others to buy into an argument is even more challenging.

You may think of the word "argue" as meaning heated conversation, with shouts flying. In the context of writing, the word is more related to discussion, reasoning, and debate, as when lawyers argue a case in court. Obviously, a judge wouldn't allow lawyers bellow at each other, and a jury wouldn't be convinced if they did. Instead, lawyers lay out their evidence and reasoning, seeking to convince.

In this chapter, you will write an argument essay that takes a position on a debatable topic and defends that position with logical and factual supporting details. Along the way, you will learn strategies to motivate your audience to side with your argument.

Learning Outcomes

LO1 Understand argument essays.

LO2 Plan an argument essay.

LO3 Write the first draft.

LO4 Revise the essay.

LO5 Edit the essay.

LO6 Reflect on the experience.

What do you think?

In what ways do you defend your point of view during an argument? Give examples.

_____

_____

_____

_____

_____

LO1 Reviewing an Argument Essay

In an argument essay, a writer takes a stance on a debatable position. In the example below, the writer argues that fighting should not be banned in professional hockey. This essay uses MLA formatting (see Chapter 9, LO3 and LO5, for more information).

Read/React Read the following essay. Then complete the analysis on the next page.

Compare

For another view of the debate over on-ice fighting, check out Raffi Cavoukian's essay titled "What's Pro Hockey Got to Do with World Peace?" in Chapter 44, Argument Essays.

Doe 1

Jane Doe

Professor Toni Starc

English 109

3 Aug 2015

On-Ice Fighting: Protecting NHL Players since 1917

The **opening** raises concern for the issue with an interesting statistic and leads to the **thesis statement**.

> In recent years, the National Hockey League (NHL) has come under increased scrutiny for allowing on-ice fighting during games. According to critics, on-ice fighting contributes to concussions and other life-threatening brain injuries. Every hockey season comes with renewed proposals to ban fighting from the game. Oddly enough, there is one group that almost unanimously rejects these proposals: NHL players. Indeed, 98% of NHL players said that they would not support a fighting ban (*2011/12 Player Poll*). What do professional hockey players know about fighting that the media and public fail to consider? Fighting actually protects players from career ending injuries caused by aggressive body checks, stick slashing, and purposeful headshots. <u>Therefore, fighting should not be banned from the NHL because it is no more dangerous than other parts of the game and actually helps protect players from unsafe play.</u>

1

5

10

The first **middle paragraph** gives reasons to support the thesis.

> While the public and media target fighting as a main cause of concussions in hockey, fighting is no more dangerous than other parts of the game. For example, NHL data from 2011 shows that fighting accounts for fewer player concussions (8 percent) than legal play (44 percent) and accidental and illegal hits (43 percent) (Benson et al. 905). Based on these statistics, removing fighting from the game would have a small impact in stopping concussions overall. A 2011 study supports this conclusion and argues that players are much more likely to be concussed from a body check from behind or into the boards than from fighting (Pasternac et al.). On-ice fighting is actually safer than it seems because the ice prevents players from getting enough traction to fully power their punches. Dr. David

15

20

25

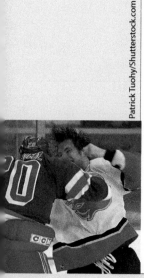

Milzman, co-author of this study, concluded that "the fights aren't causing the concussions" and that the risk of injury from fighting itself is actually quite low (Stinson).

The second **middle paragraph** gives the best reasons to support the thesis.

Fighting in professional hockey helps protect players by discouraging unsafe play. Typically, the referee's job is to ensure that players act in a safe and fair way; however, hockey is a very fast game and referees are unable to police the actions of every player. Some use this oversight to gain an advantage and they may attempt to intentionally injure another player. In response, many teams employ "enforcers," physically imposing players whose role is protect their teammates. Enforcers use the threat of fighting to confront players who break the rules and make the game unsafe. Therefore, if official penalties from the referees fail, often the simple thought of brawling with a 230-pound enforcer is enough to deter players from making a "dirty" hit.

The **closing** restates and clarifies the writer's position.

The majority of people calling for a fighting ban have never played professional hockey; they fail to consider the complex role fighting plays in keeping players safe. When it comes to on-ice fighting, the media and public need to listen to the professionals who risk injury every time they step on the ice. Players should not be forced to remove a key part of what keeps them safe. Therefore, fighting must not be banned from professional hockey.

Works Cited

2011/12 Player Poll. National Hockey League Players' Association and Hockey Night in Canada, www.nhlpa.com/news/nhlpacbcs-hockey-night-in-canada-player-poll-results-released. Accessed 14 Feb. 2014.

Benson, Brian W., et al. "A Prospective Study of Concussions among National Hockey League Players during Regular Season Games: The NHL-NHLPA Concussion Program." *Canadian Medical Association Journal*, vol. 183, no. 8, 2011, pp. 905-11.

Pasternac, Kyle, et al. "448 Results of 1,300 Consecutive NHL Fights: Fists of Fury Minimal Injuries." *Annals of Emergency Medicine: An International Journal*, vol. 58, no. 4, 2011, p. S330.

Stinson, Scott. "Brawls 'aren't causing' head trauma: Doctor." *National Post*, 21 Oct. 2011, www.news.nationalpost.com/sports/nhl/expert-fighting-isnt-causing-the-concussions. Accessed 14 Feb. 2014.

A Closer Look

This argument essay takes a defensible position on fighting in professional hockey. The writer's position is debatable, but it is supported by the details in the middle paragraphs.

Identify The argument essay "On-Ice Fighting: Protecting NHL Players since 1917" makes a pitch for keeping fighting in professional hockey and gives reasons to support it. In the chart below, identify the thesis statement and two different reasons that support the argument.

Thesis Statement

Reason 1

Reason 2

Reason 3

Explain Is the writer's argument convincing? Why or why not? Provide reasons.

_____

_____

_____

_____

_____

_____

_____

_____

LO2 Prewriting: Planning

There is no sense in debating a topic about which everyone agrees. In your own essay, you will take a position on a debatable issue. You will pick an issue that you care about and choose the side you want to defend.

Learning Outcome

Plan an argument essay.

Selecting a Topic

Prewrite To select a topic for an argument essay, start by making a cluster of subjects you have opinions about.

Tip

If you are having problems generating a topic, browse newspapers, magazines, and the Internet for current issues that you have strong feelings about.

Make a Cluster

Add more bubbles and lines as needed. Continue clustering until you have at least three debatable issues you could write about in an essay. Put a star next to your favourite idea.

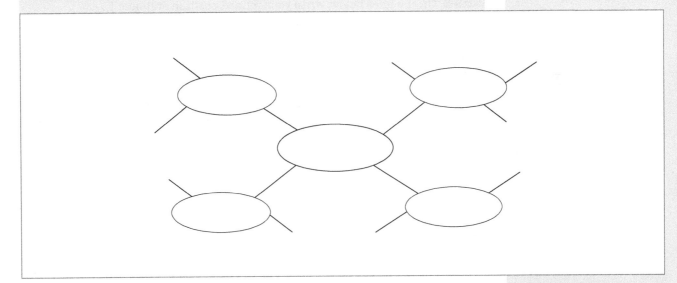

Selecting a Position

Whether in writing or speaking, a convincing argument starts with a strong position on a debatable topic.

Write Write down a defensible **position statement** that introduces the issue and expresses your opinion about it.

Vocabulary

position statement
a statement that expresses a writer's opinion on a debatable issue

Refining a Position

With your initial position written, use the following position strategies to develop and refine your opinion of the issue:

- Draw a line down the middle of a blank piece of paper. In the left column, freewrite all of the ideas you can for supporting your position. Then, on the right side, freewrite every argument you can against your position.
- Research all possible positions on your issue of debate. Who supports it and why? Who opposes it and why?
- Gather solid evidence regarding your issue. Does the most compelling evidence support or oppose your position?
- Refine your position. At this point, you may have sharpened or changed your mind about your position. Before you are ready to write, clarify your position statement.

Write On the lines below, write your refined position statement.

Gathering Details

When you take a stand on an issue, you must gather convincing support to defend your position. You can use four different types of details to support your position: **facts**, **statistics**, **testimonials**, and **predictions**.

Vocabulary

facts
statements or claims of verifiable information

statistics
concrete numbers about a topic

testimonials
insights from authorities on the topic

predictions
insights into possible outcomes or consequences, forecasting what might happen under certain conditions

Support Chart

Fact	Statistic	Testimony	Prediction
In the NHL, players who fight are removed from the game with a five-minute penalty.	The National Hockey League Players Association found that 98% of players do not support a ban on fighting.	"[Fighting] has been, and is, [part of hockey], but it's declining in its frequency." Gary Bettman, commissioner of the NHL (National Hockey League).	Banning fighting will lead to more injuries in other parts of the game.

Gather Fill in the support chart below with the research you have gathered about your issue. If you have not found supporting details to fit each category, consider doing additional research.

Fact	Statistic	Testimony	Prediction

Note

If you are using APA formatting, you need to include a title page and an abstract page (not shown here). For more information, see Chapter 9, LO6.

LO3 Writing: Creating a First Draft

Creating a first draft puts all your planning and gathering into concrete form. Provided below is a sample argument essay about marijuana legalization in Canada. This essay uses APA formatting (see Chapter 9, LO4 and LO6, for more information).

Read/React Read the essay, noting the writer's position statement and supporting details.

arindambanerjee/Shutterstock.com

POT PROHIBITION IN CANADA   4

Pot Prohibition in Canada: End the War on Weed

Canada has fallen behind when it comes to pot. For instance, on the same day in 2012 when two U.S. states decided to legalize marijuana, the Canadian government adopted stricter marijuana-related penalties (Cheadle, 2012). Under current Canadian law, those found guilty of possessing small amounts of marijuana face fines up to $1000 and/or 6 months of jail time (Theresa, 2014, para. 16). These harsh prohibition laws must be abolished because they have no scientific basis and are ineffective in protecting minors.

Racism, not research, provides the basis for Canada's prohibition laws. Many point to Judge Emily Murphy's *The Black Candle* as inspiring the Canadian government to pass the first marijuana prohibition laws in 1923. According to Murphy, racial minorities were using drugs, like marijuana, to sexually exploit Canadian women as part of a larger conspiracy to corrupt the "purity" of the white race (1922). In making this ridiculous argument, this book helped consolidate many myths that serve as the basis for prohibition—that marijuana causes addiction, laziness, mental impairment, immorality, insanity, and even death. Since the 1970s, research investigating the effects of marijuana has contradicted all of these claims (Canadian Foundation for Drug Policy, 1998). Based on this scientific evidence, a 2002 report commissioned by the Canadian government called for the outright legalization of marijuana, concluding that prohibition has "no scientific basis" (The Special Senate Committee on Illegal Drugs).

Many prohibition supporters argue that legalization will give children greater access to pot; however, prohibition is ineffective in reducing marijuana use among minors. Statistics show that Canadian children, aged 11–15, smoke more marijuana than anywhere else in the Western World. In comparison, children in countries with relaxed marijuana restrictions smoke less (Hui, 2013). If legalized in Canada, marijuana could be sold at government-run outlets that would restrict sale to minors. These outlets would put drug dealers, many who have no hesitation selling to minors, out of business. As an added bonus, marijuana would be subject to taxation: Some studies estimate that such a tax could bring in over

---

264   NEL

$7.5 billion dollars annually (Cohen & Hill, 2013). This money could be used for programs to educate youth about responsible drug use. Under the current system, this money instead helps fund drug cartels and other criminal organizations.

We need new marijuana laws based on research, not racism. We need laws that protect minors, not harm them. Most important, we need laws that reflect the desires of the Canadian people (more than two-thirds want an end to marijuana prohibition) (Bozinoff, 2013). It is time to legalize pot in Canada.

References

Bozinoff, L. (2013, August 24). More than two thirds support decriminalization/ legalization of marijuana. *Forum Research Inc*. Retrieved from http://forumresearch.com/forms/News%20Archives/News%20Releases/50140 _Federal_Trudeau_-_Marijuana_(24082013)_Forum _Research.pdf

Canadian Foundation for Drug Policy & International Harm Reduction Association. (1998). *Drugs and drug policy in Canada: A brief review and commentary*. Retrieved from http://www.parl.gc.ca/Content/SEN/Committee/362/ille/rep/rep-nov98-e.htm

Cheadle, B. (2012, November 7). Canada toughens pot laws, two U.S. states loosen up. *The Toronto Star*. Retrieved from http://www.thestar.com/news/canada/2012/11/07/canada _toughens_pot_laws_two_us_states_loosen_up.html

Cohen, T., & Hill A. (2013, August 27). Experts disagree on economic impact of legalizing marijuana in Canada. *National Post*. Retrieved from http://news.nationalpost .com/2013/08/27/experts-disagree-on-economic-impact-of -legalizing-marijuana-in-canada/

Hui, Ann. (2013, April 15). Canadian teens lead developed world in cannabis use: Unicef report. *The Globe and Mail*. Retrieved from http://www.theglobeandmail.com/news/national/canadian-teens-lead-developed-world-in-cannabis -use-unicef-report/article11221668/

Murphy, E. (1922). *The black candle*. Toronto: Thomas Allen.

Theresa, T. (2014, March 5). Government working on new pot legislation. *CBC News*. Retrieved from http://www.cbc.ca/news/politics/government-working-on-new-pot-legislation-peter-mackay-says-1.2560645

The Special Senate Committee on Illegal Drugs. (2002, September 4). *Senate committee recommends legalization of cannabis*. Retrieved from http://www.parl.gc.ca/Content/SEN/Committee/371/ille/press/04sep02-e.htm

Traits

Analyze the argument essay on the previous page using the traits. If you need to review the traits and a sample reading analysis, see Chapter 3, LO2.

A Closer Look

This essay argues that marijuana should be legalized in Canada. Answer the following questions to better understand the overall organization of the essay.

Explain What kind of opening strategy does this essay use? Is the opening effective in catching your attention? Explain.

_____

_____

_____

Identify Underline the thesis statement. Does the author take a clear stance on a debatable issue?

_____

_____

_____

Analyze Find the supporting details. Is the supporting detail a fact, statistic, testimony, or prediction? Does each fully support the thesis statement?

Support 1: _____

_____

_____

Support 2: _____

_____

_____

Support 3: _____

_____

_____

Support 4: _____

_____

_____

Explain Does the closing reaffirm the author's position? What kind of closing strategy does this essay use? Is it effective? Explain.

_____

_____

_____

Creating an Opening Paragraph

The opening paragraph of your argument essay needs to capture the reader's interest, raise concern for the issue of debate, and establish your position on the topic.

Consider these attention-grabbing strategies for your opening paragraph.

- **Ask a thought-provoking question.**
  How would you feel if you were wrongly convicted of a crime?

- **Offer a surprising statistic.**
  According to the NHL, 98 percent of professional hockey players feel that fighting should not be banned from the game.

- **Make a personal confession.**
  I can't stand cigarette smoke, but I believe adults should have the freedom to smoke in public.

- **Present yourself as an authority.**
  Having grown up with country-western music, I can attest to its essentially moral nature.

- **Make a logical claim.**
  Judging films by their special effects is like judging people by their looks.

- **Appeal to the reader's emotion.**
  Lowering a student's grades for poor class attendance is double punishment, intended to cause failure, not encourage success.

Write Create the opening paragraph for your argument essay.

Speaking & Listening

Imagine that you are giving a speech about your topic. What strategy would you use to get listeners' attention? Try a similar strategy in your writing.

Review

See Chapter 6, LO3, if you are having difficulty creating an opening paragraph.

Writing a Thesis Statement

Once you have your reader's attention, lead up to your thesis statement. Here are a few things to keep in mind when writing a thesis statement for an argument essay:

Review

If you need to review how to form a thesis statement, see Chapter 5, LO5, and Chapter 6, LO4.

(1) Choose a **controversial topic**. The best topics for an argument essay are open to debate. Avoid making an argument that is too obvious (e.g., "Racism is bad").

(2) State your **position** in your thesis statement. Again, your position is which side of the debate you stand on. Consider using one of the following verbs to strengthen the conviction of your position: *should, must, ought to, need / needs to*.

(3) Choose a topic that is **specific** and **focused**. See Chapter 5, LO5, for some suggestions on how to focus your thesis statement.

(4) Provide an **overview** of the different types of evidence that you will be using to prove your position. Each piece of evidence should correspond with one of your topic sentences. However, this overview is optional, especially in a shorter essay (see the example below on nuclear deterrence).

If expressed as a formula, an argument thesis statement would look like this.

A Debatable Topic	+	Your Position	+	Overview of Support	=	Thesis Statement
nuclear deterrence		the only way to prevent other countries from using their own nuclear weapons		X		Nuclear deterrence is the only way of preventing other countries from using nuclear weapons.
fighting in professional hockey		should not be banned		not as dangerous as it is depicted in the media (1st body paragraph) / helps protect players from unsafe play (2nd body paragraph)		Fighting should not be banned from the NHL because it is no more dangerous than other parts of the game and actually helps protect players from unsafe play.
marijuana prohibition laws in Canada		must be repealed		not based on scientific evidence (1st body paragraph) / ineffective in protecting minors (2nd body paragraph)		Marijuana prohibition must be abolished because it has no scientific basis and is ineffective in preventing minors from using pot.

Write Use this formula to create your thesis statement.

A Debatable Topic	+	Your Position	+	Overview of Support	=	Thesis Statement

Creating Middle Paragraphs

In your middle paragraphs, provide support to defend your thesis statement. Here is where your supporting details become so important. Each paragraph should use facts, statistics, testimonials, or predictions to deepen, clarify, and build upon your position statement. Be sure to review the details you gathered as part of your prewriting in LO2. Finally, address any objections to your position with a clear, well-reasoned defence.

Review

See Chapter 6, LO5, for suggestions on how to develop your middle paragraphs.

Write   Create the two middle paragraphs of your essay.

Review

See Chapter 6, LO6, to review effective closing strategies.

Creating an End Paragraph

Your final paragraph should state a firm conclusion based on the support presented in your middle paragraphs. If appropriate, make a direct or indirect plea to the reader to adopt your position.

- If the United States wants to maintain its fragile southern ecosystem, it should take a hard look at making the importation of Burmese pythons illegal.
- The majority of people calling for a fighting ban have never played professional hockey; they fail to consider the complex role fighting plays in keeping players safe.
- It's time to end marijuana prohibition in Canada.

Write Create the closing paragraph for your argument essay.

Adding a Title

Make sure to add an attention-getting title. Here are three simple strategies for writing titles

- **Use a play on words:** High Time to End Pot Prohibition
- **Sum up your argument:** Fighting Protects NHL Players
- **Create a slogan:** Ban Hockey Brawls

LO4 Revising: Improving the Writing

Revising your first draft involves adding, deleting, rearranging, and reworking parts of your writing. Revision begins with a peer review.

Peer Review

Sharing your writing at various stages—whether it is with a friend, classmate, or tutor—is an important step to improving your essay.

Respond Complete this response sheet after reading the first draft of a classmate's essay. Then share the sheet with the writer. (Keep your comments helpful and positive.)

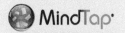

For more information, check out the Bonus Online Chapter on peer reviewing.

Essay title: _____

Writer: _____ Reviewer: _____

1. Which part of the essay seems to work best—opening, middle, or closing? Why?

   _____
   _____
   _____

2. Which part of the essay needs work—opening, middle, or closing? Why? _____

   _____
   _____
   _____

3. Do the middle paragraphs support the writer's position statement? How so?

   _____
   _____
   _____

4. Does the writer use a variety of support details? Are more needed? Why or why not?

   _____
   _____
   _____

5. Does the writer build a convincing argument? Why or why not?

   _____
   _____
   _____

Looking Out for Logical Fallacies

A logical fallacy is a false assertion that weakens an argument by distorting an issue, drawing faulty conclusions, misusing evidence, or misusing language. Below are five common logical fallacies that should be removed from your writing.

Straw Man This logical fallacy distorts an issue by exaggerating or misinterpreting an opponent's position.

> Those who consider themselves pro-choice don't value human life.

Bandwagon Mentality Such a logical fallacy appeals to "popular opinion," by implying that a claim cannot be true because most people oppose it, or must be true because most support it.

> It's obvious to everyone that cockroaches live only in the apartments of dirty people.

Broad Generalization This logical fallacy makes an all-or-nothing claim based on little evidence. The claim will often include an intensifier, such as *all, every,* or *never.*

> All athletes are driven by money.

Impressing with Numbers In this case, a writer attempts to overwhelm the reader with a deluge of statistics, some of which are unrelated to the issue at hand.

> At 35 ppm, CO levels factory-wide are only 10ppm above the OSHA recommendation, which is 25 ppm. Clearly, that 10 ppm is insignificant in the big picture.

Personal Attack In this example, writers discredit their opponent's character rather than his or her position.

> Since you are an American, your arguments about Canadian health care are invalid.

Revise Improve your writing using your partner's comments on the response sheet and the following checklist. Continue working until you can answer *yes* to each question.

Revising Checklist

Ideas:

1. Do I take a stance on a debatable issue?
2. Do I support my position with a variety of supporting details?
3. Do I avoid errors in logic?

Thesis:

4. Do I present a debatable topic?
5. Do I clearly state my position?
6. If appropriate, do I provide an overview of my support?

Organization:

7. Do I have topic, middle, and closing paragraphs?
8. Have I used transitions to connect my sentences?

Voice:

9. Do I sound knowledgeable and passionate about the issue?

Vocabulary

logical fallacy
a false assertion that may distort an issue, sabotage an argument, draw faulty conclusions, misuse evidence, or misuse language

NEL

LO5 Editing: Correcting Your Writing

The main work of editing is correcting your revised draft. Before you edit your revised essay, you can practise by editing the following model.

Editing an Essay

Edit Read the following argument essay, looking for problems listed in the checklist on the next page. Correct the model using the marks to the left. The first one has been done for you.

Correction Marks

ℑ   delete

d   capitalize

Ð   lowercase

∧   insert

⌃   add comma

?   add question
     mark
∧

word   add word
∧

⊙   add period

⬭   spelling

∿   switch

Ban Burmese Pythons

An invasive species is taking the southern tip of Florida by storm. 1
Thousands of Burmese pythons—giant snakes native to Southern asia—are
thriving in the tropical-like environment of Everglades National Park. There
presence in the park is a product of irresponsible pet owners, who intentionally
release the snakes into the wild when they become too difficult to care for. as a 5
result, Florida lawmakers have passed a law making it illigal for individuals
to own burmese pythons. In order to protect native wildlife and treasured
ecosystems of the southern United States, this law should expand nationally.

Reports show some 144 000 pythons have been imported into the United
States, many of which end up in homes of irresponsible pet owners. "All of the 10
Burmese pythons that we see in the park are a product of the international
pet trade" said Skip Snow, a wildlife biologist at Everglades National Park.
The problem is many pet owners doesn't fully understand the responsibility
of taking care of a python often the python, which grow up to between 10 and
20 feet becomes too big and to expensive to be kept in a home. In the end, the 15
owner releases the pet into the wild.

It is in the wild where Burmese pythons is causing havoc. The tropical
environment of the Everglades provides perfect conditions for the pythons to
breed and feed. With no natural competitor the strong and stealthy python is
feeding at will on native Everglade's species, Scientists worry the ecological 20
effects could be devastating. Second to habitat loss, invasive species are the
leading cause of species endangerment.

To be fair, there are no doubt thousands of responsible pet owners across
the United States. But the drawbacks of owning Burmese pythons outweigh
the benefits. These species are not meant to be pets. If the United States
wants to maintain its fragile southern ecosystem, it should take a hard look 25
at making the importation of Burmese pythons illegal.

Correcting Your Essay

Now it's time to edit your own essay.

Apply Create a clean copy of your essay and use the following checklist to check for errors. When you can answer *yes* to a question, check it off. Continue working until all items are checked off.

Editing Checklist

Words

☐ 1. Have I used specific nouns and verbs? (See Chapter 8, LO1.)

☐ 2. Have I used more action verbs than "be" verbs? (See Chapter 32, LO1.)

Sentences

☐ 3. Have I varied the beginnings and lengths of sentences? (See Chapter 25, LO2.)

☐ 4. Have I combined short choppy sentences? (See Chapter 25, LO1.)

☐ 5. Have I avoided improper shifts in sentences? (See Chapter 29, LO2.)

☐ 6. Have I avoided fragments and run-ons? (See Chapter 27, LO1 and LO2; Chapter 28, LO2.)

Conventions

☐ 7. Do I use correct verb forms (*he saw*, not *he seen*)? (See Chapter 32, LO4.)

☐ 8. Do my subjects and verbs agree (*she speaks*, not *she speak*)? (See Chapter 26, LOs 1–4.)

☐ 9. Have I used the right words (*their, there, they're*)?

☐ 10. Have I capitalized first words and proper nouns and adjectives? (See Chapter 39, LO1.)

☐ 11. Have I used commas after long introductory word groups? (See Chapter 35, LO2.)

☐ 12. Have I punctuated dialogue correctly? (See Chapter 17, LO5.)

☐ 13. Have I carefully checked my spelling?

Documentation Checklist

Format

☐ 1. Have I followed the proper formatting conventions? (See Chapter 9, LO5 and LO6.)

In-Text Citation

☐ 2. Have I properly documented any sources in the body of my writing? (See Chapter 9, LO1–LO4.)

Bibliography

☐ 3. Do I have a references or works cited page? (See Chapter 9, LO1–LO4.)

LO6 Reviewing Argument Writing

Complete these activities as needed to help you further understand how to write argument essays.

Describe A convincing argument essay requires a logical defence, based on supporting details. Describe the four types of supporting details illustrated in this chapter. Find examples of each from the sample argument essays in this chapter.

Match Draw a line to connect each logical fallacy with a claim that best demonstrates that fallacy.

Impressing with Numbers	■ My political opponent is an idiot; therefore, his views on education are incorrect.
Straw Man	■ Everyone believes the tax hike won't be beneficial, so I don't see how anyone can support it.
Bandwagon Mentality	■ Atheists couldn't care less about morality and ethics.
Broad Generalization	■ The opposition leader does not want to upgrade our aging fighter jets; he must not care about the safety of our air force pilots.
Personal Attack	■ 12% of studies show that this program has a 100% success rate, 60% of the time.

"We cannot always build the future for our youth,
but we can build our youth for the future."
—Franklin Delano Roosevelt

23 Sentence Basics

Sentences are built from some very simple parts—nouns, verbs, and modifiers. Every sentence has, at its base, the pairing of a noun and a verb, or a few of them. The other words in the sentence merely modify the noun and verb.

These are sentence basics—the building blocks of thought. With these blocks, you can build tiny towers or magnificent mansions. It all comes down to understanding how to put the pieces together and deciding what you want to create. This chapter can help.

What do you think?

How do we "build our youth for the future," as Roosevelt suggests in the quotation on the facing page? What part do language and writing have to play in building our youth?

Jupiterimages/Thinkstock

Learning Outcomes

LO1 Understand subjects, verbs, and predicates.

LO2 Work with special types of subjects.

LO3 Work with special predicates.

LO4 Understand adjectives.

LO5 Understand adverbs.

LO6 Use prepositional phrases.

LO7 Use clauses.

LO8 Apply sentence basics in a real-world context.

Eric Isselee/Shutterstock.com

LO1 Subjects, Verbs, and Predicates

The subject of a sentence tells what the sentence is about, or who or what does the action indicated by the verb. The predicate of a sentence includes a verb and tells what the subject does or is.

> Dogs bark.
> └─ Subject: what the sentence is about   └─ Predicate: what the subject does

Simple Subject and Simple Predicate

The **simple subject** is the subject without any modifiers, and the **simple predicate** is the verb without modifiers or objects.

> The brown and white spaniel barked all day long.
> simple subject   simple predicate

Complete Subject and Complete Predicate

The **complete subject** is the subject with modifiers, and the **complete predicate** is the verb plus any modifiers and objects.

> The brown and white spaniel | barked all day long.
> complete subject   complete predicate

Implied Subject

In commands, the subject *you* is implied. Commands are the only type of sentence in English that can have an **implied subject**.

> (You)   Stop barking!
> implied subject   complete predicate

Inverted Order

Most often in English, the subject comes before the verb. However, in questions and sentences that begin with *here* or *there*, the subject comes after the predicate.

>   subject   subject
> Why are you so loud?   Here is a biscuit.
>   verb   verb

Creating Subjects and Predicates

Identify/Write For each sentence below, underline and label the simple subject (SS) and simple predicate (SP). Then write a similar sentence of your own and identify the simple subject and simple predicate in the same way.

1. For thousands of years, humans have bred dogs.

   _____

   _____

2. All dog breeds descended from wolf ancestors.

   _____

   _____

3. At the end of the Ice Age, humans lived nomadically with their dogs.

   _____

   _____

4. Ever since that time, dogs have enjoyed going for walks.

   _____

   _____

Identify/Write For each sentence below, underline and label the complete subject (CS) and complete predicate (CP). Then write a similar sentence of your own and identify the complete subject and complete predicate in the same way.

1. An Irish wolfhound stands as tall as a small pony.

   _____

   _____

2. Wolfhounds were bred to hunt their wolf ancestors.

   _____

   _____

3. Wolfhounds also were used for hunting boar.

   _____

   _____

4. Is that why boars are extinct in Ireland?

   _____

5. There is little doubt.

   _____

LO2 Special Types of Subjects

As you work with subjects, watch for these special types.

Compound Subjects

A **compound subject** is two or more subjects connected by *and* or *or*.

My <u>sister and I</u> like to hike. <u>Terri, Josh, and I</u> love the outdoors.
   compound subject   compound subject

"To" Words (Infinitives) as Subjects

An **infinitive** can function as a subject. An infinitive is a verbal form that begins with *to* and may be followed by objects or modifiers.

<u>To become a park ranger</u> is my dream.
   infinitive subject

"Ing" Words as Subjects (Gerunds)

A **gerund** is a verb form that ends in *ing* and functions as a subject. It may be followed by objects or modifiers.

<u>Hiking</u> builds strong calves.   <u>Hiking the Appalachian Trail</u> is amazing.
gerund subject   gerund subject

Noun Clause as Subject

A **noun clause** can function as a subject. The clause itself has a subject and a verb but cannot stand alone as a sentence. Noun clauses are introduced by words like *what, that, why, how, whatever,* or *whichever.*

<u>Whoever hikes the trail</u> should bring replacement boots.
   noun clause subject

<u>Whatever you need</u> must be carried on your back.
   noun clause subject

Say It

Work with a partner and read each sentence aloud. Take turns identifying the type of subject–compound subject, infinitive subject, gerund subject, or noun–clause subject. Discuss your answers.

1. You and I should go hiking sometime.
2. To reach the peak of Mount Rainier would be amazing.
3. Whoever wants to go should train with mountaineering.
4. Hiking the Rockies at altitude is challenging.

Creating Special Subjects

Identify/Write For each sentence below, underline and label the complete subject: compound subject (CS), infinitive (I), gerund (G), or noun clause (NC). Then write a similar sentence of your own and identify the complete subject in the same way.

1. Planning for success is the key to success.

   _____

   _____

2. To complete the course in two years is my main goal.

   _____

   _____

3. The fan and the air conditioner are running.

   _____

   _____

4. Working through our differences won't be easy.

   _____

   _____

5. A doughnut, a cup of coffee, and good conversation make my morning.

   _____

   _____

6. Lifting the ban on street parking will help the neighbourhood.

   _____

   _____

7. To live life to its fullest is not as easy as it sounds.

   _____

   _____

8. Whoever finds the money will keep it.

   _____

   _____

9. Are Hannah, Michelle, and Sharissa going?

   _____

   _____

10. Whenever he arrives is the starting time.

    _____

    _____

LO3 Special Predicates

As you work with predicates, watch for these special types.

Compound Predicates

A **compound predicate** consists of two or more verbs joined by *and* or *or*.

> I <u>watched and laughed</u>. My cat <u>stalked, pounced, and tumbled</u>.
>   compound predicate   compound predicate

Predicates with Direct Objects

A **direct object** follows a transitive verb and tells what or who receives the action of the verb.

> I pointed the <u>laser</u>. My cat got the <u>spot</u>. He batted <u>it</u> and nipped the <u>ground</u>.
>   direct object   direct object   direct objects

Predicates with Indirect Objects

An **indirect object** comes between a transitive verb and a direct object and tells to whom or for whom an action was done.

> I gave <u>him</u> a rest. My cat shot <u>me</u> a puzzled look.
>   indirect object   indirect object

Predicates with Passive Verbs

When a verb is in the **passive** voice, the subject of the sentence is being acted upon rather than acting. Often, the actor is the object of the preposition in a phrase that starts with *by*. Using that object as the subject, the sentence can be rewritten to be in the **active** voice.

Passive

> My <u>cat</u> <u>was exhausted</u> by the <u>game</u>.
>   subject   passive verb   object of the preposition

Active

> The <u>game</u> <u>exhausted</u> <u>my cat</u>.
>   subject   active verb   direct object

> **Say It**
>
> Work with a partner and read each sentence aloud. Take turns identifying the sentence as active or passive. If the sentence is passive, speak the active version out loud.
>
> 1. My cat was mesmerized by the laser.
> 2. The light danced in his paws.
> 3. The laser glowed red on the wall.
> 4. The light was chased all down the hallway.

Creating Special Predicates

Identify/Write For each sentence below, underline and label any compound predicate (CP), direct object (DO), and indirect object (IO). Then write a similar sentence of your own and identify the compound predicate and direct or indirect object in the same way.

1. Our pet rabbits hopped and thumped.

   _____

   _____

2. The lop-ear leaped the gate.

   _____

3. I gave her a carrot.

   _____

4. She crouched and nibbled.

   _____

5. The lionhead sniffed and bounded.

   _____

6. I gave him some dried banana.

   _____

   _____

7. Those rabbits give me hours of entertainment.

   _____

   _____

Identify/Write For each passive sentence below, underline and label the simple subject (SS), the simple predicate (SP), and the object of the preposition *by* (O). Then rewrite each sentence, making it active.

1. The rabbits are fed and watered by my sister.

   _____

   _____

2. Their cages are cleaned by her as well.

   _____

   _____

3. She is seen by them as their food goddess.

   _____

   _____

Insight

It's less important to know the name of a phrase or clause than to know how it functions. If a group of words answers one of the adjective questions, the words are probably functioning as an adjective.

LO4 Adjectives

To modify a noun, use an adjective, or a phrase or clause acting as an adjective.

Adjectives

Adjectives answer these basic questions: *which, what kind of, how many, how much.*

To modify the noun **athletes,** ask . . .

Which athletes? ⟶ college athletes

What kind of athletes? ⟶ female athletes

How many athletes? ⟶ ten athletes

ten female college **athletes**

Adjective Phrases and Clauses

Phrases and clauses can also act as adjectives to modify nouns.

To modify the noun **athletes,** ask . . .

Which athletes? ⟶ **athletes** who are taking at least 12 credit hours

What kind of athletes? ⟶ **athletes** with a 3.0 average

The administration will approve loans for **athletes** with a 3.0 average who are taking at least 12 credit hours.

Say It

Pair up with a classmate to find adjectives—words, phrases, or clauses—that modify the nouns below. Take turns asking the questions while the other person answers.

1. **Sports**
   Which sports?
   What kind of sports?
   How many sports?

2. **Classes**
   Which classes?
   What kind of classes?
   How many classes?

Using Adjectives

Answer/Write For each noun, answer the questions using adjectives—words, phrases, or clauses. Then write a sentence using two or more of your answers.

1. **Tournaments**

   Which tournaments? _____

   What kind of tournaments? _____

   How many tournaments? _____

   Sentence: _____

   _____

   _____

   _____

2. **Opponents**

   Which opponents? _____

   What kind of opponents? _____

   How many opponents? _____

   Sentence: _____

   _____

   _____

   _____

3. **Victories**

   Which victories? _____

   What kind of victories? _____

   How many victories? _____

   Sentence: _____

   _____

   _____

   _____

LO5 Adverbs

To modify a verb, use an adverb or a phrase or clause acting as an adverb.

Adverbs

Adverbs answer these basic questions: *how, when, where, why, how long,* and *how often*.

To modify the verb **dance**, ask . . .

How did they dance? ⟶	danced vigorously
When did they dance? ⟶	danced yesterday
Where did they dance? ⟶	danced there
How often did they dance? ⟶	danced often

> Yesterday, **the bride and groom** often vigorously **danced,** there in the middle of the floor.

Adverb Phrases and Clauses

Phrases and clauses can also act as adverbs to modify verbs.

To modify the verb **dance**, ask . . .

How did they dance? ⟶	danced grinning and laughing
When did they dance? ⟶	danced from the first song
Where did they dance? ⟶	danced all around the room
Why did they dance? ⟶	danced to celebrate their marriage
How long did they dance? ⟶	danced until the last song

> Grinning and laughing, **the bride and groom danced** all around the room from the first song until the last song to celebrate their marriage.

Speaking & Listening

Read the last two example sentences aloud. Though they may look imposing on the page, they sound natural, probably because adverbs and adjectives are a common part of our speech. Experiment with these modifiers in your writing as well.

Using Adverbs

Answer/Write For each verb, answer the questions using adverbs—words, phrases, or clauses. Then write a sentence using three or more of your answers.

1. **Ran**

   How did they run? _____

   When did they run? _____

   Where did they run? _____

   Why did they run? _____

   How long did they run? _____

   How often did they run? _____

   Sentence: _____

   _____

   _____

   _____

   _____

2. **Jumped**

   How did they jump? _____

   When did they jump? _____

   Where did they jump? _____

   Why did they jump? _____

   How long did they jump? _____

   How often did they jump? _____

   Sentence: _____

   _____

   _____

   _____

   _____

LO6 Prepositional Phrases

One of the simplest and most versatile types of phrases in English is the prepositional phrase. A prepositional phrase can function as an adjective or an adverb.

Building Prepositional Phrases

A prepositional phrase is a preposition followed by an object (a noun or pronoun) and any modifiers.

Preposition	+	Object	=	Prepositional Phrase
at		noon		at noon
in		an hour		in an hour
beside		the green clock		beside the green clock
in front of		my aunt's vinyl purse		in front of my aunt's vinyl purse

As you can see, a prepositional phrase can be just two words long, or many words long. As you can also see, some prepositions are themselves made up of more than one word. Here is a list of common prepositions.

Prepositions

aboard	back of	except for	notwithstanding	save
about	because of	excepting	of	since
above	before	for	off	subsequent to
according to	behind	from	on	through
across	below	from among	on account of	throughout
across from	beneath	from between	on behalf of	till
after	beside	from under	onto	to
against	besides	in	on top of	together with
along	between	in addition to	opposite	toward
alongside	beyond	in front of	out	under
alongside of	but	in place of	out of	underneath
along with	by	in regard to	outside	until
amid	by means of	inside	outside of	unto
among	concerning	inside of	over	up
apart from	considering	in spite of	over to	upon
around	despite	instead of	owing to	up to
as far as	down	into	past	with
aside from	down from	like	prior to	within
at	during	near	regarding	without
away from	except	near to	round	

Insight

A preposition is pre-positioned before the other words it introduces to form a phrase. Other languages have post-positional words, which follow the words they modify.

Vocabulary

prepositional phrase
a group of words beginning with a preposition and including an object (noun or pronoun) and any modifiers

Using Phrases

Create For each item below, create a prepositional phrase by writing a preposition in the first box and an object (and any modifiers) in the second box. Then write a sentence using the prepositional phrase.

1. Preposition   **+**   Object (and any modifiers)

Sentence: _____

2. Preposition   **+**   Object (and any modifiers)

Sentence: _____

3. Preposition   **+**   Object (and any modifiers)

Sentence: _____

4. Preposition   **+**   Object (and any modifiers)

Sentence: _____

5. Preposition   **+**   Object (and any modifiers)

Sentence: _____

LO7 Clauses

A clause is a group of words with a subject and a predicate. If a clause can stand on its own as a sentence, it is an **independent clause**, but if it cannot, it is a **dependent clause**.

Independent Clause

An independent clause has a subject and a verb and expresses a complete thought. It is the same as a simple sentence.

> Clouds piled up in the stormy sky.

Dependent Clause

A dependent clause has a subject and a verb but does not express a complete thought. Instead, it is used as an **adverb clause**, an **adjective clause**, or a **noun clause**.

An adverb clause begins with a subordinating conjunction and functions as an adverb, so it must be connected to an independent clause to be complete. Here is a list of words commonly used as subordinating conjunctions:

after	before	since	when
although	even though	so that	whenever
as	given that	that	where
as if	if	though	whereas
as long as	in order that	unless	while
because	provided that	until	

> Even though the forecast said clear skies, **the storms rolled in.**

An adjective clause begins with a relative pronoun *(which, that, who)* and functions as an adjective, so it must be connected to an independent clause to be complete.

> I don't like a **meteorologist** who often gets the forecast wrong.

A noun clause functions as a noun. It is used as a subject or an object in a sentence. Noun clauses usually begin with one of these words:

how	what	whoever	whomever
that	whatever	whom	why

> I wish he had known what the weather would be.

Speaking & Listening

In each example, read the dependent clause out loud. (The dependent clause is in red.) Can you hear how each dependent clause sounds incomplete? Read it to another person, and the listener will probably say, "What about it?" These clauses depend on a complete thought to make sense.

Vocabulary

independent clause
a group of words with a subject and predicate that expresses a complete thought

dependent clause
a group of words with a subject and predicate that does not express a complete thought

adverb clause
a dependent clause beginning with a subordinating conjunction and functioning as an adverb

adjective clause
a dependent clause beginning with a relative pronoun and functioning as an adjective

noun clause
a dependent clause beginning with a subordinating word and functioning as a noun

Using Clauses

Identify/Write For each sentence below, underline and label any adverb clauses (ADVC), adjective clauses (ADJC), or noun clauses (NC). Then write a similar sentence of your own and identify the clauses.

1. I wonder why weather is so unpredictable.

_____

_____

2. Though we have satellites, storms still surprise us.

_____

_____

3. Many different factors determine what will happen in the sky.

_____

_____

4. Until we can track all factors, we can't predict perfectly.

_____

_____

5. Whoever gives a forecast is making a guess.

_____

_____

6. Since weather is so uncertain, predictions have percentages.

_____

_____

7. A 50 percent chance of rain means that there is a 50 percent chance of fair weather.

_____

_____

8. When air crosses a large lake, it picks up moisture.

_____

_____

9. Because of lake-effect rain, Valparaiso is called "Vapor Rain Snow."

_____

_____

10. Halifax gets as precipitation whatever moisture the Atlantic Ocean dishes up.

_____

_____

NEL   **Chapter 23** Sentence Basics   291

LO8 Real-World Application

Identify In the e-mail below, underline simple subjects once and simple predicates twice. Circle dependent clauses.

Send	Attach	Fonts	Colors	Save As Draft

To: Teri Bell

Subject: Revision Suggestions

Hi, Teri:

I enjoyed your article, "What Is New in *BattleTown 2*," submitted for publication on MMORPNews2.com. We are very interested in publishing your article but would like to request a few revisions before we send contracts.

This is a quick rundown of our revision suggestions:

1. The opening could be more gripping. The title works well to grab the reader's interest, but the opening feels flat. Perhaps you could provide a glimpse of new features of game play, or even give a scenario that wasn't possible in *BattleTown 1*.

2. A direct quotation from Todd Allen would strengthen the centre section. Though you allude to your interview on many occasions, Todd never gets to speak for himself, and he is a definite name in the industry.

3. Can you get permission to use the visuals? AssemblyArts would love the free publicity, but you need written permission to include the screenshots.

If you could make these changes, we would be very interested in publishing your article. Once I see the revised piece, I can send a contract for you to sign.

Thanks,
Richard Prince

Expand Consider the short sentence below, and answer the adjective and adverb questions underneath. Then expand the sentence using some of the words, phrases, and clauses you created in your answers.

The agent called.

Which agent? _____

What kind of agent? _____

Called *when*? _____

Called *how*? _____

Sentence: _____

> "A complex system that works is invariably found to have evolved from a simple system that works."
>
> —John Gaule

Simple, Compound, and Complex Sentences

24

Most leaves have a central stem with veins extending from it. Sometimes this structure forms a simple oval, but at other times, two or more ovals connect to form a compound leaf. And the shape of some leaves is complex, as if a number of leaves were fused together.

Sentences are similar. All have a noun and a verb, but some stop at this simple structure. In other cases, two or more sentences combine to make a compound sentence. And when a sentence has one or more dependent clauses fused to it, it becomes complex.

This chapter shows how to create simple, compound, and complex sentences. As with leaves, variety makes sentences beautiful.

Learning Outcomes

LO1 Create simple sentences.

LO2 Create simple sentences with compound subjects.

LO3 Create simple sentences with compound predicates.

LO4 Create compound sentences.

LO5 Create complex sentences.

LO6 Create complex sentences with relative clauses.

LO7 Apply parallelism at the clause level.

LO8 Apply simple, compound, and complex sentences in a real-world document.

Test Your Knowledge

Determine if the following sentences are simple, compound, or complex. Come back to any sentences you are unsure of after you have read the chapter.

1. Bruce Lee and Chuck Norris starred together in the film. _____
2. Lee stretched to warm up his muscles. _____
3. The cameras couldn't capture Lee's punches because they were too fast. _____
4. Lee kicked the boxing bag and it broke in two. _____
5. They kicked and punched each other. _____

LO1 Simple Sentences

A **simple sentence** consists of a subject and a verb. The subject is a noun or pronoun that names what the sentence is about. The verb tells what the subject does or is.

Rachel sang.
subject verb

Modifiers

Other words can be added to modify the subject. Words that modify the subject answer the adjective questions: *which, what kind of, how many, how much.*

My new roommate Rachel sang.
(Which Rachel do you mean?)

Other words can also modify the verb. These words and phrases answer the adverb questions: *how, when, where, why, to what degree,* and *how often.*

Rachel sang **in the shower at the top of her lungs.**
            (Where and how did Rachel sing?)

Direct and Indirect Objects

The verb might also be followed by a noun or pronoun that receives the action of the verb. Such a word is called the **direct object**, and it answers the question *what* or *whom?*

Rachel sang **"I Need a Hero."**
        (What did Rachel sing?)

Another noun or pronoun could come between the verb and the direct object, telling *to whom* or *for whom* an action is done. Such a word is the **indirect object**.

I gave **her** a picture of Chuck Norris.
        (I gave a picture of Chuck Norris to whom?)

> ### Say It
>
> Team up with a partner and follow these steps: One of you speaks the sentence aloud, and the other asks the question in italics. Then the first person says the sentence again, inserting an answer.
>
> 1. We sang songs. (*Where did you sing songs?*)
> 2. The song was our favourite. (*Which song was your favourite?*)
> 3. Rachel sang. (*What did Rachel sing?*)
> 4. I sang a song. (*To whom did you sing a song?*)

Creating Simple Sentences

Create Provide a noun for a subject and a verb for a predicate. Then write a sentence with the noun and verb, adding modifiers that answer the question asked in each case.

1. | Subject | Verb |

Which?

_____

_____

2. | Subject | Verb |

What kind of?

_____

_____

3. | Subject | Verb |

When?

_____

_____

4. | Subject | Verb |

Where?

_____

_____

5. | Subject | Verb |

How?

_____

_____

LO2 Simple Sentences with Compound Subjects

A simple sentence can have a **compound subject** (two or more subjects).

A Simple Sentence with Two Subjects

To write a simple sentence with two subjects, join them using *and* or *or*.

> **One Subject:** Lee worked on the Rube Goldberg machine.
> **Two Subjects:** Lee **and** Jerome will add the lever arm that tips the bucket.
> Lee **or** Jerome will add the lever arm that tips the bucket.
>
> **One Subject:** Ms. Claymore will help them attach the flywheel.
> **Two Subjects:** Ms. Claymore **and** her aide will help them attach the flywheel.
> Ms. Claymore **or** her aide will help them attach the flywheel.

A Simple Sentence with Three or More Subjects

To write a simple sentence with three or more subjects, create a series. List each subject, placing a comma after all but the last, and place an *and* or *or* before the last.

> **Three Subjects:** Jerome, Lee, and Sandra are finishing the machine soon.
> **Five Subjects:** Jerome, Lee, Sandra, Ms. Claymore, **and** her aide will enter the machine in a contest.

Note: When a compound subject is joined by *and*, the subject is plural and requires a plural verb. When a compound subject is joined by *or*, the verb should match the last subject.

> **Ms. Claymore and her aide need** to submit the entry form.
> **Ms. Claymore or her aide needs** to submit the entry form.

Say It

Speak each of the following sentences out loud.

1. Jerome *loves* the Rube Goldberg project.
2. Jerome *and* Sandra *love* the Rube Goldberg project.
3. Jerome *or* Sandra *works* on it every day after school.
4. Jerome, Sandra, *and* Lee *have* contributed most.
5. Jerome, Sandra, *or* Lee *has* contributed most.

Using Compound Subjects

Create Write subjects in each of the boxes provided. Then write a sentence that combines these subjects as a compound subject using *and* or *or*.

1. | Subject | Subject |

_____

_____

2. | Subject | Subject |

_____

_____

3. | Subject | Subject | Subject |

_____

_____

4. | Subject | Subject | Subject |

_____

_____

5. | Subject | Subject | Subject | Subject |

_____

_____

6. | Subject | Subject | Subject | Subject |

_____

_____

LO3 Simple Sentences with Compound Predicates

A simple sentence can also have a compound predicate—one that contains two or more verbs. Remember that the predicate tells what the subject is doing or being, so as long as all the verbs in it connect to the same subject, the sentence is still a simple sentence.

Two Verbs

To create simple sentence with two verbs, join the two verbs using *and* or *or*.

> **One Verb:** The band **rocked.**
> **Two Verbs:** The band **rocked and danced.**

Remember that the predicate includes not just the verbs, but also words that modify or complete the verbs.

> **One Verb:** The band **played** their hit single.
> **Two Verbs:** The band **played** their hit single **and covered** other songs.

Three or More Verbs

To create a compound predicate with three or more verbs, list the verbs in a series, with a comma after each except the last, and the word *and* or *or* before the last.

> **Three Verbs:** The lead singer **crooned, wailed, and roared.**
> **Five Verbs:** The fans **clapped, screamed, danced, cheered, and swayed.**

If any or all of the verbs in the series are accompanied by modifiers and/or completing words (direct or indirect objects), place the commas after these elements.

> The crowd members **got** to their feet, **waved** their hands back and forth, **and sang** along with the band.

Fuse/Thinkstock

Using Compound Predicates

Write For each subject below, create a compound predicate. Begin by writing a verb, along with any modifiers or completing words, in each box. Then write a simple sentence that joins the parts into a compound predicate with *and* or *or*.

1. The reporters

Predicate, Part 1

Predicate, Part 2

_____

_____

2. The police

Predicate, Part 1

Predicate, Part 2

_____

_____

3. The manager

Predicate, Part 1

Predicate, Part 2

_____

_____

4. The bouncer

Predicate, Part 1

Predicate, Part 2

Predicate, Part 3

_____

_____

_____

Learning Outcome

Create compound sentences.

LO4 Compound Sentences

A **compound sentence** is made out of simple sentences joined by a coordinating conjunction: *for, and, nor, but, or, yet,* or *so.* (You can remember these conjunctions using the **acronym** FANBOYS.)

Compound of Two Sentences

Insight

The word *and* indicates that the second clause provides additional information. The words *but, or, nor,* and *yet* create a contrast. The words *for* and *so* indicate that one clause is the cause of the other.

Most compound sentences connect two simple sentences, which are also called independent clauses. Connect the sentences by placing a comma after the first sentence and using a coordinating conjunction after the comma.

> **Two Sentences:** We ordered pizza. I got just one piece.
> **Compound Sentence:** We ordered pizza, **but** I got just one piece.

Compound of Three or More Sentences

Sometimes, you might want to join three or more short sentences in a compound sentence.

> **Two Sentences:** Tim likes cheese. Jan likes veggie. I like pepperoni.
> **Compound Sentence:** Tim likes cheese, Jan likes veggie, **and** I like pepperoni.

You can also join the sentences using semicolons. Authors sometimes use this approach to describe a long, involved process or a flurry of activity.

> Tim ate the cheese pizza; Jan ate the veggie pizza; Ray showed up and ate the pepperoni pizza; I got back in time for the last slice.

Note: Remember that a compound sentence is made of two or more complete sentences. Each part needs to have its own subject and predicate.

Vocabulary

compound sentence
two or more simple sentences joined with a coordinating conjunction

acronym
a word formed with the first letters of a group of other words

professionnelphoto/iStock/Thinkstock

Creating Compound Sentences

Write Write a simple sentence for each prompt, then combine the simple sentences to form a compound sentence.

1. What pizza do you like? _____

   What pizza does a friend like? _____

   Compound Sentence: _____

   _____

2. Where do you go for pizza? _____

   What other place do people go? _____

   Compound Sentence: _____

   _____

3. Who likes thin crust pizza? _____

   Who likes pan pizza? _____

   Who likes stuffed pizza? _____

   Compound Sentence: _____

   _____

4. What is the weirdest pizza? _____

   What is the grossest pizza? _____

   What is the stinkiest pizza? _____

   Compound Sentence: _____

   _____

   _____

5. When do you eat pizza? _____

   When do your friends eat pizza? _____

   When does your family eat pizza? _____

   Compound Sentence: _____

   _____

   _____

LO5 Complex Sentences

A complex sentence shows a special relationship between two ideas. Instead of connecting two sentences as equal ideas (as in a compound sentence), a complex sentence shows that one idea depends on the other.

Using a Subordinating Conjunction

You can create a complex sentence out of two simple sentences by placing a subordinating conjunction before the sentence that is less important. Here are some common subordinating conjunctions:

after	before	so that	where
although	even though	that	whereas
as	if	though	while
as if	in order that	till	
as long as	provided that	until	
because	since	when	

Adding a subordinating conjunction turns the simple sentence into a dependent clause—one that depends on the rest of the sentence and cannot stand on its own. The conjunction shows the relationship between the two ideas in the complex sentence.

Two Sentences:	We played strong offence. We won the football game.
Complex Sentence:	**Because** we played strong offence, we won the football game.
	We won the football game **because** we played strong offence.

Note: The subordinating conjunction goes at the beginning of the less important clause, but the two clauses could go in either order. When the dependent clause comes second, it usually isn't set off with a comma.

Compound-Complex

You can also create a compound-complex sentence by placing a subordinating conjunction before a simple sentence and connecting it to a compound sentence.

Simple Sentence:	I threw two touchdown passes.
Compound Sentence:	Jake kicked the extra points and the other team couldn't catch up.
Compound-Complex:	**After I threw two touchdown passes,** Jake kicked the extra points, and the other team couldn't catch up.

Speaking & Listening

Read the example complex and compound-complex sentences aloud. Despite their daunting names, these sentences aren't that complicated. You use them all the time in speech. Experiment with them in your writing.

Creating Complex Sentences

Write Write a simple sentence after each prompt. Then select a subordinating conjunction from the list above, place it at the beginning of one sentence, and combine the two sentences into a single complex sentence.

1. What did you play?_____

   Did you win or lose?_____

   Complex sentence: _____

2. Against whom did you play?_____

   Why did you play the opponent?_____

   Complex sentence: _____

3. Who won the game?_____

   Why did that side win?_____

   Complex sentence: _____

4. Where did you play?_____

   Where else could you have played?_____

   Complex sentence: _____

5. What surprised you?_____

   Why did it surprise you?_____

   Complex sentence: _____

6. How long did you play?_____

   When did you stop?_____

   Complex sentence: _____

LO6 Complex Sentences with Relative Clauses

In a complex sentence, one idea depends on the other. You've seen how a dependent clause can start with a subordinating conjunction. Another type of dependent clause starts with a relative pronoun.

Relative Clauses

Insight

In some languages, if the relative pronoun is the object of the clause it introduces, another pronoun is inserted in the clause creating a structure like this:

I liked the gift that my boss gave it *to me.*

In English, no additional pronoun is inserted:

I liked the gift that my boss gave to me.

A relative clause is a group of words that begins with a relative pronoun *(that, which, who, whom)* and includes a verb and any words that modify or complete it:

> **Relative Clauses:** that leads into the garden
> which usually leans against the shed
> who planted the scallions
> whom I asked to help me weed

Each relative clause above has a subject and a verb, but none of the clauses is a complete sentence. All need to be connected to a complete sentence.

> **Complex Sentences:** I followed the path that leads into the garden.
> I looked for the shovel, which usually leans against the shed.
> We have many onions thanks to a friend who planted the scallions.
> I worked with Tina, whom I asked to help me weed.

That and *Which*

The relative pronoun *that* signals that the information after it is necessary to the sentence. The relative pronoun *which* signals that the information is not necessary, so the clause is set off with a comma.

> ***That:*** The scallions **that** we planted this spring taste strongest. (*That* introduces the clause that explains which scallions you are talking about.)
> ***Which:*** I love scallions, **which** I eat raw or fried. (The clause beginning with *which* does not define the scallions but just adds more information about them.)

Who and *Whom*

Vocabulary

relative clause
a group of words that begins with a relative pronoun and includes a verb; it cannot stand alone as a sentence

relative pronoun
a pronoun *(that, which, who, whom)* that relates a relative clause with another word in the sentence

The pronoun *who* is the subject of the relative clause that it introduces. The pronoun *whom* is a direct object of a clause it introduces.

> ***Who:*** I helped the woman **who** harvested scallions. (*Who* is the subject.)
> ***Whom:*** I thanked the woman **whom** I helped. (*Whom* is the direct object.)

Creating Complex Sentences with Relative Clauses

Create For each item, write a relative clause beginning with the pronoun provided. Then write a complex sentence that includes the relative clause. In case you need a topic idea, think of a party you have attended or one that you would like to attend.

1. Relative clause: _that_____

   Complex sentence: _____

   _____

   _____

2. Relative clause: _who_____

   Complex sentence: _____

   _____

   _____

3. Relative clause: _which_____

   Complex sentence: _____

   _____

   _____

4. Relative clause: _whom_____

   Complex sentence: _____

   _____

   _____

5. Relative clause: _that_____

   Complex sentence: _____

   _____

   _____

6. Relative clause: _which_____

   Complex sentence: _____

   _____

   _____

Review

See Chapter 29, LO3, for more information on faulty parallelism.

LO7 Applying Parallelism at the Clause Level

Patterns help people make sense of their world. In writing, repeated patterns are called *parallelism* or *parallel structure*, and sound parallelism helps readers understand a piece of writing.

Clause-Level Parallelism

Although parallelism is often talked about with lists, the principle applies at the clause level, too. For example, joining two independent clauses with a coordinating conjunction is only part of the job; both clauses should also follow the same grammatical pattern. See how the sentences below read more smoothly with correct parallelism. The first is a compound sentence, the second a complex sentence with one subordinate clause, the third a complex sentence with series of subordinate clauses.

Faulty parallelism:	Because of the storm, the school board cancelled buses, but transit was kept running by the city.
Corrected:	Because of the storm, the school board cancelled buses, but the city kept transit running.
Faulty parallelism:	To play defence was Kari's preference even though she played centre well.
Corrected:	Kari preferred to play defence even though she played centre well.
Faulty parallelism:	The court heard that the criminal planned ahead, the crime involved significant violence, and that four bystanders were injured.
Corrected:	The court heard that the criminal planned ahead, that he used significant violence, and that he injured four bystanders.

Creating Parallelism at the Clause Level

Correct Rewrite these examples to correct the faulty parallelism.

1. Although the negotiator worked all night, he claimed that he was wide awake, needed no break, and that he was ready to go back for more discussion.

_____

_____

_____

_____

2. Dawn spent four hours on the Internet looking for closet hangers, and she chooses expensive teak ones for her front hall closet.

_____

_____

_____

3. Billie applied to Metro College, and she was given a scholarship.

_____

_____

_____

_____

4. Lise's mother would not let her go to the movie version of *The Golden Compass* because her mother was told by a priest that the movie was anti-Catholic.

_____

_____

_____

5. Despite having finished all his work in the warehouse, created a new front page for the company website, and despite having worked overtime the night before, the manager refuses to let Kelsey go home an hour early the day before Thanksgiving.

_____

_____

_____

_____

Chapter 24 Simple, Compound, and Complex Sentences

Learning Outcome

Apply simple, compound, and complex sentences in a real-world document.

LO8 Real-World Application

Rewrite Read the following message about a meeting. Note how every sentence is a simple sentence. Rewrite the message, combining sentences into some compound or complex sentences and improving the flow.

Workplace

Using a variety of sentences in workplace writing will help ideas flow and will present a polished image.

Dear Mr. Lindau:

You asked about the Monday production meeting. I will summarize it. The production staff met with the editors. The writers explained their new project. It focuses on twenty-first century skills. The writers presented two chapters. They will become a prototype.

The new project needs to be visual. It should appeal to students and teachers. The design needs to make text accessible. The writing has an open quality. It still feels academic. The book should be available for sale in the fall. A teacher's edition will follow.

The designers are beginning work on a prototype. The writers continue to create chapters.

Dear Mr. Lindau:

_____

_____

_____

_____

_____

_____

_____

_____

_____

_____

_____

_____

_____

_____

_____

_____

_____

_____

© Aurelie and Morgan David de Lossy/cultura/Corbis

25

Sentence Style

The purpose of makeup is to accentuate a person's natural beauty. Mascara that thickens lashes, blush that lends colour to cheeks, lipstick that tastefully outlines the contours of a person's lips—these are the appropriate uses of makeup.

Curly moustaches and goatees are not.

In the same way, sentence style is not about putting on a false face or making elaborate curlicues in your writing. It's about saying what you want to say and expressing who you really are. This chapter will help you create effective sentence style.

Learning Outcomes

LO1 Vary sentence lengths.

LO2 Vary sentence beginnings.

LO3 Combine with coordination.

LO4 Combine with subordination.

LO5 Combine by moving parts.

LO6 Combine by deleting.

LO7 Expand sentences.

LO8 Model professional sentences.

LO9 Revise a real-world document for sentence style.

What do you think?

What will this young man think of his makeup? What do others think? What do readers think of a sentence style that is equally fake and "dressed up"?

L◯1 Varying Sentence Lengths

To create a smooth flow of thought, use a variety of sentence lengths.

Short Sentences

Short sentences can be powerful. They make a point. In dramatic circumstances, a series of short sentences can create a staccato effect:

> I like pigs. Dogs look up to us. Cats look down on us. Pigs treat us as equals.
>
> —Sir Winston Churchill

Sometimes a series of short sentences will start to sound choppy. It is usually best to use short sentences in combination with longer sentences.

Other Classes

Read an article or a speech in your major, noting the lengths of the sentences. Count the words in each. What effect does the variety of sentences (or lack of variety) have on readability?

Medium-Length Sentences

Medium-length sentences do most of the work in everyday writing. They are not overly punchy or overly complicated, and so they communicate well.

> I look to the future because that's where I'm going to spend the rest of my life.
>
> —George Burns

Long Sentences

Long sentences express complex ideas and create an expansive feeling. The long sentence may be the hardest type to pull off because it needs to have a clear sense of direction. Otherwise, it may begin to ramble.

> I write entirely to find out what I'm thinking, what I'm looking at, what I see and what it means, what I want and what I fear.
>
> —Joan Didion

Varying Lengths

The most effective writing includes sentences of different lengths, serving different purposes. Read this call to action, noting the different lengths of sentences and their effect on the whole.

> You're alive. Do something. The directive in life, the moral imperative was so uncomplicated. It could be expressed in single words, not complete sentences. It sounded like this: Look. Listen. Choose. Act.
>
> —Barbara Hall

Varying Sentence Lengths

Create Write the types of sentences requested below. Use the third person (*he/she/it/they*).

1. Write a short sentence naming a popular TV show or film.

   _____

2. Write a medium sentence describing this show or film.

   _____

   _____

3. Write a long sentence indicating what people like most about this show or film.

   _____

   _____

   _____

4. Write a medium sentence providing a final thought about this popular TV show or film.

   _____

   _____

Create Write the types of sentences requested below. Use the first person (*I/we*).

1. Write a short sentence indicating your course of study.

   _____

2. Write a medium sentence describing your course of study.

   _____

   _____

3. Write a long sentence explaining why you chose to follow this course.

   _____

   _____

   _____

4. Write a medium sentence providing a final thought about the course of study.

   _____

   _____

LO2 New Beginnings 1

If every sentence begins with the subject, writing can become monotonous. Vary sentence beginnings by starting in these different ways.

Prepositional Phrase

Test Taking

It is more important to be able to use prepositional phrases and infinitive phrases than to be able to identify them. However, some tests require the ability to identify phrases. For more practice, see Chapter 23, LO6, and Chapter 34, LO3.

A **prepositional phrase** is formed from a preposition (*in, at, through*) followed by an object (a noun and any modifiers). (For more about prepositions, see Chapter 34, LO3, Common Prepositions.)

PR = Preposition
O = Object

After the game ...	For that matter ...	With a renewed interest ...
PR O	PR O	PR O

A prepositional phrase functions as an adjective or an adverb. That means that a prepositional phrase can answer any of the adjective or adverb questions:

Adjective Questions	Adverb Questions
Which?	How?
What kind of?	When?
How many?	Where?
How much?	Why?
	How often?
	To what degree?

Infinitive Phrase

An **infinitive phrase** is formed from the word *to* followed by a verb and any objects and modifiers.

V = Verb
O = Object

To prove my point ...	To complete the comparison ...	To be specific ...
V O	V O	V O

Vocabulary

prepositional phrase
phrase formed from a preposition followed by an object and any modifiers; it can function as an adjective or adverb

infinitive phrase
verbal phrase that begins with *to* followed by a verb and any objects; it can function as a noun, an adjective, or an adverb

An infinitive phrase functions as a noun, an adjective, or an adverb. It can answer any of the adjective and adverb questions above, but it can also serve as the subject of the sentence:

To complete my degree is my goal.
(*To complete my degree* functions as the subject of the sentence.)

Creating Sentence Variety with Prepositional and Infinitive Phrases

Vary For each sentence below, add the requested type of beginning.

1. (Prepositional phrase):

   _____

   they decided to go out for ice cream.

2. (Infinitive phrase):

   _____

   they bought homemade frozen custard instead.

3. (Prepositional phrase):

   _____

   the custard was richer and creamier.

4. (Infinitive phrase):

   _____

   an occasional treat like this helps keep life in balance.

Create Write the types of sentences requested below. Use the first person (*I/we*).

1. Write a short sentence about a treat you like. (Begin with a prepositional phrase.)

   _____

2. Write a medium sentence about the treat. (Begin with an infinitive phrase.)

   _____

   _____

3. Write a long sentence about the treat. (Begin with a prepositional phrase.)

   _____

   _____

   _____

4. Write a medium sentence about the treat. (Begin with an infinitive phrase.)

   _____

   _____

Chapter 25 Sentence Style

LO2 New Beginnings II

If sentences still sound repetitive, you can start with two other constructions—participial phrases and adverb clauses.

Participial Phrase

Insight

Participial phrases and gerund phrases both can start with verbal forms ending in *ing*, but participial phrases function as adjectives, and gerund phrases function as nouns. For a closer look at these phrases, see Chapter 32, LO7, Verbals.

A participial phrase is formed from a participle (a verbal form ending in *ing* or *ed*) and any objects and modifiers. (For more on participles, see Chapter 32, LO7, Verbals.)

PA = Participle
O = Object

Expecting the best . . .	Considering the source . . .	Concerned the plan . . .
PA O	PA O	PA O

A participial phrase functions as an adjective. That means that the phrase answers one of the adjective questions.

Adjective Questions	
Which?	How many?
What kind of?	How much?

Adverb Clause

An adverb clause is formed from a subordinating conjunction followed by a noun (or pronoun) and verb (and any objects and modifiers).

SC = Subordinating Conjunction   N = Noun   V = Verb

When Bill arrived . . .	Because Jan climbed so high . . .	While Ted watched . . .
SC N V	SC N V	SC N V

Subordinating Conjunctions			
after	before	since	when
although	even though	so that	whenever
as	given that	that	where
as if	if	though	whereas
as long as	in order that	unless	while
because	provided that	until	

An adverb clause functions as an adverb, answering one of the adverb questions.

Adverb Questions	
How?	Why?
When?	How often?
Where?	To what degree?

Vocabulary

participial phrase
phrase beginning with a participle (*ing* or *ed* form of verb) plus objects and modifiers; used as an adjective

adverb clause
clause beginning with a subordinating conjunction and functioning as an adverb

Creating Sentence Variety with Participial Phrases and Adverb Clauses

Vary For each sentence below, add the requested type of beginning.

---

1. (Participial phrase):

   _____

   we worked all through the evening.

2. (Adverb clause):

   _____

   the lights from our office shone out on the people passing by.

3. (Participial phrase):

   _____

   I smiled at my colleagues and shook their hands.

4. (Adverb clause):

   _____

   the project was finished, and we could at last go home.

Create Write the types of sentences requested below. Write these sentences in the third person (he/she/it).

---

1. Write a short sentence about working. (Begin with a participial phrase.)

   _____

2. Write a medium sentence about working. (Begin with an adverb clause.)

   _____

   _____

3. Write a long sentence about working. (Begin with an adverb clause.)

   _____

   _____

   _____

4. Write a medium sentence about working. (Begin with a participial phrase.)

   _____

   _____

Chapter 25   Sentence Style

LO3 Using Coordination

When you have too many short sentences, writing begins to sound choppy. If you notice this problem in your writing, look for sentences that have related ideas and combine them.

Coordination

Insight

The word *coordinate*
means "to place
together." A *coordinating
conjunction*, then, is a
word that connects ideas
of equal importance,
placing them together.

If two sentences express ideas of equal importance, you can combine the sentences by connecting them with a **coordinating conjunction**. (See the box below; remember the acronym *fanboys*.)

Coordinating Conjunctions						
for	and	nor	but	or	yet	so

Choppy: Human beings are self-aware. Animals may or may not be.

Combined: Human beings are self-aware, **but** animals may or may not be.

Note: Remember to place a comma before the conjunction.

The different coordinating conjunctions make different connections between ideas:

Comparison → and
Contrast → but, yet
Options → or, nor
Cause → so, for

Human beings recognize themselves in mirrors, **and** great apes can as well. Dolphins recognize themselves in mirrors, **so** they must be self-aware. Dogs, cats, and babies do not, **so** their self-awareness is in question.

Scorpp/Shutterstock.com

Vocabulary

coordinating conjunction
a word that connects
sentence parts that are of
equal importance

Combining Using Coordination

Coordinate Mark the sentences below to show how you would combine them using coordinating conjunctions. Use the correction marks as needed to add words and change punctuation and capitalization.

1. Gordon Gallup created the mirror test. He was testing self-awareness.

2. Gallup put odourless dye on an animal. Spots were in front and in back.

3. The animal looked in a mirror. Some animals noticed the front spot.

4. The animal shifted to see better. Pawing the body part showed awareness.

5. Other animals did not notice the spot. The mirror image seemed to be another animal.

6. Great apes, dolphins and orcas, and elephants passed. Monkeys did not.

7. Pigeons could be trained to pass. Magpies passed without training.

8. A sticker was under the magpie's beak. The bird tried to pull it off.

9. The other passing creatures had big brains. Magpies have small brains.

10. Magpies are visual creatures. Shiny things attract them.

11. Dogs are more olfactory. Smell is used to identify themselves and others.

12. Dogs might need an olfactory test. Smell is a better indicator for them.

13. Humans would fail an olfactory test. We don't want to smell ourselves.

14. Pigs passed a modified test. Food was reflected in a mirror.

15. Most pigs turned around to find the food. One in eight looked behind the mirror.

16. Pigs may not be self-aware. Food-aware is a different story.

17. Squid are very intelligent. Perhaps the mirror test would work for them.

18. Squid have big eyes and brains. Both are needed to succeed on the mirror test.

LO4 Using Subordination

If sentences sound choppy, you can combine them using subordination.

Subordination

If one sentence is more important than the other, you can combine the sentences by connecting them with a subordinating conjunction. (See the box below for examples.) Place the subordinating conjunction before the less important part.

Subordinating Conjunctions

after	before	since	when
although	even though	so that	whenever
as	given that	that	where
as if	if	though	whereas
as long as	in order that	unless	while
because	provided that	until	

Choppy: Every culture has music. Music is an innate part of being human.
Combined: **Because** every culture has music, music is an innate part of being human.

Choppy: Music is a language of emotion. It first touches one's feelings.
Combined: Music is a language of emotion **because** it first touches one's feelings.

Note: If the subordinate clause comes first, put a comma between the clauses. Usually, no comma is used if the subordinate clause follows the main clause.

Different subordinating conjunctions show different kinds of connections:

Time → after, as, as long as, before, since, until, when, whenever, while
Cause → because, given that, if, in order that, provided that, since, so that
Contrast → although, as if, even though, though, unless, whereas, while

sextoacto/Shutterstock.com

Combining Using Subordination

Subordinate Mark the sentences below to show what subordinating conjunction you would use to combine them. Use the correction marks as needed to add words and add and delete punctuation.

Correction Marks	
⌐	delete
d̲	capitalize
D̸	lowercase
∧	insert
⌃	add comma
? ⌃	add question mark
word ⌃	add word
⊙	add period
◯	spelling
∽	switch

1. A note can be high or low. The pitch is the frequency of wavelength.

2. A note can be short or long. The duration is its length in time.

3. Changes in duration make rhythm. Changes in pitch make melodies.

4. Sound is waves. Waves move through air, water, and other substances.

5. We use sound to communicate in speech. Music is the cousin of speech.

6. A spoken sentence can become a melody. The program Autotune can do it.

7. Language communicates emotion. Music communicates emotion even more.

8. Music is also mathematical. It measures pitch and time.

9. Mathematical patterns repeat throughout. Music makes the math emotional.

10. Science designs instruments. Musicians make science into art.

Write For each prompt, write a simple sentence, with a subject and predicate. Then combine the two sentences, using subordination.

1. What music do you like most? _____

   What music do your friends like? _____

   Combine: _____

   _____

2. Where do you get your music? _____

   Where do your friends get their music? _____

   Combine: _____

   _____

LO5 Combining by Moving Parts

Sometimes sentences need to be combined because they cover the same material. The way to combine such sentences is to move one part of one sentence into the other sentence.

Moving a Word

Before: Chinese New Year lasts for 15 days. Each day is festive.

After: Chinese New Year lasts for 15 festive days.

Moving a Phrase

Before: Red lanterns and scare off the monster Nien. Children dressed in red scare him, too.

After: Red lanterns and children dressed in red scare off the monster Nien.

Before: People clean their houses. They try to sweep away bad luck.

After: People clean their houses to sweep away bad luck.

Reworking Sentences

Before: Chinese New Year changes each year. It falls between January 21 and February 20. The date is usually on the second new moon after the winter solstice.

After: Chinese New Year falls between January 21 and February 20, usually on the second new moon after the winter solstice.

NEL

Combining by Moving Parts

Combine Combine each pair of sentences below by moving a word or phrase or by reworking the sentences.

1. Nien used to stalk villages. The monster would devour animals, plants, and people.

   _____

   _____

2. Villagers left food offerings. The offerings would satisfy Nien's hunger.

   _____

   _____

3. A child wearing red confronted Nien. The child in red scared the monster.

   _____

   _____

4. Red became a lucky colour. It was used with lanterns and spring scrolls.

   _____

   _____

5. Firecrackers also scared Nien. They were loud and bright.

   _____

   _____

6. Nien was driven off. The monster was tamed by a Taoist monk.

   _____

   _____

7. The monk rode Nien. The monster never bothered anyone again.

   _____

   _____

8. People cleaned house. They wanted to get rid of bad luck.

   _____

   _____

9. The clean houses were ready. Good luck could come into them.

   _____

   _____

10. Villagers gave each other red envelopes. The envelopes had money inside.

   _____

   _____

Chapter 25 Sentence Style

LO6 Combining by Deleting

When writing is wordy or repetitious, the best way to combine sentences is by finding the key pieces of information, deleting the rest, and writing new sentences from what is left.

Finding the Key Pieces

Read the following paragraph, noting how wordy and repetitious it is. Afterward, note the important ideas that the writer underlined.

> What is the difference between science fiction and fantasy? Well, it seems when you look at it at first that the main difference is that science fiction is about technology while fantasy is about magic. That definition might seem pretty good at first, but when you think about it, the difference between science fiction and fantasy goes deeper. Science fiction is all about achieving the new. In a science fiction story, usually the world is changed by what happens in the story and it will never be the same again. Fantasy is just the opposite. In a fantasy story, the whole point is to get things back to the way they used to be, for example restoring a king or rediscovering an ancient and lost treasure or artifact. When you think of it that way, science fiction is revolutionary and fantasy is reactionary. So, though it is true that science fiction features technology and fantasy features magic, the deeper difference is that science fiction looks to the future and change while fantasy looks to the past and continuity.

Workplace

Workplace writing needs to be concise, clear, and compelling. By finding the important points and deleting the unimportant ones, you can create a message that reaches colleagues and clients.

Rewriting and Combining

Now read the much shorter and more effective sentences that the writer created from the main ideas.

> What is the difference between science fiction and fantasy? Some say science fiction is about technology while fantasy is about magic, but the difference goes deeper. Science fiction is all about achieving the new, while fantasy is about returning to what is old. In that way, science fiction is revolutionary and fantasy is reactionary.

Combining by Deleting

Underline Read the following wordy, repetitive paragraph. Afterward, go back through and reread the paragraph, looking for important details. Underline them.

Let's look at two classic films, one from science fiction and the other from fantasy. The science fiction film is *2001: A Space Odyssey*. The film shows a lot of technology, which may or may not look really impressive now because the film was made in the '60s. The main point of the film is to show the conflict between the human astronauts and their thinking computer, HAL, who tries to take over the ship. The astronauts manage to shut down the computer, but they and the computer are drawn into connection with a mysterious object in space and the people and computer fuse to become a new life form. The world will never be the same. Now think of *The Lord of the Rings*. In it, the whole point is to stop an ancient evil from rising and save the world from being destroyed. This film is all about trying to save something that is important, and even the last part—*The Return of the King*—tells about restoring the ancient lineage of human beings to return their age of glory. The world is renewed. Note how *2001: A Space Odyssey* focuses on plunging headlong into an unknowable future, while *The Lord of the Rings* focuses on returning to a better past.

Combine Rewrite the paragraph above without unimportant details, combining important details into new sentences. Make the new paragraph concise and smooth.

_____

_____

_____

_____

_____

_____

_____

_____

_____

LO7 Sentence Expanding

Sometimes a sentence does not say enough, or it is too general. When that happens, the sentence needs to be expanded. Sentence expanding simply means adding details. The best way to expand a sentence is to answer the 5 W's about the topic.

Speaking & Listening

Imagine each sentence-expanding activity that follows as a conversation you are having with a friend. You might even read the sentence aloud and have a friend ask you each of the questions beneath. Then roll some of your answers into a single, more-informative sentence.

Original Sentence: My friend likes extreme sports.

Who likes extreme sports? my friend Liam

What sports does he like? He likes BMX biking and jumping.

Where does he train? He trains in a field beside his yard.

When did he start? about eight years ago

Why does he do it? He loves the adrenaline rush.

Expanded Sentence: My friend Liam likes the extreme sport of BMX biking and jumping, and he trains in a field beside his house.

Note: The expanded sentence does not use all of the answers to the 5 W's, but a second sentence could cover the other details:

> He started BMX jumping about eight years ago and says he loves the adrenaline rush.

niderlander/Shutterstock.com

Expanding Sentences

Expand Expand the sentences below by answering the questions provided.

1. **Short Sentence:** My friend needs help.

   a. Who is your friend?_____

   b. What help does the person need?_____

   c. Where does the friend need help?_____

   d. When does the person need help?_____

   e. Why does the person need help?_____

   Expanded Sentence: _____

   _____

   _____

   _____

   _____

   _____

2. **Short Sentence:** My friend got hurt.

   a. Who is your friend?_____

   b. What happened to the person?_____

   c. Where did the person get hurt?_____

   d. When did the person get hurt?_____

   e. Why did the person get hurt?_____

   Expanded Sentence: _____

   _____

   _____

   _____

   _____

   _____

LO8 Sentence Modelling

Sentence modelling helps you see new ways to put sentences together. Modelling involves reading a well-written sentence and then writing a similar sentence by substituting words. Here are two **examples** of original sentences, each with a new sentence modelled after it.

Original Sentence: It seemed the world was divided into good and bad people. The good ones slept better, while the bad ones seemed to enjoy the waking hours much more.

—Woody Allen

Modelled Sentence: I figured the school was divided into talkers and listeners. The talkers dominated in class, while the listeners got better grades on the tests.

Note: The new sentence doesn't *exactly* match the model. Writers always make adjustments to make their sentences work.

Original Sentence: Storms are sensual feasts—the cold wet touch of rain, the smell of damp soil, the percussive crack of thunder, the brilliant flashes of lightning.

—Eli King

Modelled Sentence: Morning on the lake was a languid treat—the soft wet slap of oars, the coils of rising mist, the watery murmur of waves, the dark, welling depths.

Note: In the sentence above, the writer chose words that had an opposite feeling from the ones in the original and created a passage with a very different impact. Notice, however, that the sentence still works and makes sense.

Richard Bowden/Shutterstock.com

Modelling Sentences

Model Create sentences that model the ones below.

1. A voice is a human gift; it should be cherished and used, to utter fully human speech as possible. Powerlessness and silence go together.
   —Margaret Atwood

   _____

   _____

2. It was a bright cold day in April, and the clocks were striking thirteen.
   —George Orwell

   _____

   _____

3. The average, healthy, well-adjusted adult gets up at seven-thirty in the morning feeling just plain terrible.
   —Jean Kerr

   _____

   _____

4. Arranging a bowl of flowers in the morning can give a sense of quiet in a crowded day—like writing a poem, or saying a prayer.
   —Anne Morrow Lindberg

   _____

   _____

5. The secret of staying young is to live honestly, eat slowly, and lie about your age.
   —Lucille Ball

   _____

   _____

6. A boy can learn a lot from a dog: obedience, loyalty, and the importance of turning around three times before lying down.
   —Robert Benchley

   _____

   _____

7. She had always wanted words; she loved them, grew up on them. Words gave her clarity, brought reason, shape.
   —Michael Ondaatje

   _____

   _____

Chapter 25 Sentence Style

LO9 Real-World Application

Read the following cover letter, written to present a resumé for a job. Note how the writer uses a lot of short, say-nothing sentences that could refer to anyone. Then rewrite the letter below, expanding the sentences with details you either make up or take from your own life. Make the letter interesting, informative, and engaging by improving the sentence style and enriching the content.

Learning Outcome

Revise a real-world document for sentence style.

Workplace

As you can see from this exercise, bland sentences can cost you a job, and great sentences can land you one.

Dear Mr. Dawson:

Do you need a good worker? I need a good employer. My education is good. I have work experience.

Many traits make me a good worker. I do well with many things.

Do you need a good worker? If so, please contact me.

I look forward to hearing from you.

Sincerely,

Dear Mr. Dawson:

"My idea of an agreeable person is a person
who agrees with me."

—Benjamin Disraeli

26

Subject–Verb Agreement

When two people agree, they can work together. They have the same goals and outlook, and they can become a team.

Subjects and verbs are much the same. If the subject is plural, the verb needs to be as well, or they can't work together. Without agreement, these words fight each other; instead of conveying ideas, they disrupt communication.

This chapter focuses on the agreement between subjects and verbs. After you work through the exercises here, you'll find it easy to write agreeable sentences.

Learning Outcomes

LO1 Make subjects and verbs agree.

LO2 Make two subjects agree with verbs.

LO3 Practise agreement with *I* and *you*.

LO4 Practise agreement with indefinite pronouns.

LO5 Practise agreement with collective nouns and measurements.

Test Your Knowledge

In the following sentences, correct any subject–verb agreement errors by deleting the wrong verb forms and writing the correct verbs above.

1. My new car are an automatic.

2. Both the new car and the old car is ice blue.

3. The Prius and the Taurus has front-wheel drive.

4. A car become your best friend when you commute.

5. The Prius have four speakers, but the Taurus have just two.

LO1 Basic Subject–Verb Agreement

A **verb** must **agree in number** with the **subject** of the sentence. If the subject is singular, the verb must be singular. If the subject is plural, the verb must be plural.

singular subject	+	singular verb	= agreement		plural subject	+	plural verb	= agreement

The truck needs a tune-up.
This book is my sister's.

The trucks need tune-ups.
The other books are mine.

Note how plural subjects often end in *s*, but plural verbs usually do not. Also note that other than certain *be* verbs, only present tense verbs have separate singular and plural forms, and only in the third person (e.g., singular *he/she*/it vs. plural *they*).

Present:	singular	plural	Past:	singular	plural
	she walks	they walk		she walked	they walked
	he sees	they see		he saw	they saw
	the dog eats	the dogs eat		the dog ate	the dogs ate
	it is	they are		it was	they were

To make most third-person verbs singular, add just an *s*.

run—runs   write—writes   stay—stays

The verbs *do* and *go* are made third-person singular by adding an *es*.

do—does   go—goes

When a verb ends in *ch, sh, x,* or *z*, create the third-person singular form by adding *es*.

latch—latches   wish—wishes   fix—fixes   buzz—buzzes

When a verb ends in a consonant followed by a *y*, change the *y* to *i* and add *es* to form the third-person singular.

try—tries   fly—flies   cry—cries   quantify—quantifies

Take Special Care

When correcting for subject–verb agreement, do **not** change the verb tense (see Chapter 32, LOs 4, 5, and 6) instead of changing the form of the verb to make it singular or plural.

Subject–Verb Error: The painting attract attention.

Verb Tense Changed: The painting attracted attention.

Corrected: The painting attracts attention.

Vocabulary

verb
tells what is happening and gives us a time frame for the action

agree in number
match, as when a subject and verb are both singular, or when they are both plural

subject
indicates who or what is doing the action

Correcting Basic Subject–Verb Agreement

Write In each sentence below, write a correct form of the verb in parentheses.

1. A philosophy major _____ about thinking. (know)

2. A philosopher _____ to find philosophical work. (try)

3. An employer rarely _____ to hire philosophers. (wish)

4. But such students _____ able to think. (is)

5. My roommate _____ philosophy. (study)

6. He also _____ to study the want ads for jobs. (need)

7. He _____ employers need thinkers. (say)

8. That idea _____ sense. (make)

9. But that idea doesn't _____ people hire him. (make)

10. At his job, he _____ lawn mowers very philosophically. (fix)

Speaking & Listening

After completing the sentences in the first activity, say them aloud, emphasizing the underlined verbs.

Correct Read the following paragraph. Correct any agreement errors you find by crossing out the incorrect verb and writing the correct present tense verb above.

The philosopher Plato say the material world aren't the real world. He say we sees shadows on a cave wall. Plato believe in eternal forms of perfection. Every real table in the world are patterned after the perfect form of a table. In that way, people too is patterned after the perfect form of people. Though Plato live more than three hundred years before Jesus, many Christian thinkers likes his concept of eternal forms. The idea fit well with the ideas of a soul and a creator. Many modern thinkers, though, has the opposite idea. They says that only physical things is real. Plato, of course, disagree.

Write For each verb below, write one sentence using the verb in its third-person singular form.

1. fly _____

2. do _____

3. fish _____

4. wax _____

5. go _____

6. deny _____

LO2 Agreement with Two Subjects

Sentences with **compound subjects** have special rules to make sure that they agree.

Two or More Subjects

When a sentence has two or more subjects joined by *and,* the verb should be plural.

Serge Vero/Shutterstock.com

plural
subject + plural
verb = agreement

Jumbo and Dumbo march.

Review

For more practice with
compound subjects, see
Chapter 24, LO2.

When a sentence has two or more subjects joined by *or, nor,* or *but also,* the verb should agree with the last subject.

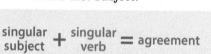

Serge Vero/Shutterstock.com

singular
subject + singular
verb = agreement

Either Jumbo or Dumbo trumpets.

Not only Jumbo but also Dumbo trumpets.

plural
subject + plural
verb = agreement

Neither the mother lion nor the cubs are asleep.

Take Special Care

Being able to locate the subject and verb in a sentence is crucial for correcting agreement errors. If you have difficulty locating the subject of a sentence, remember …

(a) The subject is never found in a short introductory word or phrase.

On Tuesdays, Bill meets his brother for lunch.

Be careful to check introductory clauses, though, because a sentence can have more than one subject and verb. See the following example and Chapter 23, LO7, Clauses, for review.

When the students sit outside, they watch the turtles in the pond.

(b) A subject is never found in a parenthetical comment (see Chapter 35, LO3, for review).

My brother, *as well as my sister,* has qualified for the track meet.

(c) A subject is never found in a prepositional phrase (see Chapter 23, LO6, Prepositional Phrases, and Chapter 34, LO3, Common Prepositions, for review).

Neither *of my brothers* is going *to the party* tonight.

Vocabulary

compound subject
two or more subjects that
share the same verb or verbs

Fixing Agreement with Two Subjects

Write In each sentence below, write the correct form of the present tense of the verb in parentheses.

1. The acrobat and clown _____ the crowd. (entertain)

2. The acrobat or clown _____ a pie in the face. (get)

3. A trapeze artist and a tightrope walker _____ an ovation. (receive)

4. Not only the acrobat but also the clown _____ highly paid. (are)

5. Neither the lion tamer nor the sword swallower _____ insurance. (have)

6. The human cannonball or the lion tamer _____ the scariest job. (have)

7. Either Todd or Lewis _____ to join the circus. (plan)

8. Thrills and hard work _____ Todd or Lewis. (await)

9. Not only Todd but also Lewis _____ a daredevil. (are)

10. The clowns or the ringmaster _____ each act. (introduce)

Correct Read the following paragraph. Correct any agreement errors you find by crossing out the incorrect verb and writing the correct present tense verb above.

Childhood dreams and fantasies rarely comes true. A firefighter or police officer are what many children dream of being. Imagine a world filled with firefighters and police! Neither the accountant nor the landscaper figure big in childhood plans. A princess or a wizard are also a popular choice for kids. Job openings and pay for both careers is pretty slim. Even the job of astronaut or explorer have become scarce. The trials of joblessness and the responsibilities of adulthood conspires to convince people to seek other careers. Childhood stars sometimes get "real" jobs, too. Johnny Whitaker and Wil Wheaton works with computers. They traded childhood dreams for adult ones.

Write Write a sentence with a compound subject joined by *and*. Write a sentence with a compound subject joined by *or*. Check subject–verb agreement.

L○3 Agreement with *I* and *You*

For most verbs, the form that goes with the singular pronouns *I* and *you* looks the same as the form that goes with the plural pronoun *they*.

Correct: I go to La Ronde and ride roller coasters. You do too.

Incorrect: I goes to La Ronde and rides roller coasters. You does too.

Note: The pronoun *I* takes the singular verbs *am* and *was*. **Do not** use *I* with *be* or *is*.

Correct: I am excited. I was nervous. I am eager to ride the roller coaster.

Incorrect: I are happy. I were nervous. I is eager to ride the roller coaster.

Quick Guide

Using *am, is, are, was,* and *were*

	Singular	**Plural**
Present Tense	I *am* you *are* he *is* she *is* it *is*	we *are* you *are* they *are*
Past Tense	I *was* you *were* he *was* she *was* it *was*	we *were* you *were* they *were*

Insight

The word *am* exists for one reason only, to go along with the word *I*. There is no other subject for the verb *am*. In academic or formal writing, *I* should never be used with *be* or *is*. Think of René Descartes saying, "I think, therefore I am."

Take Special Care

When proofreading for subject–verb agreement, find the verb or the action of the sentence and then ask yourself who's doing the action to find the subject. For example, in the following sentence, the action word is <u>*helps*</u>. If you ask who or what does the helping, the answer is <u>*arrangement*</u>, not <u>*pamphlets*</u>.

The arrangement of the pamphlets helps students to find them more easily.

Correcting Agreement with *I* and *You*

Speaking & Listening

After completing the sentences in the first exercise, say them aloud, emphasizing the underlined verbs.

Write In each sentence below, write the correct forms of the present tense of the verb in parentheses.

1. I _____ louder than he _____ . (laugh)

2. You _____ as well as she _____ . (climb)

3. We _____ together, or you _____ alone. (work)

4. Stan _____ silverware while I _____ pans. (wash)

5. I _____ often, but he _____ rarely. (help)

6. The group _____ on Sunday, but I _____ later. (watch)

7. I _____ first and she _____ after. (eat)

8. You _____ tired, and I _____ too. (is)

9. I _____ short, but you _____ tall. (is)

10. You _____ helpful; I hope I _____ also. (is)

Correct Read the following paragraphs. Correct any agreement errors you find by crossing out the incorrect verb and writing the correct verb above.

I is starting a class in astronomy, and I wonders if I can borrow your telescope. You rarely uses it anymore, and I needs it to be able to look at the moons of Jupiter. My professor says that even a moderate-size telescope will show the moons. She have instructions for finding Jupiter. I knows how to use the telescope, but if you is afraid I would break it, you could set it up for me.

Another idea would be for us to stargaze together. I has a place away from city lights, and I has lawn chairs and blankets we could use. If you agrees to come along and set up the telescope, I agrees to bring snacks for us.

What do you think? I hopes I'm not asking too much and that you isn't mad about the request. I just is excited to see Jupiter's moons, and I thinks you might like to see them, too.

Write Write two sentences using "I" as the subject. Then write two more using "you" as the subject. Check your subject–verb agreement.

_____

_____

_____

_____

LO4 Agreement with Singular Indefinite Pronouns

An **indefinite pronoun** is intentionally vague. Instead of referring to a specific person, place, or thing, it refers to something general or unknown.

Singular Indefinite Pronouns

Singular **indefinite pronouns** take singular verbs:

Someone cooks every night.
No one gets out of kitchen duty.
Everyone benefits from the chore schedule.

Note that indefinite pronouns that end in *one, body,* or *thing* are singular, just as these words themselves are singular. Just as you would write, "That thing is missing," so you would write "Something is missing." The words *one, each, either,* and *neither* can be tricky because they are often followed by a prepositional phrase that contains a plural noun. The verb should still be singular.

One of my friends is a great cook.

Each of us wants to cook as well as he does.

Remember that a compound subject joined with *and* needs a plural verb, and a compound subject joined with *or* needs a verb that matches the last subject.

Anything and everything taste terrific in his meals.
No one or nothing keeps him from making a wonderful meal.

Singular
someone
somebody
something
anyone
anybody
anything
no one
nobody
nothing
everyone
everybody
everything
one
each
either
neither

Take Special Care

When you're checking the verbs in your sentences, don't include any infinitive forms (e.g., to walk, to remember, to run, to think). The infinitive doesn't affect the subject–verb agreement of your sentence.

The superb **organization** of the activities **is helping** the volunteers **to make** the charity a success.

Tip

When you're proofreading for subject–verb agreement, don't worry too much about the content of the sentences. Instead, focus on spotting key words like *neither, either, each, every, another,* or words ending in *one, body,* or *thing.*

Correcting Indefinite Pronoun Agreement I

Write In each sentence below, write the correct present-tense form of the verb in parentheses.

1. Everyone _____ an application. (complete)

2. Somebody _____ to get the job. (have)

3. Each of the jobs _____ available. (are)

4. Neither of the applicants _____ qualified. (are)

5. Either of the prospects _____ to be trained. (hope)

6. Nobody _____ to go home empty-handed. (want)

7. Everybody _____ bills to pay. (have)

8. Someone or something _____ to give. (have)

9. Either of the positions _____ well. (pay)

10. One of my friends _____ for word on the job. (wait)

Write Write sentences using each indefinite pronoun as a subject. Choose present tense verbs and check subject–verb agreement.

1. Someone _____

_____

2. Nothing _____

_____

3. Neither _____

_____

4. Everyone _____

_____

5. Each _____

_____

6. Anybody _____

_____

Agreement with Other Indefinite Pronouns

Some other indefinite pronouns are always plural, while some can be treated as either singular or plural depending on how they are used.

Plural Indefinite Pronouns

Plural
both
few
many
several

Plural indefinite pronouns take plural verbs:

Many of us follow classical music.
Several are big fans.

Singular or Plural Indefinite Pronouns

Singular or Plural
all
any
half
part
most
none
some

Some indefinite pronouns or quantity words can be singular or plural. If the object of the preposition in the phrase following the pronoun is singular, the pronoun takes a singular verb; if the object is plural, the pronoun takes a plural verb.

Most of the song thrills us.
Most of the songs thrill us.

Notice the shift in meaning, depending on the prepositional phrase. "Most of the song" means that one song is mostly thrilling. "Most of the songs" means that all but a few of many songs are thrilling. Here's another startling difference.

Half of the concert features Tchaikovsky.
Half of the concerts feature Tchaikovsky.

In the first example, half of one concert features the Russian composer. In the second, half of a number of concerts feature Tchaikovsky's music. What a difference one *s* can make!

Take Special Care

If you're having trouble remembering which form of a verb is singular, substitute the word *Bob* as the subject of the sentence and read the sentence out loud.

Neither of the students *has/have* finished the essay.

(*Neither* takes a singular verb when it's used alone, but which verb is singular?)

Bob *has/have* finished the essay. (Read the sentence out loud both ways to determine which sounds correct).

Neither of the students *has* finished the essay (correct answer).

Correcting Indefinite Pronoun Agreement II

Write In each sentence below, write the correct present-tense forms of the verb in parentheses. See also Chapter 29, LO2, Shifts in Sentences.

After completing the sentences in the first exercise, say them aloud, emphasizing the underlined verbs.

1. Several _____ attending, and all of us _____ listening. (are)

2. All of the songs _____ dramatic, but all of the drama _____ intentional. (is)

3. One of my friends _____ a radio program; several episodes _____ in a row. (broadcast)

4. Everyone _____ Tchaikovsky, but few _____ only him. (like)

5. One of my friends _____ to classical radio; several _____ to MP3's. (listen)

6. Half of the album _____ symphonies, and half of the symphonies _____ brass fanfares. (feature)

7. Most of us _____ about music, and some of us _____ music, too. (read)

8. Of the music fans, several _____ hard core, but none of them _____ a composer. (is)

9. One of my friends _____ trombone, and some of my friends _____ piano. (play)

10. Few _____ played in an orchestra, but one of us _____ played in a band. (has)

Write Write sentences using each indefinite pronoun as a subject. Choose present tense verbs and check subject–verb agreement.

1. Part _____

_____

2. Most _____

_____

3. Few _____

_____

4. Several _____

_____

5. Both _____

_____

6. All _____

_____

LO5 Agreement with Collective Nouns and Terms of Measurement

Collective Nouns

Collective nouns (like *committee*, *family*, or *team*) take a singular verb if the group acts as a unit but a plural verb if the members act individually.

The class has agreed on a date for the final exam. (The class is acting together as a group.)

The class are unable to agree on the best date for the final exam. (The different members of the class are acting as individuals.)

If you are applying the collective noun rule and the singular form sounds odd, try to make the noun more obviously plural and use a plural verb instead.

The faculty has agreed on a new code of conduct. (option 1)

Faculty *members* have agreed on a new code of conduct. (option 2)

Terms of Measurement

Units of money, time, volume, mass, length, or distance take singular verbs.

Two hundred dollars seems like a lot to pay for a parking spot.
Seven hours is too long to wait for the ferry.

Practising Agreement with Collective Nouns and Terms of Measurement

Write Write sentences using the following collective nouns. Choose present tense verbs and check subject–verb agreement.

1. Staff

_____

2. Swarm

_____

3. Family

_____

4. Class

_____

5. Horde

_____

Review

See Chapter 30, LO2, to review collective nouns.

Vocabulary

collective noun
a noun that is usually grammatically singular but denotes a collection or number of individuals; e.g., flock, team

Write Write sentences using the following types of measurements. Choose present tense verbs and check subject–verb agreement.

1. Money

_____

2. Time

_____

3. Length

_____

4. Distance

_____

5. Weight

_____

Correct In each sentence below, identify any agreement errors you find by crossing out the incorrect verb and writing the correction above. Some sentences may be correct.

1. The class have learned a lot about computers.

2. Two-thirds of the project have been finished.

3. Ten kilometres is too far to walk to get to the theatre.

4. The team need time to learn to play well together.

5. On my trip to Europe, I realized that five euros equal seven dollars.

6. After a long period of deliberation, the jury find the defendant "not guilty."

7. Bob discovered that fifty pounds were quite heavy when he carried his groceries home in his knapsack.

8. The band are playing better now that a new guitarist has been hired.

9. Two hours goes by quickly when you're working out at the gym.

10. Ten yards of cloth are needed for the costumes.

Chapter 26 Subject–Verb Agreement

Correcting Subject–Verb Agreement: More Practice

Correct In each sentence below, identify any agreement errors you find by crossing out the incorrect verb and writing the correction above. Some sentences may be correct.

1. On Saturday night, everyone in my class are going to the local pub.

2. Either of the contractors are capable of doing the job.

3. Anyone at the party who need a ride home can talk to Frank.

4. The new meat thermometer I bought online are digital.

5. The coach, along with her players, thinks that twelve pizzas are sufficient for the party.

6. The repetition of the lessons helps the students to remember the material.

7. Neither the teachers nor the janitor are responsible for the broken window.

8. Both my brother and my step-sister needs a car for their jobs.

9. Many of the boarder guards is polite.

10. The baker's daughters is walking to the theatre down the road.

11. Each of the plants on the patio needs to be watered every morning.

12. An umbrella, a rain jacket, and a good pair of shoes is essential in Vancouver.

13. The computer and the calculator was assembled in China.

14. The bees buzz loudly as they flies through her brother's flower garden.

15. Neither of the students wants to read the passage out loud in front of the class.

16. The number of jobs created in B.C. seem to be steadily increasing.

17. My old car have a stick shift and are really loud above 55 k.p.h.

18. A cook, in addition to a nanny and a maid, have been hired by my grandmother.

19. On Wednesdays and Thursdays, each girl and boy in the summer day camp are allowed to bring a special snack from home.

20. Not only all my friends but my aunts want to come to my grad.

> "The fragments of the world seek each other
> so that the world may come into being."
>
> —Pierre Teilhard de Chardin

Mircea Simu/Shutterstock.com

27

Sentence Fragments

Once upon a time, someone spent days carving letters the size of a man's head into a solid block of stone. What message would be important enough to inscribe in that way? A couple thousand years later, we don't know. All that remains is a fragment of the stone, and of the meaning.

Sometimes in writing, sentences get broken into fragments as well. The subject gets knocked away, or the verb drops out, or some other important part goes missing. The reader then has to puzzle out the meaning—or just skips the sentence entirely.

This chapter focuses on sentence fragments, on recognizing them and repairing them. The exercises here will help you to put the pieces of sentence fragments back together.

Learning Outcomes

LO1 Correct common fragments.

LO2 Correct tricky fragments.

LO3 Check for fragments in a real-world context.

Test Your Knowledge

Read these fragments aloud. Then correct them by supplying the necessary words to form a complete sentence.

1. The overweight personal trainer. _____

2. Played guitar until her fingers bled. _____

3. Because he needed money to buy ice cream. _____

4. Requested an after-dinner mint to freshen his bad breath. _____

5. Especially honey badgers. _____

6. The boy who walks his dog in the park every morning. _____

LO1 Common Fragments

In spoken communication and informal writing, sentence fragments are occasionally used and understood. In formal academic writing, however, fragments should be avoided.

Missing Parts

A sentence requires a subject and a predicate. If one or the other or both are missing, the sentence is a fragment. Such fragments can be fixed by supplying the missing part.

Fragment:	Went to the concert.
Fragment + Subject:	We went to the concert.
Fragment:	Everyone from Westville Community College.
Fragment + Predicate:	Everyone from Westville Community College may participate.
Fragment:	For the sake of student safety.
Fragment + Subject and Predicate:	The president set up a curfew for the sake of student safety.

Incomplete Thoughts

A sentence must express a complete thought. Some fragments have a subject and a verb but do not express a complete thought. These fragments can be corrected by providing words that complete the thought.

Fragment:	The concert will include.
Completing Thought:	The concert will include an amazing light show.
Fragment:	If we arrive in time.
Completing Thought:	If we arrive in time, we'll get front-row seats.
Fragment:	That opened the concert.
Completing Thought:	I liked the band that opened the concert.

Say It

Read these fragments aloud. Then read each one again, but this time supply the necessary words to form a complete thought.

1. The student union building.
2. Where you can buy used books.
3. Walked to class every morning.
4. When the instructor is sick.
5. The cop was.

Vocabulary

fragment
a group of words that is missing a subject or a predicate (or both) or that does not express a complete thought

Correct Add words to correct each fragment below. Write the complete sentence on the lines provided.

1. Went to the office. _____

_____

2. The photographer, standing at the door. _____

_____

3. Will debate the pros and cons of tanning. _____

_____

4. The goalie. _____

_____

5. Is one of the benefits of art class. _____

_____

Correct The following paragraph contains numerous fragments. Either add what is missing or combine fragments with other sentences to make them complete. Use the correction marks shown to the right.

Some people are good at memorizing facts. They piece things together. Like the inside of a jigsaw puzzle. Slowly build a big picture. Others are better at grasping overall shapes. Then filling in the middle with facts. Either way, have to finish the puzzle.

Correct On your own paper or orally, correct the following fragments by supplying the missing parts. Use your imagination.

1. In the newspaper.
2. We bought.
3. The purpose of sociology class.
4. Somewhere above the clouds tonight.
5. Was the reason.

LO2 Tricky Fragments

Some fragments are more difficult to find and correct. They creep into our writing because they are often part of the way we communicate when we speak.

Absolute Phrases

An **absolute phrase** looks like a sentence that is missing its helping verb. An absolute phrase can be made into a sentence by adding the helping verb or by connecting the phrase to a complete sentence.

Absolute Phrase (Fragment):	Our legs trembling from the hike.
Absolute Phrase + Helping Verb:	Our legs were trembling from the hike.
Absolute Phrase + Complete Sentence:	We collapsed on the couch, our legs trembling from the hike.

Informal Fragments

Fragments that are commonly used in speech should be eliminated from formal writing. Avoid the following types of fragments unless you are writing dialogue.

Interjections:	Hey! Yeah!
Exclamations:	What a nuisance! How fun!
Greetings:	Hi, everybody. Good afternoon.
Questions:	How come? Why not? What?
Answers:	About three or four. As soon as possible.

Note: Sentences that begin with *here* or *there* have a **delayed subject**, which appears after the verb. Command sentences have an **implied subject** (*you*). Such sentences are not fragments.

Delayed Subject:	Here are some crazy fans wearing wild hats.
Delayed Subject:	Where is the mascot?
Implied Subject:	Tackle him! Bring him down!

Say It

Read these fragments aloud. Then read each one again, but this time supply the necessary words to form a complete thought.

1. Three types of laptop computers.
2. Our instructor explaining the assignment.
3. About two in the morning.
4. Is my favourite website
5. My friend working at a thrift shop.

Vocabulary

absolute phrase
a group of words with a noun and a participle (a word ending in *ing* or *ed*) and the words that modify them

delayed subject
a subject that appears after the verb, as in a sentence that begins with *here* or *there* or a sentence that asks a question

implied subject
the word *you*, assumed to begin command sentences

Complete Rewrite each tricky fragment below, making it a sentence.

1. Our boisterous behaviour announcing our approach.

   _____

   _____

2. A tidy hedge surrounding the trimmed lawn.

   _____

   _____

3. The owner's gaze tracking us from the front porch.

   _____

   _____

4. His dogs barking loudly from the backyard.

   _____

   _____

5. Our welcome feeling less likely with each step.

   _____

   _____

Delete The following paragraph contains a number of informal fragments. Identify and delete each one. Reread the paragraph and listen for the difference.

Wow! It's amazing what archaeologists can discover from bones. Did you know that Cro-Magnon (our ancestors) and Neanderthal tribes sometimes lived side by side? Sure did! In other places, when climate change drove our ancestors south, Neanderthals took their place. Neanderthals were tough and had stronger arms and hands than Cro-Magnons had. Neanderthal brains were bigger, too. What? So why aren't there any Neanderthals around now? Huh? Well, although Neanderthal tribes used spears and stone tools, our ancestors were much better toolmakers. Yeah! Also, Neanderthals mainly ate big animals, while Cro-Magnon ate anything from fish to pigs to roots and berries. So in the long run, Cro-Magnon hominids prospered while Neanderthal tribes dwindled away.

Correction Marks

℘	delete
d̲	capitalize
Ɖ	lowercase
∧	insert
∧̑	add comma
? ∧	add question mark
word ∧	add word
⊙	add period
⬭	spelling
∿	switch

LO3 Real-World Application

Correct Correct any sentence fragments in the following business memo.

Slovik Manufacturing

Date: August 8, 2015

To: Jerome James, Personnel Director

From: Ike Harris, Graphic Arts Director

Subject: Promotion of Mona Veal from Intern to Full-Time Graphic Artist

For the past five months, Mona Veal as an intern in our Marketing Department. I recommend that she be offered a position as a full-time designer. The two main reasons behind this recommendation.

1. Mona has shown the traits that Slovik Manufacturing values in a graphic designer. Creative, dependable, and easy to work with.
2. Presently, we have two full-time graphic designers and one intern. While this group has worked well. The full-time designers have averaged 3.5 hours of overtime per week. Given this fact. Our new contract with Lee-Stamp Industries will require more help, including at least one additional designer.

If you approve this recommendation. Please initial below and return this memo.

Yes, I approve the recommendation to offer Mona Veal a full-time position. _____

Attachment: Evaluation report of Mona Veal

cc: Elizabeth Zoe
   Mark Moon

Answer Team up with a classmate to discuss answers to the following questions about sentence fragments.

1. What is a sentence fragment?
2. What is a delayed subject?
3. What is an absolute phrase?
4. What are the two ways to correct a sentence fragment?

Photograph by Erin O'Connor

> "If we can connect in some tiny way with a human that doesn't agree with us, then maybe we won't blow up the planet."
>
> —Nancy White

28

Comma Splices, Run-Ons, and Ramblers

Sometimes people fail to connect. Two sides try to come together, but they can't communicate.

Sometimes sentences have the same trouble. Comma splices and run-on sentences occur when sentences are joined in ways that just don't connect grammatically; rambling sentences result when too many ideas get crammed in between the first capital letter and the period. This chapter focuses on fixing these three types of problems.

Test Your Knowledge

Identify and correct any errors in the following paragraph. After you read the chapter, come back and check your answers.

Video games are fun, but they shouldn't take over your life. I enjoy many types of video games, my friends and I play together, sometimes we are in the same room often we play together online. We like first-person shooters mostly online role-playing games are also fun. Some video games are designed to be addictive a balance of life and games is crucial, you can't just live in the game.

L◯1 Comma Splices

Comma splices occur when two complete sentences are connected with only a comma. A comma splice can be fixed by adding a coordinating conjunction (*for, and, nor, but, or, yet,* or *so*) or a subordinating conjunction (*while, after, when,* and so on). The two sentences could also be joined by a semicolon (;) or separated by a period.

Comma Splice: The Eiffel Tower was a main attraction at the Paris Exposition, the Ferris wheel was its equivalent at the Chicago Exposition.

Corrected by adding a coordinating conjunction:	The Eiffel Tower was a main attraction at the Paris Exposition, and the Ferris wheel was its equivalent at the Chicago Exposition.
Corrected by adding a subordinating conjunction:	While the Eiffel Tower was a main attraction at the Paris Exposition, the Ferris wheel was its equivalent at the Chicago Exposition.
Corrected by replacing the comma with a semicolon:	The Eiffel Tower was a main attraction at the Paris Exposition; the Ferris wheel was its equivalent at the Chicago Exposition.

Comma Splice: An engineer named George Washington Gale Ferris planned the first Ferris wheel, many people thought he was crazy.

Corrected by adding a coordinating conjunction:	An engineer named George Washington Gale Ferris planned the first Ferris wheel, but many people thought he was crazy.
Corrected by adding a subordinating conjunction:	When an engineer named George Washington Gale Ferris planned the first Ferris wheel, many people thought he was crazy.
Corrected by replacing the comma with a period:	An engineer named George Washington Gale Ferris planned the first Ferris wheel. Many people thought he was crazy.

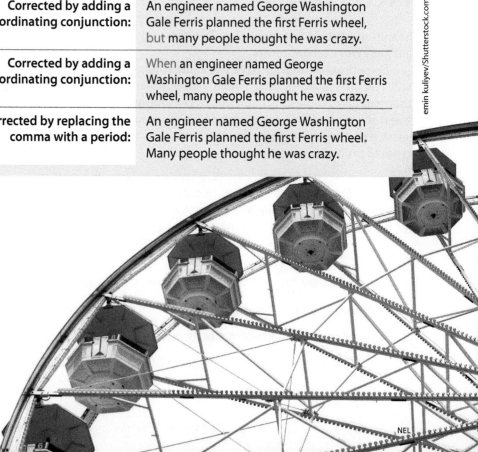

emin kuliyev/Shutterstock.com

Correcting Comma Splices

Correct Correct the following comma splices by adding a coordinating conjunction (*and, but, yet, or, nor, for, so*), adding a subordinating conjunction (*when, while, because,* and so on), or replacing the comma with a semicolon or period. Use the approach that makes the sentence read most smoothly and meaningfully. (The first one has been done for you.)

1. We set out for a morning hike,_∧ *but* it was raining.

2. The weather cleared by the afternoon, we hit the trail.

3. Both Jill and I were expecting wonderful scenery, we were not disappointed.

4. The view of the valley was spectacular, it was like a portrait.

5. We snacked on granola bars and apples, we enjoyed the view.

6. Then we strapped on our backpacks, the final leg of the hike awaited us.

7. The trail became rockier, we had to watch our step.

8. We reached the end of our hike, the sun was setting.

9. We're on the lookout for a new trail, it will be tough to beat this one.

10. We're done with our physical activities, it is time to watch a movie.

Correct Correct any comma splices in the following e-mail message.

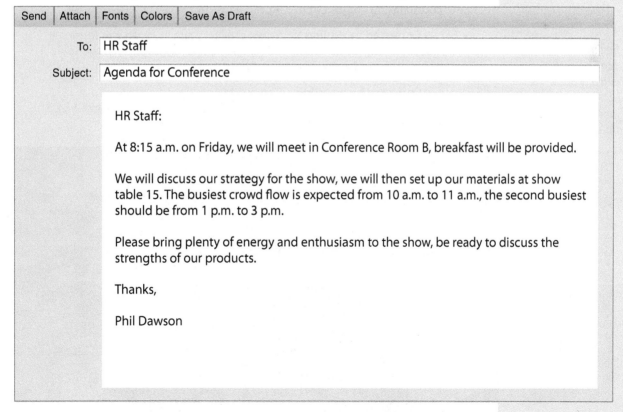

| Send | Attach | Fonts | Colors | Save As Draft |

To: HR Staff

Subject: Agenda for Conference

HR Staff:

At 8:15 a.m. on Friday, we will meet in Conference Room B, breakfast will be provided.

We will discuss our strategy for the show, we will then set up our materials at show table 15. The busiest crowd flow is expected from 10 a.m. to 11 a.m., the second busiest should be from 1 p.m. to 3 p.m.

Please bring plenty of energy and enthusiasm to the show, be ready to discuss the strengths of our products.

Thanks,

Phil Dawson

LO2 Run-On Sentences

A **run-on sentence** (sometimes just called a "run-on") occurs when two sentences are joined without punctuation or a connecting word. A run-on can be corrected by adding a comma and a conjunction, or by inserting a semicolon or period between the two sentences.

Insight

As you can see, run-ons and comma splices are very similar. They can be corrected in the same basic ways.

Run-On: Horace Wilson taught in Tokyo in 1872 he introduced the Japanese to baseball.

Corrected by adding a comma and coordinating conjunction:	Horace Wilson taught in Tokyo in 1872, and he introduced the Japanese to baseball.
Corrected by adding a subordinating conjunction and a comma:	While Horace Wilson taught in Tokyo in 1872, he introduced the Japanese to baseball.
Corrected by inserting a semicolon:	Horace Wilson taught in Tokyo in 1872; he introduced the Japanese to baseball.

Tip

Here's an additional way to correct a run-on sentence: Turn one of the sentences into a phrase or series of phrases; then combine it with the other sentence.

The first team in Japan was formed in 1878 without a thought about how popular the sport would become.

Run-On: The first team in Japan was formed in 1878 no one knew how popular the sport would become.

Corrected by adding a comma and a coordinating conjunction:	The first team in Japan was formed in 1878, yet no one knew how popular the sport would become.
Corrected by adding a subordinating conjunction and a comma:	When the first team in Japan was formed in 1878, no one knew how popular the sport would become.
Corrected by inserting a period:	The first team in Japan was formed in 1878. No one knew how popular the sport would become.

Alan C. Heison/Shutterstock.com

Correcting Run-On Sentences

Correct Correct the following run-on sentences. Use the approach that makes the sentence read most smoothly and meaningfully. The first one has been done for you.

1. In 1767, English scientist Joseph Priestley discovered a way to infuse water with carbon dioxide this invention led to carbonated water.

2. Carbonated water is one of the main components of soft drinks it gives soft drinks the fizz and bubbles we enjoy.

3. The first soft drinks were dispensed out of soda fountains they were most often found at drug stores and ice-cream parlours.

4. Interestingly, pop was sold at drug stores it promised healing properties.

5. Most of the formulas for soft drinks were invented by pharmacists the idea was to create non-alcoholic alternatives to traditional medicines.

6. The first carbonated drink bottles could not keep bubbles from escaping it was more popular to buy a soft drink from a soda fountain.

7. A successful method of keeping bubbles in a bottle was not invented until 1892 it was called a crowned bottle cap.

8. The first diet pop to be sold was known as "No-Cal Beverage" in 1959 the first diet cola hit the stores.

Rewrite Rewrite the following paragraph, correcting any run-on sentences or comma splices that you find. Remember that there are different ways to correct these types of errors; use the combination of approaches that makes the paragraph read most smoothly.

Video game technology is always changing, it's exciting to see what inventors come up with next. Motion-capture games get players moving some people use them as their primary form of exercise. Virtual reality headsets, like the Oculus Rift, are wearable goggles that totally immerse players in the game world. Secondary screens are also quite popular one screen displays the action of the game the other screen displays status information similar to movie streaming, cloud gaming gives players access to a vast library of games.

LO3 Rambling Sentences

A **rambling sentence** (or "rambler") occurs when many separate ideas are connected by one *and*, *but*, or *so* after another. The result is an unfocused sentence that goes on and on. To correct a rambling sentence, break it into smaller units, adding and cutting words as needed.

Rambling: When we signed up for the two-on-two tournament, I had no thoughts about winning, but then my brother started talking about spending his prize money and he asked me how I would spend my share so we were counting on winning when we really had little chance and as it turned out, we lost in the second round.

Corrected: When we signed up for the two-on-two tournament, I had no thoughts about winning. Then my brother started talking about spending the prize money. He even asked me how I would spend my share. Soon, we were counting on winning when we really had little chance. As it turned out, we lost in the second round.

Say It

Read the following rambling sentences aloud. Afterward, circle all of the connecting words (*and*, *but*, *so*), and be prepared to suggest different ways to break each rambling idea into more manageable units.

1. The electronics store claims to offer "one-stop shopping" and they can take care of all of a customer's computer needs and they have a fully trained staff to answer questions and solve problems so there is really no need to go anywhere else.

2. I enjoyed touring the hospital and I would enjoy joining the nursing staff and I believe that my prior work experience will be an asset but I also know that I have a lot more to learn.

Vocabulary

rambling sentence
a sentence error that occurs
when many separate ideas
are connected by one
conjunction after another

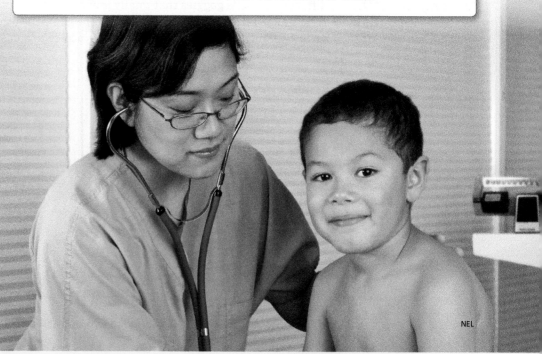

forestpath/Shutterstock.com

Correcting Rambling Sentences

Correct Correct the following rambling sentences by dividing them into separate sentences. Afterward, share your corrections with a classmate. Did you both change each rambling sentence in the same way?

1. The dancer entered gracefully onto the stage and she twirled around twice and then tiptoed to the front of the stage and the crowd applauded.

   _____

   _____

2. I went to the movies last night and when I got to the theatre, I had to wait in a super-slow line and when I finally got to the front, the show I wanted to see was sold out.

   _____

   _____

   _____

3. I like to listen to music everywhere but I especially like to rock out in my car so I scream and dance and I don't care if anyone sees me through the windows.

   _____

   _____

   _____

Answer Answer the following questions about rambling sentences.

1. How can you recognize a rambling sentence?

   _____

   _____

2. Why is a rambling sentence a problem?

   _____

   _____

   _____

3. How can you correct one?

   _____

   _____

   _____

LO4 Real-World Application

Correct Correct any comma splices or run-on sentences in the following e-mail message.

| Send | Attach | Fonts | Colors | Save As Draft |

To: StaplePro Employees

Subject: Inventory Management

Good morning:

This Saturday, from 8:00 a.m. to noon, StaplePro will conduct its quarterly inventory check the warehouse supervisors and I will lead the inventory teams. Please provide any assistance the inventory teams require of you.

After this check, the paper inventory forms will be discontinued, all shipments in and out must be inventoried using the hand scanners. There should be fewer errors when using StaplePro's electronic system, the supervisors will schedule training for their employees who are unfamiliar with the scanners.

Thanks for your cooperation StaplePro's new system will help us store and ship staples more effectively and provide better service for our customers.

Best regards,

Kevin Dooley

Warehouse Director

Reflect Reflect on what you have learned about comma splices and run-on sentences by answering the following questions.

1. What is the difference between a comma splice and a run-on sentence?

_____

_____

2. How can you correct comma splices and run-on sentences? (List at least three ways.)

_____

_____

3. What are three common coordinating conjunctions that you can use to connect two sentences?

_____

_____

> "I say that what we really need is a car that can be shot when it breaks down."
> —Russell Baker

Jupiterimages/Thinkstock

29

Additional Sentence Problems

Cars are great when they go, but when a car breaks down, it is a huge headache. There's going to be a look under the hood, a bit of scrabbling beneath the thing, maybe a push, maybe a jack, maybe a tow truck, and probably a big bill.

Sentences also are great until they break down. But you don't have to be a skilled mechanic to fix sentences. This chapter outlines a few common sentence problems and shows how to fix them. You'll be on your way in no time!

Learning Outcomes

LO1 Correct misplaced and dangling modifiers.

LO2 Correct shifts in sentence construction.

LO3 Correct faulty parallelism.

LO4 Correct sentence problems in a real-world context.

Test Your Knowledge

The following sentences have "broken down." See if you can get them up and running again. Come back to any sentences you are unsure of after you have read the chapter.

1. Because he was robbing the bank, the police officer tackled the criminal.

2. Of the five bank robbers, he was the one wearing only a mask.

3. They jump into their car and sped away from the scene of the crime.

4. With sirens blaring, the police officer went after them.

5. This story shows the importance of honour, and being loyal to your friends is essential.

LO1 Misplaced/Dangling Modifiers

Dangling Modifiers

A modifier is a word, phrase, or clause that functions as an adjective or adverb. When the modifier does not clearly modify another word in the sentence, it is called a dangling modifier. This error can be corrected by inserting the missing word and/or rewriting the sentence.

Dangling Modifier:	After strapping the toy cowboy to his back, my cat stalked sullenly around the house. *(The cat could strap the toy cowboy to his own back?)*
Corrected:	After I strapped the toy cowboy to his back, my cat stalked sullenly around the house.
Dangling Modifier:	Trying to get the cowboy off, the bowl got knocked off the shelf. *(The bowl was trying to get the cowboy off?)*
Corrected:	Trying to get the cowboy off, the cat knocked the bowl off the shelf.

Misplaced Modifiers

When a modifier is placed beside a word that it does not modify, the modifier is misplaced. The result is often an amusing or illogical statement. A misplaced modifier can be corrected by moving it next to the word that it modifies.

Misplaced Modifier:	My cat was diagnosed by the vet with fleas. *(The vet has fleas?)*
Corrected:	The vet diagnosed my cat with fleas.
Misplaced Modifier:	The vet gave a pill to my cat tasting like fish. *(The cat tastes like fish?)*
Corrected:	The vet gave my cat a pill tasting like fish.

> ### Say It
>
> Read the following sentences aloud, noting the dangling or misplaced modifier in each one. Then discuss with a classmate how you would correct each error.
>
> 1. The climbing tower on the front porch is the place to find my cat called Feline Paradise.
>
> 2. You will often see him climbing up the shag-carpeted towers and ramps with sharp claws.
>
> 3. Though just three months old, I have taught my cat his name.
>
> 4. After tearing up the couch, I decided to get my cat a scratching post.
>
> 5. I have worked to teach my cat to beg for three weeks.

Correcting Dangling and Misplaced Modifiers

Rewrite Rewrite each of the sentences below, correcting the misplaced and dangling modifiers.

1. I bought a hound dog for my brother named Rover.

_____

2. The doctor diagnosed me and referred me to a specialist with scoliosis.

_____

3. The man was reported murdered by the coroner.

_____

4. Please present the recommendation that is attached to Mrs. Burble.

_____

5. Jack drove me to our home in a Chevy.

_____

6. I couldn't believe my brother would hire a DJ who hates hip hop.

_____

7. We saw a fox and a vixen on the way to the psychiatrist.

_____

8. I gave the secretary my phone number that works in reception.

_____

9. I found a pair of underwear in the drawer that doesn't belong to me.

_____

10. We offer jackets for trendy teens with gold piping.

_____

Correct For each sentence, correct the placement of the adverb.

1. Give quickly the report to your boss.

_____

_____

2. We will provide immediately an explanation.

_____

_____

3. Fill completely out the test sheet.

_____

_____

Graham Taylor/Shutterstock.com

Insight

When a modifier comes at the beginning or end of the sentence, make sure it is intended to modify the word or phrase closest to it. Ask yourself, "Who or what is being described?"

LO2 Shifts in Sentences

Shift in Person

A **shift in person** is an error that occurs when first, second, and/or third person are improperly mixed in a sentence.

Shift in person: If you exercise and eat right, anyone can lose weight. (The sentence improperly shifts from second person—*you*—to third person—*anyone*.)

Corrected: If you exercise and eat right, you can lose weight.

Shift in Tense

A **shift in tense** is an error that occurs when different verb tenses are improperly mixed in a sentence. (See Chapter 32, LOs 4, 5, and 6 for more about verb tenses.)

Shift in tense: He tried every other option before he agrees to do it my way. (The sentence improperly shifts from past tense—*tried*—to present tense—*agree*.)

Corrected: He tried every other option before he agreed to do it my way.

Note: Writers are more likely to create inadvertent verb tense shifts between sentences or between paragraphs, rather than within sentences.

Shift in Voice

A **shift in voice** is an error that occurs when active voice and passive voice are mixed in a sentence.

Shift in voice: When she fixes the radiator, other repairs may be suggested. (The sentence improperly shifts from active voice—*fixes*—to passive voice—*may be suggested*.)

Corrected: When she fixes the radiator, she may suggest other repairs.

Vocabulary

person
first person (*I* or *we*—the person speaking), second person (*you*—the person spoken to), or third person (*he, she, it,* or *they*—the person or thing spoken about)

shift in person
an error that occurs when first, second, and third person are improperly mixed in a sentence

shift in tense
an error that occurs when different verb tenses are improperly mixed in a sentence

voice
property of a verb that shows whether the subject is doing the action (active voice) or is being acted upon (passive voice) (See Chapter 32, LO3, Voice of Verb).

shift in voice
an error that occurs when active voice and passive voice are mixed in a sentence

> ### Say It
>
> Read the following sentences aloud, paying careful attention to the improper shift each one contains. Then tell a classmate how you would correct each error.
>
> 1. David exercises daily and ate well.
> 2. Marianne goes running each morning and new friends might be met.
> 3. After you choose an exercise routine, a person should stick to it.
> 4. Lamar swam every morning and does ten laps.
> 5. The personal trainer made a schedule for me, and a diet was suggested by her.

Correcting Improper Shifts in Sentences

Rewrite Rewrite each sentence below, correcting any improper shifts in construction.

1. You should be ready for each class in a person's schedule.

_____

2. I work for my brother most days and classes are attended by me at night.

_____

_____

3. When you give me a review, can he also give me a raise?

_____

_____

4. As we walked to school, last night's football game was discussed by us.

_____

_____

5. I hoped to catch the bus until I see it leave.

_____

_____

Correct Correct the improper shifts in person, tense, or voice in the following paragraph. Use the correction marks to the right when you make your changes.

Some people are early adopters, which means technology is adopted by them when it is new. Other people are technophobes because you are afraid of technology, period. I am not an early adopter or a technophobe, but a person has to see the value in technology before I use it. Technology has to be cheap, intuitive, reliable, and truly helpful before you start using it. I let others work out the bugs and pay the high prices before a piece of technology is adopted by me. But when I decide it is time to get a new gadget or program, you buy it and use it until it is worn out. Then I look for something else that is even cheaper and more intuitive, reliable, and helpful, which is then bought by me.

Correction Marks	
ℐ	delete
d̲	capitalize
ⅅ	lowercase
∧	insert
⌃	add comma
?	add question
∧	mark
word ∧	add word
⊙	add period
⬭	spelling
∿	switch

LO3 Faulty Parallelism

Parallelism: Coordinating Conjunctions

Parallelism means using the same grammatical form to list two or more parallel ideas. To correct faulty parallelism, make sure that any matching parts of your sentence use the same grammatical form.

Ideas in lists, and those linked with **coordinating conjunctions** (*for*, *and*, *nor*, *but*, *or*, *yet*, *so*) must have grammatically equal parts.

Error: He likes bullfighting, auto racing, **and** to mountaineer. (The first two items end in *ing*, but the third, *to mountaineer*, is the infinitive verb form.)

Corrected A: He likes bullfighting, auto racing, **and** mountaineering.

Corrected B: He likes to bullfight, to auto race, **and** to mountaineer.

There is often more than one way to correct a parallelism error, but the different options are not equal. Some are more formal than others, and different approaches may result in different emphasis. Usually, the most concise option is the best. For example, compare the following three corrections:

Error: Fred's father asked him to stay home and that he should wash the car.

Corrected A: Fred's father asked him to stay home and to wash the car.

Corrected B: Fred's father asked him to stay home and wash the car.

Corrected C: Fred's father asked that he stay home and that he wash the car.

Parallelism: Correlative Conjunctions

Ideas linked with **correlative conjunctions** (*either / or, neither / nor, whether / or, both / and, not only / but also*) must be parallel. Make sure the grammatical structure used in the first half of the pair is exactly the same as that used in the second half.

Error: The tomatoes were **not only** overripe **but also** were expensive.

Corrected A: The tomatoes were **not only** overripe **but also** expensive.

Corrected B: The tomatoes **not only** were overripe **but also** were expensive.

Parallelism: Comparisons

Review

See Chapter 34, LO1, to review conjunctions.

Vocabulary

Conjunction
word or word group that joins parts of a sentence

Coordinating conjunction
conjunction that joins grammatically equal components

correlative conjunction
pair of conjunctions that stress the equality of the parts that are joined

Comparisons linked with *than* or *as* must be parallel.

Error: The preparation of food is more satisfying **than** purchasing prepackaged meals.

Corrected A: Preparing food is more satisfying **than** purchasing prepackaged meals.

Corrected B: The preparation of food is more satisfying **than** the purchase of prepackaged meals.

Rewrite Rewrite any sentences that have parallelism errors. Some sentences may be correct.

1. A person who is depressed might sleep a lot, lose motivation, and the person might skip work.

_____

2. For some people, the acquisition of property is more important than owning stocks and bonds.

_____

3. He is both smart and known for his humour.

_____

4. He found playing online role-playing games as addictive as cigarettes.

_____

5. George spent his summer hiking, fishing, water skiing, canoeing, and cooking over a bonfire.

_____

6. The courageous police officer shouted "freeze!" and his gun was pulled out.

_____

7. She is a teacher with a real dedication to her job and who genuinely cares about people too.

_____

8. Playing video games is much more stimulating than watching television.

_____

9. Bob had to decide on either the fruit salad or he also wanted to eat soup for lunch.

_____

10. Ayesha wanted neither the fruit salad nor the soup for lunch.

_____

11. Stu was delighted to discover that he could prepare popcorn in a microwave oven twice as fast as using a pot on the stove.

_____

12. Both the aging superintendent and the grumpy lawyer needed a cup of coffee.

_____

13. The old clock needed a new dial hand and the pendulum was broken as well.

_____

14. Steve is talented, popular, and has lots of money, but he is still unlikely to be chosen for the job.

_____

15. The new writing class covers essay structure, how to write an effective conclusion is introduced and thesis statement development.

_____

Chapter 29   Additional Sentence Problems

Learning Outcome

Correct sentence problems in a real-world context.

LO4 Real-World Application

Correct Correct any dangling modifiers, misplaced modifiers, shifts in construction, and parallelism errors in the following message. Use the correction marks to the left.

| Send | Attach | Fonts | Colors | Save As Draft |

From: Julia Armstrong

To: Human Resources Staff

Cc: Richard Montgomery

Subject: Monthly Human Resources Staff Meeting with President Smith

Correction Marks

℘	delete
d̲	capitalize
D̸	lowercase
∧	insert
∧̓	add comma
?∧	add question mark
word ∧	add word
⊙	add period
⬭	spelling
∿	switch

Dear HR Team:

Monday, September 12, will be the Human Resources staff meeting with the first monthly president and the head of human resources will be there as well. A person should plan to attend these meetings on the second Monday of each month from 8:30 to 9:30 a.m., and you should go to the Human Resources conference room.

To help make these meetings productive, a staff member can prepare in two ways:

1. You should review and bring any periodic reports that are generated by you—hiring stats, exit interviews, medical or worker's comp claims, and so on. He or she should bring 11 copies and an electronic file of each document.

2. Questions or concerns should be brought. However, if an issue is significant, the person should review it with Richard before you bring it to a monthly meeting.

This monthly meeting is a big commitment of time from everyone needing regular attendance. If you can't make the meeting, send an e-mail and attach to Richard a note.

Thanks for your cooperation. If you have questions or suggestions about the meeting, Richard or I should be contacted by you.

Thanks,

Julia

364   NEL

Rewrite The sentences that follow come from church bulletins and are amusing due to misplaced or dangling modifiers or other sentence problems. Rewrite each sentence to remove these problems.

1. Remember in prayer the many who are sick of our church and community.

   _____

   _____

   _____

2. For those of you who have children and don't know it, we have a nursery downstairs.

   _____

   _____

   _____

3. The ladies of the church have cast off clothing of every kind. They can be seen in the church basement Saturday.

   _____

   _____

   _____

4. The third verse of "Blessed Assurance" will be sung without musical accomplishment.

   _____

   _____

   _____

Workplace

Journalists and publishers need to be especially careful to avoid mistakes in their writing. Errors in writing reflect badly on all professionals.

Write Write the first draft of a personal narrative (true story) in which you share a time when you misplaced or lost something important to you or to someone else. Here are some tips for adding interest to your story:

- Start right in the middle of the action.
- Build suspense to keep the reader's interest.
- Use dialogue.
- Use sensory details (what you heard, saw, felt, and so on).

Afterward, exchange your writing with a classmate. Read each other's narratives, first for enjoyment and then a second time to check it for the sentence errors discussed in this chapter.

"If you want to make an apple pie from scratch,
you must first create the universe."
—Carl Sagan

Stocktrek Images/Thinkstock

30 Noun

Astrophysicists tell us that the universe is made up of two things—matter and energy. Matter is the stuff, and energy is the movement or heat of the stuff.

Grammarians tell us that thoughts are made up of two things—nouns and verbs. Nouns name the stuff, and verbs capture the energy. In that way, the sentence reflects the universe itself. You can't express a complete thought unless you are talking about matter and energy. Each sentence, then, is the basic particle of thought.

This chapter focuses on nouns, which label not just things you can see—such as people, places, or objects—but also things you can't see—such as ideas. The exercises in this chapter will help you sort out the stuff of thinking.

What do you think?

Write a short paragraph about your dream job. Then read over your paragraph and underline all of the nouns. After you have finished the chapter, read your paragraph again to confirm you have properly identified each noun. Correct any errors with nouns, articles, or other noun markers.

Learning Outcomes

LO1 Understand classes of nouns.

LO2 Use singular and plural nouns.

LO3 Form tricky plurals.

LO4 Use count and non-count nouns.

LO5 Use articles.

LO6 Use other noun markers.

LO7 Use nouns correctly in a real-world context.

LO1 Classes of Nouns

All nouns are either *common* or *proper*. They can also be *individual* or *collective*, *concrete* or *abstract*.

Common or Proper Nouns

A common noun names a general person, place, thing, or idea. It is not capitalized. A proper noun names a specific person, place, thing, or idea, and is capitalized.

	Common Nouns	**Proper Nouns**
Person:	politician	Justin Trudeau
Place:	park	Gros Morne
Thing:	marker	Sharpie
Idea:	religion	Hinduism

Individual or Collective Nouns

Most nouns are individual: They refer to one person or thing. Other nouns are collective, referring most commonly to a group of people or animals.

	Individual Nouns	**Collective Nouns**
Person:	secretary	staff
	catcher	team
	student	class
	daughter	family
Animal:	lamb	herd
	locust	swarm
	wolf	pack
	kitten	litter
	goose	gaggle

Concrete or Abstract

If a noun refers to something that can be seen, heard, smelled, tasted, or touched, it is a concrete noun. If a noun refers to something that can't be sensed, it is an abstract noun. Abstract nouns name ideas, conditions, or feelings.

Concrete Nouns	**Abstract Nouns**
judge	impartiality
brain	mind
heart	courage
train	transportation

common noun
noun referring to a general person, place, thing, or idea; it is not capitalized

proper noun
noun referring to a specific person, place, thing, or idea; it is capitalized

individual noun
noun referring to one person or thing

collective noun
noun referring to a group of people or animals

concrete noun
noun referring to something that can be sensed

abstract noun
noun referring to an idea, a condition, or a feeling—something that cannot be sensed

Using Different Classes of Nouns

Identify In each sentence below, identify the underlined nouns as common (C) or proper (P).

1. <u>Margaret Atwood</u> is an acclaimed Canadian <u>author</u>.

   _____   _____

2. Her most famous <u>novel</u> is <u>_The Handmaid's Tale_</u>.

   _____   _____

3. This dystopian novel is set in the <u>Republic of Gilead</u> in the <u>future</u>.

   _____   _____

4. Her novel <u>_Oryx and Crake_</u> also depicts the <u>collapse</u> of <u>civilization</u>.

   _____   _____   _____

Identify In each sentence below, identify the underlined nouns as individual (I) or collective (CL).

1. <u>Quentin Compson</u> appears often in the collected <u>works</u> of William Faulkner.

   _____   _____

2. The Compson <u>family</u> is the <u>centrepiece</u> of Yoknapatawpha County.

   _____   _____

3. The novel <u>_The Sound and the Fury_</u> tells of the plight of the <u>Compsons</u>.

   _____   _____

4. <u>Benjamin Compson</u> watches a <u>group</u> golf in what was once their farm field.

   _____   _____

Identify In each sentence below, identify the underlined nouns as concrete (CT) or abstract (A).

1. <u>J.K. Rowling</u> is the author of the popular Harry Potter book <u>series</u>.

   _____   _____

2. Harry's childhood is full of <u>hardship</u> until he attends a <u>school</u> that trains <u>wizards</u>.

   _____   _____   _____

3. <u>Bravery</u> is the most important trait for <u>students</u> in Gryffindor House.

   _____   _____

4. The importance of <u>friendship</u> is a major <u>theme</u> in the <u>story</u>.

   _____   _____   _____

LO2 Singular or Plural

The **number** of a noun indicates whether it is singular or plural. A **singular** noun refers to one person, place, thing, or idea. A **plural** noun refers to more than one person, place, thing or idea. For most words, the plural is formed by adding *s*. For nouns ending in *ch, s, sh, x,* or *z*, add *es*.

	Most Nouns Add *s*		Nouns Ending in *ch, s, sh, x,* or *z* Add *es*	
	Singular	**Plural**	**Singular**	**Plural**
Person:	sister	sisters	coach	coaches
Place:	park	parks	church	churches
Thing:	spoon	spoons	kiss	kisses
Idea:	solution	solutions	wish	wishes

Same in Both Forms or Usually Plural

Some nouns are the same in both singular and plural forms, and others are usually used only in the plural.

Same in Both Forms		Usually Plural	
Singular	**Plural**	**Plural**	
deer	deer	clothes	series
fish	fish	glasses	shears
moose	moose	pants	shorts
salmon	salmon	proceeds	species
sheep	sheep	savings	tongs
swine	swine	scissors	trousers

Irregular Plurals

Irregular plurals are formed by changing the words themselves. These irregular plurals come from Old English or Latin.

From Old English		From Latin	
Singular	**Plural**	**Singular**	**Plural**
child	children	alumnus	alumni
foot	feet	axis	axes
goose	geese	crisis	crises
man	men	datum	data
mouse	mice	millennium	millennia
person	people	medium	media
tooth	teeth	nucleus	nuclei
woman	women	phenomenon	phenomena

Using Singular and Plural Nouns

Identify For each word, fill in the blank with either the singular or the plural form, whichever is missing. If the word usually uses the plural form, write an X on the line.

1. crisis _____

2. _____ species

3. child _____

4. sheep _____

5. _____ shears

6. _____ teeth

7. _____ clothes

8. deer _____

9. swine _____

10. phenomenon _____

11. _____ scissors

12. _____ millennia

13. man _____

14. fish _____

15. _____ pants

16. _____ moose

17. axis _____

18. shorts _____

19. _____ mice

20. goose _____

21. _____ data

22. alumnus _____

23. _____ savings

24. tree _____

25. _____ women

LO3 Tricky Plurals

Some plural nouns are more challenging to form. Words ending in *y*, *f*, or *fe* and certain compound nouns require special consideration.

Nouns Ending in *y*

If a common noun ends in *y* after a consonant, change the *y* to *i* and add *es*. If the noun ends in *y* after a vowel, leave the *y* and add *s*.

y after a Consonant		*y* after a Vowel	
Singular	**Plural**	**Singular**	**Plural**
fly	flies	bay	bays
lady	ladies	key	keys
story	stories	tray	trays

Nouns Ending in *f* or *fe*

If a common noun ends in *f* or *fe*, change the *f* or *fe* to a *v* and add *es*—unless the *f* sound remains in the plural form. Then just add an *s*.

v Sound in Plural		*f* Sound in Plural	
Singular	**Plural**	**Singular**	**Plural**
calf	calves	belief	beliefs
life	lives	chef	chefs
self	selves	proof	proofs
shelf	shelves	safe	safes

Compound Nouns

A compound noun is made up of two or more words that function together as a single noun. Whether the compound is hyphenated or not, make it plural by placing the *s* or *es* on the most important word in the compound.

Important Word First		Important Word Last	
Singular	**Plural**	**Singular**	**Plural**
editor-in-chief	editors-in-chief	bird-watcher	bird-watchers
mother-in-law	mothers-in-law	human being	human beings
professor emeritus	professors emeritus	test tube	test tubes

Forming Tricky Plurals

Form Plurals For each word below, create the correct plural form.

1. day _____

2. shelf _____

3. middle school _____

4. pony _____

5. bay _____

6. life _____

7. chief _____

8. loaf _____

9. tray _____

10. compact car _____

11. mother-in-law _____

12. ray _____

13. lady _____

14. carafe _____

15. stepsister _____

16. proof _____

17. nose tackle _____

18. party _____

19. son-in-law _____

20. baby _____

Form Plurals In the sentences below, correct the plural errors by circling them and writing the correct forms above.

1. If I give you two pennys for your thoughts, will you give me two cents' worths?

2. Have you read *The Secret Lifes of Cheves*?

3. The professor emerituses are working on two mathematical prooves.

4. I won't question your believes or insult your wells-wisher.

5. The ladys tried to quiet their screaming babys.

6. Time is sure fun when you're having flys.

7. The compacts car are equipped with remote-access keis.

8. I like chicken pattys but don't like salmons patty.

9. I read about dwarves and elfs.

10. Stack those books on the shelfs above the saves.

LO4 Count and Non-Count Nouns

Some nouns name things that can be counted, and other nouns name things that cannot. Different rules apply to each type.

Count Nouns

Count nouns name things that can be counted—*pens, people, votes, cats,* and so forth. They can be singular or plural, and they can be preceded by numbers or articles (*a, an,* or *the*).

Insight

Many native English speakers aren't even aware of count and non-count nouns, though they use them correctly out of habit. Listen for their use of count and non-count nouns.

Singular	Plural
apple	apples
iguana	iguanas
thought	thoughts
room	rooms

think4photop/Shutterstock.com

Non-Count Nouns

Non-count nouns name things that cannot be counted. They are used in singular form, and they can be preceded by *the,* but not by *a* or *an.*

This semester, I'm taking **mathematics** and **biology** as well as **Spanish**.

Substances	Foods	Activities	Science	Languages	Abstractions
wood	water	flying	oxygen	Spanish	experience
cloth	milk	boating	weather	English	harm
ice	wine	smoking	heat	Mandarin	publicity
plastic	sugar	dancing	sunshine	Farsi	advice
wool	rice	swimming	electricity	Greek	happiness
steel	meat	soccer	lightning	Latin	health
aluminum	cheese	hockey	biology	French	wealth
metal	flour	photography	history	Japanese	love
leather	pasta	writing	mathematics	Afrikaans	anger
porcelain	gravy	homework	economics	German	fame

Two-Way Nouns

Two-way nouns can function as count or non-count nouns, depending on their context.

Please set a **glass** in front of each place mat. (count noun)

The display case was made of tempered **glass**. (non-count noun)

Vocabulary

count noun
noun naming something that can be counted

non-count noun
noun naming something that cannot be counted

two-way noun
noun that can function as either a count or a non-count noun

Using Count and Non-Count Nouns

Sort Read the list of nouns below and sort the words into columns of count and non-count nouns.

window	aluminum	holiday	health	rain
English	shoe	tricycle	poetry	ice
bowling	plum	Japanese	lawyer	teaspoon

Count Nouns

_____

_____

_____

_____

_____

_____

_____

Non-Count Nouns

_____

_____

_____

_____

_____

_____

_____

Correct Read the following paragraph and correct the noun errors. The first sentence has been corrected for you.

Our kitchen redesign involved tearing out the plastics that covered the counter and removing the flashings around the edges. We installed new aluminums to replace the old metals. Also, the cupboard doors, which used to be made of woods, were replaced by doors made of glasses. We have a new jar for holding flours and a new refrigerator with a special place for milks and a dispenser for waters. Everything is illuminated by new lightings, and a larger window lets more sunlights in.

Correction Marks

- ꝗ delete
- d̲ capitalize
- Ꝺ lowercase
- ∧ insert
- ⌄ add comma
- ? add question
- ∧ mark
- word ∧ add word
- ⊙ add period
- ◯ spelling
- ∿ switch

Chapter 30 Noun

L◯5 Articles

Articles help you to know if a noun refers to a specific thing or to a general thing. There are two basic types of articles—definite and indefinite.

Definite Article

The **definite article** is the word *the*. It signals that the noun refers to one specific person, place, thing, or idea. The definite article *the* is used before both singular and plural nouns.

Look at the rainbow.
(Look at a specific rainbow.)

> ***Note:*** *The* can be used with most nouns, but usually not with proper nouns.

Incorrect: The Joe looked at the rainbow.
Correct: Joe looked at the rainbow.

James Wheeler/Shutterstock.com

Indefinite Articles

The **indefinite articles** are the words *a, an,* and *some*. They signal that the noun refers to a general person, place, thing, or idea. The word *a* is used before singular nouns that begin with consonant sounds, and the word *an* is used before singular nouns that begin with vowel sounds. The word *some* is used before plural nouns and non-count nouns.

I enjoy seeing a rainbow.
(I enjoy seeing any rainbow.)

> ***Note:*** Don't use *a* or *an* with plural count nouns or with non-count nouns.

Incorrect: I love a sunshine.
Correct: I love the sunshine.

Incorrect: I can see a clouds.
Correct: I can see some clouds.

> ***Note:*** If a word begins with an *h* that is pronounced, use *a*. If the *h* is silent, use *an*.

Incorrect: I stared for a hour.
Correct: I stared for an hour.

Jenn Huls/Shutterstock.com

Using Articles

Identify Add the appropriate indefinite article (*a*, *an* or *some*) to each of the words below. The first one has been done for you.

1. _____*an*_____ orchard
2. _____ petunia
3. _____ hose
4. _____ honour
5. _____ avocado

6. _____ milk
7. _____ house
8. _____ hour
9. _____ shark
10. _____ honey

11. _____ error
12. _____ trees
13. _____ honest mistake
14. _____ emblem
15. _____ handkerchief

Correct Either delete or replace any articles that are incorrectly used in the following paragraph. The first sentence has been done for you.

Climate scientists see a shift in ~~a~~ *the* weather. With a increase in the levels of carbon dioxide, the atmosphere traps a heat of the sun. More heat in an air means more heat in the oceans. If a ocean gets warmer, the storms it creates are more intense. An hurricane could develop to an higher category, with stronger winds and a increase in a lightning. A Earth is already an stormy world, but with a rise in global temperatures, a weather could become more extreme.

razlomov/Shutterstock.com

ꝑ delete
d̲ capitalize
ᴅ lowercase
∧ insert
⌃ add comma
? ∧ add question mark
word ∧ add word
⊙ add period
⬭ spelling
∿ switch

Traits

Noun markers show if a noun is owned, if it is very general, if it is very specific, or if it is numerous or plentiful. Using noun markers correctly helps to make your writing clear.

LO6 Other Noun Markers

Other words help provide information about nouns.

Possessive Adjectives and Pronouns

A **possessive adjective** is the possessive form of a noun or pronoun. Possessive adjectives formed from nouns can be formed by adding *'s* to singular nouns and *'* to plural nouns. The pronoun forms are found in the chart below.

Paul's car is in the shop, but **Taylor's** is fixed.

That is **my** pen.

It's **your** choice.

Possessive Adjectives

	Singular	Plural
First Person	my	our
Second Person	your	your
Third Person	his	their
	her	their
	its	their

A **possessive pronoun** replaces both a noun and a possessive adjective modifying it.

The sweater you are wearing is **mine**.

His is the oldest car I've every seen.

The dog that barks all day is **theirs**.

Possessive Pronouns

Singular	Plural
mine	ours
yours	yours
his	theirs
hers	theirs
its	theirs

Note: The possessive adjective is used before the noun, and the possessive pronoun is often used after.

Indefinite Adjectives

An **indefinite adjective** signals that the noun it marks refers to a non-specific person, place, thing, or idea. Some indefinite adjectives mark count nouns and others mark non-count nouns.

Each person brought food. **Much** food was set out.

With Count Nouns		With Non-Count Nouns	With Count or Non-Count		
each either every		much	all	any	more
few many neither			most	some	
several					

Demonstrative Adjectives

A **demonstrative adjective** marks a specific noun. The words *this* and *that* (singular) or *these* and *those* (plural) demonstrate exactly which one (or ones) is (or are) meant.

These pickles are from **that** jar.   **This** taste comes from **those** spices.

Vocabulary

possessive adjective
the possessive form of a noun, showing ownership of another noun

possessive pronoun
a pronoun that replaces both a noun and the possessive adjective modifying it

indefinite adjective
an indefinite pronoun (*many, much, some*) used as an adjective to mark a non-specific noun

demonstrative adjective
the words *this, that,* and *those* used as an adjective to mark a specific noun

Quantifiers

A **quantifier** tells *how many* or *how much* there is of something.

With Count Nouns		With Non-Count Nouns		With Count or Non-Count		
each	a couple of	a bag of	a little	no	a lot of	most
several	every	a bowl of	much	not any	lots of	all
a number of	many	a piece of	a great deal of	some	plenty of	
both	a few					
nine						

Vocabulary

quantifier
a modifier that tells *how many* or *how much*

Using Noun Markers

Identify Circle the appropriate noun marker in parentheses for each sentence.

1. I brought one of (*my, mine*) favourite recipes, and you brought one of (*your, yours*).

2. Is this (*her, hers*) recipe, or is it (*their, theirs*)?

3. How (*many, much*) sugar should I add to the batter?

4. I can't believe the recipe does not use (*any, each*) flour.

5. Next, we should make (*this, these*) casserole.

6. Your face tells me you don't like (*that, those*) idea.

7. After making the dough, we had (*several, a little*) butter left over.

8. We liked (*a number of, much*) the recipes.

9. The best pie of all was (*her, hers*).

10. Let's make sure everyone has a copy in (*their, theirs*) recipe files.

Correct Delete and replace any incorrectly used noun markers in the following paragraph. The first one has been done for you.

An omelet can contain as few or as ~~much~~ many ingredients as you wish. Of *1* course, a good omelette starts with three or four eggs. Blend the eggs in yours biggest bowl and add a couple of milk. Next, you can include much vegetables. Try fresh ingredients from yours garden. Add a cup of chopped scallions, fresh tomatoes, or green peppers. And a number of spinach can *5* give the omelette a savoury flavour. You can also add several meat. Mix in a couple of bacon or many ham. Or you might include several sausage. Fry the omelette, fold it, sprinkle it with a couple of cheese, and enjoy!

Correction Marks

ࡏ	delete
d̲	capitalize
Ɗ	lowercase
∧	insert
⌄	add comma
? ∧	add question mark
word ∧	add word
⊙	add period
◯	spelling
∩	switch

Andrew Buckin/Shutterstock.com

LO7 Real-World Application

Correct In the e-mail that follows, correct any errors with nouns, articles, or other noun markers. Use the correction marks to the left.

Send	Attach	Fonts	Colors	Save As Draft

From: Melissa St. James

To: Design and Printing Staff

Cc:

Subject: Internship Program for College Students

Correction Marks

ℐ	delete
d ͇	capitalize
Ɗ	lowercase
∧	insert
∧	add comma
? ∧	add question mark
word ∧	add word
⊙	add period
⬭	spelling
∿	switch

Hi, Team:

Could you use a assistant—a extra pair of hands at little cost?

The head of the Graphic Arts Department at Western College has asked us if we'd be interested in developing internships for third-year students in a college's three-year graphic-arts program.

Internships could be the real win–win proposition because internes would
- work on tasks that you assign,
- give you 20 hours of work per week for 15 weeks,
- get excellent professional experience by working with you, and
- allow us an opportunity to work with potential employees.

Please consider working with an student intern during the fall semester. If you are interested, let me know before January 28.

Thanks for considering these invitation to help future member of a graphic arts profession.

Melissa

Workplace

Note how the errors in nouns and noun markers make this letter less persuasive. Readers focus on the errors instead of hearing the persuasive pitch.

"Clothes make the man. Naked people have little or no influence on society."

—Mark Twain

© Beathan/Corbis

31
Pronoun

An old saying goes that clothes make the man. Well, not quite. Just because a suit is sitting there with a laptop on its, well, lap doesn't mean that a living, breathing, and thinking person is in the room. The clothes are just temporary stand-ins.

Pronouns, similarly, are stand-ins for nouns. They aren't nouns, but they suggest nouns or refer back to them. That's why it's especially important for every pronoun to connect clearly to whatever it is replacing.

This chapter will help you make sure your pronoun stand-ins work well.

Learning Outcomes

LO1 Understand personal pronouns.

LO2 Create pronoun–antecedent agreement.

LO3 Correct other pronoun problems.

LO4 Create agreement with indefinite pronouns.

LO5 Use relative pronouns.

LO6 Use other pronouns.

LO7 Use pronouns correctly in a real-world context.

What do you think?

How could clothes make the man (or woman)? How do pronouns help nouns?

LO1 Personal Pronouns

A **pronoun** is a word that takes the place of a noun or another pronoun. The most common type of pronoun is the **personal pronoun**. Personal pronouns indicate whether the person is speaking, is being spoken to, or is being spoken about.

Person	Singular			Plural		
	Nom.	**Obj.**	**Poss.**	**Nom.**	**Obj.**	**Poss.**
First (speaking)	I	me	mine	we	us	ours
Second (spoken to)	you	you	yours	you	you	yours
Third (spoken about) masculine	he	him	his	they	them	theirs
feminine	she	her	hers	they	them	theirs
neuter	it	it	its	they	them	theirs

Nom.=nominative case / **Obj.**=objective case / **Poss.**=possessive case

Case of Pronouns

The **case** of a personal pronoun indicates how it can be used.

- **Nominative** pronouns are used as the subjects of sentences or as subject complements (following the linking verbs *am, is, are, was, were, be, being,* or *been*).

  > **He** applied for the job, but the person hired was **she**.

- **Objective** pronouns are used as direct objects, indirect objects, or objects of prepositions.

  > The police officer warned **us** about **them**.

- **Possessive** pronouns show ownership and function as adjectives.

  > Her lawn looks much greener than **mine**.

Gender

Pronouns can be **masculine**, **feminine**, or **neuter**.

> **He** showed **her** how to fix **it**.

Say It

Read the following aloud.

1. *I* am / *You* are / *He* is / *She* is / *It* is / *We* are / *They* are

2. Show *me* / Show *you* / Show *him* / Show *her* / Show *us* / Show *them*

3. *My* car / *Your* car / *His* car / *Her* car / *Their* car

4. The car is *mine.* / The car is *yours.* / The car is *his.* / The car is *hers.* / The car is *theirs.*

Vocabulary

pronoun
a word that takes the place of a noun or other pronoun

personal pronoun
a pronoun that indicates whether the person is speaking, is spoken to, or is spoken about

case
property of a pronoun showing whether it is used as a subject, an object, or a possessive

nominative
used as a subject or subject complement

objective
used as a direct object, an indirect object, or an object of a preposition

possessive
used to show ownership

masculine
male

feminine
female

neuter
neither male nor female

Using Personal Pronouns

Select For each sentence below, circle the correct personal pronoun in parentheses.

1. *(I, me, my)* love to hang out at the corner coffee shop.

2. *(I, Me, My)* friends and I gather there on Saturday morning.

3. One friend, Zach, is making a film, and *(he, him, his)* asked me to be in it.

4. We read over the lines, and other patrons listened to *(we, us, our)*.

5. *(We, Us, Our)* friend Rachel is also in the film.

6. At one point, I have to give *(she, her, hers)* a kiss.

7. The other people in the coffee shop applauded *(we, us, our.)*

8. Rachel and *(I, me, my)* blushed and stared into *(we, us, our)* lattes.

9. Zach thought it was great, and *(he, him, his)* set up a shooting schedule.

10. Whoever comes to the coffee shop that day will be *(we, us, our)* extras.

Correct In the following paragraph, correct the pronouns by crossing out the incorrect forms and writing the correct forms above.

Zach, Rachel, and me went to the coffee shop on Saturday afternoon, when them are usually closed. The owners agreed to let we film there. Zach rearranged the tables a little to make room for the camera, and him and me set up the equipment. The camera rolled, and Rachel and me started into our lines. A couple of times, we had to stop because the owners were laughing so much them couldn't hold a straight face. Rachel and me had a hard time being straight when it came to ours kissing scene. It went well, and her and me got through it in one take. Zach took the footage away, and he told us he would send a disk of the rough cut to she and I.

LO2 Pronoun-Antecedent Agreement

The antecedent is the word that a pronoun refers to or replaces. A pronoun must have the same person, number, and gender as its antecedent, creating pronoun–antecedent agreement.

third-person	singular feminine	singular feminine

Padma thought she would need a lift, but her car started.

Agreement in Person

A pronoun needs to match its antecedent in person (first, second, or third).

	third person	second person

Incorrect: If **people** keep going, **you** can usually reach the goal.
Correct: If **you** keep going, **you** can usually reach the goal.
Correct: If **people** keep going, **they** can usually reach the goal.

Agreement in Number

A pronoun needs to match its antecedent in number (singular or plural).

	singular	plural

Incorrect: Each **lifeguard** must buy **their** own uniform.
Correct: **Lifeguards** must buy **their** own uniforms.
Correct: Each **lifeguard** must buy **her** or **his** own uniform.

Agreement in Gender

A pronoun needs to match its antecedent in gender (masculine, feminine, or neuter).

	feminine	masculine

Incorrect: **Mrs. Miller** will present **his** speech.
Correct: **Mrs. Miller** will present **her** speech.

> **Say It**
>
> Speak the following pronouns aloud.
> 1. First person: *I, me, mine; we, us, ours*
> 2. Second person: *you, yours*
> 3. Third person feminine: *she, her, hers; they, them, theirs*
> 4. Third person masculine: *he, him, his; they, them, theirs*
> 5. Third person neuter: *it, its; they, them, theirs*

Correcting Agreement Errors

Revise Rewrite each sentence to correct the person error.

1. When you go to the multiplex, a person has a lot of movies to choose from.

   _____

2. Each of us has to buy their own ticket and snacks.

   _____

3. If the viewer arrives early enough, you can see a triple feature.

   _____

4. One can be overwhelmed by how many movies you can see.

   _____

Revise Rewrite each sentence to correct the number error.

5. Each moviegoer chooses what movies they want to see.

   _____

6. A snack-counter attendant serves treats, and they also clean up messes.

   _____

7. Movie critics give his opinion about different films.

   _____

8. A critic shouldn't give away the ending because they would ruin the movie.

   _____

Revise Rewrite each of the following sentences to avoid sexism.

9. A critic shouldn't give away the ending because he would ruin the movie.

   _____

10. Every acrobat should check his equipment.

   _____

11. Each acrobat must keep her balance.

   _____

12. One of the acrobats left his stilts at the park.

   _____

LO3 Other Pronoun Problems

Pronouns are very useful parts of speech, but if they are mishandled, they can cause problems.

Vague Pronoun

Do not use a pronoun that could refer to more than one antecedent.

> **Unclear:** Raul played baseball with his friend and **his** brother.
> **Clear:** Raul played baseball with his friend and **his friend's** brother.

Missing Antecedent

Avoid using *it* or *they* without clear antecedents.

> **Unclear:** **They** say humans share 97 percent of DNA with chimps.
> **Clear:** **Scientists** say humans share 97 percent of DNA with chimps.

> **Unclear:** **It** says in the *Star* that the Conservatives back the bill.
> **Clear:** The *Star* says that the Conservatives back the bill.

Double Subjects

Do not place a pronoun right after the subject. Doing so creates an error called a double subject, which is not a standard construction in English.

> **Nonstandard:** Rudy and Amar, **they** went fishing.
> **Standard:** Rudy and Amar went fishing.

Pronoun Usage Errors *(They're, You're, It's)*

Do not confuse possessive adjectives *(your, their, its)* with contractions *(you're, they're, it's)*. Remember that the contractions use apostrophes in place of missing letters.

> **Incorrect:** Keep **you're** car in **it's** own lane.
> **Correct:** Keep **your** car in **its** own lane.

Speaking & Listening

The pronoun problems on this page may not cause confusion in spoken English, which is assisted with gestures, body language, and other context cues. In written English, these problems can derail meaning. Watch for these problems and correct them in your writing.

George Fairbairn/Shutterstock.com

Correcting Other Pronoun Problems

Rewrite Rewrite each sentence to correct the pronoun–antecedent problems.

1. Sarah asked her sister and her friend to help her move.

   _____

2. It said on the news that the accident will cost billions to fix.

   _____

3. They say that dark energy takes up 75 percent of the universe.

   _____

4. Dan wants his father and his friend to help.

   _____

5. They have found a way to make deep-water drilling safer.

   _____

6. It says on the parking ticket that I have to pay $50.

   _____

Correct In the following paragraph, correct the pronoun errors. Use the correction marks to the right.

For 28 years, it reported in the *Weekly World News* all kinds of outlandish stories. Often the paper reported about Elvis or the Loch Ness Monster being spotted and his impromptu concerts for die-hard fans. A bat-human hybrid named Bat Boy and an alien named P'lod appeared repeatedly in the tabloid, and he even supposedly had an affair with Hillary Clinton. Since this was during the Monica Lewinski scandal, maybe she was getting back at him. The writers and editors of the *Weekly World News*, they rarely publicly acknowledged that their stories were jokes, but said that he or she had to "suspend disbelief for the sake of enjoyment."

Correction Marks

- ꝰ delete
- d̲ capitalize
- ⅅ lowercase
- ∧ insert
- ⸜ add comma
- ? add question
- ∧ mark
- word∧ add word
- ⊙ add period
- ◯ spelling
- ∿ switch

LO4 Indefinite Pronouns

An **indefinite pronoun** does not have an antecedent, and it does not refer to a specific person, place, thing, or idea. These pronouns pose unique issues with subject–verb and pronoun–antecedent agreement.

Singular Indefinite Pronouns

Some indefinite pronouns are singular. When they are used as subjects, they require a singular verb. As antecedents, they must be matched to singular pronouns.

each	anyone	anybody	anything
either	someone	somebody	something
neither	everyone	everybody	everything
another	no one	nobody	nothing
one			

Nobody is expecting to see Bigfoot on our camping trip.

Someone used **his** or **her** own money to buy a Bigfoot detector at a novelty shop.

Plural Indefinite Pronouns

Some indefinite pronouns are plural. As subjects, they require a plural verb; as antecedents, they require a plural pronoun.

both	few	several	many

A few of the campers **hear** thumps in the night.

Several of my friends swear **they** can see eyes glowing eight feet off the ground.

Singular or Plural Indefinite Pronouns

Some indefinite pronouns can be either singular or plural, depending on the object of the preposition in the phrase that follows them.

all	any	most	none	some

Most of **us are** too frightened to sleep.

Most of the **night is** over already anyway.

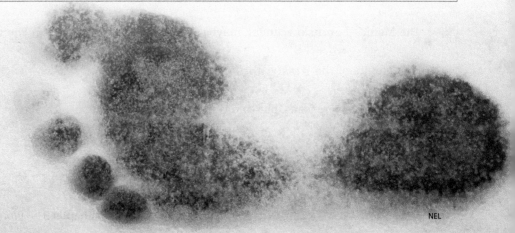

Correcting Agreement

Correct Rewrite each sentence to correct the agreement errors. The sentences are about a group of female campers.

1. Everyone needs to set up their own tent.

2. No one are getting out of work.

3. Anyone who wants to be dry should make sure they have a rain fly.

4. Nothing are more miserable than a wet sleeping bag.

5. Few is wanting to end up drenched.

6. Several wants to go hiking to look for Bigfoot.

7. Many has doubts that he exists.

8. A few says they might have dated him in high school.

9. A Bigfoot hunter should make sure they have a camera along.

10. Most of the hunters is also going to carry a big stick.

11. Most of the afternoon are available for different activities.

12. None of the girls is planning to hike after dark.

13. None of the food are to be left out to attract animals or Bigfoot.

Chapter 31 Pronoun

LO5 Relative Pronouns

A **relative pronoun** introduces a dependent clause and relates it to the rest of the sentence.

who	whom	which	whose
whoever	whomever	that	

relative clause

I would like to meet the woman **who** discovered dark matter.

Who/Whoever and Whom/Whomever

Who, whoever, whom, and *whomever* refer to people. *Who* or *whoever* functions as the subject of the relative clause, while *whom* or *whomever* functions as the object of the clause.

relative clause

I am amazed by a person **who** could imagine matter that can't be seen.
The woman **whom** I met was named Vera Rubin.
relative clause

Note: In the second relative clause, *whom* introduces the clause even though it is the direct object, not the subject *(I met whom).*

That and Which

That and *which* usually refer to things. Use *that* when the clause is restrictive—essential to the meaning of the sentence. Use *which* when the clause is non-restrictive—unnecessary to the meaning of the sentence. When *that* introduces the clause, the clause **is not** set off with commas. When *which* introduces the clause, the clause **is** set off with commas.

relative clause

I saw a documentary **that** explained about dark matter and dark energy.
The show is *Into the Wormhole,* **which** is on the Discovery Channel.
relative clause

Whose

Whose shows ownership or connection.

relative clause

Morgan Freeman, **whose** voice is soothing, hosts the show.

Note: Do not confuse *whose* with the contraction *who's* (who is).

Insight

For more practice with relative pronouns, see Chapter 24, LO6, Complex Sentences with Relative Clauses.

Vocabulary

relative pronoun
a pronoun that begins a relative clause, connecting it to a sentence

relative clause
a type of dependent clause that begins with a relative pronoun that is either the subject or the direct object of the clause

Using Relative Pronouns

Select For each sentence, circle the correct relative pronoun.

1. Vera Rubin, *(who, whom)* first discovered dark matter, wasn't seeking fame.

2. In the 1960s, she avoided black holes, *(that, which)* were a hot topic.

3. Instead, Rubin focused on the rotation of spiral galaxies, *(that, which)* few other people studied.

4. She expected that stars *(that, which)* were on the outside of galaxies would move faster than stars *(that, which)* were near the centre.

5. Instead, Rubin discovered that stars *(that, which)* were in different parts of the galaxy moved at the same speed.

6. The only way for the galaxy to move that way would be if it had ten times the mass *(that, which)* was visible.

7. Rubin, *(who, whom, whose)* had never courted fame, became a very controversial figure when she presented her findings about dark matter.

8. Other astrophysicists *(who, whom)* disbelieved her did similar observations and calculations and confirmed her findings.

9. Rubin, *(who, whom, whose)* theory once was radical, became one of the great contributors to modern science.

10. *(Whoever, Whomever)* wrestles with the idea of dark matter should remember that over fifty years ago, one woman was the first to wrestle with the idea.

© Stocktrek Images/Corbis

Write On your own paper, write a relative clause introduced by each of these relative pronouns:

1. who   3. whom   5. which   7. whose
2. whoever   4. whomever   6. that

Then use each clause correctly in a sentence.

L○6 Other Pronoun Types

Other types of pronouns have specific uses in your writing: asking questions, pointing to specific things, reflecting back on a noun (or pronoun), or intensifying a noun (or other pronoun).

Interrogative Pronoun

An **interrogative pronoun** asks a question—*who, whose, whom, which, what.*

> **What** should we call our band? **Who** will be in it?

Demonstrative Pronoun

A **demonstrative pronoun** points to a specific thing—*this, that, these, those.*

> **That** is a great name! **This** will look terrific on a cover!

Reflexive Pronoun

A **reflexive pronoun** reflects back to the subject of a sentence or clause—*myself, ourselves, yourself, yourselves, himself, herself, itself, themselves.*

> I credit **myself** for the name. You can credit **yourself** for the logo.

Intensive Pronoun

An **intensive pronoun** emphasizes the noun or pronoun it refers to—*myself, ourselves, yourself, yourselves, himself, herself, itself, themselves.*

> You **yourself** love the name Psycho Drummer. Siobhan **herself** couldn't be happier.

Reciprocal Pronoun

A **reciprocal pronoun** refers to two things in an equal way—*each other, one another.*

> We shouldn't fight with **each other**. We should support **one another**.

Say It

Speak the following words aloud.
1. Interrogative: *Who* is? / *Whose* is? / *Which* is? / *What* is? / *Whom* do you see?
2. Demonstrative: *This* is / *That* is / *These* are / *Those* are
3. Reflexive: I helped *myself.* / You helped *yourself.* / They helped *themselves.*
4. Intensive: I *myself* / You *yourself* / She *herself* / He *himself* / They *themselves.*
5. Reciprocal: We helped *each other.* / We helped *one another.*

Using Other Types of Pronouns

Indicate the type of each underlined pronoun: *interrogative, demonstrative, reflexive, intensive,* or *reciprocal.*

1. <u>That</u> is why this band needs a road crew. _____

2. <u>What</u> are we supposed to do without power cords? _____

3. I <u>myself</u> would not mind playing unplugged. _____

4. You need to remind <u>yourself</u> that we don't have acoustic guitars. _____

5. <u>That</u> is the whole problem. _____

6. The guitars <u>themselves</u> prevent us from playing unplugged. _____

7. <u>Who</u> could hear an unplugged electric guitar? _____

8. <u>What</u> person will stand a foot away to listen? _____

9. <u>This</u> is ridiculous. _____

10. <u>That</u> won't work as a power cord. _____

11. I <u>myself</u> am about to quit this band. _____

12. We should be ashamed of <u>ourselves</u>. _____

13. We shouldn't blame <u>each other</u>. _____

14. As a band, we should help <u>one another</u> get through this. _____

15. Let's buy <u>ourselves</u> another set of cords. _____

Write Create a sentence using *myself* as a reflexive pronoun, and a second using *myself* as an intensive pronoun.

1. _____

_____

_____

2. _____

_____

_____

LO7 Real-World Application

Correct In the letter that follows, correct any pronoun errors. Use the correction marks to the left.

Psycho Drummer
2457 Centre Street, Langley, BC V1W 2X3 ▪ Ph: 250.555.7188

July 30, 2015

Ms. Marcia Schwamps, Manager
Piedog Studios
350 Jackson Street
Vancouver, BC V7U 6T5

Dear Ms. Schwamps:

One of your recording technicians says that you are looking for session musicians whom could play instruments for other artists. My bandmate Jerome and me would like to offer ours services.

Jerome and me are the power duo whom are called Psycho Drummer, a name that refers to Jerome hisself. He is a master percussionist, and him has trained hisself in many styles from heavy metal to rock, pop, jazz, blues, and even classical.

I am the guitarist in Psycho Drummer. I play electric and acoustic (six- and 12-string) guitars as well as electric bass, and I too have trained myself in them.

Attached, you will find ours resumés, a list of recent gigs us have played, and a review of we from the *Langley Times*.

Please consider Jerome and I for work as session musicians at Piedog Studios. We look forward to hearing from yous and would very much appreciate an interview/audition.

Sincerely,

Terrance "Tear-It-Up" Clark

Terrance "Tear-It-Up" Clark
Guitarist
Enclosures 3

"There are 350 varieties of shark, not counting loan and pool."

—L.M. Boyd

Design Pics/Thinkstock

32
Verb

You've probably heard that a shark has to keep swimming or it suffocates. That's not entirely true. Yes, sharks breathe by moving water across their gills, but they can also lie on the bottom and push water through their gills or let currents do the work. Still, most sharks stay on the move, and when a shark is still, it has to work harder to breathe.

Verbs are much the same way. They like to stay on the move. Most verbs are action words, describing what is happening. Some verbs describe states of being—much like sharks sitting on the bottom, breathing. Either way, though, the verb gives life to the sentence, and often it is a word with big teeth. This chapter gives a view into the compelling world of verbs.

Learning Outcomes

LO1 Understand and use verb classes.

LO2 Work with number and person.

LO3 Work with voice.

LO4 Form basic verb tenses.

LO5 Form progressive tenses.

LO6 Form perfect tenses.

LO7 Understand verbals.

LO8 Use verbals as objects.

LO9 Apply learning to real-world examples.

What do you think?

Do you prefer doing or being? Why?

LO1 Verb Classes

Verbs show action or states of being. Different classes of verbs do these jobs.

Action Verbs

Verbs that show action are called action verbs. Some action verbs are transitive verbs, which means that they transfer action to a direct object.

> Trina **hurled** the softball.
> (The verb *hurled* transfers action to the direct object *softball*.)

Others are intransitive verbs: They don't transfer action to a direct object.

> Trina **pitches**.
> (The verb *pitches* does not transfer action to a direct object.)

Linking Verbs

Verbs that link the subject to a noun, a pronoun, or an adjective in the predicate are linking (or copula) verbs. Predicates with linking verbs express a state of being.

> Trina **is** a pitcher.
> (The linking verb *is* connects *Trina* to the noun *pitcher*.)
> She **seems** unbeatable.
> (The linking verb *seems* connects *She* to the adjective *unbeatable*.)

Linking Verbs

is	am	are	was	were	be	being	been	become
grow	feel	seem	look	smell	taste	sound	appear	remain

Note: The bottom-row words can also be action verbs; they are linking verbs if they don't show action.

Helping Verbs

A verb that works with an action or linking verb is a helping (or auxiliary) verb. A helping verb helps the main verb form tense, mood, and voice.

> Trina **has** pitched two shut-out games, and today she **may be** pitching her third.
> (The helping verb *has* works with the main verb *pitched*; the helping verbs *may be* work with *pitching*. Both form special tenses.)

See the chart in LO3 below for many examples of helping verbs at work.

Helping Verbs

am	been	could	does	have	might	should	will
are	being	did	had	is	must	was	would
be	can	do	has	may	shall	were	

Vocabulary

action verb
word that expresses action

transitive verb
action verb that transfers action to a direct object

intransitive verb
action verb that does not transfer action to a direct object

linking verb
verb that connects the subject with a noun, a pronoun, or an adjective in the predicate

helping (auxiliary) verb
verb that works with a main verb to form tense, mood, and voice

Using Verb Classes

Identify/Write For each sentence below, identify the underlined verbs as transitive action verbs (T), intransitive action verbs (I), linking verbs (L), or helping verbs (H). Then write your own sentence using the same class of verb.

1. I <u>love</u> fast-pitch softball, but I rarely <u>pitch</u>.

   _____

   _____

2. I <u>play</u> first base; it <u>is</u> a pressure-filled position.

   _____

   _____

3. Runners <u>charge</u> first base, and I <u>tag</u> them out.

   _____

   _____

4. Double plays <u>require</u> on-target throws, clean catches, and timing.

   _____

   _____

5. If a runner <u>steals</u>, the pitcher and player on second base <u>work</u> with me.

   _____

   _____

6. We <u>catch</u> the runner in a "pickle" and <u>tag</u> her out.

   _____

   _____

7. Softball <u>is</u> exciting, and I <u>will</u> play all summer.

   _____

   _____

8. I <u>look</u> worn out after a game, but I <u>feel</u> completely exhilarated.

   _____

   _____

L◯2 Number and Person of Verb

Verbs reflect number (singular or plural) and person (first person, second person, or third person).

Number

The **number** of the verb indicates whether the subject is singular or plural. Note that most present tense singular verbs end in *s*, while most present tense plural verbs do not.

> **Singular:** A War of 1812 re-enactment **involves** infantry, cavalry, and artillery units.
>
> **Plural:** Re-enactors **stage** amazing battle scenes from the war.

Person

The **person** of the verb indicates whether the subject is speaking, being spoken to, or being spoken about.

	Singular	Plural	Singular	Plural
First Person:	(I) am	(we) are	(I) play	(we) play
Second Person:	(you) are	(you) are	(you) play	(you) play
Third Person:	(he/she/it) is	(they) are	(he/she/it) plays	(they) play

Note that the pronoun *I* takes a special form of the *be* verb—*am*.

> I am eager to see the cannons fire.

Note that the second person (you) form of the *be* verb is the same in the singular and plural: *are* for present and *were* for past.

> **Singular:** Angela, you are in for a treat when the battle begins.
>
> **Plural:** Folks, you are in for a treat when the battle begins.
>
> **Singular:** Max, I see you were surprised at how steady the horses were in combat.
>
> **Plural:** Folks, I see you were surprised at how steady the horses were in combat.

In regular verbs, note that all the forms are the same except for the third-person singular.

> I **play** bass, you **play** drums, and Sanjay **plays** keyboard. My two brothers **play** guitar. Together, we **play** pretty well.

Uwe Bumann/Shutterstock.com

Vocabulary

number
singular or plural

person
whether the subject is speaking (*I, we*), is being spoken to (*you*), or is being spoken about (*he, she, it, they*)

Using Number and Person

Provide For each sentence below, provide the correct person and number of present tense *be* verb *(is, am, are)*.

1. We _____ at Old Fort Niagara.

2. It _____ a gathering of British and American regiments.

3. You _____ in the blue American uniform.

4. I _____ in the red uniform worn by the British.

5. A light artillery brigade _____ a group of mobile cannons.

6. A cavalry regiment _____ a group of mounted soldiers.

7. The camp doctors _____ equipped to do amputations.

8. The medicine they use _____ sometimes worse than the disease.

9. I _____ amazed by all of the tent encampments.

10. You _____ interested in becoming a re-enactor.

Rewrite Rewrite each sentence below to fix the errors in the number and person of the verb.

1. I jumps the first time a cannon goes off.

_____

2. The guns blows huge white smoke rings whirling into the air.

_____

3. The cavalry regiments charges together and battles with sabers.

_____

4. You was shocked when one cavalry officer fall from his horse.

_____

5. The infantry soldiers lines up in two rows and sends out volleys of bullets.

_____

6. After the battle, the general deliver a solemn address.

_____

LO3 Voice of the Verb

The **voice** of the verb indicates whether the subject is acting or being acted upon.

Voice

An **active voice** means that the subject is acting. A **passive voice** means that the subject is acted on.

> **Active:** The cast **sang** the song "Our State Fair."
> **Passive:** The song "Our State Fair" **was sung** by the cast.

	Active Voice		**Passive Voice**	
	Singular	Plural	Singular	Plural
Present Tense	I see you see he/she/it sees	we see you see they see	I am seen you are seen he/she/it is seen	we are seen you are seen they are seen
Past Tense	I saw you saw he saw	we saw you saw they saw	I was seen you were seen it was seen	we were seen you were seen they were seen
Future Tense	I will see you will see he will see	we will see you will see they will see	I will be seen you will be seen it will be seen	we will be seen you will be seen they will be seen
Present Perfect Tense	I have seen you have seen he has seen	we have seen you have seen they have seen	I have been seen you have been seen it has been seen	we have been seen you have been seen they have been seen
Past Perfect Tense	I had seen you had seen he had seen	we had seen you had seen they had seen	I had been seen you had been seen it had been seen	we had been seen you had been seen they had been seen
Future Perfect Tense	I will have seen you will have seen he will have seen	we will have seen you will have seen they will have seen	I will have been seen you will have been seen it will have been seen	we will have been seen you will have been seen they will have been seen

Active voice is preferred for most writing because it is direct and energetic.

> **Active:** The crowd gave the cast a standing ovation.
> **Passive:** The cast was given a standing ovation by the crowd.

Passive voice is preferred when the focus is on the receiver of the action or when the subject is unknown.

> **Passive:** A donation was left at the ticket office.
> **Active:** Someone left a donation at the ticket office.

Workplace

In workplace writing, use active voice for most messages. Use passive voice to soften bad news.

Vocabulary

voice
active or passive

active voice
voice created when the subject is performing the action of the verb

passive voice
voice created when the subject is receiving the action of the verb

© Antenna/fstop/Corbis

Using Voice of a Verb

Rewrite Read each passive sentence below and rewrite it to be active. Think about what is performing the action and make that the subject. The first one is done for you.

1. *State Fair* was put on by the community theatre group.
   The community theatre group put on State Fair.

2. The Frake family was featured in the musical.
   _____

3. Many songs were sung and danced by the cast.
   _____

4. Pickles and mincemeat were rated by judges at the fair.
   _____

5. Mrs. Frake's mincemeat was spiked with too much brandy.
   _____

6. The judges of the contest were overcome by the strength of the mincemeat.
   _____

7. Two couples were shown falling in love at the fair.
   _____

8. The singers were assisted by a stalwart piano player in the orchestra pit.
   _____

9. The song "It's a Grand Night for Singing" was the climax of the first half.
   _____

10. The cast was applauded gratefully by the crowd.
    _____

Write Using the chart showing active and passive voice, write a sentence for each situation below.

1. (A present tense singular active sentence) _____
   _____
   _____

2. (A past tense plural passive sentence) _____
   _____
   _____

LO4 Present and Future Tense Verbs

Basic verb tenses tell whether action happens in the past, in the present, or in the future.

Present Tense

Present tense verbs indicate that action is happening right now.

> Master classical musicians and new professionals **gather** at the Marlboro Music Festival.

Present tense verbs also can indicate that action happens routinely or continually.

> Every summer, they **spend** seven weeks together learning music.

Present Tense in Academic Writing

Use present tense verbs to describe current conditions.

> Pianist Richard Goode **plays** beside talented young artists.

Use present tense verbs also to discuss the ideas in literature or to use historical quotations in a modern context. This use is called the "historical present."

> The audiences at Marlboro **rave** about the quality of the music, or as the *New York Times* **says**, "No matter what is played . . . the performances at Marlboro are usually extraordinary."

Note: It is important to write a paragraph or an essay in one tense. Avoid shifting needlessly from tense to tense as you write. (See also Chapter 29, LO2, Shifts in Sentences.)

Future Tense

Future tense verbs indicate that action will happen later on.

> Marlboro music **will launch** the careers of many more young stars.

Kokhanchikov/Shutterstock.com

Using Present and Future Verb Tenses

Write For each sentence below, fill in the blank with the present tense form of the verb indicated in parentheses.

1. Young musicians _____ to the Marlboro Music Festival by special invitation. (came)

2. Seasoned professionals _____ them like colleagues, not students. (treated)

3. Musicians _____ side by side for weeks before performing. (worked)

4. The town of Marlboro, Vermont, _____ only 987 citizens. (had)

5. Many times that number _____ to the concerts each summer. (came)

Change Cross out and replace the verbs in the following paragraph, making them all present tense.

A sixteen-year-old cellist named Yo Yo Ma arrived at Marlboro. He couldn't believe his fortune to be surrounded by such great musicians. He began to play and soon fell in love with music. A festival administrator named Jill Hornor also caught his eye, and he fell in love with her as well. They were married.

Write Write a sentence of your own, using each verb below in the form indicated in parentheses.

1. thought (present) _____

_____

2. lived (future) _____

_____

3. hoped (present) _____

_____

4. cooperated (future) _____

_____

Past Tense Verbs

Past tense verbs indicate that action has already happened.

> When referring to his campaign in England, Julius Caesar **reported**, "I **came**. I **saw**. I **conquered**."

Forming Past Tense

Most verbs form their past tense by adding *ed*. If the word ends in a silent *e*, drop the *e* before adding *ed*.

help → helped	love → loved
look → looked	hope → hoped

If the word ends in a consonant before a single vowel and the last syllable is stressed, double the final consonant before adding *ed*.

stop → stopped	occur → occurred
plan → planned	refer → referred

If the word ends in a *y* preceded by a consonant, change the *y* to *i* before adding *ed*.

study → studied	hurry → hurried
worry → worried	carry → carried

Irregular Verbs

Insight

Note that some of the irregular verbs presented in the chart are among the oldest verbs in the English language. That's why they are irregular. Sadly, they are used quite often because they describe the everyday tasks that English speakers have been doing for more than a thousand years.

Vocabulary

past tense
verb tense indicating that action happened previously

Some of the most commonly used verbs form past tense by changing the verb itself. See the chart below:

Present	Past	Present	Past	Present	Past
am	was, were	fly	flew	see	saw
become	became	forget	forgot	shake	shook
begin	began	freeze	froze	shine	shone
blow	blew	get	got	show	showed
break	broke	give	gave	shrink	shrank
bring	brought	go	went	sing	sang
buy	bought	grow	grew	sink	sank
catch	caught	hang	hung	sit	sat
choose	chose	have	had	sleep	slept
come	came	hear	heard	speak	spoke
dig	dug	hide	hid	stand	stood
do	did	keep	kept	steal	stole
draw	drew	know	knew	swim	swam
drink	drank	lead	led	swing	swung
drive	drove	pay	paid	take	took
eat	ate	prove	proved	teach	taught
fall	fell	ride	rode	tear	tore
feel	felt	ring	rang	throw	threw
fight	fought	rise	rose	wear	wore
find	found	run	ran	write	wrote

Using Past Tense Verbs

Write For each verb, write the correct past tense form.

1. swing _____
2. think _____
3. slip _____
4. reply _____
5. teach _____
6. cry _____
7. sing _____
8. give _____
9. cap _____
10. fly _____

11. type _____
12. cope _____
13. shop _____
14. grip _____
15. gripe _____
16. pour _____
17. soap _____
18. trick _____
19. try _____
20. tip _____

Edit Make changes to the following paragraph, converting it from present tense to past tense. Use the correction marks to the right.

When I am fresh out of college, I get my first job as an assistant editor at a sports publisher. At this company, acquisitions editors follow trends, talk with authors, and work with them to create a manuscript. Developmental editors then work with the manuscript to develop it into a worthwhile book. Assistant editors help with all stages of production. They edit manuscripts and typemark them. Then they check the galleys—or long sheets of printout film that paste-up artists cut and wax to create pages. Those are the days of manual layout. Assistant editors have to check the paste-up pages for dropped copy. They also proofread and enter changes, and check bluelines. Publishing is completely different now, but back then, I get my first experience in real-world work. I am glad just to have an office of my own.

Correction Marks

୬	delete
d̲	capitalize
Ɖ	lowercase
∧	insert
⌃	add comma
? ∧	add question mark
word ∧	add word
⊙	add period
◯	spelling
∿	switch

LO5 Progressive Tense Verbs

The basic tenses of past, present, and future tell when action takes place. The progressive tenses tell that action is ongoing—whether in the past, the present, or the future.

Progressive Tenses

Progressive tenses indicate that action is ongoing. A progressive tense is formed by using a helping verb along with the *ing* form of the main verb.

> Work habits **were changing** rapidly.

There are past, present, and future progressive tenses. Each uses a helping verb in the appropriate tense.

> For thousands of years, most humans **were working** in agriculture.
>
> Currently in the West, most humans **are working** in non-agricultural jobs.
>
> In the future, people **will be making** their living in unimaginable ways.

Forming Progressive Tense

Past:	was/were	+	main verb	+	ing
Present:	am/is/are	+	main verb	+	ing
Future:	will be	+	main verb	+	ing

Insight

Avoid using progressive tense with the following:

- Verbs that express thoughts, attitudes, and desires: *know, understand, want, prefer*

- Verbs that describe appearances: *seem, resemble*

- Verbs that indicate possession: *belong, have own, possess*

- Verbs that signify inclusion: *contain, hold*

  I **know** your name, not I **am knowing** your name.

Vocabulary

progressive tenses
verb tenses that express ongoing action

Using Progressive Tense

Form Rewrite each sentence three times, changing the tenses as requested in parentheses.

> Everyone needs food, but agribusiness makes food production very efficient.

1. (present progressive) _____

_____

2. (past progressive) _____

_____

3. (future progressive) _____

_____

> People provide a product or service, and others pay for it.

4. (present progressive) _____

_____

5. (past progressive) _____

_____

6. (future progressive) _____

_____

> The products and services in greatest demand produce the most wealth.

7. (present progressive) _____

_____

8. (past progressive) _____

_____

9. (future progressive) _____

_____

LO6 Perfect Tense Verbs

The perfect tenses tell that the action of a verb is not ongoing, but is finished, whether in the past, present, or future.

Perfect Tenses

Perfect tenses indicate that action is completed. A perfect tense is formed by using a helping verb along with the past tense form of the main verb.

Each year of my career, I **have learned** something new.

There are past, present, and future perfect tenses. These tenses are formed by using helping verbs in past, present, and future tenses.

By the end of my first year, I **had learned** to get along in a corporate structure.
This year, I **have learned** new technology skills.
By this time next year, I **will have learned** how to be an effective salesperson.

	Forming Perfect Tense		
Past:	had	+	past tense main verb
Present:	has/have	+	past tense main verb
Future:	will have	+	past tense main verb

Perfect Tense with Irregular Verbs

Insight

For the simple past tense form of these irregular verbs, see the Irregular Verbs chart earlier in this chapter (LO4).

To form a perfect tense with an irregular verb, use the past participle form instead of the past tense form. Here are the past participles of some common irregular verbs.

Present	Past Part.	Present	Past Part.	Present	Past Part.
am, be	been	fly	flown	see	seen
become	become	forget	forgotten	shake	shaken
begin	begun	freeze	frozen	shine	shone
blow	blown	get	gotten	show	shown
break	broken	give	given	shrink	shrunk
bring	brought	go	gone	sing	sung
buy	bought	grow	grown	sink	sunk
catch	caught	hang	hung	sit	sat
choose	chosen	have	had	sleep	slept
come	come	hear	heard	speak	spoken
dig	dug	hide	hidden	stand	stood
do	done	keep	kept	steal	stolen
draw	drawn	know	known	swim	swum
drink	drunk	lead	led	swing	swung
drive	driven	pay	paid	take	taken
eat	eaten	prove	proven	teach	taught
fall	fallen	ride	ridden	tear	torn
feel	felt	ring	rung	throw	thrown
fight	fought	rise	risen	wear	worn
find	found	run	run	write	written

Using Perfect Tense

Form Rewrite each sentence three times, changing the tenses as requested in parentheses.

I work hard and listen carefully.

1. (past perfect) _____

_____

2. (present perfect) _____

_____

3. (future perfect) _____

_____

I gain my position by being helpful, and I keep it the same way.

4. (past perfect) _____

_____

5. (present perfect) _____

_____

6. (future perfect) _____

_____

My colleagues depend on me, and I deliver what they need.

7. (past perfect) _____

_____

8. (present perfect) _____

_____

9. (future perfect) _____

_____

LO7 Verbals

A verbal is formed from a verb but functions as a noun, an adjective, or an adverb. Each type of verbal—gerund, participle, and infinitive—can appear alone or can begin a verbal phrase.

Gerund

A gerund is a verb form ending in *ing* and functioning as a noun.

> **Kayaking** is a fun type of exercise. (subject)
>
> I love **kayaking**. (direct object)

A gerund phrase includes not only a gerund but also any associated objects and modifiers.

> **Running rapids in a kayak** is exhilarating. (subject)
>
> I enjoy **paddling a kayak through white water**. (direct object)

Participle

A participle is a verb form ending in *ing* or *ed* and functioning as an adjective.

> **Exhilarated**, I ran my first rapids at age 15. (*exhilarated* modifies *I*)
>
> That was an **exhilarating** ride! (*exhilarating* modifies *ride*)

A participial phrase includes not only a participle but also any associated objects and modifiers.

> **Shocking my parents**, I said I wanted to go again.

Infinitive

An infinitive is formed from *to* and a present tense verb, and it functions as a noun, an adjective, or an adverb.

> **To kayak** is to live. (noun)
>
> I will schedule more time **to kayak**. (adjective)
>
> You need courage and a little craziness **to kayak**. (adverb)

An infinitive phrase includes not only a participle but also any associated objects or modifiers.

> I want **to kayak the Colorado River through the Grand Canyon**.

Vocabulary

verbal
gerund, participle, or infinitive; a construction formed from a verb but functioning as a noun, an adjective, or an adverb

verbal phrase
phrase formed around a gerund, a participle, or an infinitive

gerund
verbal ending in *ing* and functioning as a noun

gerund phrase
phrase including a gerund and any accompanying objects and modifiers

participle
verbal ending in *ing* or *ed* and functioning as an adjective

participial phrase
phrase including a participle and any accompanying objects and modifiers

infinitive
verbal beginning with *to* and functioning as a noun, an adjective, or an adverb

infinitive phrase
phrase including an infinitive and any accompanying objects and modifiers

Using Verbals

Identify Identify each underlined verbal by circling the correct choice in parentheses (gerund, participle, infinitive).

1. <u>Rock climbing</u> is an extreme sport. (gerund, participle, infinitive)

2. I'd like <u>to climb</u> Mt. Logan one day. (gerund, participle, infinitive)

3. <u>Rappelling down a cliff in Arizona</u>, I almost slipped. (gerund, participle, infinitive)

4. <u>Catching myself</u>, I checked my lines and carabiners. (gerund, participle, infinitive)

5. <u>To fall while climbing</u> could be fatal. (gerund, participle, infinitive)

6. I keep my equipment in top shape <u>to avoid a mishap</u>. (gerund, participle, infinitive)

Form Complete each sentence below by supplying the type of verbal requested in parentheses.

1. My favourite exercise is _____. (gerund)

2. _____ would get me into shape. (gerund)

3. _____, I could stay in shape. (participle)

4. Perhaps I will also try _____. (gerund)

5. When exercising, remember _____. (infinitive)

6. _____, I'll lose weight. (participle)

Write Write a sentence that correctly uses each verbal phrase listed below.

1. to work out _____

_____

2. choosing a type of exercise _____

_____

3. excited by the idea _____

_____

LO8 Verbals as Objects

Though both infinitives and gerunds can function as nouns, they can't be used interchangeably as direct objects. Some verbs take infinitives and not gerunds. Other verbs take only gerunds and not infinitives.

Gerunds as Objects

Verbs that express facts are followed by **gerunds**.

admit	deny	enjoy	miss	recommend
avoid	discuss	finish	quit	regret
consider	dislike	imagine	recall	

> I miss **walking** along the beach.
> **not** I miss to walk along the beach.
>
> I regret **cutting** our vacation short.
> **not** I regret to cut our vacation short.

Infinitives as Objects

Verbs that express intentions, hopes, and desires are followed by **infinitives**.

agree	decide	fail	need	promise	volunteer
appear	demand	hesitate	offer	refuse	want
attempt	deserve	hope	plan	seem	wish
consent	endeavour	intend	prepare	tend	

> We should plan **to go** back to the ocean.
> **not** We should plan going back to the ocean.
>
> We will endeavour **to save** money for the trip.
> **not** We will endeavour saving money for the trip.

Gerunds or Infinitives as Objects

Some verbs can be followed by either a gerund or an infinitive.

begin	hate	love	remember	stop
continue	like	prefer	start	try

> I love **walking** by the ocean.
> **or** I love **to walk** by the ocean.

Using Verbals as Objects

Select For each sentence below, circle the appropriate verbal in parentheses.

1. I imagine (walking, to walk) along the Pacific Coast.

2. We want (seeing, to see) whales or dolphins when we are there.

3. I hope (getting, to get) some beautiful shots of the ocean.

4. We should avoid (getting, to get) sunburned when we are on the beach.

5. I enjoy (getting, to get) sand between my toes.

6. Maybe a surfer will offer (showing, to show) me how to surf.

7. We deserve (going, to go) on vacation more often.

8. Later, we will regret not (taking, to take) the time for ourselves.

9. I have never regretted (taking, to take) a vacation.

10. I wish (having, to have) a vacation right now.

Write For each verb below, write your own sentence using the verb and following it with a gerund or an infinitive, as appropriate.

1. quit _____

_____

2. recall _____

_____

3. tend _____

_____

4. volunteer _____

_____

5. discuss _____

_____

6. decide _____

_____

LO9 Real-World Application

Revise Rewrite the following paragraph, changing passive verbs to active verbs. (See LO3.)

Bedford's school music program should be supported by Grohling Music Suppliers. Our instrument rentals and our sheet-music services have been used extensively by the school system. In these tough economic times, the school should be assisted by us.

_____

_____

_____

_____

_____

_____

_____

_____

Revise In the following paragraph, change future perfect verbs into past perfect verbs by crossing out helping verbs and writing new helping verbs. (See LO6.)

We will have provided reduced-cost sheet music to the school system and will have added used and refurbished instrument rentals. In addition, we will have provided best-customer discounts to schools that will have rented and bought in volume.

Revise In the following paragraph, correct misused verbals by crossing out the gerund or infinitive and replacing it with the correct verbal form. (See LO7.)

I hope exploring these possibilities with you. We could recommend to make some of these changes the first year. I admit to have a soft spot for student performers. I recall to get my first flute as a student and to begin with music then.

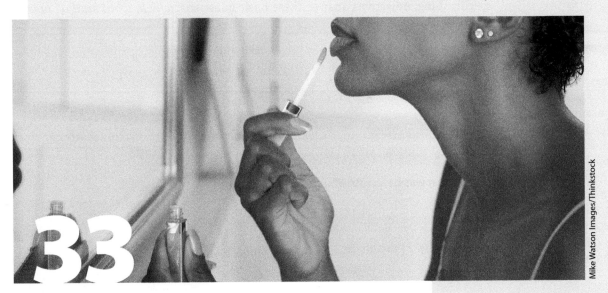

"Where lipstick is concerned, the important thing is not colour, but to accept God's final word on where your lips end."

—Jerry Seinfeld

33
Adjective and Adverb

The purpose of makeup is to accentuate the beauty that is already in your face. The focus should be on you, not on the mascara, lipstick, foundation, or blush you use.

In the same way, the real beauty of a sentence lies in the nouns and verbs. Adjectives and adverbs can modify those nouns and verbs, bringing out their true beauty, but these modifiers should not overwhelm the sentence. Use them sparingly to make your meaning clear, not to distract with flash. This chapter will show you how to get the most out of a few adjectives and adverbs.

Learning Outcomes

LO1 Understand adjective basics.

LO2 Put adjectives in order.

LO3 Use adjectivals.

LO4 Understand adverb basics.

LO5 Place adverbs well.

LO6 Use adverbials.

LO7 Apply adjectives and adverbs in real-world contexts.

What do you think?

What effect is created when lipstick overwhelms lips? What effect is created when adjectives overload nouns?

L◯1 Adjective Basics

An **adjective** is a word that modifies a noun or pronoun. Even **articles** such as *a, an,* and *the* are adjectives, because they indicate whether you mean a general or specific thing. Adjectives answer these basic questions: *which, what kind of, how many/how much.*

Speaking & Listening

Read the first example sentence aloud. Then read it without the adjectives. Note how adjectives add spice to the description. Like spice, though, adjectives should be used sparingly, to "season" nouns, not to overwhelm them.

Adjectives often appear before the word they modify.

> I saw a **beautiful grey tabby** cat.

A **predicate adjective** appears after the noun it modifies and is linked to the word by a linking verb.

> The cat was **beautiful** and **grey**.

Proper adjectives come from **proper nouns** and are capitalized.

> I also saw a **Persian** cat.

Forms of Adjectives

Adjectives come in three forms: positive, comparative, and superlative.

- **Positive adjectives** describe one thing without making any comparisons.

> Fred is a **graceful** cat.

- **Comparative adjectives** compare the thing to something else.

> Fred is **more graceful** than our dog, Barney.

- **Superlative adjectives** compare the thing to two or more other things.

> He is the **most graceful** cat you will ever see.

Vocabulary

adjective
word that modifies a noun or pronoun

articles
the adjectives *a, an,* and *the*

predicate adjective
adjective that appears after a linking verb and describes the subject

proper adjective
adjective that derives from a proper noun

proper noun
noun referring to a specific person, place, thing, or idea; capitalized as a name

positive adjective
word that modifies a noun or pronoun without comparing it

comparative adjective
word that modifies a noun or pronoun by comparing it to something else

superlative adjective
word that modifies a noun or pronoun by comparing it to two or more things

Note: For one- and two-syllable words, create the comparative form by adding *er*, and create the superlative form by added *est*. For words of three syllables or more, use *more* (or *less*) for comparatives and *most* (or *least*) for superlatives as in the example above. Also note that *good* and *bad* have special superlative forms:

Positive	Comparative	Superlative
good	better	best
bad	worse	worst
big	bigger	biggest
happy	happier	happiest
wonderful	more wonderful	most wonderful

Using the Forms of Adjectives

Identify/Write In each sentence below, identify the underlined adjectives as positive (P), comparative (C), or superlative (S). Then write a new sentence about a different topic, but use the same adjectives.

1. The shelter had a <u>Siamese</u> cat with <u>crossed</u> eyes and <u>black</u> feet.

   _____

   _____

2. She was <u>more inquisitive</u> than the other cats.

   _____

   _____

3. Her eyes were the <u>bluest</u> I had ever seen on a cat.

   _____

   _____

4. Her <u>surprising</u> meow was <u>loud</u> and <u>insistent</u>.

   _____

   _____

5. But her name—Monkey—was the <u>most surprising</u> fact of all.

   _____

   _____

Correct Read the paragraph below and correct adjective errors, using the correction marks to the right. The first one has been done for you.

Some people say dogs are ~~more~~ tamer than cats, but cats have a more great place in some people's hearts. Cats were probably first attracted to human civilizations during the most early days of the agricultural revolution. The sudden surplus of grains attracted many mice, which in turn attracted cats. Cats that were the most best mousers were welcomed by humans. In time, more cute and more cuddly cats became pets. But cats have never given up their wildness. Even now, a barn cat that is not used to human touch can be feraler than a dog.

Correction Marks

- ℐ delete
- d̲ capitalize
- ꟿ lowercase
- ∧ insert
- ⌃ add comma
- ? add question
- ∧ mark
- word̂ add word
- ⊙ add period
- ⬭ spelling
- ꝏ switch

Insight

Native English speakers use this order unconsciously because it sounds right to them. If you put adjectives in a different order, a native English speaker might say, "That's not how anybody says it." One way to avoid this issue is to avoid stacking multiple adjectives before nouns.

JeremyRichards/Shutterstock.com

LO2 Adjective Order

Adjectives aren't all created equal. Native English speakers use a specific order when putting multiple adjectives before a noun, and all speakers of English can benefit from understanding this order.

Begin with . . .

1. articles	a, an, the
demonstrative adjectives	that, this, these, those
possessives	my, our, her, their, Kayla's

Then position adjectives that tell . . .

2. sequence	first, second, next, last
3. how many	three, few, some, many
4. value	important, prized, fine
5. size	giant, puny, hulking
6. shape	spiky, blocky, square
7. condition	clean, tattered, repaired
8. age	old, new, classic
9. colour	blue, scarlet, salmon
10. nationality	French, Chinese, Cuban
11. religion	Baptist, Buddhist, Hindu
12. material	cloth, stone, wood, bronze

Finally place . . .

13. nouns used as adjectives	baby [seat], shoe [lace]

Example:

that ruined ancient stone temple

(**1** + **7** + **8** + **12** + **noun**)

Note: Avoid using too many adjectives before a noun. An article and one or two adjectives are usually enough. More adjectives may overload the noun.

Too many:	their first few expensive delicious French bread appetizers
Effective:	their first French bread appetizers

Placing Adjectives in Order

Order Rearrange each set of adjectives and articles so that they are in the correct order. The first one has been done for you.

1. blue   square   that

   _____ that square blue _____ button

2. my   Scottish   rugged

   _____ kilt

3. plastic   brand-new   few

   _____ beads

4. worthless   a   brass

   _____ tack

5. classic   many   Kenyan

   _____ masks

6. aluminum   pop   Jayden's

   _____ can

7. key   Catholic   my

   _____ chain

8. dilapidated   this   old

   _____ shack

9. wool   her   woven

   _____ cardigan

10. identical   seven   music

    _____ stands

11. young   the   bright

    _____ faces

12. last   real   our

    _____ option

LO3 Adjective Questions and Adjectivals

Adjectives answer these basic questions: *which, what kind of, how many / how much.*

Stockbyte/Thinkstock

	Guy
Which?	that guy
What kind of?	cool tattooed guy
How many/how much?	one guy

that one cool tattooed guy

Insight

Instead of trying to memorize the names of different types of phrases and clauses, just remember the adjective questions. Turn them into a cheer—*which, what kind of, how many/ how much!*

Adjectivals

A single word that answers one of these questions is called an adjective. If a phrase or clause answers one of these questions, it is an **adjectival** phrase or clause.

	Guy
Which?	guy sitting in the Mustang
What kind of?	guy who exudes attitude

Look at that guy, **who exudes attitude,** sitting in the Mustang.

The following types of phrases and clauses can be adjectivals:

Prepositional phrase:	with his arms crossed
Participial phrase:	staring at something
Adjective clause:	who doesn't even own the Mustang

Vocabulary

adjectival
phrase or clause that answers one of the adjective questions and modifies a noun or pronoun

prepositional phrase
phrase that starts with a preposition and includes an object and modifiers

participial phrase
phrase made up of a participle (*ing* or *ed* form of verb) plus any accompanying objects and modifiers; used as an adjective

adjective clause
clause beginning with a relative pronoun and including a verb, but not able to stand alone; functioning as an adjective

> ## Say It
>
> Partner with a classmate. One of you should say the noun, and the other should ask the adjective questions. Then the first person should answer each question with adjectives or adjectivals.
>
> 1. **convertibles**
>   Which convertibles?
>   What kind of convertibles?
>   How many convertibles?
>
> 2. **detergent**
>   Which detergent?
>   What kind of detergent?
>   How much detergent?

Using Adjectives and Adjectivals

Answer/Write For each word, answer the adjective questions using adjectives and adjectivals. Then write a sentence using two or more of your answers.

1. Dogs

Which dogs? _____

What kind of dogs? _____

How many dogs? _____

Sentence: _____

_____

_____

_____

2. Sports

Which sports? _____

What kind of sports? _____

How many sports? _____

Sentence: _____

_____

_____

_____

3. Proposals

Which proposals? _____

What kind of proposals? _____

How many proposals? _____

Sentence: _____

_____

_____

_____

LO4 Adverb Basics

An **adverb** can modify a verb, a **verbal**, an adjective, an adverb, or occasionally a whole sentence. An adverb answers one of these basic questions: *how, when, where, why, to what degree, how often.*

Sheri leaped **fearlessly**.
(*Fearlessly* modifies the verb *leaped*.)

Sheri leaped **quite readily**.
(*Quite* modifies *readily*, which modifies *leaped*.)

Obviously, she wants to fly.
(*Obviously* modifies the whole sentence.)

Note: Most adverbs end in *ly*. Some can be written with or without the *ly*, but when in doubt, use the *ly* form.

loud ⟶ loud**ly**   tight ⟶ tight**ly**
deep ⟶ deep**ly**

Forms of Adverbs

Like adjectives, adverbs have three forms: positive, comparative, and superlative.

■ **Positive adverbs** describe without comparing.

Sheri leaped **high** and **fearlessly**.

■ **Comparative adverbs** (*-er, more,* or *less*) describe by comparing with one other action.

She leaped **higher** and **more fearlessly** than I did.

■ **Superlative adverbs** (*-est, most,* or *least*) describe by comparing with more than one action.

She leaped **highest** and **most fearlessly** of any of us.

Note: Some adverbs change form to create comparative or superlative forms.

well ⟶ better ⟶ best   badly ⟶ worse ⟶ worst

Traits

Intensifying adverbs such as *very* and *really* are best used sparingly. In academic writing, it is considered better to choose a precise, vivid verb than to prop up an imprecise verb with an adverb.

Vocabulary

adverb
word that modifies a verb, a verbal, an adjective, an adverb, or a whole sentence

verbal
word formed from a verb but functioning as a noun, an adjective, or an adverb

positive adverb
adverb that modifies without comparing

comparative adverb
adverb that modifies by comparing with one other action

superlative adverb
adverb that modifies by comparing to two or more actions

Using the Forms of Adverbs

Provide In each sentence below, provide the correct form of the adverb in parentheses—positive, comparative, or superlative.

1. My friend likes to eat _____ (quickly).

2. She eats _____ (quickly) than I do.

3. She eats _____ (quickly) of anyone I know.

4. My brother eats _____ (reluctantly).

5. He eats _____ (reluctantly) than a spoiled child.

6. He eats _____ (reluctantly) of anyone on Earth.

7. I eat _____ (slowly).

8. I eat _____ (slowly) than I used to.

9. I eat _____ (slowly) of anytime in my life.

10. I suppose the three of us eat pretty _____ (badly).

Choose In each sentence, circle the correct word in parentheses. If the word modifies a noun or pronoun, choose the adjective form (good, bad). If the word modifies a verb, a verbal, an adjective, or an adverb, choose the adverb form (well, badly.)

1. My brother went to a (good, well) play.

2. He said the actors did (good, well), and that the plot was (good, well).

3. He even got a (good, well) deal on tickets for (good, well) seats.

4. He wanted (bad, badly) to see this play.

5. The problem was that one patron behaved (bad, badly).

6. He had a (bad, badly) attitude and once even booed.

7. My brother told him to stop, but the guy took it (bad, badly).

8. The ushers did (good, well) when they removed the guy.

9. The audience even gave them a (good, well) ovation.

10. My brother says the overall evening went (good, well).

My Good Images/Shutterstock.com

LO5 Placement of Adverbs

Adverbs should be placed in different locations in sentences, depending on their use.

How Adverbs

Adverbs that tell *how* can appear anywhere except between a verb and a direct object.

> **Steadily** we hiked the trail.
> We **steadily** hiked the trail.
> We hiked the trail **steadily**.
>
> `not` We hiked **steadily** the trail.

When Adverbs

Adverbs that tell *when* should go at the beginning or end of the sentence (or clause).

> We hiked to base camp **yesterday**. **Today** we'll reach the peak.

Where Adverbs

Adverbs that tell *where* should follow the verb they modify, but should not come between the verb and the direct object. (**Note:** Prepositional phrases often function as *where* adverbs.)

> The trail wound **uphill** and passed **through rockslide debris**.
> We avoided falling rocks **throughout our journey.**
>
> `not` We avoided **throughout our journey** falling rocks.

To What Degree Adverbs

Adverbs that tell *to what degree* go right before the adverb they modify.

> I learned **very** definitely the value of good hiking boots.

How Often Adverbs

Adverbs that tell *how often* should go right before an action verb, even if the verb has a helping verb.

> I **often** remember that wonderful hike.
> I will **never** forget the sights I saw.

Placing Adverbs Well

Place For each sentence below, insert the adverb (in parentheses) in the most appropriate position. The first one has been done for you.

1. In order to scare off bears, we *occasionally* made noise. (occasionally)

2. Bears avoid contact with human beings. (usually)

3. A bear surprised or cornered by people will turn to attack. (often)

4. A mother bear with cubs is likely to attack. (very)

5. If a bear approaches, playing dead may work. (sometimes)

6. Climbing a tree is not the best idea. (usually)

7. Black bears climb trees. (often)

8. Grizzly bears just knock the tree down. (usually)

9. Another defence is to open your coat to look large. (especially)

10. At the same time, try to make a loud noise. (very)

Revise In the paragraph below, use the transpose mark (‿) to move adverbs into their correct positions.

Spotting wildlife is one often of the highlights of a hiking trip. Deer appear in fields occasionally, and lucky hikers might glimpse a bear sometimes in the distance. Porcupines, raccoons, and other creatures amble out of the woods curiously. Not usually hikers will see mountain lions because the cats are ambush predators. Mountain lions attack groups of people rarely and usually avoid human contact. Do keep children from behind straggling.

LO6 Adverb Questions and Adverbials

As you know, adverbs answer these basic questions: *how, when, where, why, to what degree,* and *how often.*

Donald Iain Smith/Getty Images

	Children splashed.
How?	splashed barefoot
When?	splashed today
Where?	splashed outside
Why?	splashed excitedly
To what degree?	splashed very excitedly
How often?	splashed repeatedly

Today, the children **repeatedly** and **very excitedly** splashed **barefoot outside.**

Note: Avoid this sort of adverb overload in your sentences.

Adverbials

Often, the adverb questions are answered by adverbial phrases and clauses, which answer the same six questions.

	Children splashed.
How?	splashed jumping up and down
When?	splashed during the downpour
Where?	splashed in the puddles in the driveway
Why?	splashed for the joy of being wet
To what degree?	splashed until they were drenched
How often?	splashed throughout the storm

During the downpour and **throughout the storm,** the children splashed, **jumping up and down in the puddles in the driveway for the joy of being wet** and **until they were drenched.**

Note: Again, avoid this sort of adverbial overload in your sentences.

The following types of phrases and clauses can be adverbials:

Prepositional phrase:	in the puddles in the driveway
Participial phrase:	jumping up and down
Dependent clause:	until they were drenched

Vocabulary

adverbial
phrase or clause that answers
one of the adverb questions

Using Adverbials

Answer/Write For each sentence, answer the adverb questions using adverbs and adverbials. Then write a sentence using three or more of your answers.

1. **They danced.**

   How did they dance? _____

   When did they dance? _____

   Where did they dance? _____

   Why did they dance? _____

   To what degree did they dance? _____

   How often did they dance? _____

   Sentence: _____

   _____

   _____

   _____

2. **They sang.**

   How did they sing? _____

   When did they sing? _____

   Where did they sing? _____

   Why did they sing? _____

   To what degree did they sing? _____

   How often did they sing? _____

   Sentence: _____

   _____

   _____

   _____

LO7 Real-World Application

Correct In the following document, correct the use of adjectives and adverbs. Use the correction marks to the left.

Clowning Around

1328 West Road
Digby, NS B4C 5D6
902-555-8180

January 6, 2015

Mrs. Judy Bednar
14 Truro Drive
Digby, NS B4C 4D4

Dear Ms. Bednar:

It's time for a party birthday! You've thought of everything—balloons, decorations, cake . . . But what about awesomely entertainment? How many kids are coming and how much time do you have to keep them entertained?

Fear not. At Clowning Around, we specialize in making every birthday the funnest and memorablest it can be. For young kids, we offer balloon colourful animals, magic amazing tricks, and backyard goofy games. For older kids, we have water wild games and magic street illusions. And for kids of all ages, we have the most funny clowns, the most bravest superheroes, and most amazingest impressionists.

That's right. You can throw a terrific party for your loved one worrying without about the entertainment—and paying without a lot either. See the enclosed brochure for our services and rates. Then give us a call at Clowning Around, and we'll make your party next an event to remember.

Let's talk soon!

Dave Jenkins

Dave Jenkins
CEO, Clowning Around

Enclosure: Brochure

> "A family is a unit composed not only of children but of men, women, an occasional animal, and the common cold."
>
> —Ogden Nash

Hill Street Studios/Thinkstock

34

Conjunction and Preposition

A family is a network of relationships. Some people have an equivalent relationship, like wives and husbands or brothers and sisters. Some people have unequal relationships, like mothers and daughters or fathers and sons. And the very young or very old are often considered dependent on those in their middle age.

Ideas also have relationships, and conjunctions and prepositions show those relationships. When two ideas are equally important, a coordinating conjunction connects them. When two ideas are not equally important, a subordinating conjunction makes one idea dependent on the other. And prepositions create special relationships between nouns and other words.

Conjunctions and prepositions help you connect ideas and build whole families of thought.

Learning Outcomes

LO1 Use coordinating and correlative conjunctions.

LO2 Use subordinating conjunctions.

LO3 Understand common prepositions.

LO4 Use *by*, *at*, *on*, and *in*.

LO5 Use conjunctions and prepositions in real-world documents.

What do you think?

What equal relationships do you have? What dependent relationships do you have?

_____

_____

_____

LO1 Coordinating and Correlative Conjunctions

A conjunction is a word or word group that joins parts of a sentence—words, phrases, or clauses.

Coordinating Conjunctions

A coordinating conjunction joins grammatically equal elements—a word to a word, a phrase to a phrase, or a clause to a clause. (A clause is a group of words that contains a subject–verb combination. An independent clause is basically a sentence.)

Coordinating Conjunctions						
and	but	or	nor	for	so	yet

Equal importance: A coordinating conjunction shows that the two elements joined are of equal importance.

Sherise and Lydia enjoy arts and crafts.
(*And* joins words in an equal way.)

They have knitted sweaters and pieced quilts.
(*And* joins the equally important phrases *knitted sweaters* and *pieced quilts*.)

I tried to knit a sweater, but the thing unravelled.
(*But* joins the two equally important clauses, with a comma after the first.)

Items in a series: A coordinating conjunction can also join more than two equal elements in a series.

Sherise, Lydia, and I will take a class on making mosaics.
(*And* joins *Sherise, Lydia,* and *I.* A comma follows each word except the last.)

We will take the class, design a mosaic, and complete it together.
(*And* joins three parts of a compound predicate; each part is a verb plus any associated objects and modifiers.)

Correlative Conjunctions

Correlative conjunctions consist of a coordinating conjunction paired with another word. They also join equal grammatical elements: word to word, phrase to phrase, or clause to clause.

Correlative Conjunctions				
either/or	neither/nor	whether/or	both/and	not only/but also

Stressing equality: Correlative conjunctions stress the equality of parts.

Not only Sherise but also Lydia has made beautiful quilts.
(*Not only/but also* stresses the equality of *Sherise* and *Lydia*.)

Either I will learn quilting, or I will die trying.
(*Either/or* joins the two clauses, with a comma after the first.)

Stockbyte/Thinkstock

Vocabulary

conjunction
word or word group that joins parts of a sentence

coordinating conjunction
conjunction that joins grammatically equal elements

correlative conjunction
pair of conjunctions that stress the equality of the elements that are joined

Using Coordinating and Correlative Conjunctions

Choose In each sentence below, circle the best coordinating conjunction in parentheses.

1. I would like to learn knitting (but, for, or) crocheting.

2. Lydia, Sherise, (and, nor, yet) I enjoy making handmade crafts.

3. We have different talents, (or, so, yet) we teach each other what we know.

4. Lydia is best at knitting, (nor, but, for) I am best at tatting.

5. Sherise is our weaver, (but, yet, so) she is the loom master.

6. Each week, Lydia, Sherise, (and, but, or) I meet to share our works.

7. We want to broaden our skills, (and, or, yet) it's hard to learn something new.

8. I like needlepoint, Sherise likes quilting, (and, nor, so) Lydia likes knitting.

9. Come join us one day, (and, for, so) we love to teach beginners.

10. We'll show you our work, (but, nor, for) you'll decide what you want to learn.

Write Create sentences of your own, using a coordinating conjunction *(and, but, or, nor, for, so, yet)* as requested in each.

1. joining two words: _____
   _____

2. joining two phrases: _____
   _____

3. creating a series: _____
   _____

4. joining two clauses (place a comma after the first clause, before the conjunction): _____
   _____
   _____
   _____

Write Create a sentence using a pair of correlative conjunctions:

_____
_____
_____

When two ideas correlate, they work together. They co-relate. Thinking in this way can help you remember the term *correlative conjunction*.

Traits

Using conjunctions correctly helps to create fluent sentences that clearly express the connections between your ideas.

LO2 Subordinating Conjunctions

A **subordinating conjunction** is a word or word group that connects two clauses of different importance.

Subordinating Conjunctions

after	as long as	if	so that	till	whenever
although	because	in order that	than	unless	where
as	before	provided that	that	until	whereas
as if	even though	since	though	when	while

Subordinate clause: The subordinating conjunction comes at the beginning of the less-important clause, making it subordinate (it can't stand on its own). The subordinate clause can come before or after the more important clause (the independent clause).

It is too hot to cook inside during the summer. I often barbecue.
(two clauses)

Because it is too hot to cook inside during the summer, I often barbecue.
(*Because* introduces the subordinate clause, which is followed by a comma.)

I often barbecue because it is too hot to cook inside during the summer.
(If the subordinate clause comes second, a comma usually isn't needed.)

Special relationship: A subordinating conjunction shows a special relationship between ideas. Here are the relationships that subordinating conjunctions show:

Time	after, as, before, since, till, until, when, whenever, while
Cause	as, as long as, because, before, if, in order that, provided that, since, so that, that, till, until, when, whenever
Contrast	although, as if, even though, though, unless, whereas

Whenever the temperature climbs, I cook on the grill.
(time)

I barbecue because I don't want to heat up the house.
(cause)

Even though it is hot outside, I feel cool in the shade as I cook.
(contrast)

Using Subordinating Conjunctions

Write Fill in the blank in each sentence with an appropriate subordinating conjunction. Then circle what type of relationship it shows.

1. _____ I marinated the chicken, I put it on the grill.
    (time, cause, contrast)

2. Grilling bratwurst is tough _____ the grease causes big flames.   (time, cause, contrast)

3. _____ of trichinosis, many people say that pork
    (time, cause, contrast)
    should not be pink inside.

4. I like grilling chicken _____ my favourite food is steak.
    (time, cause, contrast)

5. I grill my steak rare_____ Health Canada recommends
    well done.   (time, cause, contrast)

6. Some people use barbecue sauce _____
    I prefer marinades.   (time, cause, contrast)

7. I use a gas grill _____ it is fast and
    convenient.   (time, cause, contrast)

8. Purists use only charcoal _____ it creates a nice
    flavour.   (time, cause, contrast)

9. _____ I was in Alberta, I had magnificent brisket.
    (time, cause, contrast)

10. _____ brisket can be tough, this was totally tender.
    (time, cause, contrast)

Write Create three of your own sentences containing subordinate clauses, one for each type of relationship.

1. time: _____

_____

_____

2. cause: _____

_____

_____

3. contrast: _____

_____

_____

LO3 Common Prepositions

A **preposition** is a word or word group that shows a relationship between a noun or pronoun and another word. Here are common prepositions:

Prepositions

aboard	back of	except for	near to	round
about	because of	excepting	notwithstanding	save
above	before	for	of	since
according to	behind	from	off	subsequent to
across	below	from among	on	through
across from	beneath	from between	on account of	throughout
after	beside	from under	on behalf of	'til
against	besides	in	onto	to
along	between	in addition to	on top of	together with
alongside	beyond	in behalf of	opposite	toward
alongside of	but	in front of	out	under
along with	by	in place of	out of	underneath
amid	by means of	in regard to	outside	until
among	concerning	inside	outside of	unto
apart from	considering	inside of	over	up
around	despite	in spite of	over to	upon
as far as	down	instead of	owing to	up to
aside from	down from	into	past	with
at	during	like	prior to	within
away from	except	near	regarding	without

Prepositional Phrases

A **prepositional phrase** starts with a preposition and includes an object of the preposition (a noun or pronoun) and any modifiers. A prepositional phrase functions as an adjective or adverb.

> The Basset hound flopped on his side on the rug.
> (*On his side* and *on the rug* modify the verb *flopped*.)
>
> He slept on the rug in the middle of the hallway.
> (*On the rug* modifies *slept*; *in the middle* modifies *rug*; and *of the hallway* modifies *middle*.)

Comstock/Thinkstock

Speaking & Listening

A prepositional phrase can help break up a string of adjectives. Instead of writing "the old, blue-awninged store," you can write "the old store with the blue awning." Read sentences aloud to find stacked-up adjectives and use prepositional phrases to create a better flow.

Vocabulary

preposition
word or word group that creates a relationship between a noun or pronoun and another word

prepositional phrase
phrase that starts with a preposition and includes an object of the preposition (noun or pronoun) and any modifiers; it functions as an adjective or adverb

Using Common Prepositions

Create In each sentence, fill in the blanks with prepositional phrases. Create them from the prepositions listed in the chart and nouns or pronouns of your own choosing. Be creative!

1. Yesterday, I ran _____ .

2. Another runner _____ waved at me.

3. I was so distracted, I ran _____ .

4. The other runner then ran _____ .

5. We both had looks of surprise _____ .

6. I leaped _____ .

7. The other runner jogged _____ .

8. Then we both were _____ .

9. The incident _____ was a lesson.

10. The lesson was not to run _____ .

Model Read each sentence below and write another sentence modelled on it. Note how the writer uses prepositional phrases to create specific effects.

1. The SUV shot between the semis, around the limousine, down the tunnel, and up into bright sunlight.

   _____

   _____

2. I will look for you, but I also look to you.

   _____

   _____

3. Before the freedom of the road and the fun of the trip, I have finals.

   _____

   _____

4. Walk through the hallway, down the stairs, through the door, and into the pantry.

   _____

   _____

LO4 *By, At, On,* and *In*

Prepositions often show the physical position of things—above, below, beside, around, and so on. Four specific prepositions that can show position also get a lot of other use in English.

Uses for *By, At, On,* and *In*

in a boat
on the Seine
by the roadway
in Paris
at dusk
on May 30

Rogdy Espinoza Photography/Getty Images

By means "beside" or "up to a certain place or time."

> by the creek, by the garage
>
> by noon, by August 16

At refers to a specific place or time.

> at the edge, at the coffee shop
>
> at 6:45 p.m., at midnight

On refers to a surface, a day or date, or an electronic medium.

> on the table, on the T-shirt
>
> on July 22, on Wednesday
>
> on the computer, on the DVD

In refers to an enclosed space; a geographical location; an amount of time, a month, or a year; or a print medium.

> in the hall, in the bathroom
>
> in Winnipeg, in France
>
> in a minute, in December, in 2017
>
> in the magazine, in the book

> **Say It**
>
> Team up with a partner. Have the first person read one of the words below, and have the second person use it in a prepositional phrase beginning with *by, at, on,* or *in*. The first person should check if the form is correct. (Some have more than one correct answer.) Then you should switch roles.
>
> 1. the den
> 2. June 23
> 3. 9:33 p.m.
> 4. the MP3 player
> 5. the corner
> 6. Toronto
> 7. the counter
> 8. the diner
> 9. sunset
> 10. the newspaper

Using *By*, *At*, *On*, and *In*

Provide In each sentence, circle the correct preposition in parentheses.

1. The guests arrived (by, on, in) 7:30 p.m., so we could eat (at, on, in) 8:00 p.m.

2. Put your suitcase (by, at, on, in) the trunk or (by, at, on) the rooftop luggage rack.

3. I looked for the new album (by, at, on, in) a music store, but could find it only (by, at, on, in) the Internet.

4. We waited (by, at, on, in) the lobby for a half hour, but Jerry didn't show up or even call (by, at, on, in) his cellphone.

5. Three people standing (by, at, in) the corner saw a traffic accident (by, at, on) the intersection of Queen and Monroe.

6. (By, At, On, In) April 1, many pranksters may post apocalypse hoaxes (by, at, on, in) the Internet.

7. Let's meet (by, at, on) the convenience store (at, on, in) 7:00 p.m.

8. Place your order form (by, at, on, in) the postage-paid envelope, write your return address (by, at, on, in) the envelope, and post it.

9. A cat lay (by, at, on) the windowsill and looked me (by, at, on, in) the eye.

10. (At, On, In) noon on January 7, the school's pipes (at, on, in) the basement froze and caused flooding.

Write Write a sentence that uses all four of these prepositions in phrases: *by, at, on, in.*

Chapter 34 Conjunction and Preposition

L○7 Real-World Application

Revise Read the following e-mail, noting how choppy it sounds because all of the sentences are short. Connect some of the sentences using a coordinating conjunction and a comma, and connect others using a subordinating conjunction. You can also change other words as needed. (Use the correction symbols to the left.) Reread the e-mail to make sure it sounds smooth.

Coordinating Conjunctions			
and	but	or	nor
for	so	yet	

Subordinating Conjunctions					
after	as long as	if	so that	till	whenever
although	because	in order that	than	unless	where
as	before	provided that	that	until	whereas
as if	even though	since	though	when	while

Send   Attach   Format

Correction Marks

ꝰ	delete
d̲	capitalize
ꝺ	lowercase
∧	insert
⌄	add comma
?	add question mark
word ∧	add word
⊙	add period
◯	spelling
∿	switch

From: rhaverson@haversonpublishing.com

To: dkraitsman@delafordandco.com

Subject: Completed Photo Log

Dear Deirdra:

Attached, please find the photo log. The log shows all photos on the website. Some photos are from Getty Images. Others are from Shutterstock. A few are from Corbis. All photos have been downloaded. The downloads have the right resolution.

I hope you are pleased with the log. It includes permissions details. It also shows the resolution. I included a description of each photo.

I am available for more work. I could compile another photo log. I could also do the permissions work on these photos. I do writing and editing as well.

Thank you for this project. I look forward to hearing from you.

Thanks,

Roger Haverson
Photo Editor

Correct Read the following party invitation, noting the incorrect use of the prepositions *by, at, on,* and *in*. Correct the errors by deleting the prepositions and replacing them. Use the correction marks on the facing page.

Workplace

Correct use of *by, at, on,* and *in* will mark you as a writer comfortable with English.

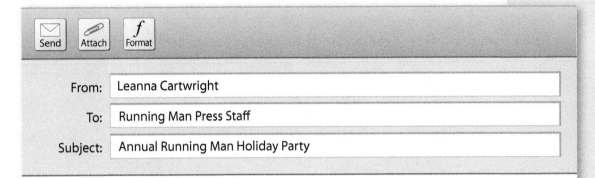

From: Leanna Cartwright

To: Running Man Press Staff

Subject: Annual Running Man Holiday Party

Dear Staff:

It's time for the Running Man Press Holiday Party!

Who? All employees and their significant others

What? Should come for dinner

Where? By the Hilton in Grand Avenue on Ballroom B

When? At December 12, beginning on 7:00 p.m. and going until 11:00 p.m.

Why? We're celebrating a great year on Running Man Press

The event is full of fun, including drinks in 7:00 p.m., dinner on 8:00 p.m., awards in 9:00 p.m., and dancing on 9:30 p.m. Prime rib, roast chicken, and vegetarian selections are at the menu, and beverages of all sorts will be available in the bar.

Please RSVP at December 2 to let us know how many people will join us on the Hilton. We look forward to having a great night with everyone at December 12.

Sincerely,

Leanna Cartwright
Human Resources

"The writer who neglects punctuation, or mispunctuates, is liable to be misunderstood for the want of merely a comma."

—Edgar Allan Poe

35 Comma

When you speak, you communicate with much more than words. You pause, raise or lower your pitch, change your tone or volume, and use facial expressions and body language to get your point across.

When you write, you can forget about pitch or volume, facial expressions or body language. You're left with the tone of your words and with the pauses that you put in them. Commas give you one way to create a soft pause. They help to show which words belong together, which should be separated, and which line up in parallel. Commas are key to being understood.

In this chapter, you will learn about the conventional use of commas. Understanding the correct comma usage is an important step in improving your writing.

Test Your Knowledge

Indicate where commas are needed in the following sentences. As you read through this chapter, check your answers to see if you have used each punctuation mark correctly.

1. Internship coordinators found at most colleges and universities help students apply for and gain valuable internship experience.

2. Shakira a Colombian recording artist has enjoyed crossover success in the Latin pop and American pop markets.

3. Even before turning around to check Vince sensed someone was following him.

4. At risk of sounding outlandish the smell of chocolate-covered bacon is making my mouth water.

5. In *Slumdog Millionaire* which won ten Academy Awards a young man from the slums wins the Indian version of *Who Wants to Be a Millionaire?*

6. Before making any harsh judgments you should know I considered all options prior to deciding.

7. Based on her preliminary research Hanna felt she was ready to begin drafting an essay.

8. The road construction barrels which were orange with white stripes littered the side of the highway.

9. Despite her craving for ice cream Candace opted for an apple.

10. Marc Jacobs a famous American designer is the creative director for the Louis Vuitton fashion line.

Learning Outcomes

LO1 Use commas in compound and complex sentences.

LO2 Use commas with introductory phrases.

LO3 Use commas with equal modifiers.

LO4 Use commas between items in a series.

LO5 Use commas with appositives and non-restrictive modifiers.

LO6 Use commas correctly in other ways.

LO7 Use commas in real-world writing.

Traits

Make sure to use both a comma and a coordinating conjunction in a compound sentence, or you will create a comma splice or a run-on. For more information, see Chapter 28.

LO1 In Compound and Complex Sentences

The following principles will guide the conventional use of commas in your writing.

In Compound Sentences

Use a comma before the coordinating conjunction *(and, but, or, nor, for, yet, so)* in a compound sentence. (See Chapter 24, LO4, Compound Sentences, to review.)

Heath Ledger completed his brilliant portrayal as the Joker in *The Dark Knight,* **but** he died before the film was released.

Many people believe that Ledger's Joker is the best movie villain ever portrayed, **and** I agree with them.

Note: Do not confuse a compound predicate (see Chapter 24 for review) with a compound sentence.

Ledger's Joker became instantly iconic and won him the Oscar for best supporting actor. (compound predicate: two verbs governed by a single subject, forming one independent clause)

His death resulted from the abuse of prescription drugs, but it was ruled an accident. (compound sentence: two independent clauses, each with a subject and verb)

In Complex Sentences

In a complex sentence, use a comma after a dependent clause at the beginning of a sentence. (See Chapter 24, LO5, Complex Sentences, to review.)

Although Charlemagne was a great patron of learning, he never learned to write properly. (dependent adverb clause)

When the dependent clause follows the independent clause and is not essential to the meaning of the sentence, use a comma. This comma use generally applies to clauses beginning with *even though, although, while,* or some other conjunction expressing a contrast.

Charlemagne never learned to write properly, **even though he continued to practise**.

Do *not* use a comma if the dependent clause following the independent clause is essential to the meaning of the sentence.

Charlemagne nevertheless must have had intelligence since he united most of Western Europe.

Correcting Comma Errors

Correct For each sentence below, add a comma (⋀) before the coordinating conjunction *(and, but, or, nor, for, so, yet)* if the clause on each side could stand alone as a sentence. Write "correct" if the conjunction separates word groups that can't stand alone.

1. Catherine had questions about her class schedule so she set up an
   appointment with her academic adviser.   _____

2. I was going to play in the beach volleyball league but it conflicted with
   my work schedule.   _____

3. Trisha picked up some groceries and stopped by the bank.   _____

4. I normally don't listen to jazz music yet I love going to summer jazz
   concerts in the park.   _____

5. Should I finish my essay a day early or should I go to my friend's house
   party?   _____

6. Kevin has a job interview at the advertisement agency and he hopes he
   can make a good impression.   _____

7. Creativity is his best quality but leadership is not far behind.   _____

Correct For each sentence below, add a comma after any introductory clauses. If no comma is needed, write "correct" next to the sentence.

1. Even though e-books are the craze I prefer paperbacks.   _____

2. Although the crab dip appetizer was delicious my entrée left something
   to be desired.   _____

3. Because I'm starved for time online shopping is a convenient alternative
   to mall shopping.   _____

4. I toggled through radio stations while I waited at the tollbooth.   _____

5. Erin worried about giving her speech even though she had practised for
   weeks.   _____

L○2 With Introductory Phrases and Clauses

Use a comma after introductory phrases.

In spite of his friend's prodding, Jared decided to stay home and study.

Use a comma after an introductory phrase is not at the beginning of the sentence.

You may omit a comma after a short (four or fewer words) introductory phrase—unless it is needed to ensure clarity.

At 10:30 p.m. he would quit and go to sleep.

Use a comma after an introductory clause.

Although **Jared's friends tried to convince him to go to the movies,** Jared decided to stay home and study.

L○3 With Equal Modifiers

To Separate Adjectives

Use commas to separate adjectives that equally modify the same noun. Remember that no comma separates the last adjective from the noun.

You should exercise regularly and follow a **sensible, healthy** diet.
A good diet includes lots of **high-protein, low-fat** foods.

To Determine Equal Modifiers

Speaking & Listening

Try the strategies below by speaking the words aloud. If it sounds strange to switch the order of the adjectives or to insert an *and* between them, do not separate them with a comma.

To determine whether adjectives modify a noun equally, use these two tests.

1. Reverse the order of the adjectives; if the sentence is still clear, the adjectives modify equally. (In the example below, *hot* and *crowded* can be switched, but *short* and *coffee* cannot.)

   Matt was tired of working in the **hot, crowded** lab and decided to take a **short coffee** break.

2. Insert *and* between the adjectives; if the sentence still reads well, use a comma when *and* is omitted. (The word *and* can be inserted between *hot* and *crowded*, but *and* does not make sense between *short* and *coffee*.)

Brian Kinney/Shutterstock.com

Correcting Comma Errors

Correct For each sentence below, insert a comma after the introductory phrases and clauses if a comma is needed. If no comma is needed, write "correct" next to the sentence.

1. Before you send the e-mail make sure you reread it for errors in clarity. _____

2. In accordance with the academic code plagiarism is deemed a major offence. _____

3. After she hit the 10-kilometre jogging plateau Heather felt a great rush of adrenaline. _____

4. Heather felt a great rush of adrenaline after hitting the 10-kilometre jogging plateau. _____

5. Thankfully DeMarcus stopped the leak before it could do any real damage. _____

6. After Wilson checked his bank balance he decided against going to the concert. _____

7. To train for the triathlon Ajay altered his diet. _____

8. At the end of the day Erin recorded her favourite show. _____

Correct For each sentence below, determine whether or not a comma is needed to separate the adjectives that modify the same noun. Add any needed commas (∧). Write "no" next to the sentence if a comma is not needed.

1. I'm expecting this to be a **rocking after** party. _____

2. There's nothing like the **warm emerald** water in the Caribbean Sea. _____

3. The exercise program included a **calorie-burning cardio** session. _____

4. My **surly economics** professor is one of a kind. _____

5. I'm in desperate need of a **relaxing summer** vacation. _____

6. Marathon runners favor **light comfortable** shorts. _____

LO4 Between Items in a Series

Use commas to separate individual words, phrases, or clauses in a series. (A series contains at least three items.)

> Tobias always attended his **philosophy, political science,** and **English** classes.
>
> After Helene packed **her books, her clothes,** and **her chihuahua,** she was ready to go.
>
> Many college students must balance studying with **taking care of a family, working, getting exercise,** and **finding time to relax.**

Do not use commas when all the items in a series are connected with *or, nor,* or *and.*

> Hmm . . . should I study **or** do laundry **or** go out?

3dfoto/Shutterstock.com

LO5 With Appositives and Non-Restrictive Modifiers

Learning Outcome

Use commas with appositives and non-restrictive modifiers.

To Set Off Some Appositives

A specific kind of explanatory word or phrase called an appositive identifies or renames a preceding noun or pronoun. Appositives are surrounded by commas if they add information that is non-restrictive (not necessary to identify the noun).

> Albert Einstein, **the famous mathematician and physicist,** developed the theory of relativity.

Do not use commas if the appositive is important to the basic meaning of the sentence.

> The famous physicist **Albert Einstein** developed the theory of relativity.

With Non-Restrictive Clauses and Phrases

Traits

Do not use commas to set off restrictive clauses and phrases: those that add information that a reader needs to understand the sentence.

Example: Only the professors **who run at noon** use the locker rooms in Swain Hall to shower. (restrictive clause)

Use commas to enclose phrases or clauses that are non-restrictive: phrases or clauses that add information that is not necessary to the basic meaning of the sentence. For example, if the clause or phrase (in **boldface**) were left out of the two examples below, the meaning of the sentences would remain clear. Therefore, commas are used to set off the information.

> The locker rooms in Swain Hall, **which were painted and updated last summer,** give professors a place to shower. (non-restrictive clause)
>
> Work-study programs, **offered on many campuses,** give students the opportunity to earn tuition money. (non-restrictive phrase)

Using *That* or *Which*

Vocabulary

appositive
a noun or noun phrase that identifies or renames another noun right beside it

non-restrictive
adding information that is not essential to the meaning of the sentence

Use *that* to introduce restrictive clauses; use *which* to introduce non-restrictive clauses. (See also Chapter 31, LO5, Relative Pronouns.)

> Campus jobs **that are funded by the university** are awarded to students only. (necessary)
>
> The cafeteria, **which is run by an independent contractor,** can hire nonstudents. (unnecessary)

Correcting Comma Errors

Correct Indicate where commas are needed in the following sentences. If no commas are needed, write "correct" next to the sentence.

1. The Artificial Reef Society of B.C. plans to sink HMCS *Annapolis* a _____ decommissioned warship to create a new scuba diving site off the coast of British Columbia.

2. Gordon Ramsay the fiery chef and television star specializes in French _____ Italian and British cuisines.

3. Hall of Fame baseball player and notable philanthropist Roberto _____ Clemente died in a plane crash while en route to Nicaragua to deliver aid to earthquake victims.

4. The concert hall which is on the corner of Meridian Avenue and _____ 1st Street is expected to revitalize the downtown district.

5. Press passes that allow for backstage access are given out to special _____ media members.

6. Michel Pleau who later became the Canadian Parliamentary Poet _____ Laureate won the Governor General's Award for poetry in 2008.

Write The following sentences contain clauses using *that*. Rewrite the sentences with clauses using *which*, and insert commas correctly. You may need to reword some parts.

1. The mechanical issue that delayed the flight should be corrected within 25 minutes.

_____

_____

2. The wind farm that was built along Highway 1 is scheduled to double in size by 2016.

_____

_____

3. Scholarships that are sponsored by the Kiwanis Club are awarded to local high school students.

_____

_____

LO6 Other Uses of the Comma

Learning Outcome

Use commas correctly in other ways.

To Set Off Transitional Expressions

Use a comma to set off conjunctive adverbs and transitional phrases.

> Handwriting is not, **as a matter of fact**, easy to improve upon later in life; **however**, it can be done if you are determined enough.

If a transitional expression blends smoothly with the rest of the sentence, it does not need to be set off.

> If you are **in fact** coming, I'll see you there.

To Set Off Dialogue

Use commas to set off the words of the speaker from the rest of the sentence.

> **"Never be afraid to ask for help,"** advised Ms. Kane.
>
> **"With the evidence that we now have,"** Professor Thom said, **"many scientists believe there could be life on Mars."**

Do not use a comma before an indirect quotation.

> **Incorrect:** My roommate said, that she didn't understand the notes I took.
>
> **Correct:** My roommate said that she didn't understand the notes I took.

To Enclose Explanatory Words

Use commas to enclose an explanatory word or phrase.

> Time management, **according to many professionals**, is an important skill that should be taught in college.

Correcting Comma Errors

Correct Indicate where commas are needed in the following sentences.

1. I considered becoming a lawyer; however law school wasn't for me.

2. "Never, never, never give up" advised the Winston Churchill.

3. MGMT's music is infused with electronic beats catchy lyrics and a pop-friendly sound.

4. British Columbia as opposed to Alberta is relatively mountainous.

5. In London I visited Tower Bridge Buckingham Palace and Westminster Abbey.

6. Chen as you may have noticed is eager to share his vast knowledge of random facts.

7. In regard to public transportation, you may decide between the subway buses or taxis.

8. "While it certainly offers a convenient alternative to paper maps" said Emilie "my car's navigational system more often gets me lost."

9. Avocados the key ingredient of guacamole are a good source of fibre.

10. Secondly determine if weather price or transportation will factor into your decision.

Correct Indicate where commas are needed in the following paragraph.

On an early summer morning in July I sat slumped in a terminal at Vancouver International Airport reminiscing about my time in Vancouver British Columbia. It had been a fun trip. I visited all the usual landmarks including the Vancouver Art Gallery Granville Island Kitsilano Beach and the Dr. Sun Yat-Sen Chinese Garden. However my favourite landmark was the Seawall a 8.8 km trail that loops around Stanley Park. With West Coast rainforests on one side and the Pacific Ocean on the other it's easy to see why both tourists and locals adore this route for walking running and biking. Besides the Seawall Stanley Park also includes an aquarium First Nations art and totem poles forest trails and gardens. If you're ever in Vancouver I highly recommend a trip to the Seawall and Stanley Park.

LO7 Real-World Application

Correct Indicate where commas are needed in the following e-mail message.

Hi, Michael:

I've attached the agenda for the quarterly update with the marketing team. Daniel Gilchrest senior marketing coordinator will moderate the meeting but I want you to familiarize yourself with the material. Here are some highlights of the new agenda:

1. The advertising allowance for Gillette Hillsboro Farms and Justice Inc. has increased by 5 percent.
2. The penetrated market which accounts for actual users of products declined in the health-care sector.
3. We will shift the focus of marketing efforts to meet the digital and social media demands of today's market.

Please review the agenda by the end of the day and let me know if you have any additions or corrections.

Thanks

Tru Sha

Marketing Associate

Correction Marks

ℐ	delete
d̲	capitalize
Ð	lowercase
∧	insert
⌃	add comma
? ∧	add question mark
word ∧	add word
⊙	add period
◯	spelling
∿	switch

billdayone/Shutterstock

The study habit that sets you apart.

www.nelson.com/student

> "There is virtue in work and there is virtue in rest. Use both and overlook neither."
>
> —Alan Cohen

Patrizia Tilly/Shutterstock.com

36

Semicolon, Colon, Hyphen, Dash

Work is important, of course. Progress. Motion. Getting somewhere. And yet, sometimes it's important to pause and take a breath. Breaks allow you to work even more effectively afterward.

Written materials need pauses and breaks, too. It doesn't have to be a full stop (a period); maybe something softer will do. Semicolons, colons, hyphens, and dashes can give the reader just the right break to be refreshed, directed, and prepared to set out again. This chapter covers these punctuation marks.

Test Your Knowledge

Write a short paragraph about a favourite vacation spot. Make sure to use one of each of the following punctuation marks: a semicolon, a colon, a hyphen, and a dash. After you work through this chapter, check your paragraph to see if you have used each punctuation mark correctly.

Learning Outcomes

LO1 Use semicolons and colons correctly.

LO2 Understand hyphen use.

LO3 Use dashes well.

LO4 Apply punctuation in real-world documents.

LO1 Semicolons and Colons

Semicolons and colons have specific uses in writing.

Semicolon

Between Two Closely-Related Sentences

A semicolon can be called a soft period. Use the semicolon to join two sentences that are closely related.

> The mosquitoes have returned; it must be July in Quebec.

Before a Conjunctive Adverb

Often, the second sentence will begin with a conjunctive adverb *(also, besides, however, instead, meanwhile, therefore)*, which signals the relationship between the sentences. Place a semicolon before the conjunctive adverb, and place a comma after it.

> The outdoor mosquito treatment was rated for six weeks; however, it lasted only four.

With Series

Use a semicolon to separate items in a series if any of the items already include commas.

> Before the party, I'll cut the grass and treat the lawn; buy a bug zapper, citronella candles, and bug spray; and get ready to swat and scratch.

Colon

To Introduce an Example or List

The main use of a colon is to introduce an example or a list. Write a complete sentence as an introduction, place the colon, and then provide the example or list.

> Here's one other mosquito treatment: napalm.
>
> I have one motto: No bug is going to use my blood to reproduce!

Note: If a complete sentence follows the colon, it should be capitalized.

After Salutations

In business documents, use a colon after salutations and in memo headings.

> Dear Ms. Alvarez: To: Tawnya Smith

Times and Ratios

Use a colon to separate hours, minutes, and seconds. Also use a colon between the numbers in a ratio.

> 8:23 a.m.   4:15 p.m.   14:32:46   The mosquito–person ratio is 5:1.

Other Classes

In addition to the colon uses listed on this page, a colon is often used in academic writing to separate the main title of a paper from its subtitle.

Mosquitos: The World's Deadliest Creatures

Vocabulary

semicolon
a punctuation mark (;) that connects sentences and separates items in some series

conjunctive adverb
an adverb that joins one independent clause to another, signalling the relationship between them

colon
a punctuation mark (:) that introduces an example or list and has other special uses

salutation
the formal greeting in a letter, usually starting with "Dear"

Using Semicolons and Colons

Correct Add semicolons (⌄) and commas (⌄) as needed in the sentences below.

1. Mosquitoes here are a nuisance however in some places they are deadly.

2. Malaria kills many in Africa and South America it is carried by mosquitoes.

3. Each year, mosquito-borne illnesses affect 700 million victims many of them die.

4. Mosquitoes breed in stagnant water they need only a small amount.

5. Ponds would produce more mosquitoes however, many fish eat mosquito eggs and larvae.

6. A female mosquito inserts her proboscis, injects an anti-clotting agent, and draws blood into her abdomen then she uses the blood proteins to create her eggs.

7. A mosquito bites you and gets away afterward she uses your blood to create more little horrors.

8. Bats rely on mosquitoes for much of their food frogs and birds eat them as well.

9. A friend of mine says a bug zapper does not get rid of mosquitoes it only reduces the "mosquito pressure."

10. The oldest known mosquito was trapped in amber in the Cretaceous period 73 million years ago perhaps it inspired the dinosaur mosquito in *Jurassic Park*.

Correct Add colons (⌄) where needed in the sentences below.

1. Mosquitoes in Egypt can carry a deadly disease yellow fever.

2. Here's the real shame the mosquitoes don't catch the disease.

3. Thankfully, mosquitoes don't pass along one terrible disease Ebola.

4. A mosquito can, however, pass along another nasty payload parasites.

5. Millions die per year because of one critter the mosquito.

6. A world without mosquitoes would be utterly different for one species *Homo sapiens*.

LO2 Hyphens

A hyphen joins words to each other—or to letters or numbers—to form compounds.

Compound Nouns

Use hyphens to create compound nouns.

city-state	fail-safe	fact-check	T-shirt	mother-in-law

Compound Adjectives

Use hyphens to create compound adjectives that appear before the noun. If the adjective appears after, it usually is not hyphenated.

peer-reviewed article	an article that was peer reviewed
ready-made solution	a solution that is ready made
a 200-pound bag	a bag that weighs 200 pounds

Note: Don't hyphenate a compound made from an *-ly* adverb and an adjective, or a compound that ends with a single letter.

newly acquired songs	grade B plywood

Compound Numbers

Use hyphens for compound numbers from twenty-one to ninety-nine. Also use hyphens for numbers in fractions and other number compounds.

twenty-two	fifty-fifty	three-quarters	seven thirty-seconds

With Letters

Use a hyphen to join a letter to a word that follows it.

L-bracket	U-shaped	O-ring	G-rated	X-ray

With Common Elements

Use hyphens to show that two or more words share a common element included in only the final term.

We offer low-, middle-, and high-coverage plans.

hyphen
a short, horizontal line (-) used to form compound words

compound noun
a noun made of two or more words; compounds nouns are often hyphenated

compound adjective
an adjective made of two or more words; usually it is hyphenated before the noun but not afterward

compound numbers
two-word numbers from twenty-one to ninety-nine

Using Hyphens

Correct Add hyphens ($\wedge$) to the following sentences as needed.

1. The United Nations secretary general ruled the vote fifty fifty.

2. I replaced the U bend and made a new P trap under the sink.

3. He guessed the board was three eighths inch thick.

4. Would you like to purchase low , medium , or high deductible insurance?

5. The double decker sandwich includes low fat ham and fat free mayonnaise.

6. The ham is low fat, and the mayonnaise is fat free.

7. In your graph, make sure to label the x and y axes.

8. The sales tax percentage is at an all time high.

9. My father in law is an attorney at law.

10. The T shirt showed the X ray of a ribcage.

Divide Follow the guidelines for word division to decide on the best way to divide each word at the end of a line. Use hyphens to show the possible breaks. If a word should not be broken, write NB for "no break."

1. opinion _____

2. repossess _____

3. paperboy _____

4. omit _____

5. mother-in-law _____

6. apple _____

7. couldn't _____

8. hopelessly _____

9. maple _____

10. 6 324 000 _____

LO3 Dashes

Unlike the hyphen, the **dash** does more to separate words than to join them together. There is no key for a dash on a computer keyboard, but most word-processing programs convert two hyphens into a dash.

Tip

If your word processor doesn't turn a double hyphen into a dash automatically, you may be able to insert a dash as a symbol or special character. Or simply use two hyphens with no space before or after; most readers (and instructors) will understand that a dash is meant.

Other Classes

In most academic writing, use dashes sparingly. If they are overused, they lose their emphasis.

Vocabulary

dash
a long horizontal line that separates words, creating emphasis

For Emphasis

Use a dash instead of a colon if you want to emphasize a word, phrase, clause, or series.

> Doughnuts—they're not just for police officers anymore.
>
> There's only one thing better than a doughnut—two doughnuts.
>
> I like all kinds of doughnuts—fritters, crullers, and cake doughnuts.

To Set Off a Series

Use a dash to set off a series of items.

> Elephant ears, Danish pastries, funnel cakes—they just aren't as cool as doughnuts.
>
> They have many similarities—batter, frosting, and sugar—but where's the hole?

With Non-Essential Elements

Use a dash to set off explanations, examples, and definitions, especially when these elements already include commas.

> The hole—which is where the "dough nut" got its name, originally—is a key component.

To Show Interrupted Speech

Use a dash to show that a speaker has been interrupted or has started and stopped while speaking.

> "I'd like a—um—how about a fritter?"
>
> "You want an apple—"
>
> "Yes, an apple fritter, well—make it two."

Using Dashes

In the sentences below, add a dash ($\overline{\wedge}$) where needed.

1. Which would you prefer a cruller, a glazed doughnut, or a Boston cream?

2. I love a nice blintz basically like a crepe but from Eastern Europe.

3. Doughnuts or do you prefer the spelling "donuts" are yummy.

4. "Could I have a dozen of Do you have a sale on doughnuts or on "Today our sale is on wait, let me check yes, on doughnuts. Get a dozen for $3.00."

5. Batter, hot fat, frosting, sprinkles that's how you make a doughnut.

6. Making your own doughnuts is fun fattening, too!

7. A deep fat fryer basically a deep pot filled with oil is needed to make doughnuts.

8. Let the doughnut cool before taking a bite extremely hot!

9. Then decorate your doughnut with frosting, cinnamon, jelly whatever you want.

10. Don't eat too many doughnuts you'll end up with one around the middle.

Correct Write your own sentence, correctly using dashes for each of the situations indicated below:

1. For emphasis: _____

_____

_____

2. To set off a series: _____

_____

_____

3. With non-essential elements: _____

_____

_____

_____

LO4 Real-World Application

Correct In the following e-mail message, insert semicolons (), colons (), hyphens (), and dashes ( ) where necessary. (Clearly distinguish short hyphens from long dashes.)

Correction Marks

𝓎 delete

d̲ capitalize

𝒟 lowercase

∧ insert

∜ add comma

? add question
∧ mark

word
∧ add word

⊙ add period

spelling

switch

Send **Attach** ***f* Format**

From:	Marissa Rogers
To:	All Staff
Subject:	Parking During Parking-Lot Resurfacing

Hello, everyone:

Fall is here, and we know what that means parking lot resurfacing. The east, west, and south lots will be resurfaced on separate days please follow this schedule

- Monday, September 20 Do not park in the east lot.
- Tuesday, September 21 Do not park in the west lot.
- Wednesday, September 22 Do not park in the south lot.

Spaces in the available lots may be tight please be considerate and take only one space. You can also park on the grass along the edges of the lot. Still, space will be tight. I have one suggestion car pool.

Thanks for your cooperation. Let's work together to achieve our goal resurfacing blacktop without ruining shoes.

Thanks,

Marissa Rogers

Krom1975/Shutterstock.com

NEL

"I get the Reese's candy bar. If you read it, there's an apostrophe. The candy bar is his.
Next time you're eating a Reese's and some guy named Reese comes up to you and says,
'Let me have that,' you better give it to him."

—Mitch Hedberg

Suzanne Tucker/Shutterstock.com

37

Apostrophe

The position of an apostrophe makes a world of a difference to the meaning of a sentence. Take a close look at the following two examples:

■ My brother's girlfriend is having a beach party.
■ My brothers' girlfriend is having a beach party.

The meaning of the first sentence is clear: The girlfriend of the writer's brother is having a beach party. In the second sentence, the writer of the second example has more than one brother dating the same girl, who is throwing a beach party. Not a good scenario!

Apostrophes have two main uses: to form possessives and to create contractions. The rules and activities in this chapter will help you understand their usage.

Learning Outcomes

LO1 Use apostrophes for contractions.

LO2 Apply apostrophes in real-world documents.

Test Your Knowledge

Do an Internet search for "funny apostrophe errors" and find three examples of misused apostrophes. In the space below, write the incorrect examples, make notes about their meanings, and provide corrected versions.

LO1 Contractions and Possessives

Apostrophes are used primarily to show that a letter, a group of letters, or a number has been left out, or that a noun is possessive.

Contractions

When one or more letters are left out of a word, use an apostrophe to form the contraction.

don't	he'd	would've
(*o* is left out)	(*woul* is left out)	(*ha* is left out)

Missing Characters

Use an apostrophe to signal when one or more characters are left out.

class of '16	rock 'n' roll	good mornin'
(*20* is left out)	(*a* and *d* are left out)	(*g* is left out)

Possessives

Use an apostrophe to show possession or ownership. Form possessives of singular nouns by adding an apostrophe and an *s*.

Sharla's pen	the man's coat	*The Pilgrim's Progress*

Singular Noun Ending in *s* (One Syllable)

Form the possessive by adding an apostrophe and an *s*.

the boss's idea	the lass's purse	the bass's teeth

Singular Noun Ending in *s* (Two or More Syllables)

Form the possessive by adding an apostrophe and an *s*—or by adding just an apostrophe. If the construction becomes too awkward, you can also rephrase it to avoid the apostrophe altogether.

Kansas's plains	*or*	the plains of Kansas

Plural Noun Ending in *s*

Form the possessive by adding just an apostrophe.

the bosses' preference	the Smiths' home

Binkski/Shutterstock.com

Note: The word before the apostrophe is the owner.

the girl's ball
(*girl* is the owner)

the girls' ball
(*girls* are the owners)

Plural Noun Not Ending in *s*

Form the possessive by adding an apostrophe and an *s*.

the children's toys   the women's room

Forming Contractions and Possessives

Write For each contraction below, write the words that formed the contraction. For each pair of words, write the contraction that would be formed.

1. you're _____

2. John is _____

3. would have _____

4. she'd _____

5. you would _____

6. shouldn't _____

7. I had _____

8. they are _____

9. we've _____

10. it is _____

Rewrite Rework the following sentences, replacing the "of" phrases with possessives using apostrophes.

1. I'm going to the house of Jeremy.

   _____

2. The ice cream of the corner stand is amazing.

   _____

3. The pace of the track star is impressive.

   _____

4. I like the early work of the Rolling Stones.

   _____

5. The persona of Texas is well represented in the slogan "Everything is bigger in Texas."

   _____

Rewrite Rework the following sentences, replacing the "of" phrases with possessives using apostrophes.

1. The paintings of the artist were outstanding.

_____

2. I discovered the best pizza spot of Calgary.

_____

3. She reviewed the notes of Kimbra.

_____

4. The contractor assessed the structure of the house.

_____

5. The position of the politician on health care remained firm.

_____

Correct In the following sentences, correct any errors related to apostrophe use.

1. Bobs TV has been broken for the past two weeks.

2. *Super Mario Brothers'* is my all-time favourite video game series; lets play it!

3. Its a shame that people arent as respectful of other peoples privacy as they used to be.

4. She's going to Freds house to play video games' and watch movies.

5. Todays video games are quite easy compared with games made in the nineties'.

6. Fred three his' new gamepad across the room and broke its' screen.

7. I'm better than my brother at most video games especially at first person shooters.

8. The boys work schedules prevented them from playing video games late into the evening.

9. The movie theatre was booked by Joans girlfriend for her' party.

10. Whose in charge here? Get me you're manager!

11. Dont eat the food in the office fridge. Its my bosses lunch.

12. The local high school students save all they're money for video games.

Tip

Before adding an apostrophe to indicate possession, always make sure a noun follows the word. If not, the word cannot be possessive.

Tip

Don't confuse pronoun possessives with similar-sounding contractions:

its / it's

whose / who's

their / they're

your / you're

L○2 Real-World Application

Correct The following letter sounds too informal because it contains too many contractions. Cross out contractions and replace them with full forms of the words. Also, correct any errors with apostrophes. Use the correction marks to the left.

☞ REDLAND BANK ☜

October 13, 2015

Phillip Jones
2398 10th Ave.
Vancouver, BC V9R 8S7

Dear Mr. Jones:

This letter's a response to your inquiry about financing your housing project. Its been a pleasure discussing your project and I appreciated your honesty about your current loan.

As of today, we've decided to make a commitment to your project. I've enclosed Redland Banks' commitment letter. Please take time to read the terms of agreement.

If there's any part you don't understand, don't hesitate to call or e-mail us. We'd be happy to answer any questions. As always's, we look forward to serving you.

Sincerely,

Melinda Erson

Melinda Erson
Loan Officer

Enclosure: Commitment Letter

Correction Marks

♃ delete

d̲ capitalize

𝒟 lowercase

∧ insert

⌄ add comma

? add question
∧ mark

word
∧ add word

⊙ add period

◯ spelling

∿ switch

Learning like never before.

4LTR
P·R·E·S·S

www.nelson.com/student

"Sometimes people give [book] titles to me,
and sometimes I see them on a billboard."
—Robert Penn Warren

Image Source/Getty Images

38

Quotation Marks and Italics

Broadway is plastered with billboards five storeys high and is jammed with marquees that flash in the night. They advertise plays and movies, books and magazines, albums and TV shows— all in spotlights or neon to make people take notice.

In writing, there are no spotlights, there is no neon. Instead of writing the names of plays, movies, books, and so forth in giant, flashing letters, writers set them off with appropriate punctuation. This chapter will show you how to correctly punctuate titles of works big and small and how to indicate words used as words.

What do you think?

How are quotation marks and italics like flashing lights in writing? How are they different?

_____

_____

_____

_____

_____

_____

Learning Outcomes

LO1 Apply quotation marks correctly.

LO2 Understand the use of italics.

LO3 Apply quotation marks and italics in a real-world document.

LO1 Quotation Marks

To Punctuate Dialogue

Use quotation marks to set dialogue apart from the rest of a sentence.

> "Make sure to finish your homework before class tomorrow," instructed the teacher.

To Punctuate Titles (Smaller Works)

Use quotation marks to enclose the titles of smaller works, including speeches, short stories, songs, poems, episodes of audio or video programs, chapters or sections of books, unpublished works, and articles from magazines, journals, newspapers, or encyclopedias. (For titles of longer works, see LO2, Italics.)

Speech:	"I Have a Dream"
Song:	"Royals"
Short Story:	"Boys and Girls"
Magazine Article:	"Is Google Making Us Stupid?"
Chapter in a Book:	"The Second Eve"
Television Episode:	"Felina"
Encyclopedia Article:	"Autoban"
A Page on a Website:	"Grammar Girl"

Insight

In British English, a single quotation mark is used instead of double quotation marks. Also, British English has slightly different rules for using other punctuation with quotation marks. When writing in a Canadian or U.S. setting, use the rules on this page.

For Special Words

Quotation marks can be used (1) to show that a word is being referred to as the word itself; (2) to indicate that it is jargon, slang, or a coined term; or (3) to show that it is used in an ironic or sarcastic sense.

> (1) The word "chuffed" is British slang for "very excited."
> (2) I'm "chuffed" about my new computer.
> (3) I'm "chuffed" about getting a root canal.

Placement of Periods and Commas

When quoted words end in a period or comma, always place that punctuation inside the quotation marks.

> "When you leave the kitchen," Tim said, "turn out the light."

Placement of Semicolons and Colons

When a quotation is followed by a semicolon or colon, always place that punctuation outside the quotation marks.

> I finally read "The Celebrated Jumping Frog of Calaveras County"; it is a hoot!

Placement of Exclamation Points and Question Marks

If an exclamation point or a question mark is part of the quotation, place it inside the quotation marks. Otherwise, place it outside.

> Shawndra asked me, "Would you like to go to the movies?" What could I say except, "That sounds great"?

Using Quotation Marks

Correct In the following sentences, insert quotation marks ("") where needed.

1. Tim loves the short story The Bear Came Over the Mountain by Alice Munro.

2. Stephen King's short story The Body was made into a movie.

3. Anna Quindlen wrote the article Uncle Sam and Aunt Samantha.

4. Lisa told Jennie, Tonight is the pizza and pasta buffet.

5. Jennie asked, Isn't it buy one, get one free?

6. Was she thinking, That's a lot better than cooking?

7. Here is the main conflict of the story To Build a Fire: Man versus nature.

8. I read an article entitled The Obese Fruit of Capitalism; it suggested that our modern obesity epidemic demonstrates the tremendous achievements of fast food and agribusiness.

9. What does the word hypertrophy mean?

10. I was thrilled to receive the unexpected bill.

Write Write a sentence that indicates the actual meaning of each sentence below.

1. The fully loaded logging truck "tiptoed" across the one-lane bridge.

_____

_____

2. Enjoy our "fast" and "friendly" service.

_____

_____

3. We had a "fun" time at our Canada Revenue audit.

_____

_____

Other Classes

While the rules given here are widely accepted, different academic disciplines may have their own specific rules for identifying titles. As you write research reports in different classes, find out which style your discipline uses for reporting titles of larger and smaller works.

LO2 Italics

To Punctuate Titles (Larger Works)

Use italics to indicate the titles of larger works, including newspapers, magazines, journals, pamphlets, books, plays, films, radio and television programs, movies, ballets, operas, long musical compositions, CD's, DVD's, software programs, and legal cases, as well as the names of ships, trains, aircraft, and spacecraft. (For titles of shorter works, see LO1, Quotation Marks.)

Magazine: *Canadian Living*

Play: *The Rez Sisters*

Film: *Mon oncle Antoine*

Book: *The English Patient*

Website: *YouTube*

Newspaper: *The Star Phoenix*

Journal: *Nature*

Software Program: *Final Draft*

Television Program: *Doctor Who*

For a Word, Letter, or Number Referred to as Itself

To show that a word, letter, or number is being referred to as itself, you can use quotation marks (as already discussed in LO1). It is also acceptable to use italics for this purpose. If a definition follows a word used in this way, place that definition in quotation marks.

The word *courage* comes from the French word *coeur*, which means "heart."

In the handwritten note, I couldn't distinguish an *N* from an *M*.

For Foreign Words

Use italics to indicate a word that is being borrowed from a foreign language.

The phrase *et cetera ad nauseum* is a Latin phrase meaning "and so on until vomiting."

For Technical Terms

Use italics to introduce a technical term for the first time in a piece of writing. After that, the term may be used without italics.

Particle physicists are seeking the elusive *Higgs boson*—a subatomic particle thought to provide mass to all other particles. The Higgs boson has become a sort of Holy Grail of quantum mechanics.

Note: If a technical term is being used within an organization or field of study where it is common, it may be used without italics even the first time in a piece of writing.

Using Italics

Correct In the following sentences, underline words that should be in italics.

1. One of my favourite novels is The Curious Incident of the Dog in the Night-Time by Mark Haddon.

2. Have you seen the amazing movie Memento?

3. The name of the paso doble dance comes from the Spanish word for "double step."

4. In 1945, the bomber called the Enola Gay dropped the first atomic bomb, a weapon predicted in 1914 in the H. G. Wells novel The World Set Free.

5. She always has a real joie de vivre.

6. To look at the PDF, you need Adobe Reader or Adobe Acrobat.

7. In this context, the words profane and profanity do not refer to swearing but simply to things that are not divine.

8. The television show Project Runway pits fashion designers against each other.

9. In the musical A Funny Thing Happened on the Way to the Forum, the slave Pseudolus spells out his hope to be F – R – E – E.

10. The enlargement of muscles through weightlifting is known as hypertrophy.

Write Write three sentences, each demonstrating your understanding of one or more rules for using italics.

1. _____

_____

_____

_____

2. _____

_____

_____

_____

3. _____

_____

_____

_____

Learning Outcome

Apply quotation marks and italics in a real-world document.

Practise In the following business e-mail, underline any words that should be italicized and add quotation marks (" ") where needed.

Workplace

Note how improperly punctuated titles can lead to confusion in business writing. Correct punctuation makes for clear communication.

Send | Attach | *f* Format

From: John Metrameme

To: Will McMartin

Subject: Metrameme Author Bio

Hi, Will:

Here is the author bio you requested from me to be published in my next book, War Child:

John Metrameme has published over a dozen novels, most recently the historical epic Sons of Thunder and the romp Daddy Zeus. He has written articles also for The Atlantic and The New Yorker, and his short story Me and the Mudman won the Rubel Prize. Metrameme is perhaps best known for his novel Darling Buds of May.

In his spare time, Metrameme enjoys acting in productions at his community theatre. He played himself in the three-man show The Complete Works of William Shakespeare (Abridged). He also starred as Kit Gill in No Way to Treat a Lady and as Jonathan in Arsenic and Old Lace.

Will, please let me know if you need anything more from me.

Thanks,

John

> "The rules of capitalization are so unfair to words in the middle of a sentence."
>
> —John Green, *Paper Towns*

Richard Newstead/Getty Images

3❾

Capitalization

Why is the word *mom* capitalized in "Did Mom call?" and not in "Did my mom call?" This is just one vagary when it comes to proper capitalization in our language. As you page through this section, you will find others.

One of the best ways to learn about the eccentricities in capitalization is to become a reader and writer yourself. Combine regular reading and writing with the practice in this chapter and you will be well on your way to mastering correct capitalization. You can also use this chapter as a reference whenever you have questions about capitalization; it provides an easy-to-use set of rules and examples.

Learning Outcomes

LO1 Understand basic capitalization rules.

LO2 Understand advanced capitalization rules.

LO3 Understand capitalization of titles, organizations, abbreviations, and letters.

LO4 Understand capitalization of names, courses, and Web terms.

LO5 Apply capitalization in real-world documents.

Vocabulary

vagary
an unexpected change; an eccentric idea

L○1 Basic Capitalization

All first words, proper nouns, and proper adjectives must be capitalized. The following guidelines and examples will help illustrate these rules.

Proper Nouns and Adjectives

Capitalize all proper nouns and all proper adjectives (adjectives derived from proper nouns). The chart below provides a quick overview of capitalization.

Quick Guide: Capitalization at a Glance

Days of the week	Saturday, Sunday, Tuesday
Months	March, August, December
Holidays, holy days	Christmas, Hanukah, Canada Day
Periods, events in history	the Renaissance, Middle Ages
Special events	Tate Memorial Dedication Ceremony
Political parties	Conservative Party, Green Party
Official documents	Canadian Charter of Rights and Freedoms
Trade names	Frisbee disc, Heinz ketchup
Formal epithets	Alexander the Great
Official titles	Prime Minister Stephen Harper, Senator Baker
Planets, heavenly bodies	Earth, Mars, the Milky Way
Continents	Asia, Australia, Europe
Countries	France, Brazil, Japan, Pakistan
Provinces, states	Alberta, Ontario, Manitoba, Nebraska
Cities, towns, villages	Winnipeg, Carberry, Benito
Streets, roads, highways	Sussex Drive, Route 66, Trans Canada Highway
Sections of Canada and the world	the West Coast, the Middle East
Landforms	Rocky Mountains, Kalahari Desert
Bodies of water	Lake Erie, Tiber River, Atlantic Ocean
Public areas	Banff National Park, High Park

First Words

Capitalize the first word in every sentence and the first word in a direct quotation.

Professional sports has become far too important in Canada.

Yvonne asked, "**Why** do baseball players spit all of the time?"

Correcting Capitalization

Capitalize In each sentence below, place capitalization marks (≡) under any letters that should be capitalized.

1. Musician louis armstrong helped make jazz popular to north american and european audiences.

2. Armstrong grew up in new Orleans in a rough neighborhood called the "battleground."

3. he was sent to reform school because he fired a gun in the air on new year's eve.

4. Upon his release, he visited music halls like funky butt hall to hear king oliver play.

5. Oliver gave armstrong his first real cornet, and he played with oliver's band in storyville, the red-light district in New orleans.

6. He also played with the allen brass band on the strekfus line of riverboats.

7. In 1919, Armstrong left new Orleans for Chicago and played with kid orv.

8. He really began to make a name for himself in the creole jazz band that played at Lincoln gardens in Chicago.

Correct Read the following paragraph. Place capitalization marks (≡) under any letters that should be capitalized in proper nouns, proper adjectives, or first words.

My great-grandfather John grew up in saskatoon, saskatchewan, during the great depression. He lived in two different houses on third avenue just south of the downtown area. John attended holy name catholic school and franklin school when he was a kid. His dad, my great-great-grandfather, came from Poland and started out by selling hot dogs. Because money was scarce, great-grandfather's family sometimes had only corn on the cob for dinner. After high school, he enlisted in the navy, but he was turned down because of poor eyesight. He then joined the army and fought in europe during world war II. when John returned to saskatoon, he went to work at harris falcon, a company that made tractors.

LO2 Other Guidelines for Capitalization

Sentences in Parentheses

Capitalize the first word in a sentence that is enclosed in parentheses if that sentence is not combined within another complete sentence.

> Missy needs to learn more about the health care system in Canada. (**She** just moved from Australia to marry a guy from Toronto.)

Note: Do *not* capitalize a sentence that is enclosed in parentheses and is located in the middle of another sentence.

> Missy's husband (his name is André) works in a family business.

Sentences Following Colons

Do not capitalize a complete sentence that follows a colon unless it is a quotation.

> Seldom have I heard such encouraging words: **the** economy is on the rebound.

Salutation and Complimentary Closing

In a letter, capitalize the first and all major words of the salutation. Capitalize only the first word of the complimentary closing.

> **Dear Mayor Nenshi:**   **Sincerely** yours,

Sections of the Country

Words that indicate sections of the country are proper nouns and should be capitalized; words that simply indicate directions are not proper nouns.

> The **Prairies** are suffering from a drought. *(section of country)*
> I live a few blocks **southwest** of here. *(direction)*

Languages, Ethnic Groups, Nationalities, and Religions

Capitalize languages, ethnic groups, nationalities, religions, Supreme Beings, and holy books.

> **African**   **Navajo**   **Islam**   **God**   **Allah**
> **Jehovah**   **the Koran**   **Exodus**   **the Bible**

Tip

You may not be familiar with the names of sections of a country. For example, the Lake District is a region in Great Britain; the Corn Belt refers to a section of the United States. If you are not sure whether a geographical term should be capitalized, look it up in a good dictionary or on a reliable website (like the one for the tourist bureau of the country).

Correcting Capitalization

Capitalize In each sentence below, place capitalization marks (≡) under any letters that should be capitalized.

1. The high plains is a subregion in the great plains.

2. Golda Meir once said this about women: "whether women are better than men I cannot say—but I can say they are certainly no worse."

3. The inuit descend from a group known as the thule.

4. My dad is already planning for his retirement. (what will he do with so much free time?)

5. Many people from Mexico prefer Mexican Canadian more than hispanic or latino.

6. Don't visit the deep south in August unless you like stifling heat and humidity.

7. The third largest religion, hinduism, does not have a single founder or a single sacred text.

8. My mechanic made a bad day even worse: he told me that my car needed four new tires.

Correct Read the following paragraph. Place capitalization marks (≡) under any letters that should be capitalized and cross out (X) any letters that should not be capitalized.

In 1871, prime minister John a. Macdonald promised to build a Transcontinental Railroad to unite British Columbia with eastern Canada. Construction on the canadian pacific railway began ten years later. Building the railway was difficult work: the mountain ranges of British Columbia were especially treacherous. Andrew Onderdonk, the Construction Contractor, hired chinese migrant workers to lay track through this region (these workers were paid pitiful wages and faced dangerous conditions). The last spike was driven in at craigellachie (a site West of the Eagle pass summit) on November 7, 1885.

Capitalize Place capitalization marks (≡) under any letters that should be capitalized.

kleenex tissue	the koran	holiday	asian	forest
thanksgiving day	sherwood forest	tissue paper	the middle east	

LO3 Other Capitalization Rules I

Titles

Capitalize every word in a title except articles *(a, an, the),* short prepositions, *to* in an infinitive, and coordinating conjunctions. Follow this rule for titles of books, newspapers, magazines, poems, plays, songs, articles, films, works of art, and stories.

Knight and Day (movie)	*Chronicle Herald* (newspaper)
"Lovers in a Dangerous Time" (song)	"Boycott the 2016 Olympic Games" (essay)
Comedy of Errors (play)	*Anne of Green Gables* (novel)

Organizations

Capitalize the name of an organization or a team and its members.

Habitat for Humanity	Liberal Party
The Bill & Melinda Gates Foundation	Toronto Raptors
Special Olympics	Hamilton Tiger-Cats

Abbreviations

Capitalize abbreviations of titles and organizations.

M.D.	Ph.D.	U.N.	C.E.	B.C.E.	GPA

Letters

Capitalize letters used to indicate a form or shape.

S-curve	T-shirt	R-rated	C-section

(right) Brent Hofacker/Shutterstock.com
(left) Brent Hofacker/Shutterstock.com

Correcting Capitalization

Correct In each sentence below, place capitalization marks (≡) under any letters that should be capitalized.

1. To me, *a midsummer night's dream* is one of Shakespeare's best plays.

2. The San Francisco giants used to play in Candlestick park.

3. I enjoyed reading *city of thieves,* a novel by David Benioff.

4. Do you know the song "don't drink the water" by dave matthews?

5. My brother splattered some paint on my favourite Calgary flames t-shirt.

6. Newman's own foundation donates to charities all net royalties and profits after taxes it receives from Newman's own products.

7. Javier Lopez, an old friend from the neighbourhood, earned a ph.d in history.

8. Perhaps the least known of the beatles is George Harrison; I love his song "while my guitar gently weeps."

9. The oscar-winning movie "12 years a slave" was rated 18A according to the *Vancouver sun*.

10. Anna Quindlen's article "uncle sam and aunt samantha" first appeared in *newsweek*.

11. People attend aa (alcoholics anonymous) meetings to support each other as they battle their alcoholism.

Practise Read the paragraph below, placing capitalization marks (≡) under letters that should be capitalized.

An article in last week's *standard press* promoted the city's farmer's market. The market, held every Thursday afternoon, is sponsored by the Brighton chamber of commerce. The vendors, who must reside within the local area, sell everything from fresh produce to tie-dyed t-shirts. In addition, organizations such as the red cross and Brighton little league have informational booths at the market. A special feature is the live entertainment supplied by rainbow road, a local folk rock band. They play a lot of Gordon Lightfoot, singing favourites like "if you could read my mind."

Understand capitalization of names, courses, and Web terms.

LO4 Other Capitalization Rules II

Words Used as Names

Capitalize words like father, mother, uncle, senator, and professor only when they are parts of titles that include a personal name or when they are substitutes for proper nouns (especially in direct address).

> Hello, **Professor** Baldwin. (*Professor* is part of the name.)
>
> It's good to meet you, **Professor**. (*Professor* is a substitute for the name.)
>
> Our **professor** is a member of two important committees.
>
> Who was the volleyball **coach** last year?
>
> We had **Coach Snyder** for two years.
>
> I met **Coach** in the athletic office.

Do not capitalize common nouns and titles that appear near, but are not part of, a proper noun.

Chancellor John Bohm...
(Chancellor *is a title being used as part of the name.*)

John Bohm, our chancellor,...
(Chancellor *appears near, but is not part of, the proper noun.*)

Note: To test whether a word is being substituted for a proper noun, simply read the sentence with a proper noun in place of the word. If the proper noun fits in the sentence, the word being tested should be capitalized. Usually the word is not capitalized if it follows a possessive—*my, his, our, your,* and so on.

> Did **Mom** (Yvonne) pick up the dry cleaning?
> (*Yvonne* works in the sentence.)
>
> Did your **mom** (Yvonne) pick up the dry cleaning?
> (*Yvonne* does not work in the sentence; the word *mom* follows *your*.)

Titles of Courses

Words such as technology, history, and science are proper nouns when they are included in the titles of specific courses; they are common nouns when they name a field of study.

> The only course that fits my schedule is **Introduction to Oil Painting**.
> (title of a specific course)
>
> Judy Kenner advises anyone interested in **oil painting**.
> (a field of study)

Internet and E-Mail

The words *Internet* and *World Wide Web* are capitalized because they are considered proper nouns. When your writing includes a Web address (URL), capitalize any letters that the site's owner does (on printed materials or on the site itself).

> When doing research on the **Internet**, be sure to record each site's **Web** address (URL) and each contact's **e-mail** address.

Correcting Capitalization

Capitalize In each sentence below, place capitalization marks (≡) under any words that should be capitalized.

1. Every summer, pastor bachman leads the youth group on a hike around lake geneva.

2. Claude Dickert, our current mayor, writes blog entries on *brightontoday.ca,* the city's official website.

3. At the celebration, dad asked senator ryan about health care.

4. The easiest course I ever took in high school was called leisure reading.

5. When I'm on the internet, I use google to answer all kinds of questions.

6. My night course, contemporary history, is always packed because professor scharfenburg presents such interesting lectures.

7. When it comes to shopping for books, I often go to amazon.ca for ideas and information.

8. Our instructor had us bookmark *grammar girl,* a website that provides grammar tips and practice.

Correct Read the paragraph below, placing capitalization marks (≡) under any words or letters that should be capitalized.

Internet art does not consist of existing pieces of artwork digitized to be seen using a web browser. Instead, it is art that is created on or with the net, and it comes into being using websites, e-mail options, virtual worlds such as *second life,* and so on. Steve Dietz, formerly the curator of the Walker art center, defines internet art as art that has "the internet as a necessary condition of viewing/participating/experiencing." Martin Wattenberg has created a Website called *idea line,* which provides "a timeline of net artwork" to help people experience this type of art.

LO5 Real-World Application

Correct In the following e-mail, place capitalization marks (≡) under letters that should be capitalized. If a letter is capitalized but shouldn't be, put a lowercase editing mark (/) through the letter.

Send	Attach	Fonts	Colors	Save As Draft

From: Rodell Williams rodellwilliams2@earthlink.net

To: Professor Jean Leuinski

Subject: Thank You for Your Recommendation

Dear professor Leuinski,

Thank you for recommending me for the internship at Bismark laboratories. During my interview last Monday, Dr. Lemark said that he had received your letter and had talked with you by phone. Apparently you said, "clearly Rodell has demonstrated meticulous and thorough Lab techniques." I really appreciate this description of my work habits.

The outcome of the application and interviewing process could not have been any better, because this morning Dr. Lemark offered me the position. I will be working at Conway science centre, one of Bismark's newest Labs, helping various chemists with their work.

I am so glad that I had you for biochemistry I. You made that course so interesting, and I learned so much. Dr. Lemark also was impressed that I had taken analytical chemistry I and II taught by professor Khan.

Again, I can't thank you enough, professor, for your help. I know I will be busy next semester with the Internship, but I can't wait to get started. (you can expect to hear from me about my work.)

sincerely,

Rodell Williams

Special Challenge Write one sentence in which you use the same regional or directional word twice—with the word correctly capitalized in one case and correctly lowercase in the other case.

The study habit that sets you apart.

www.nelson.com/student

"How we remember, what we remember,
and why we remember form the most
personal map of our individuality."
—Christina Baldwin

iofoto/Shutterstock.com

40 Narrative Essays

This chapter contains two example narrative essays, along with questions to help you analyze each reading.

SQ3R When you read, become involved with the text by using the SQ3R approach.

- **Survey:** Prepare by reading "About the Author," skimming the essay, and noting any vocabulary words.
- **Question:** Ask yourself what the title and the author description might lead you to expect from the essay. List any questions that come to mind.
- **Read:** Read the essay for effect, allowing the story to carry you along.
- **Recite:** Recite especially effective or enjoyable sections aloud to better understand and remember them.
- **Review:** Scan the essay again, asking yourself what the author sought to accomplish and how successful you believe he or she was. Answer the questions provided to help you analyze the essay.

Learning Outcomes

LO1 Understand, read, and analyze personal narratives.

Essay List:

"Shark Bait": In this narrative from the book *Dave Barry Is Not Making This Up,* Dave Barry tells of a day spent on a boat off the shore of Miami, with five other men and four 10-year-olds. Things get interesting when a barracuda shows up where they have been swimming.

"A Doctor's Dilemma": James N. Dillard revisits a life-or-death decision he faced as a young doctor in training, and explains why he would choose differently if he were facing the same situation today.

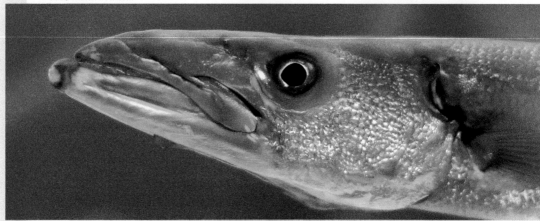

About the Author

Dave Barry is a book author and Pulitzer Prize–winning humour columnist whose work has appeared in over 500 newspapers.

Dave Berry "Shark Bait," *Dave Barry Is Not Making This Up*, Random House, 2001.

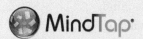

You will find another example narrative essay online.

Vocabulary

cholesterol
a waxy substance in animal cells, sometimes leading to clogged arteries, heart disease, and/or stroke

cardiac arrest
a heart stoppage, heart attack

stereotyping
applying an oversimplified mental attitude toward some group

genetic
having to do with DNA, encoded in a creature's genes

Shark Bait
by Dave Barry

It began as a fun nautical outing, 10 of us in a motorboat off the coast of Miami. The weather was sunny and we saw no signs of danger, other than the risk of sliding overboard because every exposed surface on the boat was covered with a layer of snack-related grease. We had enough cholesterol on board to put the entire U.S. Olympic team into cardiac arrest. This is because all 10 of us were guys. 5

I hate to engage in gender stereotyping, but when women plan the menu for a recreational outing, they usually come up with a nutritionally balanced menu featuring all the major food groups, including the Sliced Carrots Group, the Pieces of Fruit Cut into Cubes Group, the Utensils Group, and the Plate Group. Whereas 10 guys tend to focus on the Carbonated Malt Beverages Group and the Fatal Snacks Group. On this particular trip, our food supply consisted of about 14 bags of potato chips and one fast-food fried-chicken Giant Economy Tub o' Fat. Nobody brought, for example, napkins, the theory being that you could just wipe your hands on your stomach. Then you could burp. This is what guys on all-guy boats are doing 15 while women are thinking about their relationships.

The reason the grease got smeared everywhere was that four of the guys on the boat were 10-year-olds, who, because of the way their still-developing digestive systems work, cannot chew without punching. This results in a lot of dropped and thrown food. On this boat, you regularly encountered semi-gnawed 20 pieces of chicken skittering across the deck toward you like small but hostile alien creatures from the Kentucky Fried Planet. Periodically a man would yell "CUT THAT OUT!" at the boys, then burp to indicate the depth of his concern. Discipline is vital on a boat.

We motored through random-looking ocean until we found exactly what 25 we were looking for: a patch of random-looking ocean. There we dropped anchor and dove for Florida lobsters, which protect themselves by using their tails to scoot backward really fast. They've been fooling predators with this move for millions of years, but the guys on our boat, being advanced life forms, including a dentist, figured it out in under three hours. I myself did not participate, because I 30 believe that lobsters are the result of a terrible genetic accident involving nuclear radiation and cockroaches. I mostly sat around, watching guys lunge out of the water, heave lobsters into the boat, burp, and plunge back in. Meanwhile, the lobsters were scrabbling around in the chicken grease, frantically trying to shoot

35 backward through the forest of legs belonging to 10-year-old boys squirting each other with gobs of the No. 197 000 000 000 Sun Block that their moms had sent along. It was a total Guy Day, very relaxing, until the arrival of the barracuda.

This occurred just after we'd all gotten out of the water. One of the men, Larry, was fishing, and he hooked a barracuda right where we had been swimming. This

40 was unsettling. The books all say that barracuda rarely eat people, but very few barracuda can read, and they have far more teeth than would be necessary for a strictly seafood diet. Their mouths look like the entire $39.95 set of Ginsu knives, including the handy Arm Slicer.

We gathered around to watch Larry fight the barracuda. His plan was to

45 catch it, weigh it, and release it with a warning. After 10 minutes he almost had it to the boat, and we were all pretty excited for him, when all of a sudden . . .

Ba-DUMP . . . Ba-DUMP . . .

Those of you who read music recognize this as the sound track from the motion picture *Jaws*. Sure enough, cruising right behind Larry's barracuda,

50 thinking sushi, was a shark. And not just any shark. It was a hammerhead shark, perennial winner of the coveted Oscar for Ugliest Fish. It has a weird, T-shaped head with a big eyeball on each tip, so that it can see around both sides of a telephone pole. This ability is of course useless for a fish, but nobody would dare try to explain this to a hammerhead.

55 The hammerhead, its fin breaking the surface, zigzagged closer to Larry's barracuda, then surged forward.

"Oh ****!" went Larry, reeling furiously.

CHOMP went the hammerhead, and suddenly Larry's barracuda was in a new weight division.

60 *CHOMP* went the hammerhead again, and now Larry was competing in an entirely new category, Fish Consisting of Only a Head.

The boys were staring at the remainder of the barracuda, deeply impressed.

"This is your leg," said the dentist. "This is your leg on *Jaws*. Any

65 questions?"

The boys, for the first time all day, were quiet.

Summarize In one or two sentences, sum up what happened in this narrative.

_____

_____

Comment Did you enjoy this story? Why or why not?

_____

_____

About the Author

Dr. Dillard served for 12 years as an assistant professor at Columbia University's College of Physicians and Surgeons, and as medical director for its Rosenthal Center for Complementary and Alternative Medicine. Since 2006 he has worked in private practice. He is also an author and television personality.

James Dillard, "A Doctor's Dilemma," *Newsweek*, June 12, 1995.

A Doctor's Dilemma
by James N. Dillard

Helping an accident victim on the road could land you in court.

It was a bright, clear February afternoon in Gettysburg. A strong sun and layers of **down** did little to ease the biting cold. Our climb to the crest of **Little Roundtop** wound past somber monuments, barren trees and polished cannon. From the top, we peered down on the wheat field where men had fallen so close together that one could not see the ground. Rifle balls had whined as thick as bee swarms through the trees, and cannon shots had torn limbs from the young men fighting there. A frozen wind whipped tears from our eyes. My friend Amy huddled close, using me as a wind breaker. Despite the cold, it was hard to leave this place.

Driving east out of Gettysburg on a country blacktop, the gray Bronco ahead of us passed through a rural crossroad just as a small pickup truck tried to take a left turn. The Bronco swerved, but slammed into the pickup on the passenger side. We immediately slowed to a crawl as we passed the scene. The Bronco's driver looked fine, but we couldn't see the driver of the pickup. I pulled over on the shoulder and got out to investigate.

The right side of the truck was smashed in, and the side window was shattered. The driver was partly out of the truck. His head hung forward over the edge of the passenger-side window, the front of his neck crushed on the shattered windowsill. He was unconscious and starting to turn a dusky blue. His chest slowly heaved against a blocked windpipe.

A young man ran out of a house at the crossroad. "Get an ambulance out here," I shouted against the wind. "Tell them a man is dying."

I looked down again at the driver hanging from the windowsill. There were six empty beer bottles on the floor of the truck. I could smell the beer through the window. I knew I had to move him, to open his airway. I had no idea what neck injuries he had sustained. He could easily end up a **quadriplegic**. But I thought: he'll be dead by the time the ambulance gets here if I don't move him and try to do something to help him.

An image flashed before my mind. I could see the courtroom and the driver of the truck sitting in a wheelchair. I could see his attorney pointing at me and

1

5

10

15

20

25

30

thundering at the jury: "This young doctor, with still a year left in his residency training, took it upon himself to play God. He took it upon himself to move this gravely injured man, condemning him forever to this wheelchair . . ." I imagined the millions of dollars in award money. And all the years of hard work lost. I'd be
35 paying him off for the rest of my life. Amy touched my shoulder. "What are you going to do?"

The automatic response from long hours in the emergency room kicked in. I pulled off my overcoat and rolled up my sleeves. The trick would be to keep enough traction straight up on his head while I moved his torso, so that his probable
40 broken neck and spinal-cord injury wouldn't be made worse. Amy came around the driver's side, climbed half in and grabbed his belt and shirt collar. Together we lifted him off the windowsill.

He was still out cold, limp as a rag doll. His throat was crushed and blood from the jugular vein was running down my arms. He still couldn't breathe. He
45 was deep blue-magenta now, his pulse was rapid and thready. The stench of alcohol turned my stomach, but I positioned his jaw and tried to blow air down into his lungs. It wouldn't go.

Amy had brought some supplies from my car. I opened an oversize intravenous needle and groped on the man's neck. My hands were numb, covered with freezing
50 blood and bits of broken glass. Hyoid bone—God, I can't even feel the thyroid cartilage, it's gone . . . OK, the thyroid gland is about there, cricoid rings are here . . . we'll go in right here . . .

It was a lucky first shot. Pink air sprayed through the IV needle. I placed a second needle next to the first. The air began whistling through it. Almost
55 immediately, the driver's face turned bright red. After a minute, his pulse slowed down and his eyes moved slightly. I stood up, took a step back and looked down. He was going to make it. He was going to live. A siren wailed in the distance. I turned and saw Amy holding my overcoat. I was shivering and my arms were turning white with cold.

60 The ambulance captain looked around and bellowed, "What the hell . . . who did this?" as his team scurried over to the man lying in the truck.

"I did," I replied. He took down my name and address for his reports. I had just destroyed my career. I would never be able to finish my residency with a massive lawsuit pending. My life was over.

65 The truck driver was strapped onto a backboard, his neck in a stiff collar. The ambulance crew had controlled the bleeding and started intravenous fluid. He was slowly waking up. As they loaded him into the ambulance, I saw him move his feet. Maybe my future wasn't lost.

A police sergeant called me from Pennsylvania three weeks later. Six days
70 after successful throat-reconstruction surgery, the driver had signed out, against medical advice, from the hospital because he couldn't get a drink on the ward. He was being arraigned on drunk-driving charges.

A few days later, I went into the office of one of my senior professors, to tell the story. He peered over his half glasses and his eyes narrowed. "Well, you did the
75 right thing medically of course. But, James, do you know what you put at risk by doing that?" he said sternly. "What was I supposed to do?" I asked.

"Drive on," he replied. "There is an army of lawyers out there who would stand in line to get a case like that. If that driver had turned out to be a quadriplegic, you might never have practiced medicine again. You were a very lucky young man." 80

The day I graduated from medical school, I took an oath to serve the sick and the injured. I remember truly believing I would be able to do just that. But I have found out it isn't so simple. I understand now what a foolish thing I did that day. Despite my oath, I know what I would do on that cold roadside near Gettysburg today. I would drive on. 85

Map Along the timeline below, list the most important details of Dr. Dillard's story.

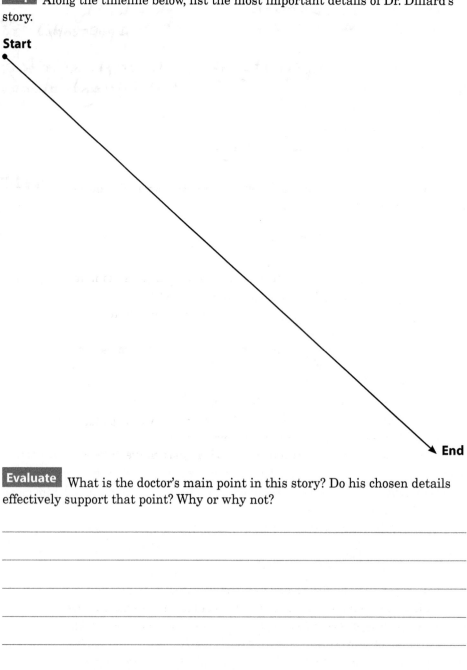

Start

End

Evaluate What is the doctor's main point in this story? Do his chosen details effectively support that point? Why or why not?

_____

_____

_____

_____

_____

_____

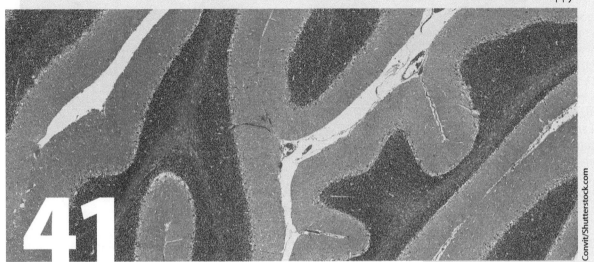

"Aristotle was famous for knowing everything. He taught that the brain exists merely to cool the blood and is not involved in the process of thinking. This is true only of certain persons."

—Will Cuppy

41

Process Essays

This chapter contains two example process essays, along with questions you can use as tools to help analyze each reading.

SQ3R When you read, become involved with the text by using the SQ3R approach.

- ■ **Survey:** Prepare by reading "About the Author," skimming the essay, and noting any vocabulary words.
- ■ **Question:** Make a list of questions you expect to have answered by the essay.
- ■ **Read:** Read the essay, noting the steps in the process that is being described.
- ■ **Recite:** Recite the steps in order to make sure you understand and remember them.
- ■ **Review:** Scan the essay again, looking for details you might have missed or answers to any remaining questions you may have. Answer the questions provided to help you analyze the essay.

Learning Outcomes

LO1 Understand, read, and analyze process essays.

Essay List:

"Conversational Ballgames": Nancy Masterson Sakamoto uses two very different types of ball games as analogies to contrast Japanese and North American conversational styles.

"How Our Skins Got Their Color": Dr. Marvin Harris argues that the natural skin tone of the human race is brown, then explains how Europeans developed white skin from that base, and the parallel development of black skin in sub-Saharan Africa. His essay is based upon explanation of another process: the human body's use of sunlight to create vitamin D, and its use of that substance to absorb calcium.

About the Author

Nancy Masterson Sakamoto is the author of the book *Polite Fiction: Why Japanese and Americans Seem Rude to Each Other*. Born in Los Angeles in 1931, she married a Japanese man and taught American studies in Japan from 1972 to 1982. She then returned to the U.S.A. and became a professor at Shitennoji Gakuen University in Honolulu.

Conversational Ballgames
by Nancy Masterson Sakamoto

After I was married and had lived in Japan for a while, my Japanese gradu- 1
ally improved to the point where I could take part in simple conversations with my husband, his friends, and family. And I began to notice that often, when I joined in, the others would look startled, and the conversation would come to a halt. After this happened several times, it became clear to me that I was doing 5
something wrong. But for a long time, I didn't know what it was.

Finally, after listening carefully to many Japanese conversations, I discovered what my problem was. Even though I was speaking Japanese, I was handling the conversation in a Western way.

Japanese-style conversations develop quite differently from Western-style 10
conversations. And the difference isn't only in the languages. I realized that just as I kept trying to hold Western-style conversations even when I was speaking Japanese, so were my English students trying to hold Japanese-style conversations even when they were speaking English. We were unconsciously playing entirely different conversational ballgames. 15

A Western-style conversation between two people is like a game of tennis. If I introduce a topic, a conversational ball, I expect you to hit it back. If you agree with me, I don't expect you simply to agree and do nothing more. I expect you to add something—a reason for agreeing, another example, or a remark to carry the idea further. But I don't expect you always to agree. I am just as happy if you 20
question me, or challenge me, or completely disagree with me. Whether you agree or disagree, your response will return the ball to me.

And then it is my turn again. I don't serve a new ball from my original starting line. I hit your ball back again from where it has bounced. I carry your idea further, or answer your questions or objections, or challenge or question you. And 25
so the ball goes back and forth.

If there are more than two people in the conversation, then it is like doubles in tennis, or like volleyball. There's no waiting in line. Whoever is nearest and quickest hits the ball, and if you step back, someone else will hit it. No one stops the game to give you a turn. You're responsible for taking your own turn and no 30
one person has the ball for very long.

A Japanese-style conversation, however, is not at all like tennis or volleyball, it's like bowling. You wait for your turn, and you always know your place in line. It depends on such things as whether you are older or younger, a close friend or a relative stranger to the previous speaker, in a senior or junior position, and so on.

The first thing is to wait for your turn, patiently and politely. When your moment comes, you step up to the starting line with your bowling ball, and carefully bowl it. Everyone else stands back, making sounds of polite encouragement. Everyone waits until your ball has reached the end of the lane, and watches to see if it knocks down all the pins, or only some of them, or none of them. Then there is a pause, while everyone registers your score.

Then, after everyone is sure that you are done, the next person in line steps up to the same startling line, with a different ball. He doesn't return your ball. There is no back and forth at all. And there is always a suitable pause between turns. There is no rush, no impatience.

No wonder everyone looked startled when I took part in Japanese conversations. I paid no attention to whose turn it was, and kept snatching the ball halfway down the alley and throwing it back at the bowler. Of course the conversation fell apart, I was playing the wrong game.

This explains why it can be so difficult to get a Western-style discussion going with Japanese students of English. Whenever I serve a volleyball, everyone just stands back and watches it fall. No one hits it back. Everyone waits until I call on someone to take a turn. And when that person speaks, he doesn't hit my ball back. He serves a new ball. Again, everyone just watches it fall. So I call on someone else. This person does not refer to what the previous speaker has said. He also serves a new ball. Everyone begins again from the same starting line, and all the balls run parallel. There is never any back and forth.

Now that you know about the difference in the conversational ballgames, you may think that all your troubles are over. But if you have been trained all your life to play one game, it is no simple matter to switch to another, even if you know the rules. Tennis, after all, is different from bowling.

Think Critically Review the process diagrams to the left. Which do you think best suits a North an American conversation and which a Japanese? Explain.

_____

_____

_____

_____

_____

_____

Process Diagrams

I. Topic _____
(Chronological Order)

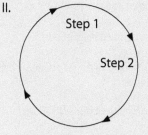

II.

About the Author

Dr. Marvin Harris (1927–2001) was chair of the anthropology department at Columbia University, then a Graduate Research Professor at the University of Florida. He also served as the Chair of the General Anthropology Division for the American Anthropological Association. During his life, he published 16 books and wrote a series of essays he titled *Our Kind*.

How Our Skins Got Their Color
by Marvin Harris

Most human beings are neither very fair nor very dark, but brown. The 1
extremely fair skin of northern Europeans and their descendants, and the very
black skins of central Africans and their descendants, are probably special adap-
tations. Brown-skinned ancestors may have been shared by modern-day blacks
and whites as recently as 10 000 years ago. 5

Human skin owes its color to the presence of particles known as melanin.
The primary function of melanin is to protect the upper levels of the skin from being damaged by the sun's ultraviolet rays. This radiation poses a critical problem
for our kind because we lack the dense coat of hair that acts as a sunscreen for
most mammals. . . . Hairlessness exposes us to two kinds of radiation hazards: 10
ordinary sunburn, with its blisters, rashes, and risk of infection; and skin cancers,
including malignant melanoma, one of the deadliest diseases known. Melanin is
the body's first line of defense against these afflictions. The more melanin particles, the darker the skin, and the lower the risk of sunburn and all forms of skin
cancer. This explains why the highest rates for skin cancer are found in sun- 15
drenched lands such as Australia, where light-skinned people of European descent
spend a good part of their lives outdoors wearing scanty attire. Very dark-skinned
people such as heavily pigmented Africans of Zaire seldom get skin cancer, but
when they do, they get it on depigmented parts of their bodies—palms and lips.

If exposure to solar radiation had nothing but harmful effects, natural selec- 20
tion would have favored inky black as the color for all human populations. But the
sun's rays do not present an unmitigated threat. As it falls on the skin, sunshine
converts a fatty substance in the epidermis into vitamin D. The blood carries
vitamin D from the skin to the intestines (technically making it a hormone rather
than a vitamin), where it plays a vital role in the absorption of calcium. In turn, 25
calcium is vital for strong bones. Without it, people fall victim to the crippling
diseases rickets and osteomalacia. In women, calcium deficiencies can result in a
deformed birth canal, which makes childbirth lethal for both mother and fetus.

Vitamin D can be obtained from a few foods, primarily the oils and liv-
ers of marine fish. But inland populations must rely on the sun's rays and their 30

Vocabulary

pigmented
colored by pigment

unmitigated
not made less severe

epidermis
uppermost layer of skin

rickets
softening of bones in the young

osteomalacia
softening of bones in adults

own skins for the supply of this crucial substance. The particular color of a human population's skin, therefore, represents in large degree a trade-off between the hazards of too much versus too little solar radiation: acute sunburn and skin cancer on the one hand, and rickets and osteomalacia on the other. It is this trade-off
35 that largely accounts for the preponderance of brown people in the world and for the general tendency for skin color to be darkest among equatorial populations and lightest among populations dwelling at higher latitudes.

At middle latitudes, the skin follows a strategy of changing colors with the seasons. Around the Mediterranean basin, for example, exposure to the summer
40 sun brings high risk of cancer but low risk for rickets; the body produces more melanin and people grow darker (i.e., they get suntans). Winter reduces the risk of sunburn and cancer; the body produces less melanin, and the tan wears off.

The correlation between skin color and latitude is not perfect because other factors—such as the availability of foods containing vitamin D and calcium, regional
45 cloud cover during the winter, amount of clothing worn, and cultural preferences—may work for or against the predicted relationship. Arctic-dwelling Eskimo, for example, are not as light-skinned as expected, but their habitat and economy afford them a diet that is exceptionally rich in both vitamin D and calcium.

Northern Europeans, obliged to wear heavy garments for protection
50 against the long, cold, cloudy winters, were always at risk for rickets and osteomalacia from too little vitamin D and calcium. This risk increased sometime after 6000 B.C., when pioneer cattle herders who did not exploit marine resources began to appear in northern Europe. The risk would have been especially great for the brown-skinned Mediterranean peoples who migrated
55 northward along with the crops and farm animals. Samples of Caucasian skin (infant penile foreskin obtained at the time of circumcision) exposed to sunlight on cloudless days in Boston (42°N) from November through February produced no vitamin D. In Edmonton (52°N) this period extended from October to March. But further south (34°N) sunlight was effective in producing vitamin D in the
60 middle of the winter. Almost all of Europe lies north of 42°N. Fair-skinned, nontanning individuals who could utilize the weakest and briefest doses of sunlight to synthesize vitamin D were strongly favored by natural selection. During the frigid winters, only a small circle of a child's face could be left to peek out at the sun through the heavy clothing, thereby favoring the survival
65 of individuals with translucent patches of pink on their cheeks characteristic of many northern Europeans. (People who could get calcium by drinking cow's milk would also be favored by natural selection. . . .)

If light-skinned individuals on the average had only 2 percent more children survive per generation, the changeover in the skin color could have begun
70 5000 years ago and reached present levels well before the beginning of the Christian era. But natural selection need not have acted alone. Cultural selection may also have played a role. It seems likely that whenever people consciously or unconsciously had to decide which infants to nourish and which to neglect, the advantage would go to those with lighter skin, experience having show that such
75 individuals tended to grow up to be taller, stronger, and healthier than their darker siblings. White was beautiful because white was healthy.

preponderance
majority

latitude
imaginary line marking a distance from the earth's equator

Mediterranean
coastal lands of Southern Europe, Southwest Asia, and Northern Africa

correlation
relationship of two things often occurring together

habitat
environment in which a person or an animal lives

Caucasian
light-skinned people originating in the Caucasus Mountains region

penile foreskin
fold of skin surrounding the tip of the penis

circumcision
surgical removal of the foreskin

translucent
nearly transparent

To account for the evolution of black skin in equatorial latitudes, one has merely to reverse the combined effects of natural and cultural selection. With the sun directly overhead most of the year, and clothing a hindrance to work and survival, vitamin D was never in short supply (and calcium was easily obtained 80 from vegetables). Rickets and osteomalacia were rare. Skin cancer was the main problem, and what nature started culture amplified. Darker infants were favored by parents because experience showed that they grew up to be freer of disfiguring and lethal malignancies. Black was beautiful because black was healthy.

Vocabulary

malignant
malicious, intending damage

Evaluate What processes are explained in this essay?

_____

_____

_____

_____

Diagram Label the diagram below with steps from one of the processes in the essay. (Add more arrows as needed.)

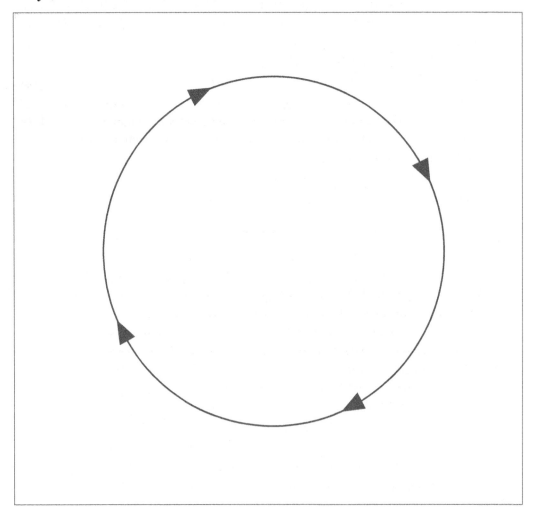

"Shall I compare thee to a summer's day?"

—William Shakespeare

Jeanette Dietl/Shutterstock.com

42

Comparison–
Contrast Essays

One of the best ways to understand a subject is to compare and contrast it with another. This chapter contains two example comparison–contrast pieces, along with questions and graphics for analyzing each.

SQ3R When you read, become involved with the text by using the SQ3R approach.

- **Survey:** Prepare by reading "About the Author," skimming the writing, and noting any vocabulary words.
- **Question:** Ask yourself what topics are being compared and contrasted and what organizational pattern is used. Three common patterns are provided on the next page.
- **Read:** Carefully read the piece, reviewing the vocabulary words as you encounter them, finding answers to your questions, and judging the effectiveness of the author's comparison and contrast.
- **Recite:** Stop to repeat important points silently or aloud.
- **Review:** Analyze the writing by filling in the graphic organizer and answering the questions provided.

Learning Outcomes

LO1 Understand, read, and analyze comparison–contrast essays.

Essays

"Religious Faith Versus Spirituality": Neil Bissoondath uses his mother's death and cremation to distinguish between faith and spirituality.

"For Minorities, Timing Is Everything": Olive Skene Johnson explores changing social attitudes towards left-handedness and homosexuality.

Point-by-Point

Beginning

Point 1	Subject 1
	Subject 2
Point 2	Subject 1
	Subject 2
Point 3	Subject 1
	Subject 2

Ending

Subject-to-Subject

Beginning

Subject 1
Subject 2

Ending

Similarities-Differences

Beginning

Similarities
Differences

Ending

© Remi Benali/Corbis

About the Author

Neil Bissoondath is a journalist and author who was born in Trinidad and later immigrated to Canada. In this essay, he explores his own spiritual experience following his mother's death, comparing and contrasting it with religious faith (and, glancingly, with scientific certainty).

Religious Faith Versus Spirituality by Neil Bissoondath. Reprinted by permission of the author.

Religious Faith Versus Spirituality
by Neil Bissoondath

1   *Wait till someone you love dies. You'll see. You'll know God exists. You'll want Him to.* The prediction, repeated with minimal variation through the years by believers challenged by my nonbelief, was never offered as a promise but as a vague threat, and always with a sense of satisfied superiority, as if the speakers
5   relished the thought that one day I would get my comeuppance.

They were, without exception, enthusiastic practitioners of their respective faiths—Roman Catholics, Presbyterians, Hindus, Muslims, God-fearing people all. Which was, to me, precisely the problem: Why all this fear?

And then one day, without warning, my mother died. Hers was the first
10 death to touch me to the quick. Her cremation was done in the traditional Hindu manner. Under the direction of a pundit, my brother and I performed the ceremony, preparing the body with our bare hands, a contact more intimate than we'd ever had when she was alive.

As I walked away from her flaming pyre, I felt myself soaring with a lightness
15 I'd never known before. I was suddenly freed from days of physical and emotional lassitude, and felt my first inkling of the healing power of ritual, the solace that ceremony can bring.

Still, despite the pain and the unspeakable sense of loss, the oft-predicted discovery of faith eluded me. I remained, as I do today, a nonbeliever, but I have no
20 doubt that I underwent a deeply spiritual experience. This was when I began to understand that religious faith and spirituality do not necessarily have anything to do with each other—not that they are incompatible but that they are often mutually exclusive.

Western civilization has spent two thousand years blurring the distinction
25 between the two, and as we enter the third millennium we are hardly more at peace with ourselves than people were a thousand years ago. Appreciating the distinction could help soothe our anxieties about the days to come.

Spirituality is the individual's ability to wonder at, and delight in, the indecipherable, like a baby marveling at the wiggling of its own toes. It is to be

Vocabulary

comeuppance
deserved repayment for a wrong act or attitude

pundit
a Hindu scholar or "wise man"

pyre
a pile of wood for cremating a body

lassitude
weariness, fatigue, or lethargy

at ease with speculation, asking the unanswerable question and accepting that any answer would necessarily be incomplete, even false. It is recognizing that if scientific inquiry has inevitable limits, so too do religious explanations, which base themselves on unquestioning acceptance of the unprovable: neither can ever fully satisfy. 30

A sense of the spiritual comes from staring deep into the formation of a rose or a hibiscus and being astonished at the intricate delicacy of its symmetry without needing to see behind its perfection of form the fashioning hand of a deity. 35

It comes from watching your child being born and gazing for the first time into those newly opened eyes, from holding that child against your chest and feeling his or her heartbeat melding with yours. 40

It comes from gazing up into the sparkling solitude of a clear midnight sky, secure in the knowledge that, no matter how alone you may feel at moments, the message of the stars appears to be that you most indisputably are not.

At such moments, you need no dogma to tell you that the world seen or unseen, near or distant, is a wonderful and mysterious place. Spirituality, then, requires neither science nor religion, both of which hunger after answers and reassurance—while the essence of spirituality lies in the opening up of the individual to dazzlement. Spirituality entails no worship. 45

At the very moment of my mother's cremation, her brother, trapped thousands of miles away in England by airline schedules, got out his photographs of her and spread them on his coffee table. He reread her old letters and spent some time meditating on the life that had been lived—his way, at the very moment flames consumed her body, of celebrating the life and saying farewell, his way of engaging with the spiritual. 50

Analyze Complete the T-graph to analyze Bissoondath's comparison of faith and spirituality. In the left column, list details about faith; in the right, list details about spirituality.

Religious Faith	Spirituality

Think Critically How does science fit into Bissoondath's essay? Where would you place it in the T-graph above? How does your placement reflect on your own experiences with science and with religion?

For Minorities, Timing Is Everything
by Olive Skene Johnson

About the Author

Olive Skene Johnson was a neuropsychologist, social activist, counselor and author. She wrote *The Sexual Spectrum* (2007) and has published work in *MacLean's, Star Weekly, Vancouver Life,* and *Canadian Living.*

1   Left-handedness and homosexuality both tend to run in families. As my husband's family and mine have some of each, it is not surprising that one of our children is left-handed and another homosexual. Both my left-handed daughter and my homosexual son turned out to be bright, funny, talented people with loving

5   friends and family. But their experience of growing up in different minority groups was a striking contrast and an interesting illustration of how societal attitudes change as sufficient knowledge accumulates to make old beliefs untenable.

By the time my daughter was growing up, left-handedness was no longer regarded as a sign of immorality or mental deficiency. Almost everybody knew

10   "openly" left-handed friends, teachers and relatives and viewed them as normal people who wrote differently. Except for a little awkwardness in learning to write at school, my daughter's hand preference was simply never an issue. If people noticed it at all, they did so with a shrug. Nobody called her nasty names or banned school library books about left-handed families, as school trustees in Surrey, B.C., recently

15   banned books about gay families. Nobody criticized her left-handed "lifestyle" or suggested that she might be an unfit role model for young children. Nobody claimed that she *chose* to be left-handed and should suffer the consequences.

My gay son did not choose to be different either, but when he was growing up, homosexuality was still too misunderstood to be accepted as just another variant

20   of human sexuality. Because gay people still felt unsafe revealing their sexual orientation, he was deprived of the opportunity of knowing openly gay teachers, friends and relatives. He grew up hearing crude jokes and nasty names for people like him, and he entered adulthood knowing that being openly gay could prevent you from getting a job or renting an apartment. It could also get you assaulted.

25   Bigotry has never been reserved for homosexuality, of course. I am old enough to remember the time when bigotry directed toward other minorities in Canada was similar to that which is still sometimes aimed at homosexuals. In my Vancouver childhood, Chinese were regularly called "Chinks" (the boys in my high school

Vocabulary Practice

Look up the following words using an online dictionary, thesaurus, or encyclopedia.

minority groups

_____
_____
_____

untenable

_____
_____
_____

deficiency

_____
_____
_____

variant

_____
_____
_____

bigotry

_____
_____
_____

wore black denim "Chink pants" tailored for them in Chinatown). Black people were "niggers," prohibited from staying in most Vancouver hotels. Kids in the special class were "retards" or "morons." Jews were suspected of all sorts of crazy things, and physically disabled people were often regarded as mental defectives. 30

When I was a child, left-handed children were still being punished for writing with their left hand, particularly in the more religious parts of Canada. (When I was a graduate psychology student in Newfoundland doing research on handedness, 35 I discovered that several of my "righthanded" subjects were actually left-handers; at school their left hands had been tied behind their backs by zealous nuns.)

The gay children and teachers of my childhood were simply invisible. Two female teachers could live together without raising eyebrows, chiefly because women in those days (especially women *teachers*) were not generally thought of as 40 sexual persons. Two male "bachelors" living together did tend to be suspect, and so gay men brave enough to live together usually kept their living arrangements quiet. "Sissy" boys and "boyish" girls took a lot of teasing, but most people knew too little about homosexuality to draw any conclusions. These boys and girls were expected to grow up and marry people of the opposite sex. Some of them did, 45 divorcing years later to live with one of their own.

Many of the teachers and parents of my childhood who tried to convert left-handed children into right-handers probably believed they were helping children avoid the stigma of being left-handed, just as many misguided therapists tried to "cure" patients of their homosexuality to enable them to avoid the stigma of being 50 gay in a heterosexual world.

Thanks to advances in our understanding, left-handedness gradually came to be seen as a natural and innate trait. We know now that people do not *choose* to be more skillful with one hand than the other; they simply are. While researchers are still debating the precise mechanisms that determine hand preference, there 55 is general agreement that left- and right-handedness are just two different (and valid) ways of being. Left-handers are a minority in their own right, not "deviants" from normal right-handedness.

The same is true for sexual orientation. Although we do not yet clearly understand the mechanisms that determine sexual orientation, all indicators 60 point to the conclusion that it results from interactions between genetic, hormonal and possibly other factors, all beyond the individual's control. Like left-handedness, sexual orientation is an innate trait, not a choice or "lifestyle." Like left-handedness, homosexuality is a valid alternative sexuality, not a deviance from "normal" heterosexuality. 65

As with other minorities, attitudes toward homosexuality are inevitably becoming more liberal, at least in Canada. A recent poll, commissioned by the B.C. Teachers' Federation, found that almost 70 per cent of B.C. residents think students should be taught in school to accept homosexuals and treat them as they would other people. (Twenty per cent said homosexuality should be discouraged, 70 9 per cent said they didn't know and 3 per cent refused to answer.) These results

indicate that overt bigotry toward homosexuality is increasingly limited to religious extremists. The Surrey school trustees who voted against having gay and lesbian resource materials in schools are probably at about the same stage of
75 cultural evolution as were the Newfoundland nuns who tied children's left hands behind their backs 40 years ago.

Even so, I'm grateful that they're further along the path of enlightenment than their predecessors in medieval Europe, who burned many left-handers and homosexuals at the stake. Being born in the late 20th century was a wise move on
80 the part of my son and daughter. In some things, timing is everything.

Summarize Summarize the main argument of this essay in one sentence.

_____

_____

_____

Analyze Complete the following Venn diagram. In the centre section, list similarities between homosexuality and left-handedness. In the outer sections, list details unique to each subject.

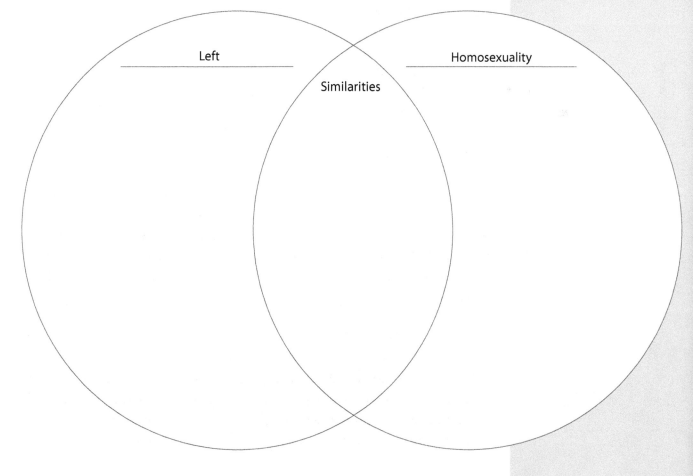

Left _____

Homosexuality _____

Similarities

Chapter 42 Comparison–Contrast Essays

Built for the way you learn.

WRITE2

www.nelson.com/student

> "The ultimate result of shielding men from the effects of folly is to fill the world with fools."
>
> —Herbert Spencer

James Steidl/Shutterstock.com

43

Cause–Effect Essays

Within this chapter, you will find two example essays using a cause–effect approach. You will also find questions and graphic organizers you can use as tools to help analyze each reading.

SQ3R When you read, become involved with the text by using the SQ3R approach.

- **Survey:** Prepare by reading "About the Author," skimming the essay, and noting any vocabulary words.
- **Question:** Ask yourself what cause-and-effect relationships you predict from the essay.
- **Read:** Read the essay, noting the causes leading to or effects resulting from the main topic.
- **Recite:** Recite the main details of the cause-and-effect relationship the author provides.
- **Review:** Answer the questions provided and use the graphic organizers to help you analyze the essay.

Learning Outcomes

LO1 Understand, read, and analyze cause–effect essays.

Essay List:

"Embraced by the Needle": Drawing on his experience working as a physician in Vancouver's Downtown Eastside, Gabor Maté examines the causes of substance abuse and addiction.

___

"Spanglish Spoken Here": Janice Castro describes the way in which the Spanish language is merging with English in the United States, creating a unique blend of the two.

___

About the Author

Gabor Maté is a physician who specializes in the treatment of addiction and attention deficit disorder. He was a medical columnist for *The Globe and Mail* and the *Vancouver Sun* and has written four books.

Gabor Maté, "Embraced by the Needle," *Nelson Maple Collection,* First Edition.

Vocabulary Practice

Look up the following words using an online dictionary, thesaurus, or encyclopedia. Be sure to look up any other words not listed below that you don't understand.

anesthetics

_____
_____
_____

eloquence

_____
_____
_____

harm-reduction

_____
_____
_____

Kamira/Shutterstock.com

Embraced by the Needle
by Gabor Maté

Addictions always originate in unhappiness, even if hidden. They are emotional anesthetics; they numb pain. The first question always is not "Why the addiction?" but "Why the pain?" The answer, ever the same, is scrawled with crude eloquence on the wall of my patient Anna's room at the Portland Hotel in the heart of Vancouver's Downtown Eastside: "Any place I went to, I wasn't wanted. And that bites large." 5

The Downtown Eastside is considered to be Canada's drug capital, with an addict population of 3000 to 5000 individuals. I am a staff physician at the Portland, a non-profit harm-reduction facility where most of the clients are addicted to cocaine, to alcohol, to opiates like heroin, or to tranquilizers—or to any combination of these things. Many also suffer from mental illness. Like 10 Anna, a 32-year-old poet, many are HIV positive or have full-blown AIDS. The methadone I prescribe for their opiate dependence does little for the emotional anguish compressed in every heartbeat of these driven souls.

Methadone staves off the torment of opiate withdrawal, but, unlike heroin, it does not create a "high" for regular users. The essence of that high was best 15 expressed by a 27-year-old sex-trade worker. "The first time I did heroin," she said, "it felt like a warm, soft hug." In a phrase, she summed up the psychological and chemical cravings that make some people vulnerable to substance dependence.

No drug is, in itself, addictive. Only about 8 per cent to 15 per cent of people who try, say alcohol or marijuana, go on to addictive use. What makes them 20 vulnerable? Neither physiological predispositions nor individual moral failures explain drug addictions. Chemical and emotional vulnerability are the products of life experience, according to current brain research and developmental psychology.

Most human brain growth occurs following birth; physical and emotional interactions determine much of our brain development. Each brain's circuitry and chemistry reflects individual life experiences as much as inherited tendencies. For any drug to work in the brain, the nerve cells have to have receptors—sites where the drug can bind. We have opiate receptors because our brain has natural opiate-like substances, called endorphins, chemicals that participate in many functions, including the regulation of pain and mood. Similarly, tranquilizers of the benzodiazepine class, such as Valium, exert their effect at the brain's natural benzodiazepine receptors.

Infant rats who get less grooming from their mothers have fewer natural benzo receptors in the part of the brain that controls anxiety. Brains of infant monkeys separated from their mothers for only a few days are measurably deficient in the key neuro-chemical, dopamine.

It is the same with human beings. Endorphins are released in the infant's brain when there are warm, non-stressed, calm interactions with the parenting figures. Endorphins, in turn, promote the growth of receptors and nerve cells, and the discharge of other important brain chemicals. The fewer endorphin-enhancing experiences in infancy and early childhood, the greater the need for external sources. Hence, the greater vulnerability to addictions.

Distinguishing skid row addicts is the extreme degree of stress they had to endure early in life. Almost all women now inhabiting Canada's addiction capital suffered sexual assaults in childhood, as did many of the males. Childhood memories of serial abandonment or severe physical and psychological abuse are common. The histories of my Portland patients tell of pain upon pain.

Carl, a 36-year-old native man, was banished from one foster home after another, had dishwashing liquid poured down his throat for using foul language at age 5, and was tied to a chair in a dark room to control his hyperactivity. When angry at himself—as he was recently for using cocaine—he gouges his foot with a knife as punishment. His facial expression was that of a terrorized urchin who had just broken some family law and feared Draconian retribution. I reassured him I wasn't his foster parent, and that he didn't owe it to me not to screw up.

But what of families where there was not abuse, but love, where parents did their best to provide their children with a secure nurturing home? One also sees addictions arising in such families. The unseen factor here is the stress the parents themselves lived under even if they did not recognize it. That stress could come from relationship problems, or from outside circumstances such as economic pressure or political disruption. The most frequent source of hidden stress is the parents' own childhood histories that saddled them with emotional baggage they had never become conscious of. What we are not aware of in ourselves, we pass on to our children.

Stressed, anxious, or depressed parents have great difficulty initiating enough of those emotionally rewarding, endorphin-liberating interactions with their children. Later in life, such children may experience a hit of heroin as the "warm, soft hug" my patient described: What they didn't get enough of before, they can now inject.

Feeling alone, feeling there has never been anyone with whom to share their deepest emotions, is universal among drug addicts. That is what Anna had

deficient

_____
_____
_____

skid row

_____
_____
_____

urchin

_____
_____
_____

Draconian

_____
_____
_____

retribution

_____
_____
_____

Chapter 43 Cause–Effect Essays

lamented on her wall. No matter how much love a parent has, the child does 70
not experience being wanted unless he or she is made absolutely safe to express
exactly how unhappy, or angry, or hate-filled he or she may feel at times. The sense
of unconditional love, of being fully accepted even when most ornery, is what no
addict ever experienced in childhood—often not because the parents did not have
it to give, simply because they did not know how to transmit it to the child. 75

Addicts rarely make the connection between troubled childhood experiences
and self-harming habits. They blame themselves—and that is the greatest wound
of all, being cut off from their natural self-compassion. "I was hit a lot," 40-year-
old Wayne says, "but I asked for it. Then I made some stupid decisions." And would
he hit a child, no matter how much that child "asked for it"? Would he blame that 80
child for "stupid decisions"?

Wayne looks away. "I don't want to talk about that crap," says this tough
man, who has worked on oil rigs and construction sites and served 15 years in jail
for robbery. He looks away and wipes tears from his eyes.

Summarize According to Maté, what causes people to become addicted to drugs
or alcohol? What experience do "skid row addicts" share that the author thinks
causes their addictions?

_____

_____

_____

Explain How does Maté explain addiction among people who were loved, not
neglected or abused, by their parents as children? How would his theory explain
one addicted child in a family with non-addicted siblings?

_____

_____

_____

Evaluate Toward the end of the essay, Maté states clearly what he believes _all_
addicts lacked during their infancy and childhood. Identify his assertion. Do you
agree or disagree with him? Why?

_____

_____

_____

R. Gino Santa Maria/Shutterstock.com

About the Author

Janice Castro is an assistant professor at Northwestern University's journalism school. She served as a reporter, a writer, and an editor at *Time* magazine for over 20 years and has freelanced for many other publications.

Spanglish Spoken Here
by Janice Castro

1   In Manhattan a first-grader greets her visiting grandparents, happily exclaiming, "Come here, sientate!" Her bemused grandfather, who does not speak Spanish, nevertheless knows she is asking him to sit down. A Miami personnel officer understands what a job applicant means when he says, "Quiero un part
5   time." Nor do drivers miss a beat reading a billboard alongside a Los Angeles street advertising CERVEZA—SIX-PACK!

This free-form blend of Spanish and English, known as Spanglish, is common linguistic currency wherever concentrations of Hispanic Americans are found in the U.S. In Los Angeles, where 55 percent of the city's 3 million inhabitants
10   speak Spanish, Spanglish is as much a part of daily life as sunglasses. Unlike the broken-English efforts of earlier immigrants from Europe, Asia and other regions, Spanglish has become a widely accepted conversational mode used casually—even playfully—by Spanish-speaking immigrants and native-born Americans alike.

Consisting of one part Hispanicized English, one part Americanized Spanish
15   and more than a little fractured syntax, Spanglish is a bit like a Robin Williams comedy routine: a crackling line of cross-cultural patter straight from the melting pot. Often it enters Anglo homes and families through the children, who pick it up at school or at play with their young Hispanic contemporaries. In other cases, it comes from watching TV; many an Anglo child watching Sesame Street has
20   learned *uno dos tres* almost as quickly as one two three.

Spanglish takes a variety of forms, from the Southern California Anglos who bid farewell with the utterly silly "hasta la bye-bye" to the Cuban-American drivers in Miami who *parquean* their *carros*. Some Spanglish sentences are mostly Spanish, with a quick detour for an English word or two. A Latino friend
25   may cut short a conversation by glancing at his watch and excusing himself with the explanation that he must "ir al supermarket."

Many of the English words transplanted in this way are simply handier than their Spanish counterparts. No matter how distasteful the subject, for example, it is still easier to say "income tax" than *impuesto sobre la renta*. At the same time,
30   many Spanish-speaking immigrants have adopted such terms as VCR, microwave

Vocabulary

linguistic
concerning languages

Hispanic
a person of Latin American descent living in the U.S.A.

syntax
the ordering of words into phrases and sentences.

patter
rapid speech

Anglo
a Caucasian living in the U.S.A.

Latino
See "Hispanic," above.

Do you speak a hybrid
language? Which
languages are combined?
Where do you use this
hybrid?

and dishwasher for what they view as largely American phenomena. Still other English words convey a cultural context that is not implicit in the Spanish. A friend who invites you to *lonche* most likely has in mind the brisk American custom of "doing lunch" rather than the languorous afternoon break traditionally implied by *almuerzo*.   *35*

Mainstream Americans exposed to similar hybrids of German, Chinese or Hindi might be mystified. But even Anglos who speak little or no Spanish are somewhat familiar with Spanglish. Living among them, for one thing, are 19 million Hispanics. In addition, more American high school and university students sign up for Spanish than for any other foreign language.   *40*

Only in the past ten years, though, has Spanglish begun to turn into a national slang. Its popularity has grown with the explosive increases in U.S. immigration from Latin American countries. English has increasingly collided with Spanish in retail stores, offices and classrooms, in pop music and on street corners. Anglos whose ancestors picked up such Spanish words as *rancho, bronco,*   *45* *tornado* and *incommunicado*, for instance, now freely use such Spanish words as *gracias, bueno, amigo* and *por favor*.

Among Latinos, Spanglish conversations often flow easily from Spanish into several sentences of English and back again. "It is done unconsciously," explains Carmen Silva-Corvalan, a Chilean-born associate professor of linguistics at the   *50* University of Southern California, who speaks Spanglish with relatives and neighbors. "I couldn't even tell you minutes later if I said something in Spanish or in English."

Spanglish is a sort of code for Latinos: the speakers know Spanish, but their hybrid language reflects the American culture in which they live. Many lean to   *55* shorter, clipped phrases in place of the longer, more graceful expressions their parents used. Says Leonel de la Cuesta, an assistant professor of modern languages at Florida International University in Miami: "In the U.S., time is money, and that is showing up in Spanglish as an economy of language." Conversational examples: *taipiar* (type) and *winshi-wiper* (windshield wiper) replace *escribir a maquina*   *60* and *limpiaparabrisas*.

Major advertisers, eager to tap the estimated $134 billion in spending power wielded by Spanish-speaking Americans, have ventured into Spanglish to promote their products. In some cases, attempts to sprinkle Spanish through commercials have produced embarrassing gaffes. A Braniff airlines ad that sought   *65* to tell Spanish-speaking audiences they could settle back *en* (in) luxuriant *cuero* (leather) seats, for example, inadvertently said they could fly without clothes (*encuero*).

A fractured translation of the Miller Lite slogan told readers the beer was "Filling, and less delicious." Similar blunders are often made by Anglos trying to   *70* impress Spanish-speaking pals. But if Latinos are amused by mangled Spanglish, they also recognize these goofs as a sort of friendly acceptance. As they might put it, *no problema*.

Vocabulary

implicit
clearly conveyed, though not directly expressed

languorous
slow and relaxed

hybrid
a mixture from two or more backgrounds

Latin America
all of the Americas south of the U.S.

gaffe
an ignorant or careless mistake in language

blunder
a foolish or clumsy error

Analyze Which of these cause–effect diagrams best illustrates the essay? Why?

Cause ↘
Cause → **Effect**   **OR**   Cause → **Effect**
Cause ↗

Cause ↗ **Effect**
Cause → **Effect**
↘ **Effect**

_____

Explain What is the main effect or main cause in the essay?

_____

Analyze How do the details of the essay proceed from that cause or lead to that effect?

_____

Reflect How does Spanglish, or the melding of other languages, affect your own life? In what ways is Spanglish unique from other meldings or similar to them?

_____

Cienpies Design/Shutterstock

Monkey Business Images/Shutterstock.com

44

Argument Essays

Within this chapter you will find two example argument essays. Each is followed by questions to help analyze the reading.

SQ3R When you read, become involved with the text by using the SQ3R approach.

- **Survey:** Prepare by reading "About the Author," skimming the essay, and noting any vocabulary words.
- **Question:** Try to predict what the writer hopes to convince you of.
- **Read:** Read the essay, noting the value of supporting arguments and concessions the author makes.
- **Recite:** Recite the main points of the argument.
- **Review:** Answer the questions provided to help you analyze the essay.

Learning Outcomes

L◯1 Understand, read, and analyze argument essays.

Essays

"What's Pro Hockey Got to Do with World Peace? Stand on Guard for Kids and the Game We Love": Raffi Cavoukian claims that Canada's reputation as a peacemaker is contradicted by the violence of its national sport.

"Overpopulation Is Bad but Overconsumption Is Worse": David Suzuki argues that overconsumption, not overpopulation, is responsible for the degradation of the environment.

About the Author

Raffi Cavoukian is a children's singer-songwriter, environmentalist, author, and children's rights advocate. He was awarded the Order of Canada in 1983.

Cavoukian, Raffi "What's pro hockey got to do with world peace? Stand on guard for kids and the game we love.," Rabble .ca, January 14, 2012 <http://rabble.ca/blogs/bloggers/raffi-cavoukian/2012/01/whats-pro-hockey-got-do-world-peace>

Vocabulary Practice

Look up the following words using an online dictionary, thesaurus, or encyclopedia. Be sure to look up any other words in the essay that you don't understand.

Don Cherry (1934–)
former NHL coach, now a controversial hockey commentator for CBC.

militarization
_____
_____
_____
_____

goon (in hockey)
_____
_____
_____
_____

microcosm
_____
_____
_____
_____

Wickedgood/Dreamstime.com/GetStock.com

What's Pro Hockey Got to Do with World Peace? Stand on Guard for Kids and the Game We Love
by Raffi Cavoukian

You might wonder about pro hockey and world peace—what's this about, is he nuts? Well, maybe. But considering the NHL hockey violence often in the news, and hockey analyst Don Cherry's repeated tributes to Canada's Afghan war dead within "Coach's Corner" on CBC's *Hockey Night In Canada*, I could examine the militarization of Cherry's segment and the loss of respect for Canada as a peace-maker in the world. But I won't. I will, however, question the role of violence in Canada's fall-winter-spring passion and what that says about this country. I believe it's a lack of imagination that keeps our beloved game unchangeable in the minds of violence proponents. Canada, we're better than this. We're peacemakers.   1   5

The focus on rough and tumble hockey takes its toll: NHL teams are plagued with a rash of injuries, their player rosters get depleted and miss star players. Recently, concussions have knocked out some top NHL players, none more so than Sidney Crosby who's been out for months and is not slated for return any time soon. With all due respect to Canada's military families and their undoubted sacrifice, there's a strong case to be made for letting a game be a game, and restoring Saturday NHL telecasts to "hockey night" in Canada. Not fight night, goon night, or injury night. Not politics night. Hockey night.   10   15

When even NHL commissioner Gary Bettman admits that "sports is a microcosm of society in general," then why do we condone NHL violence that would, anywhere else, result in arrests and jail time? What does this say about pro hockey, and about our society?   20

Within the last year, with four deaths of NHL tough-guy "enforcers"—tough guys paid to provoke a fist-fight to intimidate opponents—one might ask, what's thuggery got to do with hockey? Aren't there other ways to outdo the competition? Outwit them, for example?   25

Hockey is a kids' game turned into fierce contest by professional athletes, and at the NHL level it's a tough, high-flying contact sport. Fast skating and booming shots make for exciting play, but they also bring injuries from pucks, sticks, falls, unavoidable collisions as well as body checks. All the more reason, in my view, to limit injuries to just that—the unavoidable accidents—without   30 prompting players to harm one another in the name of toughness. That's just stupid, and dangerous. It maims, and can kill.

Cherry has called for rule changes that might reduce injury: notably re-instituting the centre red line to slow the speed of the game, a return to lighter
35 shoulder pads for skaters, and no "headshots" or body checks from behind. That's fine. But then he confuses the issue by glorifying hockey violence in many other aspects. His repeated insults at players (especially Europeans) who won't fight or aren't rough enough for his taste is unwar-ranted. Graceful players from Lafleur to Gretzky to Lemieux and Bure, have been tops in their game, and their skills
40 deserve only respect. The Sedin twins are exemplars of hockey sportsmanship, all too rare in today's game; they also happen to be among the game's top scorers.

But Cherry's 23 "Rock 'Em, Sock 'Em" videos reinforce his preference for grit over grace. That's a false choice. (He's as wrong on this as he was on the Iraq invasion.) To glorify rough play as Cherry continues to do harms the game and its
45 players, and it harms our nation's impressionable young. Besides, anyone knows that to make it to the NHL level, you have to be tough. So it's illogical, and a form of bullying, to question a player's manhood by his style of play. It's also an insult to the growing number of girls and women who now play hockey—with great skill and heart.
50 We can design for a better outcome. We can remake the game.

We need a change in pro hockey culture and the minor leagues that feed it. A ban on fighting, as Ken Dryden has rightly urged, won't lessen the drive to win. But to remove fighting, you've got to start young and stay consistent through the various leagues on up.
55 Hockey Canada could design a "Smart Hockey" culture right from the start. For thousands of kids, parents and coaches in hockey at rinks all across the country, Smart Hockey could emphasize skill, grace, and sports-manship, instilling adversarial respect in the youngest players right up to the junior leagues. Imagine that!
60 Remaking the NHL into an exciting and entertaining brand—devoid of violence—may sound unthinkable to some; perhaps it's a matter of national will. For all those who contend that a fight ban would decrease the fan base, there are scores of fans turned off by the violence who might be happy to return to the game. True, there's the U.S. market and the huge TV revenues that go with that,
65 and you'll hear the dubious claim that U.S. fans demand fighting. Yet nobody complained that the 2010 Olympic hockey series lacked excitement.

And here's a critically important question: is pro hockey all about money? Should it be? Do we value money more than our kids? Don't they deserve the best we can give them, to have positive sports models? Aren't these the kind of
70 questions Canadian fans, and Americans, should be asking themselves?

A pro hockey spring won't happen overnight, but the seeds can be planted now. Imagine an NHL whose referees call all infractions by the book—the rulebook!—as they do in World Cup soccer, the NBA, baseball, and foot-ball. Consistent officiating is the backbone of a sport's integrity. And that's what we
75 need in pro hockey: refereeing by the book. Break the rules and you're penalized, you hurt your team. Fight and you're out. A goalie slashes a skater, he's out. In

maims
_____
_____
_____
_____

impressionable
_____
_____
_____

illogical
_____
_____
_____

Ken Dryden (1947-)
former goaltender, a member of The Hockey Hall of Fame. From 2004 to 2011, he served as a federal Member of Parliament.

adversarial
_____
_____
_____
_____

infractions
_____
_____
_____

officiating
_____
_____
_____

integrity
_____
_____
_____

MindTap

You will find another example of an argument essay online.

Chapter 44 Argument Essays

recent years the NHL rightly clamped down on hooking and grabbing; the same can apply to cheap shots, after whistle cross-checks and intimidation. Our game has changed, and it can change again.

Imagine a hockey culture of respect: one that balances the grit, valour and determination it takes to win with a focus on skill, grace, and sportsmanship. What hockey family wouldn't choose that? Why not go for the glamour of the high road? Why not be known worldwide for this brand of hockey? 80

Pacifying the game would have tremendous positive impacts for Canada's hockey families, officials, and the fans. Come on Canada, we can do this. Stand on guard for our kids, and for the game we love. For a smart hockey culture and a society that loves its young. 85

Canada, we can be peacemakers—on and off the ice.

React Don Cherry, and many players and fans, seems to believe that violence is a part of hockey. Do you think that fighting in hockey is necessary? Why or why not?

_____

_____

_____

_____

Think Critically Cavoukian argues that violence should not be tolerated on the rink if it is not tolerated in society. Is this argument effective? If sporting events are subject to the rules of everyday life, how can boxing and mixed martial arts continue as sports?

_____

_____

_____

React The article ends with a call to arms; that is, an invitation to the reader to take action. What steps does the author recommend to make changes to the way hockey is played? Are these suggestions reasonable? Why or why not? If you agree with the author, offer some suggestions for change.

_____

_____

_____

_____

About the Author

David Suzuki is an environmentalist, broadcaster, academic, and author. He has received numerous awards and honours throughout his career. In 2004, CBC viewers voted him one of the "Greatest" Canadians of all time.

David Suzuki, "Overpopulation Is Bad but Overconsumption Is Worse," *Nelson Maple Collection,* First Edition.

Overpopulation Is Bad but Overconsumption Is Worse
by David Suzuki

1   After a recent lecture, two people objected vehemently to my suggestion that we in industrialized countries are the major cause of global ecological degradation and pollution. They blamed overpopulation in the Third World. I countered by pointing out that the great disparity in wealth and consumption between rich
5   and poor countries has to be addressed. Excess population does lead to ecological destruction and it's made worse in the Third World by their access to little of the planet's resources.

But each Canadian consumes 16 to 20 times as much as a person in India or China and 60 to 70 times more than someone in Bangladesh. Thus we
10   1.1 billion people in industrialized nations have the same ecological impact as 17 billion to 77 billion Third World people. The planet certainly could not take 5.5 billion people living as we do. But if we don't cut back consumption and pollution, poorer nations can rightfully aim to emulate us. My disputants weren't convinced and retorted: "You're crazy if you expect people in Canada or
15   the U.S. to cut back on consumption. It's nat-ural to want more."

More than 2,000 years ago, Aristotle had come to the same conclusion: "The avarice of mankind is insatiable." Last century, Leo Tolstoy had backed him up: "Seek among men, from beggar to millionaire, one who is contented with his lot and you will not find one such in a thousand." Alan Durning of
20   the Worldwatch Institute raises the issue in his book *How Much Is Enough?* (W.W. Norton & Co., New York) which opens: "Consumption: the neglected god in the trinity of issues the world must address if we are to get on a path of development that does not lead to ruin. The other two—population growth and technological change—receive attention; but with consumption, there is often
25   only silence."

So is it human nature to want more? Durning suggests that today's appetite for more consumer goods was a deliberate goal of American busi-ness and government. Retailing analyst Victor Lebow stated shortly after World War II: "Our enormously productive economy . . . demands that we make consumption
30   our way of life, that we convert the buying and use of goods into rituals, that

Reprinted by permission of The David Suzuki Foundation.

Vocabulary Practice

Look up the following words using an online dictionary, thesaurus, or encyclopedia. Be sure to look up any other words you don't understand which are not listed below.

vehemently
_____
_____

industrialized country
_____
_____

Third World
_____
_____

ecological degradation
_____
_____

disparity
_____
_____

consumption
_____
_____

emulate
_____
_____

Vocabulary Practice

disputants
_____
_____

Aristotle
_____
_____

avarice
_____
_____

insatiable
_____
_____

Leo Tolstoy
_____
_____

trinity
_____
_____

ego
_____
_____

recession
_____
_____

accumulation
_____
_____

alienation
_____
_____

self-reliance
_____
_____

we seek our spiritual satisfaction, our ego satisfaction, in consumption. . . . We need things consumed, burned up, worn out, replaced, and discarded at an ever increasing rate."

The chairman of the U.S. Council of Economic Advisers in 1953 pronounced the ultimate goal of the American economy was "to produce more consumer goods." And they were immensely successful. The contents of the average North American home today would be the envy of kings and emperors of the past. We now classify cars, televisions, telephones, refrig-erators, microwave ovens and stereos as necessities. 35

We even think of ourselves as "consumers" and "shopping" is a recreation. Consumption has become so crucial for the economy that in periods of recession, the consumer is often blamed for not spending enough while business and government seek ways to increase consumer confidence to stimulate spending. Media propaganda pounds home the message that con-sumption brings happiness. But possessions can't fill the emotional and spiritual needs for human relationships, community and some purpose beyond accumulation of wealth and goods. 40 45

Durning quotes a psychologist who finds "there is very little difference in the levels of reported happiness found in rich and very poor countries." In spite of the steep rise in consumption, the fraction of people who feel happy with life has not changed during the past 40 years. And continued escalation in consumption is not sustainable. Durning says, "In constant dollars, the world's people have consumed as many goods and services since 1950 as all previous generations put together. Since 1940, Americans alone have used up as large a share of the Earth's mineral resources as did everyone before them combined." 50 55

It is a fact that everything on Earth is limited. So endless increase in consumption cannot continue and will fall. But that does not mean the future must be a bleak life of denial and sacrifice. Much of our consumption is based on inefficiency and waste. We can reduce our ecological impact severalfold simply by improving our efficiency. 60

Overconsumption is not a goal that society must maintain at all costs; it has become a symptom that something is wrong because no matter how much we possess, we are not fulfilled or satisfied. Our lifestyle exacts a heavy price: violence, alcoholism, burglary, vandalism, drug abuse, alienation, loneliness, pollution and disruption of family and neighbourhood. Making do with less and designing a future that is based in communities with greater self-reliance and self-sufficiency makes ecological and social sense. But we won't get started until we stop trying to shift the responsibility elsewhere. 65

Analyze What is Suzuki's main argument?

_____

_____

_____

What are his supporting points?

_____

_____

_____

Do you agree or disagree? Why?

_____

_____

_____

Respond Suzuki says that "possessions can't fill the emotional and spiritual needs for human relationships, community and some purpose beyond accumulation of wealth and goods." (para. 6) How valid is it to say that things don't make people happy?

_____

_____

_____

_____

Respond What are Suzuki's solutions to the problem of overconsumption? Are they workable in our society? Discuss.

_____

_____

_____

_____

The information you need, the textbook you want.

WRITE2

www.nelson.com/student

Index

quantifiers of, 379
singular/plural, 370–373
specific/general, 80
tricky plurals, 372–373
two-way, 374
Noun clause, 280, 290
Noun markers, 378–379
Number(s), 370
agreement in, 330, 384–385
compound, 456
fallacy of impressing with, 272
italics and, 470
of noun, 370–371
of verb, 398–399
Nutshelling strategy, 3

O

Object
direct/indirect, 282, 294
gerund/infinitive as, 412
verbal as, 412–413
Objective case, 382
Objective pronoun, 382–383
O'Brien, Sharon, 28
O'Conner, Patricia T., 68, 86
On, 436–437
Online resources, 483
Opening paragraph, 56, 57
of argument essay, 258, 267
of cause-effect essay, 244, 248, 249
of classification essay, 196, 200, 202
of comparison-contrast essay, 230, 234, 235
of narrative essay, 180, 184, 185
of process essay, 212, 216, 218
Opinion statement, 171
Order, 14
of adjectives, 418–419
chronological, 48, 128, 182
of importance, 48
inverted, 278
spatial, 48
transitional words and, 224
Organization. *See also* Graphic organizer
deductive, 48
inductive, 48
patterns of, 24, 48–49, 163, 167, 231, 242, 498
point-by-point pattern of, 163, 167, 242, 498
quick list for, 50
revising and, 70
similarities-differences pattern of, 163, 167, 242, 498
subject-to-subject pattern of, 163, 167, 231, 242, 498
of supporting information, 48, 50–51
as writing trait, 22, 23, 32–33, 36, 48–49, 68
Organization name, capitalization of, 478
Outline, 51
for argument paragraph, 172
for cause-effect paragraph, 157
for classification paragraph, 150
for comparison-contrast paragraph, 165
customized, 51
for definition paragraph, 146
for descriptive paragraph, 124
for illustration paragraph, 136
for narrative paragraph, 129

for problem-solution paragraph, 176
for process paragraph, 140
Overconsumption, essay on, 513, 517–519
"Overpopulation is Bad but Overconsumption is Worse" (Suzuki), 513, 517–519
Ovid, 243

P

Paragraph(s), 120–177. *See also specific types of paragraphs*
argument, 169–173
cause-effect, 153–159
classification, 148–154
closing. *See* Closing paragraph
comparison-contrast, 161–167
definition, 143–147
descriptive, 122–125
expanding into an essay, 124
illustration, 133–137
middle. *See* Middle paragraphs
narrative, 126–131
opening. *See* Opening paragraph
problem-solution, 174–177
process, 138–142
structure of, 56, 124
topic sentence for, 47, 50, 56
Parallelism, 306–307, 362–363
faulty, 306, 362–363
Paraphrasing, 8, 10, 13, 94, 100, 115
plagiarism and, 94
summary vs., 115
Parentheses, sentences in, 476
Parks, Suzan-Lori, 29
Participial phrase, 314–315, 410, 420–421, 426
Participle, 404, 410
Passive verbs, 85, 282, 414
Passive voice, 282, 360, 400–401
Past participles, 404
Past tense verbs, 404–405
irregular, 404
Peer review, 68, 76–77, 86
of argument essay, 271
of cause-effect essay, 252
of classification essay, 206
of comparison-contrast essay, 238
constructiveness in, 76
of narrative essay, 188
of process essay, 223
role of listeners/responders in, 76
role of writer in, 76
Percy, Benjamin, 53
Perfect tense verbs, 408–409
Period
comma splice and, 350–351
with quotation marks, 191, 468
run-on sentences and, 352–353
Perkins, Maxwell, 56
Person, 360, 384, 398
agreement in, 384–385
shift in, 360–361
of verb, 398–399
Personal attack, 272
Personal narrative, 179
Personal pronoun, 382–383
Persuasive essay. *See* Argument essay
Persuasive paragraphs. *See* Argument paragraph; Problem-solution paragraph
Phrase
absolute, 346

adjectival, 284
gerund, 410
infinitive, 312–313, 410
introductory, 444–445
non-restrictive, 90, 447–448
participial, 314–315, 410, 420–421, 426
prepositional, 288–289, 312–313, 420–421, 424, 426, 434–435
transitional. *See* Transitional words/phrases
verbal, 410
Pictograph, 17
Plagiarism, 93–95
avoiding, 95
consequences of, 95
identifying, 94
intentional vs. unintentional, 94
Plural noun, 370–373
Plural pronoun, 384, 388
Plural verb, 330, 332, 398–399
Poe, Edgar Allan, 440
Point-by-point pattern of organization, 163, 167, 242, 498
Pointed question strategy, 3
Policy, as topic, 43
Position statement, 261
Positive adjective, 416
Positive adverb, 422
Possessive adjective, 378–379, 418
Possessive case, 382
Possessive pronoun, 378–379, 382–383, 462
Possessives, 462–464
"Pot Prohibition in Canada: End the War on Weed," 264–265
Predicate, 278–279, 282–283. *See also* Verb
complete, 278
compound, 282, 298–299
with direct/indirect object, 282
inverted order of subject and, 278
with linking verb, 396
simple, 292
Predicate adjective, 416
Prediction, as supporting information, 262
Prepositional phrases, 288–289, 312–313, 420–421, 424, 426, 434–435
Prepositions, 288, 429, 434–439
common, 288, 434
real-world applications, 438–439
Present tense verbs, 402–403
Prewriting, 30, 31, 37–52
argument essay and, 261–263
argument paragraph and, 171
cause-effect essay and, 246–247
cause-effect paragraph and, 156
classification essay and, 198–199
classification paragraph and, 149
comparison-contrast essay and, 232–233
comparison-contrast paragraph and, 164, 167
definition paragraph and, 145
descriptive paragraph and, 123
finding a focus in, 46–47
gathering/organizing details in, 42–43, 127–128, 145, 164, 171, 175, 215, 233, 247, 253, 262
illustration paragraph and, 135
narrative essay and, 182–183

Reading–Writing Connection

Writing and reading are your two essential tools of learning. You gain new information by reading, and you understand this information more fully by writing about it. In addition, reading and writing stimulate your thinking, and being a post-secondary student is all about good thinking—about understanding causes and effects, about making comparisons, and about forming logical arguments.

> **1.** Think of **writing** as . . .
> - a learning tool, helping you sort out your thoughts about new information, and
> - a way to share what you have learned in paragraphs and essays.

You are writing for yourself when you use writing as a learning tool; you are writing for an audience (instructors, classmates) when you are writing to share what you've learned.

> **2.** Think of **reading** as a number of related tasks:
> - previewing the assignment,
> - writing and thinking about the text as you read, and
> - summarizing what you have learned after the reading.

If you own the book or are working with a copy, consider annotating the text (making comments on the pages) as you read.

Assess Demonstrate your understanding of the writing and reading connection by answering these two questions.

> **1.** How is writing a learning tool?
>
> _____
>
> _____
>
> **2.** How is effective, active reading more than simply following the words on the page?
>
> _____
>
> _____

Reflect Which skill challenges you more, reading or writing? Why?

> _____
>
> _____
>
> _____

Writing

Stimulates thinking and learning

Reading

Linking Writing and Reading Assignments

Three common strategies can help you carry out your writing and reading assignments: (1) using the STRAP strategy, (2) using the traits of writing, and (3) using graphic organizers.

1. The **STRAP Strategy** consists of a series of questions to answer before you start a reading or writing assignment.

For Writing Assignments		For Reading Assignments
What specific topic should I write about?	**S**ubject	What specific topic does the reading address?
What form of writing (essay, article) will I use?	**T**ype	What form (essay, text chapter, article) does the reading take?
What position (student, citizen, employee) should I assume?	**R**ole	What position (student, responder, concerned individual) does the writer assume?
Who is the intended reader?	**A**udience	Who is the intended reader?
What is the goal (to inform, to persuade) of the writing?	**P**urpose	What is the goal of the material?

2. The **Traits of Writing** identify the important features in reading and writing assignments. Use the traits to analyze each type of assignment.
   - Ideas (*The main points and details in a text*)
   - Organization (*The overall structure of the material*)
   - Voice (*The text's personality—how the writer speaks to the reader*)
   - Word Choice (*The writer's use of words and phrases*)
   - Sentence Fluency (*The flow of sentences*)
   - Conventions (*The correctness of the language*)
   - Design (*The appearance of the text*)

3. **Graphic organizers** chart the key points you collect for writing assignments and the key points you find in reading assignments.

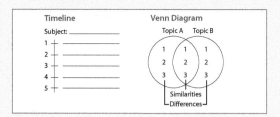

Reflect Which of these strategies would prove most helpful to you? Why?

The Writing Process

Writing is a process. It is very difficult to write a great paragraph or essay all at once. The process makes writing easy by breaking the job into five steps:

Process	Activities
Prewriting	Start the process by (1) selecting a topic to write about, (2) collecting details about it, and (3) finding your focus, the main idea or thesis.
Writing	Then write your first draft, using your prewriting plan as a general guide. Writing a first draft allows you to connect your thoughts about your topic.
Revising	Carefully review your first draft and have a classmate review it as well. Change any parts that could be clearer and more complete.
Editing	Edit your revised writing by checking for style, grammar, punctuation, and spelling errors.
Publishing	During the final step, prepare your writing to share with your instructor, your peers, or another audience.

Assess Demonstrate your understanding of the writing process by matching the steps in the process with the activities that are appropriate to each step.

1. Prewriting
2. Writing
3. Revising
4. Editing
5. Publishing

- Correcting errors in punctuation and spelling
- Posting your work online or sharing it with your instructor or family members
- Deciding what you want to write about and gathering details about it
- Asking a classmate to read your work and help you figure out the best way to fix it
- Creating a first draft and letting your planning guide the way

Reflect Which part of the writing process is most challenging to you? Why?

A "Recursive" Process

The writing process might not go in a straight line. You might be in the middle of writing when you realize you need to gather more details. After a classmate reviews your work, you might need to rewrite parts. The chart below shows how you can move back and forth in the process as necessary.

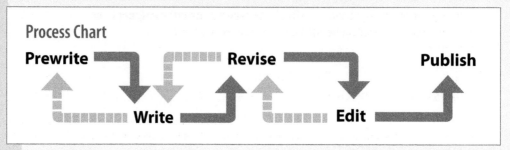

Process Chart

Prewrite **Revise** **Publish**

Write **Edit**

Assess For each situation below, tell which step you would move to in the writing process and why.

1. You are editing an essay when you realize that you need a stronger ending. What do you do now?

   _____

   _____

2. You are supposed to write a paragraph for a class assignment, but you can't think of what to write about. What do you do now?

   _____

   _____

3. A classmate has read your first draft and says you need to add some more interesting and exciting details. What do you do now?

   _____

   _____

4. You have posted your writing online, and people love it so much that they want you to write more about the same topic. What do you do now?

   _____

   _____

Reflect If you can always go backward and forward in the writing process, how do you know when you are "done"?

_____

_____

The Traits of Effective Writing

What elements make up good writing? The seven traits below provide criteria for effective writing in all forms and subject areas.

Traits	Description
Strong Ideas	Good writing contains plenty of relevant information (ideas and details), and all of the information holds the reader's interest.
Logical Organization	Effective writing has a clear overall structure—with a beginning, a middle, and an ending. Transitions link the ideas.
Fitting Voice	In the best writing, you can hear the writer's voice—his or her own unique way of saying things. Using an appropriate voice shows that the writer cares about the subject.
Well-Chosen Words	In strong writing, nouns and verbs are specific and clear, and the modifiers add important information.
Smooth Sentences	The sentences in good writing flow smoothly from one to the next. They carry the meaning of the essay or article.
Correct Copy	Strong writing is easy to read because it follows the conventions or rules of the language.
Appropriate Design	In the best academic writing, the design follows the guidelines established by the instructor or school.

Assess Demonstrate your understanding of the traits of effective writing by matching the traits with the activity that would most improve each trait.

1. Strong Ideas
2. Logical Organization
3. Fitting Voice
4. Well-Chosen Words
5. Smooth Sentences
6. Correct Copy
7. Appropriate Design

- Rearranging details into a better order
- Doing further research for more interesting details
- Making a paragraph sound as if you were explaining something to a friend
- Replacing a general verb with a more specific verb
- Fixing an error in subject–verb agreement
- Double-checking to see if you need to include a cover page for your essay
- Making sure your sentences don't sound too choppy

Reflect Which of the seven traits of effective writing is your greatest strength? Which one do you need to most work on?

Traits across the Writing Spectrum

The writing traits help you write and read in any subject area. Each writing discipline has its own ideas and organizational structures that you should learn. And whether you are writing an informal blog entry or a comparison–contrast essay, strong words, smooth sentences, correctness, and effective design will make your writing stronger.

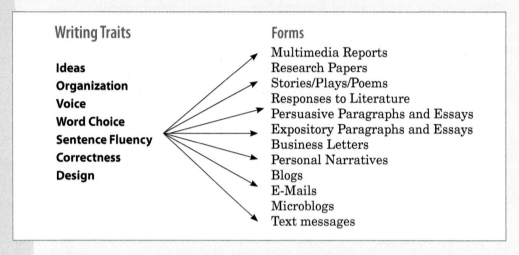

Writing Traits

Ideas
Organization
Voice
Word Choice
Sentence Fluency
Correctness
Design

Forms
Multimedia Reports
Research Papers
Stories/Plays/Poems
Responses to Literature
Persuasive Paragraphs and Essays
Expository Paragraphs and Essays
Business Letters
Personal Narratives
Blogs
E-Mails
Microblogs
Text messages

Assess For each situation below, tell which trait you would work on to improve your writing and why.

1. Your initial draft has a lot of good ideas but they seem out of order. What trait or traits could you improve upon?

   _____

   _____

2. A reader points out that your new blog entry sounds too formal and doesn't show off your personality. What trait or traits could you improve upon?

   _____

   _____

3. A number of spelling and grammar errors make your e-mail message difficult to understand. What trait or traits could you improve upon?

   _____

   _____

Reflect How can the traits help you analyze your writing and reading?

   _____

   _____

Paragraph Patterns

The structure of your paragraphs and essays will depend on a clear topic sentence or thesis. Use the following formula:

Forming a Thesis

A specific topic	**+**	A particular feeling, feature, or part	**=**	An effective thesis statement or topic sentence

Once you identify a thesis, you'll need to decide how to organize information that supports it. You have many patterns of organization to choose from.

Patterns of Organization

- Use **chronological order** (time) when you are sharing a personal experience, telling how something happened, or explaining how to do something.
- Use **spatial order** (location) for descriptions, arranging information from left to right, top to bottom, from the edge to the centre, and so on.
- Use **order of importance** when you are taking a stand or arguing for or against something. Either arrange your reasons from most important to least important or the other way around.
- Use **deductive organization** if you want to follow your thesis statement with basic information—supporting reasons, examples, and facts.
- Use **inductive organization** when you want to present specific details first and conclude with your thesis statement.
- Use **compare–contrast organization** when you want to show how one topic is different from and similar to another one.

Assess Demonstrate your understanding of the patterns of organization by choosing an appropriate method of organization for the example thesis statement. Briefly explain your choice.

Thesis Statement: _The view from the mountaintop was like nothing I'd ever seen before._

Method of Organization: _____

Explain: _____

_____

Reflect What is the difference between inductive and deductive organization? Which method do you prefer? Why?

_____

_____

Forming a Meaningful Whole

Forming a meaningful whole for a paragraph means including a topic sentence, body sentences, and a closing sentence. For an essay, it means including an opening paragraph (with a thesis statement), multiple supporting paragraphs, and a closing paragraph.

Paragraph Structure

Topic Sentence
A **topic sentence** names the topic.

Detail Sentences
Detail sentences support the topic.

Closing Sentence
A **closing sentence** wraps up the paragraph.

Essay Structure

Opening Paragraph
The **opening paragraph** draws the reader into the essay and provides information that leads to a thesis statement. The thesis statement tells what the essay is about.

Middle Paragraphs
The **middle paragraphs** support the thesis statement. Each middle paragraph needs a topic sentence, a variety of detail sentences, and a closing sentence.

Closing Paragraph
The **closing paragraph** finishes the essay by revisiting the thesis statement, emphasizing an important detail, providing the reader with an interesting final thought, and/or looking toward the future.

Assess Study the following writing sample. Put a plus (+) next to the sample if it forms a meaningful whole; put a minus (-) next to the sample if it doesn't. Explain what is missing if you label a sample with a minus.

_____ Air travel is both amazing and frustrating, and not necessarily in that order. My air travel experience from Toronto back to my hometown in southern Alberta last weekend demonstrates this point. In one sense, the convenience of the trip was extraordinary. To think I flew from Toronto, to Calgary (where I saw the Rockies outside my window), in under four hours is mind blowing. But the plane rides were less than spectacular. In fact, they were downright miserable.

Explanation: _____

_____

Reflect How do the structure of paragraphs and essays relate to each other?

_____

_____

Simple Sentences

A simple sentence consists of a subject and a verb and expresses a complete thought. The subject names what the sentence is about, and the verb says what the subject does or is. A direct object can receive the action of the verb.

Subject + Verb	**Subject + Verb + Direct Object**
Roger works.	He builds homes.

Compound Sentences

A compound sentence consists of two simple sentences joined with a comma and a coordinating conjunction (*and, but, or, nor, for, so, yet*). (The sentences can also be joined with a semicolon.)

Simple Sentence + , CC + Simple Sentence
Roger works, **for** he builds homes.

Complex Sentences

A complex sentence consists of two simple sentences joined with a subordinating conjunction. The subordinating conjunction makes one sentence depend on the other.

Dependent Clause + Simple Sentence
When Roger works, he builds homes.
Simple Sentence + Dependent Clause
Roger works whenever he builds homes.

Subordinating Conjunctions	
after	since
although	so that
as	that
as if	though
as long as	unless
because	until
before	when
even though	whenever
given that	where
if	whereas
in order that	while
provided that	

Assess Join the following simple sentences first as a compound sentence and then as a complex sentence.

Roger also builds boats. He is a novice at boat building.

Compound sentence: _____

_____

Complex sentence: _____

_____

Reflect Coordinating conjunctions connect sentences in an equal way, and subordinating conjunctions join sentences in an unequal way. Explain.

Avoiding Fragments

A sentence must have a subject and verb and must express a complete thought. Otherwise, the group of words is a sentence fragment. You can fix a fragment by supplying the part it is missing.

Fragment Missing a Subject	**Sentence with a Subject**
Works all summer. ⟶	Roger works all summer.
Fragment Missing a Verb	**Sentence with a Verb**
His construction company. ⟶	His construction company thrives.
Fragment Missing a Subject and Verb	**Sentence with a Subject and Verb**
With three projects. ⟶	They are busy with three projects.
Fragment Missing a Complete Thought	**Sentence with a Complete Thought**
When they work. ⟶	When they work, the company thrives.

Avoiding Run-On Sentences and Comma Splices

When joining two simple sentences to make a compound sentence, make sure to use both a comma and a coordinating conjunction. If you leave out both, you have a run-on, and if you leave out the conjunction, you have a comma splice.

Run-On Missing Both	**Compound Sentence Joined Correctly**
Roger works hard he is tired. ⟶	Roger works hard, and he is tired.
Comma Splice Missing Conjunction	**Compound Sentence Joined Correctly**
Roger works hard, he is tired. ⟶	Roger works hard, and he is tired.

Assess Correct each fragment, run-on, or comma splice below.

1. The Roger Davies Construction Company. _____
   _____

2. Built the convention centre. _____
   _____

3. On time and on budget. _____
   _____

4. Roger runs the company he has 12 employees. _____
   _____

Reflect Why are complete, correct sentences more important in writing than in speaking?

Varying Lengths and Beginnings

If all your sentences are the same, your writing will sound repetitive and dull. You can create interest by using different lengths of sentences and beginning them in different ways.

Sentence Lengths

Here are the three basic sentence lengths and their best uses:

> **Medium sentences (10–20 words):** Use medium sentences to express most ideas.
>
> When I saw the advertisement online, I wrote my resumé and cover letter and sent them in.
>
> **Long sentences (over 20 words):** Use long sentences to express complex ideas.
>
> After waiting anxiously to hear from the employer, I received a call requesting an interview, went in to meet the department manager, toured the facility, and completed a test.
>
> **Short sentences (under 10 words):** Use short sentences to make a point.
>
> I got the job!

Sentence Beginnings

Instead of starting each sentence with the subject, start some sentences with a transition word, phrase, or clause.

> **Transition Word**
>
> However, I won't start work until July.
>
> **Transition Phrase**
>
> With all the arrangements, I won't start work until July.
>
> **Transition Clause**
>
> Though I am eager to begin, I won't start work until July.

Assess Write each type of sentence requested below.

1. Write a medium sentence about applying for school. _____

_____

2. Write a long sentence about the process of applying. _____

_____

3. Write a short sentence about the result of applying. _____

_____

Reflect What transition word, phrase, or clause could you use to start one of the sentences you just wrote, above?

Varying Kinds of Sentences

Some sentences make statements. Others ask questions. Still others express strong emotion, give commands, or show how one condition depends on another. Here are the different kinds of sentences and their best uses.

Statements provide information about the subject. Use them most often.
   I was one of 25 applicants for the job.

Questions ask for information about the subject. Use them to engage the reader.
   What made me stand out from the other applicants?

Exclamations express strong emotion. Use them sparingly in academic writing.
   I had the best attitude!

Commands tell the reader what to do. (They have an implied subject—*you*.) Use them to call the reader to action.
   Show a positive attitude when you interview.

Conditional sentences show that one situation depends on another.
   If you have a positive attitude and an impressive resumé, then the interviewer will notice.

Assess Write each kind of sentence requested below.

1. Write a statement about finding a job. _____

2. Write a question about finding a job. _____

3. Write an exclamation about finding a job. _____

4. Write a command about finding a job. _____

5. Write a conditional (if/then) sentence about finding a job. _____

Reflect How do different kinds of sentences reflect different kinds of thinking?

Combining Sentences

Sometimes sentences are short and choppy and should be combined to improve the flow of thought. Use the following strategies.

Coordination

When two sentences share equal ideas, combine them using a comma and a coordinating conjunction (*and, but, or, nor, for, so, yet*). To combine three or more sentences, create a series, using a comma between each sentence and a coordinating conjunction before the last.

Two sentences:	I'm a nursing major. My roommate studies business.
Combined:	I'm a nursing major, but my roommate studies business.
Three sentences:	I'll heal you. She'll bill you. Mark will drive you home.
Combined:	I'll heal you, she'll bill you, and Mark will drive you home.

Subordination

When one sentence is less important than another, combine them using a subordinating conjunction. Place the subordinating conjunction before the less-important sentence, creating a dependent clause. If the dependent clause comes first, put a comma after it.

Two sentences:	Mark drives a taxi. He hopes to be an actor.
Combined:	Though Mark drives a taxi, he hopes to be an actor.
Combined:	Mark drives a taxi though he hopes to be an actor.

Subordinating Conjunctions

after	since
although	so that
as	that
as if	though
as long as	unless
because	until
before	when
even though	whenever
given that	where
if	whereas
in order that	while
provided that	

Assess Combine each pair of sentences as indicated.

Mark has appeared on stage. He has done more work backstage.

1. Coordinate _____

_____

2. Subordinate _____

_____

Acting is a tough career. Mark has talent and drive.

3. Coordinate _____

_____

4. Subordinate _____

_____

Combining by Moving and Deleting

Sometimes sentences sound repetitive and should be combined to be more concise. Combine such sentences by moving the key bits of information and deleting the rest.

Repetitive sentences:	I plan to be a nurse. I want to work in a hospital.
Combined sentences:	I plan to be a nurse in a hospital.

Expanding Sentences

Some sentences provide little information and should be expanded. Expand a sentence by answering the 5 W's and H about the sentence and then adding some of your answers to the sentence.

Say-nothing sentence:	She works there.
Who works there?	my friend Stacy
What does she do?	She's a pediatrics nurse.
Where does she work?	at Lakeside Memorial Hospital
When does she work?	She works nights.
Why does she work?	to support her son
How does she work?	cheerfully
Expanded sentence:	My friend Stacy cheerfully works nights as a pediatrics nurse at Lakeside Memorial Hospital.

Assess Combine the sentences in 1 and 2 by moving and deleting. Expand sentence 3 by answering the 5 W's and H about it.

1. Stacy's work supports her son. Her work also supports her husband. _____

_____

2. Her husband works days. He works at a canning plant. _____

_____

3. Her friend helps out.

Who helps out? _____

What does the friend do? _____

Where? _____

When? _____

Why? _____

How? _____

Expanded sentence: _____

_____

_____

Noun

A common noun refers to a general person, place, thing, or idea, and a proper noun refers to a specific person, place, thing, or idea. Proper nouns are capitalized.

	Common Nouns	**Proper Nouns**
Person:	politician	Peter MacKay
Place:	park	Banff National Park
Thing:	marker	Sharpie
Idea:	religion	Hinduism

Pronoun

There are different personal pronouns to indicate whether a person is speaking (*I, me, my, us, we*), is being spoken to (*you, your*), or is being spoken about (*he, she, they, them*).

	Singular			**Plural**		
Person	**Nom.**	**Obj.**	**Poss.**	**Nom.**	**Obj.**	**Poss.**
First (speaking)	I	me	mine	we	us	ours
Second (spoken to)	you	you	yours	you	you	yours
Third (spoken about) masculine	he	him	his	they	them	theirs
feminine	she	her	hers	they	them	theirs
neuter	it	it	its	they	them	theirs

Verb

Verbs show number (singular or plural), voice (active or passive), and tense (present, past, and future).

	Active Voice		**Passive Voice**	
	Singular	Plural	Singular	Plural
Present Tense	I see you see he/she/it sees	we see you see they see	I am seen you are seen he/she/it is seen	we are seen you are seen they are seen
Past Tense	I saw you saw he saw	we saw you saw they saw	I was seen you were seen it was seen	we were seen you were seen they were seen
Future Tense	I will see you will see he will see	we will see you will see they will see	I will be seen you will be seen it will be seen	we will be seen you will be seen they will be seen
Present Perfect Tense	I have seen you have seen he has seen	we have seen you have seen they have seen	I have been seen you have been seen it has been seen	we have been seen you have been seen they have been seen
Past Perfect Tense	I had seen you had seen he had seen	we had seen you had seen they had seen	I had been seen you had been seen it had been seen	we had been seen you had been seen they had been seen
Future Perfect Tense	I will have seen you will have seen he will have seen	we will have seen you will have seen they will have seen	I will have been seen you will have been seen it will have been seen	we will have been seen you will have been seen they will have been seen

Adjective and Adverb

Adjectives modify nouns, and adverbs modify verbs, adjectives, or other adverbs. Each type of modifier answers a different set of questions.

Adjective Questions	Adverb Questions
Which?	How?
What kind of?	When?
How many/how much?	Where?
	Why?
	To what degree?
	How often/how long?

Conjunction

Conjunctions join ideas, showing their relationship. Coordinating conjunctions join ideas in an equal way. Correlative conjunctions stress the equality of the ideas. Subordinating conjunctions show that one idea depends on another.

Coordinating Conjunctions

and   but   or   nor   for   so   yet

Correlative Conjunctions

either/or   neither/nor   whether/or   both/and   not only/but also

Subordinating Conjunctions

after	as long as	if	so that	unless	where
although	because	in order that	that	until	whereas
as	before	provided that	though	when	while
as if	even though	since	till	whenever	

Preposition

Prepositions create a special relationship between a noun or pronoun and another word or phrase in the sentence. A prepositional phrase starts with a preposition (such as *by, at, on, in*), includes an object (a noun or pronoun), and functions as an adjective or adverb, answering one of the questions listed earlier.

Assess Write examples of the parts of speech requested.

1. Nouns: common _____ proper _____

2. Pronouns: first person _____ second person _____ third person _____

3. Verbs: present _____ past _____ future _____

4. Adjective _____ adverb _____

5. Conjunction: coordinating _____ subordinating _____

6. Conjunction: correlative _____ / _____

7. Preposition _____ prepositional phrase _____